THE MYSTERY OF LIFE

WHAT'S IT ALL ABOUT?

THE MYSTERY OF LIFE
WHAT'S IT ALL ABOUT?

DISCOVERING THE TRUTH IN A SKEPTICAL WORLD

DAVID E. PEEPLES

To order additional copies of this book, contact:
Xlibris
1-888-795-4274
www.Xlibris.com
Orders@Xlibris.com
730785

CONTENTS

Born in 1950, David Peeples grew up in a small Western Washington logging town near the coast of the Pacific Northwest. As a young boy he would always prefer to be outdoors whenever possible as this afforded him the opportunity to satisfy his growing curiosity for the natural world first hand. After his graduation from high school, he attended Lower Columbia College in Longview, Washington where the focus of his academic study in the sciences would become the natural progression of a keen interest in a complex physical world and its many wonders. This led him to the discovery and understanding of many facts and details that have defined the disciplines of physics, chemistry, and biology. David went on to the University of Washington in Seattle where he studied and received an academic degree in pharmaceutical science in 1973. After combining his science background with a personal interest in history and theology, he turned to writing as a way to share the knowledge gained through many years of study, research, observation, and personal experience. As a long-term healthcare professional, he soon recognized that writing and teaching were the most effective ways to share the knowledge and understanding he had gained, which could ultimately benefit others as well. Many years of study, research, writing and editing would eventually lead to the completion of a book narrative that he had dreamed of sharing throughout much of his adult life. *The Mystery of Life* book project is not a casual stab in the dark at a few puzzling questions inherent in a complex physical world, but contains some thorough documentation of highly relevant and verifiable scientific and historical facts that have been, all too often, conveniently overlooked and even carelessly disregarded by a skeptical world.

Dedication and Acknowledgments

This book is dedicated to my dear wife Linda, my best friend and lifelong companion without whose love, patience and encouragement this book would never have become a reality. And to my four wonderful children__ Heidi, Aaron, Heather, and Travis with whom my wife and I have shared many joys, and the challenges of life that have shaped us into the people we are today.

I would also like to acknowledge and offer a special thank you to several individuals who have helped me with various aspects of this lengthy book project including editorial review, technical assistance and project management. A sincere thank you to Linda Peeples, Paul Mcintire, Heidi Codorniz , Mark Ruttan, and to the Xlibris staff who have been to very helpful in the process.

Preface

Have you ever tried to make sense of the routine struggle we engage in day after day? The sun comes up again. We go to work or school. We eat, we play, we watch some television, interact with family and friends, and we sleep. We do this over and over, day after day, and while we are doing it we grow old, and eventually we die. From the cradle to the grave, most of us go through the repetitious routines of life without ever pausing to seriously consider the most important questions presented to our minds through the struggles and triumphs we experience on life's journey. Even though we have come a long way in terms of human progress, the basic problems that have plagued our world throughout history still remain with us today. Many people are privileged enough to live in real prosperity, and yet poverty is noticeable just about everywhere we look. We living in America have had an opportunity for the best education the world can offer; yet laziness, ignorance, hatred, and prejudice are far too pervasive in our culture. The marvels of modern civilization have made all of our lives easier in so many ways, but what good is new technology when our personal relationships are falling apart? People still look to America for successful diplomacy in resolving menacing human conflict around the world, and yet war, bitter hatred, rampant lawlessness, and widespread corruption continue to dominate our news headlines.

The twenty-first century has become characterized by another new and insidious threat to civilized human culture, which could never have been imagined by the parents and grandparents of generations past. The news media is dominated by vicious crimes against humanity as radicalized religious zealots spread hatred and terror in the hope of subjugating those who view life differently than they do. By breeding and propagating violent hatred without conscience, they show no mercy to the young and old alike. We live in a dangerous world compromised by extreme political and religious views resulting in jihadist-minded violence of a type that is unprecedented in recent history. Cruel attacks of deadly brutality are often waged against Western targets for no apparent reason other than bitter hatred and a misguided ambition compelling some to dictate their preferred ideology to others as they see fit. We certainly should have provided a safer world for our children and grandchildren to grow up in; but the truth is we are living in a very dangerous, violent, and perilous time that is comparable to some degree with historical memories scarred by violent atrocities in the past. Through self-indulgence and prideful living, we have pursued pleasure and wealth only to discover these objectives to be dreadfully empty of the substance that makes life fulfilling and meaningful. What is wrong with today's modern world? Why does this life seem so empty and pointless to many people, even in a culture as affluent as ours? I invite you now to consider the content of these pages. If you should deem the basic thoughts recorded in this publication to be truthful and sincere, I believe they could have the power to transform your life and bring purpose, hope, and meaning to all of your tomorrows.

Life is a mystery, but it does not have to remain that way for you and me. I found a few definitions for the word *"mystery"* with the assistance of several sources. According to Webster's II New Riverside University Dictionary, it means: "something not fully understood; a religious truth comprehensible only by divine revelation." And Webster's New World Dictionary defines *"mystery"* as: "something beyond human knowledge or understanding; anything that remains as secret or obscure as to excite curiosity." I like to define *"mystery"* as that which is incapable of discovery by mere reason, but must be revealed. Dictionary.com also describes it this way: "any truth that is unknowable except by divine revelation."

The mystery of life has been revealed to us! You are about to discover the systematic unveiling of a philosophical enigma that has plagued our world from the beginning of time and still remains so heavily upon our hearts and minds yet today.

Introduction

In the modern technologically advanced digital world of the twenty-first century, many people are finding themselves so preoccupied with excessively busy schedules and time-consuming daily affairs that they often tend to overlook or disregard the most important questions that should be seriously considered by everyone today. Humans are naturally drawn to the question of life's meaning, although humanity's deep-seated longing for truth and purpose is easily suppressed by the hectic pace of today's modern lifestyles. We busy ourselves with many time-consuming details of living in a technologically advanced age, which may reflect an inward desire to avoid or perhaps postpone the vital question of our own mortality. I believe many people are allowing the years to slip away without ever giving serious consideration to life's most pressing questions. They wrestle with overstimulated lives and hurried schedules that force the search for meaning and the divine to the back of their minds where it's typically chalked up as a matter for future consideration. What is this life all about? What on earth am I here for? What is my purpose for living? Why do we live in such a broken world?

Are these questions too difficult to examine, or can we lay hold of answers that will satisfy our deepest longing for the truth? Perhaps many of us are simply going through the motions of everyday living without ever attempting to perceive the actual purpose and true significance revealed through the triumphs and struggles in which we engage. Until people are able to recognize the direction that was intended for their lives, many will continue to struggle in the face of mounting frustration, confusion and growing disappointment while pressing onward in a fallen world that is reeling from the trials inherently caused by death and decline. There remains today a desperate need in modern culture for individuals to take the necessary time to consider, openly and honestly, questions that pertain directly to the most critical issues of life with the overall objective of discovering life's true meaning. If you are willing to seriously consider these all-important questions, and do so with an open mind, then you are about to discover the very answers that could decisively reveal your purpose, alter your view of life, and forever shape your future. For you and me to experience the real meaning and genuine purpose for our mortal lives, it would certainly be helpful to discover the truth about several very basic questions. Before we consider these all-important questions, however, we should briefly examine the condition in which we find our world today.

Isn't it interesting that we, who are living in America, often considered to be the most progressive, affluent, and advanced culture in the world, are still desperately searching for that elusive thing called happiness. Even though we have seen tremendous progress as a nation, which has greatly impacted the quality and comfort of daily living the world over, we are still forced to admit that our world today is more corrupt and unsafe, and in a greater state of peril than most of us can remember. Recent tragic, history-altering events on America's own shores have confirmed to the whole world that the stability and peace we all desire has still eluded us, even well into a new millennium, where recent advances in modern civilization were expected to make our lives healthier, safer, and finally at lasting peace with those around us. The extraordinary progress in modern science, technology, medicine, education, travel, and communication has greatly impacted all of our lives in so many ways, but this has not provided us a better and safer world in which to grow up in and raise our families. The genuine emptiness, despair, frustration, and anxiety all around us are clearly witnessed by the fact that the second-most dominant category of prescription drugs sold in America over the last thirty years were those used to address the treatment of anxiety, depression, insomnia, and various other mental health issues.

Why, in a nation of unprecedented blessing and prosperity, are so many people in such great despair? It appears that far too many Americans find themselves to be terribly unhappy and dissatisfied with their lives, even though so many have enjoyed all the material blessings that are necessary to make one's life comfortable and content. Why does today's divorce rate now far exceed one-half of all marriages in America? Why do we find ourselves still at war in a world with brutal dictators who impose their selfish will upon the helpless? Why is this insidious brand of terrorism such a threat to the national security of America and many other freedom-loving nations throughout the world? Why have we witnessed so much blatant corruption, shameful immorality, and abuse of power in government and business, even among our most trusted elected leaders? And why do we detect so much sexual perversion, uncontrolled violence, hate crimes, drug abuse, poverty, and debt? These and other harsh realities are only outward symptoms of the most basic problems still facing humanity today, even at the dawn of a new millennium in which human progress was expected to provide solutions to many issues that have so long eluded us.

Man's problem is not in the mind to be analyzed, debated over, or negotiated! We surely do not need another nifty invention or an even bigger government. The problem we have is in the heart of man, and it needs to be healed! This dilemma we are facing stems from a basic lack of understanding of what this life is really all about and what is actually necessary to fulfill the most basic needs that we all have. How much longer can we possibly continue on the downward spiral of moral corruption we have experienced in Western culture over the last century? I now sense, more than ever, a desperate need in America, and throughout today's modern world, for many individuals to take a short pause from the hectic pace of modern living. Overly driven by time-consuming technology, we must stop to seriously consider the most important issues that all of us will face before our days here on this earth are over.

These simple and yet profound questions must be adequately addressed if we ever expect to know lasting fulfillment and the genuine happiness we all desire. Who am I? Where did I come from? Why am

I here? Where am I going? Can you honestly say, without any doubt whatsoever, that you have found reliable answers to these most puzzling questions about human life? Millions of people appear to be wandering aimlessly through life without any true sense of direction, and they are desperately lacking the contentment they were meant to enjoy. In a culture that is ripe with hedonism, many Americans are seeking after immediate gratification as they live only for the moment, driven primarily by self-serving desires, feelings, and emotions. These troubled souls are either misinformed or seriously unaware of the actual purpose for their existence. When considering the deeper questions of life, one such issue that we must all face, of course, is death. No matter what you choose to believe, I think we can all agree that life, as we now know it, will come to a screeching halt for all of us someday. Many individuals are taken from this world much younger than others__ and often quite suddenly without any warning. Countless men and women working at the Twin Towers in New York City on September 11, 2001, had no idea it would be their last day alive. Sudden death was waiting for and stalking so many innocent lives on that infamous and ominous day in American history.

We prepare for many things in life__ such as career, marriage, and retirement. But I wonder how many people have actually prepared themselves for the final call when they will face leaving this world behind forever? Having now considered, studied, and researched these questions for over thirty years, I would like to share with you what I believe to be undeniable answers to the troubling questions that we must all face at some time during our lives__ questions such as, how did life originate? What is the true nature of man? Is there really a supreme God? Has God adequately revealed himself to us?

As we examine these all-important questions in some detail, there remains a guiding principle that we must apply to our diligent search for understanding if we expect to discover the honest truth about life. We must follow wherever the evidence is leading us! I have spent a good portion of the last ten years gathering and organizing an abundance of valuable material that was collected and recorded over many years of following the evidence wherever it was leading me. I have written this material so that many other seekers of truth could, perhaps, come to know what life is really all about. It is right before our eyes, just waiting to be discovered. As you read through this carefully researched book, I only ask that you do so with an open mind. And this may, perhaps, mean that you should be open to the possibility that much of what Americans have been taught about life's purpose via secondary and higher education, in close concert with repetitive messages delivered by mass media outlets, has been and is untrue.

This reality will become evident when we consider a thorough evaluation of the basic life questions I am calling to your attention here. You will discover in these carefully researched pages that things are not always as they seem, even after having this information presented to us over and over throughout the vast public domain of a highly secularized culture. In a modern world that is mostly dominated by the wisdom of man (or lack thereof), this certainty becomes obvious when interpreting and documenting the truth about life's most pressing questions. There have been far too many scientific and historical facts that are deliberately hidden from public view for the purpose of shaping within us a worldview that is carefully controlled by modern secular institutions.

This, sadly enough, calls for a rigid ideology that has led to many erroneous conclusions, followed by a vast array of lifestyle choices resulting in terribly unfulfilled lives. When we ultimately consider the most critical questions about life, you and I cannot afford to be hoodwinked by the elite educational establishment in concert with mass media bias, because it is really our personal fulfillment and destiny that is at stake here. Therefore, we must discover the genuine meaning of life, which has been cleverly veiled behind a thick smokescreen obscuring the view of many for far too long.

In this material we will diligently follow the evidence to see where it leads. And as we do so, it will become very apparent to us that an immense cloud of deception has been hanging heavily over today's Western civilization for so long that even many very well-respected scientists, historians, and educators remain in denial when the authentic facts are finally laid out before them. For everyone who chooses to read this publication with an open mind and a searching heart, the predominant public mind-set that has drastically obscured an accurate view of life is about to change. Let us now commence with a thorough examination of the evidence associated with these and many other very important and related questions. It remains my sincere hope and prayer that this material will somehow assist those who truly desire to unravel *The Mystery of Life*.

Chapter 1

THE ORIGIN OF LIFE

Setting the Stage

Somehow life appeared on planet earth in the distant past. Without any doubt, the great mystery of our existence starts with the question, how did it all begin? At some point in our lives, all of us will have to consider the crucial question of origins. Where did we come from? How did we get here? Everyone has an opinion about the origin of life, but I wonder how many people can actually point to valid evidence that will support his or her own personal worldview. It seems to me as though few people really care enough to examine the abundant evidence offered in the physical world—evidence that will likely confirm or deny what they believe. I suppose that people are far too preoccupied with the rapid pace of modern living, and the hearts of many in affluent cultures have become overly stimulated by the time-consuming affairs of everyday life, preventing pause to consider these questions seriously. But why is this subject of such great importance? Some might even say, what difference does it make where we came from, or how we got here? The obvious fact is we are here, so we should just enjoy it while we can! I believe this cavalier approach to life will leave a serious void within the human heart and soul, which will never be fully satisfied or at peace. With this thought in mind, I would submit to you that not knowing where we came from will leave you and me with very little real understanding about who we are, or even why we are living on this earth. And without this fundamental knowledge, people are left with a genuine lack of appreciation for the real purpose and meaning that was intended for their lives.

Within this opening chapter, we will begin to investigate many of the vitally important considerations regarding the origin of life, and I am quite confident that making a thorough examination of this material will lead us toward a greater understanding of exactly why we are alive. I do not know how you feel, but not knowing the truth about life doesn't sit well with me. I want to know! I want to fully understand whatever I can about the past, present, and future! I want to comprehend the truth to the extent that it may be fully embraced by our feeble minds. I want to discern whether we decide our own future, or if the final consummation of our earthly days is simply an abrupt dead end to a difficult and exhausting journey. I believe that anyone wanting to live a significant life with purpose-filled tomorrows must be willing to carefully examine the truth about the all-important question of origins.

The two most commonly held views about life's origin, which have dominated the thinking of the vast majority of people within Western culture, are naturalism and intelligent design. Which of these ideas represent the correct worldview? Why do these thoughts present such conflicting concepts? Please join me now as I endeavor to thoroughly address the critical topic of origins, and specifically the vital question, how did life begin? I believe the vast implications inferred by the truth about our past will, ultimately, become far reaching and life changing with regard to our future. Whatever we subsequently come to accept about the past, after considering this vital question of origins, will have a profound and powerful influence in determining our entire worldview, and as a result, the knowledge generated by this encounter will have significant control over the way in which we live our lives. If there is no eternal creator God, and we are nothing but the accidental outcome of many unguided, random chance events in a vastly impersonal universe, then there really can be no absolute authority to which we, ultimately, owe a debt of gratitude for our existence. We are simply set adrift to fend for ourselves in a very hostile and often unforgiving world. Is this life plagued with pain, suffering, sorrow, and death all there is? Do we have anything significant to look forward to as we all grow old and eventually lose our will to survive? Are people just an accident? Are we some random, unexpected, and unplanned product of blind chance, or do our lives have real purpose and meaning, allowing us to make logical sense of a very troubled existence into which each of us was born?

Western civilization, including these United States of America, has become overly saturated with the strange notion that the evolution model is the only possible explanation for life as we know it; but does the evidence confirm this point of view, or have we simply become indoctrinated within modern culture by the voices of those who have long since rejected the idea of a supreme intelligence? This intelligence, many believe, speaks to us of a loving, personal God who has the power to create all things with specific purpose. As you carefully consider the material in this book, I trust it will somehow assist you in your own personal quest for knowledge and truth, knowing that the purpose for addressing the all-important question of origins is absolutely critical to an overall understanding of the meaning of life.

Creation and Evolution Defined

To refresh our thinking, let's define the concept of biological evolution that has saturated Western culture for more than a century and is now being taught exclusively in public schools and universities throughout America and many other nations of the world. The concept of evolution, with regard to organic life-forms, has been defined and redefined in a variety of ways over the last one hundred years. Sometimes it refers to very basic thoughts__ like change, species variation, and even artificial selection. Therefore, it is important for us to understand the basic concepts I am referencing whenever I mention the topic of evolution in this publication. The wide variation within established genetic boundaries is sometimes referred to by the term "microevolution." Although I would prefer not to use this confusing terminology, I do not know of anyone who would deny that genetic variation within prescribed limits has been written into the DNA code of all living organisms. In the words of MIT graduate Dr. Lee Spetner, who once served as the resident expert and chief professor of information and communication theory at the famous Johns Hopkins University, "I have studied the implications of random variations on evolution for many years, and have found contradiction after contradiction, difficulty after difficulty, with neo-Darwinian theory...A large body of evidence points to the suggestion that organisms come equipped with the ability to make heritable changes in their organs and functions in response to environmental cues."[1]

"Macroevolution," on the other hand, is a clear reference to what Mr. Charles Darwin was initially proposing. His original hypothesis has conjured up the notion of large-scale physical transformation giving rise to the appearance of new improved species over time, driven supposedly by a mechanism incorporating mutation and natural selection. This perceived drastic appearance of new organs, body structures, and innovative survival features in organic design is believed to be due to random chance alterations or, possibly, to the addition of new genetic information within a host organism's cellular DNA. Finally, there is the concept spoken of as "molecular evolution." This terminology is often used in reference to the initial emergence of a living cell from nonliving chemical elements in a primordial state. You may also remember this hypothesis by the term "spontaneous generation."

The various modern hypotheses that have incorporated both macroevolution and molecular evolution (spontaneous generation) are the popular ideas that I would vigorously question. I believe these popular concepts are dangerous and deceiving notions that have led toward an unparalleled decline in Western civilization by virtue of a steep and steady descent toward atheism. These commonly taught ideas are highly offensive to a great many Americans who have based their lifestyle choices and ethical ideals upon a firm, long-lived tradition grounded in our nation's Judeo-Christian heritage. By my way of thinking, the most troubling thing about these rather strange notions, which have now become firmly embedded in the American psyche, is that no reliable scientific evidence is found to support them, as you and I will soon discover. I would even suggest that anyone who firmly aligns themselves with the peculiar concepts of macroevolution and spontaneous generation is actually walking on very thin ice scientifically speaking, and therefore, they must ultimately rely on unfounded speculation to generate the faith to steadfastly maintain these two intellectual commitments. The following general statements are now commonly included in the basic tenets of the evolution model as I have come to understand it.

1. Perhaps ten or twenty billion years ago, all matter was concentrated in one place. While spinning at a rapid rate, it somehow exploded in what has come to be known as "the big bang." The cooling gases and debris from this spontaneous explosion of light, matter, and energy eventually resulted in the formation of a vast cosmos populated by billions of star-studded galaxies, including the spectacular Milky Way, serving as host to a fascinating solar system as we know it today. The third planet from our sun in this amazing group of celestial bodies is where our story begins.

2. As the new universe expanded and the earth cooled, water mingled with the elements, providing a primordial soup teeming with raw chemicals. By some mysterious accidental process that cannot be explained, these simple inorganic compounds began to randomly fuse themselves together to form complex molecular structures. These spontaneously generated organic molecules somehow became highly energized and subsequently were able to miraculously organize themselves under the most improbable of conditions. Some scientists believe that this random series of "lucky breaks" was necessary to accidentally produce the first self-replicating cellular life-form.

3. Over many millions of years, this spontaneously generated, primitive cellular organism eventually became a multifaceted life-form through random transmutation and was enabled, after

5

accumulating an exhaustive series of mutational variation, to somehow alter its crude physical features and gradually become much more complex in its overall anatomy, and ever fitter to survive in a hostile world.

4. After many millions of years of endless gradual change by natural processes alone, these primitive organisms began to randomly evolve into life-forms with greater complexity that were much more capable of environmental adaptation, allowing for greater survival in the extremely harsh climates of an ever-changing world.

5. Through the painfully slow process of mutation and natural selection, by pure chance, these early life-forms were continually experiencing many accidental, structurally advanced modifications, allowing one species to change itself into another in a continuous progression from simple organisms to those demonstrating far greater complexity and order. Eventually, these new emerging life-forms would gain the fitness necessary to thrive amid the harsh and unforgiving climates of earth.

6. Over several billion years, these relentless, although modest, physiological alterations were continually accumulating, allowing only the most robust organisms to survive. This drive toward transformation led to many new advanced species that were better able to adapt to the challenges presented to them by the rigorous environment. Over the vast ages of time, many increasingly unique and amazingly complex living things would appear until finally, ultimately, human life had evolved.

Evolution, as we know it today, is based on the concept of naturalism, which teaches that all organic changes occurring in nature are the result of random chance events acting totally independent of any divine force or intelligent influence. This unusually strange notion, commonly called "naturalistic evolution," has demanded that mutational changes, occurring randomly in living organisms, must provide physical advantages that will, over time, result in significant improvements in the structure and functionality of all living things.

These perceived physiologically useful benefits, which many believe will become concentrated in the population, would result in progeny exhibiting greater and greater fitness and a much higher probability of adaptive survival in the highly competitive and ever-changing environments of a hostile planet.

The other typically accepted view of the origin of life is that of "special creation," which also brings to mind the concept of "intelligent design." And in spite of the widespread dissemination of evolutionary ideas in modern American culture, national surveys are commonly suggesting that well over 60 percent of Americans still believe in this traditional view of origins. The intelligent design model has implied that an all-powerful Supreme Being is solely responsible for intelligently planning and then purposefully creating the entire universe, including our own planet, and each of the extremely complex life-forms that dwell upon it. In stark contrast with evolution, special creation teaches that life on planet earth is not accidental or random but the ingenious design of a purposeful God. A written and very detailed record of the creation account is clearly summarized for our careful examination in the first two chapters of the celebrated book of Genesis.

When considering the question of origins, the modern concept of evolution, as we know it today, is actually a fairly recent phenomenon. At the onset of the current scientific revolution, Christianity and science were considered to be totally compatible. For at least the first 300 years following the rise of the modern scientific age, Christianity clearly offered the dominant worldview, and the majority of those early scientists were devoted Christian believers. It has only been within the last 150 years or less that an evolutionary worldview has taken a strong hold upon Western civilization. This strange view, however, now appears to be the official position of public policy in the most advanced cultures of the world.

In the first generation following World War I, a survey of more than five hundred National Academy of Science members revealed that only 7 percent of them believed in the concept of a personal creator God. Nevertheless, in spite of well over 150 years of public debate, it was men who held a strong belief in a Creator that founded the primary branches of modern science, as we know them today. The long list of creation-minded scientific pioneers is really quite impressive when you consider names like Sir Isaac Newton, Michael Faraday, Louis Pasteur, William Kelvin, Robert Boyle, Gregor Mendel, Nicolaus Copernicus, Galileo Galilei, Johannes Kepler, and Blaise Pascal, just to name a very few of the most impressive scientific figures in world history. Even classical Greek philosophers like Plato and Aristotle, whose influential ideas have, no doubt, given rise to a materialistic view of the physical dimension, recognized the obvious fact that the universe is far from self-explanatory, requiring an explanation well beyond itself.

In my exhaustive search for truth and knowledge, I have discovered that many men and women of contemporary science are still continuing in the time-honored tradition of these early pioneers who had laid a firm foundation for observation and discovery. Because of their insatiable appetite for knowledge and understanding, distinguished scientists the world over have already given us a remarkable glimpse of the unknown with some surprisingly spectacular insights into the characteristics of the universe we inhabit. On a grand scale of the incomprehensible vastness of outer space, the technologically advanced Hubble Telescope is continually transmitting back to earth exceptionally stunning images of the starry heavens above. At the opposite end of this vast physical spectrum, we discover the painstakingly driven science of modern biochemistry that has utilized electron microscope technology to meticulously map the unique complexity of minute cellular physiology. This fabulous microscopic world of discernible macromolecules is constantly at work generating microminiaturized molecular machinery within every living cell. These important cellular components are specifically calibrated to consistently manufacture a wide array of essential proteins with unbelievable precision and efficiency, demonstrating very unique levels of complexity by creating living chemistry and making the most advanced engineering designs of human technology appear crude by comparison.

In recent decades, evolutionary thought has taken our Western civilization by storm, but does that necessarily make it true? When we consider what is suggested by the big bang theory, it's just not reasonable for rational man to assume that a completely random explosion, absent any intelligent oversight, could ever produce something resembling complex order and design. This is especially true when one considers the precision and mathematical symmetry in the physical laws that are governing a vast array of heavenly bodies, such as planets, stars, and galaxies. Random explosions, lacking any intelligent guidance, will always produce pure chaos and disorder; they will never produce organization, beauty, and useful complexity. That, they say, is how the universe began, and from that point on it was merely one accident after another that supposedly produced the detailed intricacy and unbelievable continuity of the material world in which we live.

The many proponents of evolution theory would have us believe that several billion years ago, random chemicals, in some imagined primordial soup, were somehow spontaneously and very unintentionally arranged, organized, and became fully energized. This pure accident, they believe, resulted in the initial spontaneous generation of the first primitive life-form. By evoking simple materialistic naturalism as the fundamental basis of their beloved theory, modern evolutionists have consistently inferred that all things became what they are today by freakish, random chance events. They aggressively and dogmatically promote the idea that organization and order in the known universe has occurred completely without the direction of intelligent agency, and therefore, the vast material world we know and experience has no specific reason for existing. On the other hand, intelligent design would suggest to us that a personal God had a very definite plan and a specifically designed purpose when he initially chose to uniquely order and intentionally fashion a vast and remarkable universe filled with exceptional beauty, complexity, and design. Fortunately for us, this exceptional creation included an extraordinary planet like earth teeming with abundant life—a planet we are all privileged to call our home.

There is obviously a considerable degree of contradiction between the two concepts of creation and evolution. How can one honestly believe in a literal interpretation of the biblical record of creation and, at the same time, accommodate evolution theory. In order to believe in creation, one must believe in a Creator as well__ perhaps the one who left a detailed record of the designs resulting from his impressive handiwork. The concepts of creation and evolution are certainly diametrically opposed to one another. However, what may surprise a lot of people is also the certainty that one cannot actually believe in a literal interpretation of the known facts of empirical science and still hold allegiance to evolution as well. The reason for this is revealed in our understanding that the facts of science do not adequately support the evolutionary model, as we will henceforth discover throughout this book's narrative. Unfortunately, however, many people have framed their position on origins based entirely upon what they consider to be the expert statements, opinions, and conclusions that have been consistently offered by others, instead of by carefully and thoroughly examining unbiased evidence for themselves.

Before we actually begin to explore the detailed material I would like to submit for your thoughtful consideration, let me state here, quite emphatically, that the conflict between the two worldviews that incorporate the naturalistic model of Darwinian evolution, as opposed to special creation by Intelligent design, is so great in scope and so critical to the formulation of a personal understanding of life that any proposed compromise, utilizing aspects of both views in an attempt to satisfy everyone, is totally out of the question. If one of these views is found to be truthful, based upon a clear consensus of the scientific evidence that is now available to us, the other view must remain utterly false and should be completely discarded.

Doubting Darwin

For thousands of years now, various philosophers have related a somewhat similar materialistic view of life in an attempt to explain the diversity set before us. However, it was Mr. Charles Darwin who, in modern times, has been credited with popularizing this commonly held view of origins. In his two major works, *On the Origin of Species* and *The Descent of Man*, Charles Darwin laid out the basic ideas and

the foundational material that has shaped the evolutionary model widely accepted today. Darwin had strongly believed that somehow the mechanism of natural selection could possibly account for the full development of all the species over vast ages of time. This is clearly evident from some of the initial statements he recorded in his original works. Darwin stated that, "Natural selection is daily and hourly scrutinizing . . . every variation, even the slightest; rejecting that which is bad, preserving and adding up all that is good; silently and insensibly working at the improvement of each organic being."[2]

Even though Darwin had intended to submit his initial conclusions as only a possible explanation for the origin of living things, his early works have received such wide acclaim that he became, to some degree, misrepresented over the years. Many have concluded that Darwin was very dogmatic about his proposed ideas and had offered sufficient evidence to support them. However, after considering some of Darwin's own personal statements, I think you and I will agree that he was actually somewhat uncertain and very careful not to overstate his intentions. From the very outset of his major work, *On the Origin of Species*, it is very obvious that Darwin himself harbored some serious doubts about the validity of his claims by frequently using thoughts of conjecture, setting a tone of uncertainty about his conclusions.

In the introductory material of his first major publication, Darwin makes this prudent statement: "A fair result can be obtained only by fully stating and balancing the facts and arguments on both sides of each question; and this is here impossible."[3] Darwin surely knew that his unique proposals could not be tested for accuracy, and therefore, he was very careful to convey the true nature of his conclusions as supposition only. His dubious conviction, when compared to the dogmatic attitude of many modern-day naturalists, would lead us to the conclusion that contemporary evolutionists have leaned heavily toward real bias in their public approach to this very controversial subject. The suggestion that many so-called *beneficial mutations* will lead to improved species over time has become a true companion concept with natural selection and survival of the fittest, which, of course, are ideas that obviously no one would deny in a world that is plagued by awful disease, disability,

and death. In adopting this overt mechanism of fitness, evolution has taught that nature will always favor and select the more robust species for survival, while the weaker, less fit, and perhaps least aggressive organisms will all tend to die off and become extinct over time.

From his various observations, Charles Darwin presumed that when a mutant variation had occurred in a given species, which could possibly improve its relative chance of survival, this resulting trait would take clear precedence over less desirable physical qualities and over time would become concentrated in the population. By this process, known as the "variation of species," Darwin eventually concluded that over millions of years, the accumulation of these (possibly beneficial) minor changes would somehow support each other in a complementary and cumulative way and therefore could, perhaps, allow for one species to successfully transform itself into another. However, his initial doubts about the accuracy of this prediction are very apparent when you consider these questioning remarks: "Why, if species have descended from other species by fine gradations, do we not everywhere see innumerable transitional forms? Why is not all nature in confusion, instead of species being, as we see them, well-defined?"[4] He continues with this perplexing observation: "But, as by this theory, innumerable transitional forms must have existed, why do we not find them embedded in countless numbers in the crust of the earth?"[5] The absence of so-called transitional forms (commonly called "missing links") has been a constant source of confusion for today's modern evolutionists. Many scientists simply assume these intermediate forms must have existed, in spite of the overwhelming lack of evidence in the fossil record. Again, Darwin expresses serious misgivings after having observed various species in the normal process of sexual reproduction. This knowledge had caused him to become admittedly puzzled by certain unexpected outcomes. In response to these observations, he again posed another very intuitive question: "How can we account for species, when crossed, being sterile and producing sterile offspring, whereas, when varieties are crossed, their fertility is unimpaired?"[6]

Apparently he was questioning how his theory could possibly hold up to scrutiny in light of obvious fixed boundaries between various animal

species. The genetic DNA chemistry in living organisms was designed to ensure that each organic kind would retain its own specific identity, while at the same time allowing for the development of wide variation within certain physical traits, making each variety most compatible with environmental change. Before his death, Darwin already knew that his theory was in serious trouble and could not account for certain unpredictable anomalies. His obvious awareness of the unfruitfulness of the fossil record to demonstrate any tangible evidence for transitional intermediates, ultimately, prompted the following regretful remarks, and this has certainly added to the speculation that Darwin had some very serious doubts about his own personal conclusions: "The number of intermediate varieties which have formerly existed on the Earth must be truly enormous. Why then is not every geological formation and every stratum full of such intermediate links? Geology assuredly does not reveal any such finely graduated organic chain; and this is perhaps the most obvious and gravest objection that can be urged against my theory."[7]

Evidently, many people today choose to overlook this distinct lack of intermediate transitions and remain confident in conveying evolution publicly as a scientific reality. This unwarranted dogmatism is offered consistently in the public domain in spite of the serious doubts Charles Darwin had appropriately expressed about his own conclusions. When Mr. Darwin initially advanced his theory in 1859, modern science was still in its formative years. Today, however, with such amazing advances in contemporary technology, new opportunities to discover the reality of our world have accelerated at a blistering pace. With the aid of the electron microscope and digital computer technology, we are now able to peer into and map the unique and vast complexity of a single cell. The fascinating physiology and complex design we have thus far discovered in this tiny speck of life is light-years beyond the imagination of the greatest scientists of Darwin's day, who considered a single cell to be a relatively simple structure. Captivating recent discoveries in the ever-advancing technical world of empirical science have now led mankind further down the road toward numerous innovative and unique frontiers of research, including molecular microbiology, astrophysics, quantum

electrodynamics, and probability analysis. Advanced research into these, and many other modern technological scientific disciplines, is now proving to be disastrous for evolutionary theory.

Many highly qualified and well-equipped researchers in the ongoing study of origins, unlike the disadvantaged and ill-equipped investigators of Darwin's day, are now finding the popular concept of evolution to be quite impractical and are, therefore, no longer taking it seriously. However, we are living in a contemporary, modern society in which evolution theory is assumed by many to be strictly factual. This commonly held position exists primarily because a blatantly materialistic view of origins has been continually and consistently embellished by media bias, while also forced upon most American citizens through a massive public-education campaign. This dogma has been presented to us over and over again as objective truth and scientific fact. Now, however, we're discovering that modern science has exposed major flaws in "the theory," having uncovered a serious lack of convincing evidence available to support the evolution model. Therefore, nearly all American families are now finding themselves repeatedly subjected to a blatant form of indoctrination funded by the government at taxpayers' expense. As it turned out historically, those who would choose not to retain God in their consideration of life were standing quietly by, ready and eager to believe that Darwin's theory had eliminated the need for an "intelligent designer," by finally demonstrating a process through which naturalistic events could account for the remarkable complexity and diversity of living things.

We now understand, however, that Darwin's theory was seriously flawed. His rather presumptuous speculation and premature guesswork about the origin of life is far from satisfactory when we consider the compelling evidence thus far uncovered by mankind's eager search for knowledge over the last 150 years of scientific investigation. By using electron microscopy, with research into biochemical cellular physiology, we are recognizing scientific realities Charles Darwin never dreamed of. Yet with today's fascinating advances in many accelerating new fields of research and discovery, scientists are now able to unveil vivid and remarkable complexity in cellular design that Darwin's outdated

theory utterly failed to account for. The living cell's delicately detailed interlocking machinery of various sensors, pumps, gates, and delivery systems unveiled by viewing microscopic cellular physiology has required that each of these critical networking components be in place simultaneously, being fully integrated together in order for active cellular function to occur. I believe that Darwin's fatal error was twofold in regard to the functioning mechanisms of living, organic cellular design. First of all, he wrongly assumed the living cell was comprised of fairly simple organic structures. Second, Darwin believed that, somehow, these vital integrated structures and interlocking molecular components could be added together very slowly, over millions of years, by the piecemeal process of mutation and natural selection.

Because the technology of Darwin's day was so limited, he was able to convince the scientific world of the nineteenth century that a rather simple design in organic, cellular physiology would allow for gradual change and increasing complexity leading toward greater organic fitness over time. Darwin would often refer to this process as the "transmutation of species," and ultimately, he believed that, somehow, these steady, gradually occurring random changes would slowly, but continually, move evolutionary biology forward toward higher, more advanced, and increasingly more complex living organisms.

Outspoken Evolutionists

In Western culture, prior to Darwin, biblical Christianity was the foundational basis of formal education in all areas of study, teaching, and research, and especially in the realm of science. After Darwin introduced his theory, however, the world of modern academia was ready and eagerly waiting to cast aside the Bible in favor of a worldview that denied God. Since that time, and with passionate zeal, liberal-minded, progressive reformers have gradually infiltrated the six major areas of public influence within American culture. These power centers include public education, government, the entertainment industry, science, journalism, and to a somewhat lesser degree, even the church.

These six most dominant public institutions within modern culture have gradually but steadily drawn an unsuspecting public further and further away from biblical truth in favor of a more secular and highly materialistic view of the world. In an effort to sway public opinion, many evolutionists have become consistently biased, often overzealous, and, in far too many cases, downright deceptive in representing the facts and the true nature of their position. Years ago, *Reader's Digest* magazine printed a condensed version of a new book entitled *The Naked Ape*. In the very first paragraph of this major book review, British zoologist Dr. Desmond Morris states rather bluntly that it is a known fact that man evolved from ancestors of apelike intelligence.[8] The enormously popular *Time* magazine, perhaps the most widely read news magazine in the world, has printed many articles about the origin of life over the years, and generally with a strong evolutionary bias toward an unproven theory, which is primarily based upon preconceived speculation and guesswork. One particular cover story was published in 1977 with the title "How Man Became Man."[9] Typical of nearly all news magazine coverage on this subject, the *Time* writers made it perfectly clear that they believe evolution is the key to understanding the origin of the human species. However, throughout the magazine article, a serious lack of convincing evidence forces anthropologists to use common words of conjecture to describe their work—phrases like "we believe," "we theorize," and "we speculate." These phrases tell us that a great deal of educated guesswork has gone into today's scientific thought on origin-of-man research. Toward the end of this interesting *Time* article, the following major concessions are offered to the reader: "Still, doubts about the sequence of man's emergence remain. Scientists concede that even their most cherished theories are based on embarrassingly few fossil fragments, and that huge gaps exist in the fossil record."[10]

Even the world's so-called greatest experts have been baffled by the obvious lack of compelling evidence from scientific study, research, and investigation over recent generations. So after more than 150 years since the time of Darwin's classic publication, intense study and painstaking research has left modern evolutionary theory in the poorhouse.

Nevertheless, its faithful proponents continue to make many profound yet unverifiable claims about their cherished ideology.

After considering a generation of skepticism represented by their highly improbable claims, we will carefully examine some of today's current scientific evidence. This new knowledge, provided for us through systematic observation and experimentation, should help us greatly in evaluating the question of whether true, contemporary science actually supports the bold and highly controversial conclusions of evolutionary theory. Allow me to share, for your consideration, a few of these especially dogmatic assertions that the so-called scientific experts of the past have made to the world over the public airwaves in recent years.

1. "The first point to make about Darwin's theory is that it is no longer a theory but a fact . . . Darwinism has come of age, so to speak. We are no longer having to bother about establishing the fact of evolution."[11] (Julian Huxley, biologist)

2. "Modern science must rule out special creation or divine guidance."[12] (Julian Huxley)

3. "Evolution is a fact, not a theory."[13] (Carl Sagan, astronomer)

4. "Natural selection is a successful theory devised to explain the fact of evolution."[14] (Carl Sagan)

5. "To those who were trained in science, creationism seems like a bad dream, a sudden reliving of a nightmare, a renewed march of an army of the night risen to challenge free thought and enlightenment."[15] (Isaac Asimov, biochemist)

6. "The process of natural selection and survival of the fittest, with the many mutations that occur over hundreds of millions of years, adequately account for the origin and development of the species."[16] (Corliss Lamont, philosopher)

7. "Man is the result of a purposeless and natural process that did not have him in mind. He was not planned. He is a state of matter, a form of life, a sort of animal and a species of the order Primates, akin nearly or remotely to all life and indeed to all that is material."[17] (George Gaylord Simpson, paleontologist)

8. "Most enlightened persons now accept as a fact that everything in the cosmos from heavenly bodies to human beings, has developed and continues to develop through evolutionary processes."[18] (René Dubos, microbiologist)

9. "Evolution . . . is the most powerful and the most comprehensive idea that has ever arisen on earth."[19] (Julian Huxley)

10. "Humanism believes that man is a part of nature, and that he has emerged as the result of a continuous process."[20] (*Humanist Manifesto I*)

11. "Science affirms that the human species is an emergence from natural evolutionary forces."[21] (*Humanist Manifesto II*)

These still unconfirmed statements and dogmatic assertions by Huxley, Sagan, and others have directly challenged the intelligence of many people who remain thoroughly unconvinced that simple materialism holds the key to explaining the origin, complexity, and diversity of living things. Publicly making unscientific statements like these speaks volumes about the inflexibility and overconfidence often seen in those who continually belittle, demean, and harass anyone who does not concur with their atheistic worldview.

In his 1980 television series *Cosmos*, atheist astronomer Carl Sagan boldly declared, "The cosmos is all there is, or was, or ever shall be."[22] Thus, the essence of naturalism proposes that there is nothing beyond nature, that we live in a closed system, and that there is no other realm or entity that has, by any means, altered the natural order by way of some transcendent supernatural power. Sagan's assertion is a statement of personal belief, not of science! It is strictly a philosophical view, not unlike believing in the Genesis account of creation. Therefore, the question we must all answer is this: which worldview does empirical science most strongly support__ naturalism or theism? To most modern-day evolutionists, the unnatural idea of an all-powerful creator God, to whom everyone will ultimately be held accountable, is absolutely unthinkable. Therefore, because the evolution theory appears to be the only explanation of origins that excludes supernatural power, those who deny God have embraced it with great tenacity. So while most naturalists continue to persist in their ceaseless effort to explain life without divine cause, it remains entirely up to each one of us to thoroughly examine this topic to see if any valid support can be found for their bold and provocative claims. Please join me with a focused mind and an open, searching heart as we thoroughly investigate what so many revealed facts, qualified expert testimony, and volumes of hard, empirically derived scientific data actually reveal to us about the validity and reliability of evolutionary claims.

Design Demands a Designer

We live in a world filled with designed physiology__ demonstrating mind-blowing complexity. Just try to explain the explosive defense mechanism of the bombardier beetle, the visual accommodation apparatus of the archerfish, the homing instinct of a carrier pigeon, the head and neck muscular and skeletal design of a woodpecker, or perhaps the migratory instinct of Canadian geese. The Australian molecular biochemist Dr. Michael Denton has concluded from his outstanding research that "it is the sheer universality of perfection, the fact that everywhere we look, to whatever depth we look, we find an elegance and integrity of an absolutely transcending quality, which so mitigates against the idea of chance."[23]

Perhaps one of the world's leading evolution advocates, renowned scholar Dr. Richard Dawkins of Oxford University, made this statement in a book he entitled *The Blind Watchmaker*: "We have seen that living things are too improbable and too beautifully 'designed' to have come into existence by chance."[24] Although we must understand that Dawkins is clearly not advocating for intelligent design, this acknowledgement, from a world-class atheist, seems to offer at least the vague notion that nature is far too remarkable to simply chalk it all up to a long series of bizarre, random accidents. In his popular book entitled *Darwin's Black Box*, Dr. Michael Behe, a well-known molecular biochemistry researcher from Lehigh University, has introduced us to a new term, "irreducible complexity," which refers to a very strict requirement in nature that all the major subcomponents of any vital organ system must be found simultaneously present, fully functioning, and completely networked together for any complex integrated system to work properly. A sample design that will illustrate this point can be found in the common five-part mousetrap. This simple mechanism, which was designed specifically to kill mice, will only function for its intended purpose if all five parts are present simultaneously. This device requires a platform, spring, catch, hammer, and hold-down bar working together all at the same time. If any single component is missing or broken, the device is basically useless for mouse removal. In a much more complex illustration, it is obvious that all of the major subcomponents of a Boeing 747 must be found networked together and fully integrated with extreme precision before the plane can fly successfully. In the same sense, all of the required primary subcomponents of any essential biological organ system, such as digestion or vision, must be simultaneously present and properly networked together before any active, useful function can occur. This suggests that the vital parts of any living biological system could not possibly have resulted from a simple piecemeal process like natural selection!

Consider Dr. Behe's comments regarding cellular design. "Now it's the turn of the fundamental science of life, modern biochemistry, to disturb . . . The simplicity that was once expected to be the foundation of life has proven to be a phantom; instead, systems of horrendous, irreducible complexity inhabit the living cell . . . The resulting realization that life was designed by an intelligence is a shock to us in the 20th century who have gotten used to thinking of life as the result of simple, natural laws. But other centuries have had their shocks, and there is no reason to suppose that we should escape them."[25]

The design principle of irreducible complexity must have struck fear in the heart of Darwin, as he began to consider the intricacy, unique design, and vast complexity of living systems, and how his theory had utterly failed to account for them. He once wrote, "If it could be demonstrated that any complex organ existed, which could not possibly have been formed by numerous, successive, slight modifications, my theory would absolutely break down."[26]

In the case of a single living cell, science has thus far identified a minimum of seventeen complex systems that must be in place and fully integrated simultaneously in order to have viable cellular function. Otherwise, the cell would be nonfunctional and totally unable to generate the minimum essential proteins required for life.

Anatomically speaking, the visual system (sight) would represent a very pronounced example of the design principle of irreducible complexity within living organisms. When you consider a complex organ system such as vision, the extreme problems for evolution encountered by irreducibly multipart design become very evident. Sight allows for electromagnetic radiation (photons or visible light energy) to be detected by a very specialized organ system and converted into chemically mediated nerve impulses that are interpreted by the brain as visual images. This detection occurs when visible light is reflected off an object and enters the cornea of the eye, where it passes through the clear lens, and is focused upon the retina. The normal refraction of light through the lens causes the image to be displayed on the retina upside down. This useful energy from visible light is then absorbed by highly sensitive pigment cells on the surface of the rods and cones lining the retina. The inner portion of the retina then converts this light energy into chemically mediated nerve impulses (electronic signals), which are then passed along to the optic chiasm and through the optic tract, resulting in transmission by the optic nerve to the brain, where the visual information is initially received at the geniculate body. The iris muscle of the human eye acts like a small mechanical diaphragm as it alters the size of the pupil, thus controlling the amount of light entering the cornea. As the optic nerve transmits all these neural impulses to the associated parts of the brain, an electronic message is received at the lateral geniculate nucleus. From there, electronic impulses are transmitted to the primary and secondary visual cortex (occipital cortex) at the back of the brain, where the image is displayed right-side up. Ultimately, each image is received at the frontal lobes of the brain where visual acuity and pattern recognition occurs and where each object is finally identified. Eyelids, nerves cells, blood vessels, tear ducts, aqueous humor, and vitreous humor are a few of the other subcomponents, which all play an important role in this complex feature that is vitally essential for a wide variety of living organisms.

The complicated system of vision (ocular perception) requires that all the necessary subcomponents be in place and fully integrated together to produce visual recognition. If any single primary component of the visual apparatus is missing or defective, this could negate the proper functioning of the entire system. It is certain that the piecemeal process of evolution cannot possibly account for any complex organic system in which all major subcomponents must appear in unison and be fully networked to allow viable functioning to occur. Charles Darwin was certainly aware that this reality presented a major obstacle for his theory. In fact, he even made a specific reference to the evolution of vision, which, of course, is an essential survival feature common to many organic life-forms and a great example of Behe's irreducible complexity. Darwin, perhaps reluctantly, recorded the following major observation: "To suppose that the eye (with so many parts, all working together) could have been formed by natural selection, seems, I freely confess, absurd to the highest degree."[27] Now, without question, irreducible complexity has revealed an undeniably complex and highly integrated design principle within living organisms that speaks volumes about the necessity for a complex-minded, ingenious design engineer. After thoroughly examining the various naturalistic hypotheses offered as an explanation for living things, biochemist Michael Behe, who has reintroduced this unique design concept to our generation, has written this compelling statement: "I conclude that another possibility is more likely: the elegant, coherent, functional systems upon which life depends are the result of deliberate, intelligent design."[28]

Have you ever stopped to consider that our remarkable solar system works like a giant clock? It is a grand geometric design that works by mathematical order based upon the fundamental laws of physics. The rotation and revolution of the planets around the sun is so precise that we can determine the exact location of each of the sun's satellites at any given moment past, present, or future. We can also predict exactly when a lunar or solar eclipse will occur and just how long it will last. Halley's Comet, which consistently speeds around our solar system in a very conventional fashion, was last viewed in 1985. We can calculate exactly when it will appear again, in the year 2060, because its passage across the solar system brings it near our planet on a reliable seventy-five-year cycle. We recently experienced a rare astronomical event causing many to look skyward to observe a brief phenomenon called the Transit of Venus. On June 5, 2012, we all witnessed the planet Venus on its passage directly between the earth and the sun. Astronomers were able to predict exactly when this unique event would begin and exactly when it would end. You and I will all be long gone the next time it is scheduled to occur, on December 10 of the year 2117.

We know exactly when the sun will rise in the east and set in the west and when it will be high tide and low tide; and we can predict these events with precise accuracy on any given day of the year at any specific location on the planet, past, present, or future. Why is this? It is because the universe precisely obeys physical laws defined by mathematical order. Would it make rational sense for any of us to think of the magnificent machinery of a fine, delicately designed watch in terms of a common freak accident? I believe that our fine-tuned, mathematically arranged solar system would speak no less of remarkable intelligent design! Men like Galileo and Kepler have long since investigated this mathematical order, and the most reasonable conclusion they could draw was that our beautiful solar system, operating with such remarkable precision according to the defined laws of physics, has resulted from the magnificently designed plan of an intelligent power, which is orderly, organized, and extremely reliable. As such, the physical universe exhibits the character and nature of its designer.

The life-giving element of water (in liquid form) so abundant on the earth (covering 350 million cubic miles) is noticeably absent or currently undetected elsewhere in our solar system. The presence of precious liquid H_2O that is so essential to life appears to have been purposely designed specifically to sustain life on planet earth. Even though some scientists have described what they believe to be evidence that water may have existed on Mars in the distant past, this has not been confirmed. Oxygen, another crucial element required for organic life, is found in abundance on earth, but this also appears to be somewhat rare beyond our planet. While the utilization of oxygen upon the earth's surface is so critical for sustaining life, there is another important reason for the world we live in to have an atmosphere containing a high level of these essential gas molecules. The intense ultraviolet light originating from solar radiation would be quite deadly on our planet's surface if it were not for the additional presence of an oxygen matrix in the earth's upper atmosphere. The life-giving oxygen molecules we breathe contain two oxygen atoms. The ozone layer high above us is also composed of pure oxygen, but its molecular structure consists of three oxygen atoms, resulting in a physical feature that was designed for another very essential purpose. The earth's ozone blanket offers a unique structural feature allowing it to block ultraviolet light. As a result, this design works to effectively filter out most of the sun's deadliest rays. Without this special filtering mechanism, these high-energy waves would become lethal to life on the planet's surface. On the other hand, the sun's visible light waves, which are, of course, essential for the energy and growth of plants, along with supporting all other life-forms, pass right on through the ozone layer, while it efficiently filters out the most harmful rays, providing the perfect shield to protect us. I'm quite certain that this unique, life-saving feature found in the atmosphere of planet earth is much more than just a random accident!

Whose idea was photosynthesis? Photosynthesis is a very unique, extremely complicated design mechanism by which plants are able to capture radiant energy from the sun and convert it into very useful chemical energy. Webster's II New Riverside University Dictionary describes photosynthesis in this manner: "the process by which chlorophyll-containing cells in green plants are able to convert the sun's visible light energy into chemical energy and synthesize organic compounds from inorganic compounds." Thanks to this complex photo-biochemical process, plants are then able to efficiently produce many important organic compounds by utilizing the soil's inorganic raw materials. This is especially true in the production of carbohydrates from carbon dioxide and water, accompanied by a simultaneous release of oxygen. Photosynthesis is the only naturally occurring process resulting in the vital storage of large amounts of solar energy. This vital solar energy is required for the growth and reproduction of all plants while they simultaneously manufacture and store vital nutrition and energy-rich compounds for the consumption of all heterotrophic organisms. With this bounty of chemical energy, the plants are able to make use of simple molecules and essential minerals from soil deposits__ such as ammonia, phosphorus, nitrogen, potassium, sulfur, and other basic minerals__ to efficiently manufacture and store many important complex organic compounds. These compounds would include essential fatty acids, sugars, proteins, carbohydrates, amino acids, hormones, and a great variety of other vibrant phytochemicals. This complex manufacturing system had to be in place from the very beginning, when plants were first created, because without the essential process of photosynthesis, living things would not survive.

By utilizing a variety of plants as their primary source of food energy, many animal as well as human populations are totally and absolutely dependent upon photosynthesis, a unique and irreducibly complex design mechanism found in nature. Photosynthesis is not some accidental apparatus that evolved over vast eons of time by some bit-by-bit process involving many randomly occurring events connecting freakish mutations of nature, as evolution theory would presume to teach. Photosynthesis is assuredly a very unique and very complicated manufacturing system demonstrating an extremely complex design mechanism that was necessary from the beginning of carbon-based life. This system has been utilized by all plants throughout the entire history of life on planet earth. It is certainly an extraordinary example of irreducible complexity that could never be explained by the gradual, piecemeal process of evolution. Since all life-forms are highly dependent upon light energy from sunrays, and plants were created with a special apparatus to capture, convert, and store that energy, this means there would be no life on earth without the astonishing design mechanism of photosynthesis. This incredible apparatus, planned and created by an ingenious intelligence, speaks volumes to us about a master design engineer and the chief architect of the universe, who was, in crafting planet earth, preparing the perfect home for mankind and the many coinhabitants with whom he would share this profoundly diverse world.

Some people have pointed to the metamorphosis of a tadpole becoming a frog or a fuzzy caterpillar transforming into a beautiful butterfly as evidence for evolution. The actual word *metamorphosis* means "to transform." This process involves a chemically mediated biological transformation in the life of a maturing organism, resulting in a uniquely marked alteration in appearance, characteristic behavior, and functioning abilities. The genetically driven metamorphosis of amphibians is chemically regulated by the thyroxin hormone in the bloodstream, which stimulates the conversion process, and by the prolactin hormone, which actively counteracts it. The unique transformation of the common tadpole moves along quite rapidly when thyroxin reaches an optimum level in the bloodstream, thus triggering the ensuing transfiguration. Tadpoles and caterpillars are definitely not the only transformers in the animal kingdom, but they are certainly the most popular of such organic specimens examined by children in fifth-grade science class. Metamorphosis is a remarkably complex biological process by which a maturing organism undergoes a completely unique hormone-driven physical modification. These many genetically induced molecular alterations involve a relatively abrupt change in body structure, resulting from a special DNA-mediated acceleration of cellular growth and differentiation. This rapid and drastic hormone-triggered transformation, when examined carefully, is really very powerful evidence of design complexity and genetic engineering that no one except an infinitely intelligent creator God could have conceived of. Metamorphosis has nothing to do with natural selection or evolution! Again and again, the powerful evidence of unique specialization and exceptional complexity in the visible organic world flatly denies fundamental evolution theory.

Thus, we see that the overwhelming impression of purposeful design in nature is causing many one-time evolutionists to abandon their initial allegiance to impersonal, unguided materialism. In regard to the common design argument, even famous atheist Bertrand Russell, whose professional life has had a profound influence on that of Richard Dawkins, was highly impressed with the logical implications of the specialized design mechanisms that he had observed. Consequently, he has offered the following response: "This argument contends that, on a survey of the known world, we find things which cannot plausibly be explained as the product of blind natural forces, but are much more reasonably to be regarded as evidences of a beneficent purpose. This argument has no formal logical defect."[29]

What Is True Science?

Evolution is a theory in crisis! Consider this comment from Dr. Colin Patterson, the well-known senior paleontologist of the British Museum of Natural History. He said, "A theory that simply accepts the diversity of life, without offering any mechanism to explain how that diversity came into being, cannot be considered a scientific theory at all."[30] Leaders of evolutionary thought have always been opposed to the idea of a Judeo-Christian God, as revealed by the Holy Scriptures. Although many of them are highly educated, well-respected professionals, their determined refusal to seriously consider even the possibility of intelligent design would suggest to me that their best possible interpretation of the evidence is terribly biased and misleading, as well as intellectually dishonest. Unfortunately though, many people have often confused objective truth with theoretical science, and therefore, they will often blindly trust the misguided philosophy of the world's so-called experts. As it turns out, many of these individuals are instructing from textbooks, not from empirical data that was actually gathered through firsthand experience in disciplined areas of serious research. Theoretical science seems to deal with speculation about what may have happened based upon a line of reasoning the investigator is most accustomed to and most comfortable with. True empirical science is defined as knowledge derived from observation. Now, even though evolution is a common topic in many scientific circles, the theory is, in fact, not very scientific in the true sense, because it has never actually been observed.

An American biochemist, the late Dr. Duane T. Gish, served as a long-term teaching associate with the Institute for Creation Research and is considered a well-respected authority on the fossil record. He said, "It is obvious, for example, that no one has observed the origin of the universe, the origin of life, the conversion of a fish into an amphibian or an ape into a man. No one, as a matter of fact, has even observed the origin of a species by naturally occurring processes. Evolution has been postulated, but it has never been observed."[31] Evolution is simply speculation about the past based on one's personal faith in an unproven hypothesis that crowns man supreme and relegates God and His Word to the realm of religious fantasy. Creation by intelligent design, on the other hand, is a reasonable faith that fits the known facts—verifiable facts, which have been observed in our world today and also painstakingly uncovered from the historical world of the past. To call the evolution model a valid theory is in itself a clear contradiction. Any valid scientific hypothesis must be formally put to the test of impartial scientific experimentation and observation, and the resulting data gathered from these experiments should either confirm or deny the validity of any such claim. In the case of evolution theory, as well as creation, no observable scientific experiments have ever been devised that could possibly validate either popular worldview in a truly empirical sense; and yet those who advocate for evolution theory as the correct mechanism for explaining life's origin have consistently insisted upon calling it factual.

So what is science? The word means "knowledge," inferring testable knowledge (not speculation) that can be logically and rationally deciphered through an ongoing scientific process, and theoretical knowledge that must be carefully weighed in the balance to determine whether the evidence actually supports a given hypothesis or not. However, it would be considered an absolute and utter misuse of scientific protocol to insist on promoting one's preferred ideology as strictly factual, when today's scientific community is utterly incapable of producing sufficient evidence to authenticate and legitimize such a claim. Science affords all of us a reliable way to explore and to analyze many details about the natural world, but true science is completely powerless to embrace questions like, "Why does the universe exist?" "Why is the physical world precisely governed by the universal laws of physics?" "Why is conscious organic life found almost everywhere on planet Earth?" "What is the true meaning and purpose for human life?" "Why is death a reality in the natural world, and what lies beyond the grave?" "How can we possibly find hope and peace in a terribly troubled, disease-ridden, and dying world?" And there are also many ethical questions that each of us must wrestle with throughout our lifetime. These basic philosophical issues remain completely outside the scope of science.

Consider the following unquestionable statement from a well-known, world-class Christian scientist: "By far the most influential argument against the Bible is the widespread belief that science has proven evolution, and therefore disproves the Biblical account of creation."[32] This insightful comment comes from Dr. Henry M. Morris, PhD, a scientist, educator, and author of more than twenty fascinating books on creation, design, and evidence. He has made a very accurate assessment of the common view liberal, theoretical science has brought to bear on the public mind-set. The late Dr. Morris, who served on the faculty of five major universities, was perhaps one of the most accomplished men of science in America over the last century. He has offered the following reaction to the very bold and demanding claim of evolution theorists, who have always insisted on circumventing standard scientific methodology in their very determined and relentless effort to promote a baseless and certainly controversial worldview. Dr. Henry Morris explains that "one of the strangest paradoxes in the history of science is that a theory so barren of scientific proof as evolution could be so universally accepted as scientific fact. Science is knowledge, and the essence of the scientific method is experimentation and observation."[33] Truthful empirical science, by definition, can only deal with observable processes occurring in the present. It does not allow for wild speculation about various unrepeatable events of the past. Given this authentic definition of testable science, the theory of evolution can and must be more accurately described as a nonscientific dogma that has managed to capture the hearts and minds of intelligent people the world over, including many Americans.

Those who have blindly followed this ideology, without doing any real homework and research on the subject, have become thoroughly indoctrinated, thinking that what they believe amounts to real science. However, as previously mentioned, many of the early scientific pioneers (great men like Copernicus, Kepler, Newton, Faraday, Boyle, Bacon, and Galileo) all believed that their acclaimed, monumental discoveries that sparked a scientific revolution were effectively revealing the magnificent design of a purposeful God. How saddened they would surely be, if they knew that many authorities in modern science who have drifted away from belief in God would now credit their epic insights to blind-chance events and nothing more. This unfortunate reality has occurred long after these brilliant men of the early scientific endeavor revealed the amazing outcomes of their monolithic search for knowledge __ a search that ultimately delivered such accurate and astonishing information to the modern world about the fundamental laws that are consistently governing the vast, created, physical reality.

At the core of science lies a firm conviction that the universe was remarkably fashioned in a very organized and orderly manner. The ancient Hebrew prophets were the first ones to articulate that the universe was created by and is governed by a single all-powerful God. It is this original monotheistic worldview that has laid the historical foundation upon which modern science sprang forth. Sir Francis Bacon, who is regarded by many as the founding father of contemporary science, taught that to be properly educated, one must have a thorough knowledge of both of the fascinating books the one true God had provided—the book of nature and the Bible. When the scientific revolution first commenced in sixteenth-century Europe, it was many God-fearing men professing profound Christian faith such as Copernicus, Kepler, and Galileo whose profound scientific observations and impressive mathematical calculations forged a successful paradigm shift in the way mankind would view the solar system. For the first time ever, the movement of the planets could be properly understood by the discovery that the earth clearly revolved around the sun, and not the sun around the earth as common tradition held for centuries through the powerful influence of the classical philosophers Socrates, Plato, and Aristotle.

Galileo was a courageous and determined young man, who remained a very strong Christian believer throughout his entire lifetime. As an early investigator, he was captivated by the exciting possibility of scientific exploration and had argued that such endeavors not only were acceptable but constituted the noblest course of action for a believer. In a famous remark that has inspired many Christians to pursue a life of science, he once said, "I do not feel obliged to believe that the same God who has endowed us with sense, reason, and intellect has intended for us to forgo their use."[34] In a gallant effort to further enhance current scientific knowledge, Galileo chose to develop theories pertaining to the physical universe that were based squarely upon the evidence. He purposely ignored and even criticized the prevailing worldview that was held by the secular philosophers of his day. Their rather strange view was quite strongly influenced by the many traditions of the well-known ancient Greek philosopher Aristotle. As a student of Plato, Aristotle had taught that the earth was the center of the universe and everything else revolved around it. He believed that ether was the material that filled the regions of space in which the celestial bodies floated. His prevailing worldview also clearly denied a personal creator and most likely led multitudes toward a naturalistic view of the cosmos, in which man is ultimately thought to be the wisest and most influential inhabitant. Galileo's firm conviction that scientific observation should always take precedence over tradition was not well received by the philosophers of his day or by the Roman Catholic Church, and he experienced serious persecution because of it.

It is a certainty that in our time, even as in Galileo's day, any criticism of the prevailing scientific worldview is an open invitation for a targeted attack involving censorship, persecution, and isolation. Tensions always seem to run high whenever empirically derived evidence is determined to be in conflict with what many consider to be the established and accepted scientific framework. It takes a very long time before the collective sum of real evidence favoring a new paradigm is truly able to successfully replace or actively supersede an existing one. This is especially true in the realm of science. The current ideological battleground within our culture is certainly very real, but it has quite often been mistakenly characterized as a war between science and religion. However, in reality, this monumental conflict is the natural outcome of an inevitable collision between two powerful, diametrically opposed worldviews that are most accurately described today as *naturalism* and *theism*.

The Laws of Thermodynamics

The first of two laws of thermodynamics (sometimes called "the law of conservation of mass and energy") states that neither matter nor energy is now being created or destroyed. The inspired record of Genesis says that God ended his work of creation (Genesis 2:2). Scientific observations have confirmed that no new matter or energy is now being created anywhere that we can observe. This means that all matter and energy resulted from an initial "first cause", which implies a creator! There exists nothing we understand in natural law that could possibly substantiate the idea that matter either created itself or has always existed. For this reason, the reality of a first cause must be embraced. Now, judging by the vast quantity and quality of mass and energy in the universe, this ingenious causing agent should be held in such high esteem as to be worthy of the devoted worship of his creation. The second universal law of thermodynamics simply teaches us that all matter (including every organized system, whether living or nonliving) is ultimately moving from a state of order and useful purpose toward a final state of disorder, uselessness, or death. The living world we experience is one in which entropy (the degree of disorder) is increasing. This fact is demonstrated everywhere as a fundamental law of physics that is described for us in the universally acknowledged second law of thermodynamics. In other words, all things, including the exceptional organic life-forms upon this earth, are under the unfortunate influence of a continual shift toward physical decline, decay, disorganization, and ultimately death, or the inevitable end of useful purpose. Evolution, on the other hand, calls for a universe that is becoming progressively more orderly, advanced, and more resistant to disease (advancing from a state of chaos toward perfection by random chance). The second law of increasing entropy would flatly deny this erroneous claim!

Recognized the world over as a universal law of true science, the second law of thermodynamics is a certain reality everywhere in the present universe, with no known exception ever observed. The laws of thermodynamics teach us that the universe has had a beginning and that what was once created new is now growing old, falling apart, dying, or becoming less useful over time. We cannot deny the fact that everywhere we look in the physical realm, we observe a constant moving from a state of order toward disorder, life toward death, useful toward useless. The undeniable reality of the second law is observed everywhere, every day, the world over; and there is no means of escape from its relentless power over us on this side of eternity. For example, we can observe this insidious curse on the physical world when we visit a sick and dying friend or when we simply throw away an old, worn-out appliance; yet the most incredible claim of the evolution model would suggest a very different physical reality—that, somehow, integrated life-forms are improving over time, developing greater complexity, becoming more resistant to disease, and better able to survive while gradually moving toward an ideal state. Without constant care and intervention, it is obvious that everything left to itself is in decline. The evidence suggests that evolution's unproven ideology amounts to little more than wishful thinking. It's really a wasted dream about some imagined, far-off utopia that has no basis in reality as observed anywhere on this planet.

What our young people really need today, in such a dreadful age of deception, is truthful, honest science that makes no biased attempt to manipulate the truth about known facts or does not withhold the new evidence of recent discoveries in order to preserve support for a strictly materialistic philosophical point of view. This rigid viewpoint refuses to consider any evidence that is deemed to be unsupportive of evolutionary thought. Let's consider the following very powerful statement from Dr. James Tour, a nano-scientist, who is a celebrated professor at Rice University's Department of Chemistry and Center for Nanoscale Science and Technology. Dr. Tour, who makes molecules for a living, has made this remarkable statement after fulfilling many years of devoted study, research, and repeated scientific observation at the molecular level: "I stand in awe of God, because of what he has done through his creation. Only a rookie, who knows nothing about science, would say science takes away from faith. If you really study science, it will bring you closer to God."[35]

Chapter 2

EVOLUTION: A THEORY IN CRISIS

What about Mutations?

For evolution to be true, there must be some mechanism that drives the process forward, resulting in new, improved species over the course of time. Evolutionists have always claimed this mechanism is mutation and natural selection. Ernst Mayr, a former professor of zoology at Harvard University, who was considered a leading authority on evolution during the 1970s and 1980s, has stressed the absolute necessity of mutations as the driving force behind evolutionary change. He made this very clear in the following written statement: "It must not be forgotten that mutation is the ultimate source of all genetic variation found in natural populations, and the only new material available for natural selection to work on."[1] As an elite scholar and a notable professor from a world-renowned university, he is telling us that for evolution theory to work, many major structural variations must randomly appear in organisms over time, resulting from new information being added to the cellular DNA by rarely occurring mutational modifications. We must keep in mind, however, that this new customized information must be correctly positioned within the host organism to make genetic transmission to future generations possible.

Theoretically speaking, these so-called beneficial mutations could be passed on to the progeny, but only if they appear within the germ cell's DNA. Of the many trillions of cells that make up complex biological systems, only the reproductive cells can possibly pass a mutated gene to future generations. Since the offspring receive characteristics from both male and female parents, the odds of a mutated germ cell passing on this information are 50 percent or less. Also, keep in mind that the chance of a mutation occurring within the germ cell DNA of an organism is very low. How then could mutations be the machinery that drives evolution forward? This is a significant question that must be addressed. By adding billions or even millions of years to the final equation of life, evolutionists believe that random mutations could eventually add up to something significant toward the upward and onward progress required by the theory. These remotely vast eons of time, which are constantly alluded to in our culture, have made evolutionary thought seem quite obscure and far beyond the comprehension of the average person. When it comes to an accurate intellectual understanding, the only option for most people has been to rely upon the dogmatic opinions of the so-called experts, who, by the way, were not there to observe naturalism occurring when life began.

Again I will make reference to the assertive and controversial statement of Corliss Lamont, which I believe we may consider to be highly representative of the unproven and overconfident remarks that have been declared publicly by many contemporary evolutionists in recent years: "The process of natural selection and survival of the fittest, with the many mutations that occur over hundreds of millions of years, adequately account for the origin and development of the species."[2]

In this chapter, we shall consider the controversial subject of organic mutations in an honest attempt to determine if they really could be the mechanism advancing evolution as so many proponents have claimed. Evolution requires that mutations must ultimately lead to improved species over time, species that are better able to adapt and are, therefore, fitter to survive the very rigorous challenges of a hostile environment. Virtually all biology and science textbooks found within public education will claim that mutation is the driving force behind evolutionary change. What we now know for certain is that without these so-called beneficial mutations, there can be no evolution. Many people believe and explain that occasional copying errors in the DNA genetic code are a probable source of mutations. However, these mistakes are very uncommon primarily because biological DNA comes equipped with its own error-correcting system that specifically prevents the occasional occurrence of genetic misinformation resulting from normal cellular duplication.

We should think of DNA like Morse code, only instead of dots and dashes organic genes use ATCG, a four-letter chemical alphabet allowing for genetic communication. If a letter is somehow misplaced or lost in the replication process, the resulting genetic signal has changed. Now, virtually all mutations will generate a net loss of information. However, on rare occasions this net loss of information can possibly generate a net gain in organic function and overall fitness resulting in a beneficial outcome. Over eons of time, however, getting from an amoeba to a man would surely require billions of beneficial mutations; but remember that nearly all mutations produce a loss of information and a net negative outcome. Also we must keep in mind that in raw nature, every potentially useful mutation would be accompanied by millions of harmful ones, so organic change is clearly moving in the wrong direction, generating a loss of fitness and working against the far-reaching claims of evolution. The theory promises progressive change over time with positive physiological transformation advancing new, improved species.

According to the information specialist Dr. Werner Gitt, a former director and a professor at the German Federal Institute of Physics and Technology, the replication of DNA in every actively dividing cell within the growing human physiology is unbelievably accurate. He once wrote, "This replication is so precise, that it can be compared to 280 clerks copying the entire Bible sequentially—each one from the previous one, with, at most, one single letter being transposed erroneously in the entire copying process."[3] Why, then, do mutations happen? Because cellular division and DNA replication occur constantly in all organic populations, mutations are inevitable. A typically harmful mutation will result from the corruption of one or more letters within a normal genetic sequence. A serious problem with random mutations as the hypothetical engine that successfully propels evolutionary change is that they are generally unable to add any new information to genetic code as required for the theory to work. Mutations can only scramble or corrupt existing information that is already present in cellular DNA. This is why these genetic mistakes will typically produce fatal, harmful, or useless outcomes. In other words, given the negative outcome of randomly mutated genes, the unique concept of a "beneficial mutation" seems somewhat like an oxymoron.

This presents a serious dilemma for evolution theory, because mutations are relied upon as the only instrument that drives organic change. Also, we should keep in mind that naturally occurring mutations are very rare, and those that do randomly occur virtually always produce a negative outcome, creating major problems and significant disadvantages for future offspring, which actually make them much *less fit* to survive. Remember that mutations are just mistakes in the genetic code. It's hard to imagine how numerous mistakes spread out over generations could ever add up to any useful, positive change. We might simply think of mutations as something like typing errors. We must recognize that typing errors generally subtract information by corrupting a sequence of letters, leaving a message less intelligible than it has been previously. This cellular DNA contains computer-code-like messages, which spell out every last detail of life's biological function, and also directs every developing physical characteristic of each living organism. Evolution theory must rely upon the hope that mutations can somehow add new intelligible information to germ cell DNA in a parent organism. Paleontologist George Gaylord Simpson once wrote, "If evolution is to occur, living things must be capable of acquiring new information or alteration of the stored information."[4]

Consider the following comments from highly qualified scientist Dr. Lee Spetner, an outstanding retired physicist and a former professor of information and communication theory at Johns Hopkins University. In his thoroughly researched book, *Not by Chance*, he has made a very startling assertion about mutations: "In this chapter I'll bring several examples of evolution, particularly mutations, and show that information is not increased . . . In all the reading I've done in the life-sciences literature, I've never found a mutation that added information."[5] His thoughts continue with this statement, "All point mutations that have been studied on the molecular level turn out to reduce the genetic information and not to increase it."[6] Unfortunately for modern neo-Darwinian evolution, mutations can produce changes in existing stored information, but they are typically unable to add new information to that which is already present in the DNA. And because of this, the resulting outcome of these changes is generally injurious. Science has demonstrated over and over again that mutations do not provide the new and beneficial structures that are required to advance new species. Without this regular addition of new information to the composition of an organic genome, Darwin's dream has become a nightmare. Not only is this a clear failure to support the theory, but it actually amounts to strong evidence against the evolution model. If, however, molecular instructions already present in DNA are somehow erased or altered by mutation, the original chemical message is left either incomplete or significantly changed, which typically leaves an overall negative outcome for the organism's biological structure and function. Therefore, the loss of information from mutated DNA will most likely lead to a flawed trait within the organism, resulting in no significant change or diminished overall fitness.

Evolution science is still hard-pressed to explain just how major evolutionary transition occurs, and the few random mistakes that have resulted from occasional mutations certainly do not appear to be supporting this cause. Because science has never clearly demonstrated just how mutations are able to break the limits of change required to advance new species, the proponents of evolution will have to begin looking for some other driving mechanism in order to explain their theory. After studying the mutations within microorganisms for many years, French zoologist Dr. Pierre-Paul Grasse offers the following assessment: "What is the use of their unceasing mutations, if they do not change? In summary, the mutations of bacteria and viruses are merely hereditary fluctuations around a median position; a swing to the right, a swing to the left, with no final evolutionary effect."[7] Pierre Grasse flatly rejects mutation-selection as the correct mechanism for evolutionary change. He further explains that mutations "are not complementary, nor are they cumulative."[8] In other words, mutations do not harmonize with or complement each other, thereby improving the original genetic blueprint. Neither do they work together, adding up to anything significant by way of synergism. "They modify what pre-exists," says Dr. Grasse; by this he means that you get nothing more from mutations than simply variation within a kind.

Over time they will tend to revert back toward the genetic composition of the original parent genome without producing any advantageous or beneficial outcome as required for evolution theory to work. He continues with this provocative thought: "The opportune appearance of mutations permitting animals and plants to meet their needs seems hard to believe. Yet the Darwinian theory is even more demanding: a single plant, a single animal would require thousands and thousands of lucky, appropriate events. Thus, miracles would become the rule: events with an infinitesimal probability, could not fail to occur . . . there is no law against daydreaming, but science must not indulge in it."[9] Dr. Grasse also reminds us that "some contemporary biologists, as soon as they observe a mutation talk about evolution. They are implicitly supporting the following syllogism: 'mutations are the only evolutionary variations, all living beings undergo mutations, and therefore all living beings evolve.' This logical scheme is, however, unacceptable: first, because its major premise is neither obvious nor general; and second, because its conclusion does not agree with the facts. No matter how numerous they may be, mutations do not produce any kind of evolution."[10]

Some have pointed to the commonly observed occurrence of antibiotic resistance as genuine evidence of evolution working today. However, it is very interesting to note that bacteria samples obtained from organic specimens, which were placed in frozen storage prior to the initial development of antibiotics, were subsequently determined to be totally antibiotic resistant. This means that many bacteria cells have actually lost their natural resistance over time, resulting in a diminished ability to survive. This really indicates a loss of fitness, not an improvement or biological advantage as many have often claimed. Antibiotic resistance again is variation within a kind with a tendency to revert back to the original genetic blueprint.[11] Even in the often-cited case of sickle cell anemia, when examined closely, the long-term result of the offending mutation is observed as having a negative overall effect on the host, even while providing added protection against malaria infection. In this instance, the survival, fitness, and longevity of the host are significantly impaired in the individuals whose lives have been genetically altered in this way. Rarely occurring genetic mistakes, which are often thought by evolutionists to be beneficial in many cases, have never actually demonstrated a unique ability to supply the additional genetic information that would be required to propel the evolution model. The reality of this observation has proven to be devastating to evolution theory because the theory is completely and utterly dependent upon the hopeful proposition of billions of beneficial mutations leading to positive evolutionary change.

Due to the harmful nature of genetic mistakes, placing one's hope in favorable mutations leading to consistently positive outcomes is like believing an electronic virus could somehow improve the working performance of your personal computer. With this said, it's impossible to understand how mutations could actually be the driving force behind evolutionary change, in light of the negative consequences observed in the few organisms they affect. Albert Szent-Gyorgyi, the Hungarian-born and Cambridge-educated biochemist, who also became the 1937 Nobel Prize winner in physiology and medicine, has informed us that "the origin of complex traits by random mutation has the probability of zero."[12] Former biology professor, former atheist, and author of the book *Creation Facts of Life*, Dr. Gary Parker, has summed up the evolution problem in this way: "Evolution demands an increase in the quantity and quality of genetic information and mutation-selection, no matter how long you wait, cannot provide it."[13] It was reported that prominent atheist Mr. Thomas Nagel also appeared to be quite impressed with the powerful argument for intelligent design. He has commented that "evolutionary biologists regularly say they are very confident that random mutations are sufficient to account for the complex chemical systems we observe in living things, yet he feels that there is a great deal of pure rhetoric in their arguments, and judges that the evidence is not sufficient to rule out the input of intelligence." [14]

The Fruit Fly Fiasco

Because of their very rapid rate of reproduction, the fruit fly (*Drosophila*) has always been one of researchers' favorite specimens to experiment on. Fruit flies represent a complex organism that scientists love to study because of their rapid growth to maturity. A fruit fly generation, from egg to adult, requires only nine days. The deliberate manipulation of fruit flies by laboratory experimentation has produced a wide variation of strange body features. By bombarding them with unusually high doses of radiation, scientists have attempted to demonstrate evidence for evolution through the driving force of mutational change. The overall outcome of these experiments has resulted in a variation of eye color, wing size, body length, and so on. Unfortunately, however, the physical changes that have been observed to occur in these small prevalent insects never seem to add up to anything significant, as Darwin's theory of evolution requires. This is because mutant flies have never had any new genetic information added to their genome, and because of this, they always remain fruit flies. After experimenting with the genetics of the fruit fly and other common insects for nearly half a century, the famous Cal-Berkley geneticist Dr. Richard Goldschmidt had virtually admitted to a complete failure to demonstrate the evolutionary process when he finally threw his hands up and exclaimed, "Even if you could accumulate a thousand mutations in a single fruit fly, it would still be nothing but an extremely odd fruit fly." [15] He reminds us that "it is good to keep in mind that nobody has ever succeeded in producing even one new species by the accumulation of micro-mutations. Darwin's theory of natural selection has never had any proof, yet it has been universally accepted." [16] After the long and laborious worldwide study of many thousands of successive fruit-fly generations, subjected to great numbers of radiation-induced mutations, consider the conclusion drawn by environmental activist and author Jeremy Rifkin: "All in all, scientists have been able to catalyze the fruit fly evolutionary process such that what has been seen to occur in 'Drosophila' (fruit fly) is the equivalent of many millions of years of normal mutations and evolution . . . Even with this tremendous speedup of mutations, scientists have never been able to come up with anything other than another fruit fly."[17]

Many years of studying countless generations of various bacteria and flies all over the world has demonstrated that evolution is not happening today, and this is strongly suggestive that it has never happened at any time in the past. According to microbiologist Dr. Gordon Taylor, "In all the thousands of fly-breeding experiments carried out all over the world for more than fifty years, a distinct new species has never been seen to emerge . . . or even a new enzyme."[18] If no evolutionary changes have ever been demonstrated in *Drosophila*, one of the most rapidly reproducing organisms on the planet, after so many years of forced manipulation, we are left with some powerful evidence that evolutionary change in organic species has never occurred anywhere on the planet at all.

To actually achieve the necessary changes that evolution theory requires, mutations would certainly have to provide significant improvements in many major organic structures resulting in the biological advantages that could be genetically passed to offspring. Eminent French biologist Pierre-Paul Grasse observed that in spite of thousands of generations of breeding experiments and millions of artificially induced mutations, fruit flies have always remained fruit flies regardless of the aggressively forced manipulation that has been imposed on them. More recent lab experimentation involving *E coli* bacteria has produced the same result. After scientists have observed no less than thirty thousand generations of *E coli* bacteria reproduction in the laboratory (equivalent to one million human years in evolutionary terms), this thorough research has also produced no significant innovative change that could remotely offer any kind of support for the evolutionary hypothesis.[19]

However, if sporadic mutations really are, as many say, the driving force behind evolutionary change, they certainly do not appear to be taking this fashionable notion anywhere at all, and, in fact, are clearly working against the theory. The Harvard evolutionary biologist Dr. Stephen J. Gould explains, "The essence of Darwinism lies in a single phrase: natural selection is the creative force of evolutionary change. No one denies that natural selection will play a negative role in eliminating the unfit. Darwinian theories require that it create the fit as well."[20] Logically speaking, if natural selection favors the fitter organisms, as everyone would agree, some very simple reasoning will surely point out the fact that rare mutations cannot possibly work to advance positive evolutionary change. Mutated structures (defects) are generally not more useful, and, therefore, typically do not add value to the overall fitness of the organisms from which they originated; as a consequence, natural selection will simply wipe out any defective creatures, and they will become consistently lost from the population. Evolutionary geneticist N. Heribert-Nilsson explains for us the serious dilemma that so many scientists are facing when they become dependent solely upon mutations to explain evolutionary transformation: "If one allows the unquestionably largest experimenter to speak, namely nature, one gets a clear and incontrovertible answer to the question about the significance of mutations for the formation of species and evolution. They disappear under the competitive conditions of natural selection, as soap bubbles burst in the breeze."[21] Even evolutionists are beginning to admit that this poses a problem. Let's consider once again the analytical thinking of world-renowned evolutionist Stephen J. Gould of Harvard University: "What good is half a jaw or half a wing?"

Gould has even been critical of various artists, often employed by museums and textbook publishers, who have actually presented publicly what amounts to hypothetical guesswork in their clever charts and drawings supporting gradual change in organic species over time. These illustrations, highlighted with evolutionary comments, are steeped in imagination that points toward extremely biased speculation. As such, Dr. Gould responded with another rather scathing rebuke: "These tales, in the 'just-so-stories' tradition of evolutionary natural history, do not prove anything; concepts salvaged only by facial speculation, do not appeal to me."[22] How very disturbing it is that our precious children are continually and consistently exposed to biased guesswork when it comes to their fragile understanding of how life began. And to make matters worse, this bizarre speculation is constantly presented to them as factual.

The Fossil Record Speaks

When considering the fossil record, it is important to understand exactly what we are dealing with. Fossils, by definition, include "the remains, or visible trace, of a plant or animal organism from the past that have been, to some degree, preserved in the crust of the earth." The fossilization of any organic specimen will only take place under certain ideal conditions, and apparently those unique conditions are rarely found on the earth today, because we are currently aware of little or no appreciable fossilization occurring at the present time. Fossil formation speaks to us of rapid death, and sudden burial through the action of water-laid sediments. This process can only occur when the proper ingredients including lime, sand, water, pressure, and other fossilizing chemicals are found present; such would be the conditions resulting from massive flood devastation. "To become fossilized, a plant or animal must usually have hard parts, such as bone, shell or wood. It must be buried quickly to prevent decay, and must be undisturbed throughout a long process."[23]

The entire entombing scenario must have occurred very rapidly; otherwise, typical agents of decay and disintegration, such as rotting, scavengers, bacteria, and moisture will destroy any organic remains. After being buried, however, each entombed specimen must lie completely undisturbed for an extended period, until the fossilization and rock-forming procedure is completed. Fossilization is a unique process that typically requires an inescapable cataclysmic event of epic proportion in order to rapidly bury and preserve the remains of plant and animal organisms. If the present is a window to the past, then we can certainly assume that various isolated local flooding throughout history would not provide an adequate explanation for the massive worldwide deposition of buried fossil remains we observe today, which have been and continue to be uncovered from the crust of the earth.

Some very unusual fossil deposits have actually been reported that contain the remains of jellyfish and other extremely soft-tissue organisms. This rather unexpected phenomenon offers evidence that can only be explained by an extremely rapid process involving very sudden burial under unusually rare and highly catastrophic conditions. Evolutionary scientists would have us believe that isolated local flooding occurring over and over again for as long as perhaps several billion years could have accounted for the vast museum of natural history that we currently find preserved within the earth's crust, representing organisms of every variety worldwide. However, judging from our current data, it is obvious that local flooding cannot possibly account for the massive fossil graveyards we have to date uncovered from the rock formations of the earth. If, indeed, the fossil record does support the broad, gradualistic claims of evolution—that the simplest life-forms should be found buried deep within the earth's crust, while the more complex and highly advanced organisms should appear closer to the surface—then we have some very important questions to consider. First of all, how can it be that the current fossil record is generally found to be so far out of its predicted order, according to naturalistic claims, almost without exception throughout the world? Many evolutionists today are hard-pressed to explain why millions of years of anticipated geologic column are completely missing, in many locations, the world over.

According to notable geology expert and former science educator Mr. John Woodmorappe, "80 to 85 percent of the earth's land surface does not have even three geological periods appearing in 'correct' consecutive order; . . . it becomes an overall exercise of gargantuan special pleading and imagination for the evolutionary uniformitarian paradigm to maintain that there ever were geologic periods."[24] At one particular site in England, evolutionary geologists once proudly pointed out the correct order of organic fossil deposition as predicted by the typical evolutionary forecast. However, some workers subsequently discovered, during a rock quarrying operation at this specific location, that a large petrified tree was embedded across the entire geologic column at a forty-degree angle. The base of this tree was positioned near the bottom of the fossil deposits, while the top portion extended very near the upper end. If it had taken several billion years to deposit the progressive geological column of fossil-bearing strata at this location, as evolutionists have claimed, then how could a whole, intact tree possibly be preserved lying across the entire bed of fossil deposition from top to bottom without any sign of decay? This fascinating discovery, along with similar documented evidence that involves coal deposits containing embedded trees, would certainly suggest to us that the various geological formations of fossil containing sediments were most likely all deposited within a relatively short, limited period of time. Therefore, our vast, immeasurable worldwide museum of fossil-bearing history may have resulted from a single cataclysmic event of epic proportion—an event like the biblical universal flood recorded in the well-known Genesis account, which thoroughly documents a global devastation during the days of Noah, the renowned Old Testament patriarch.

Unfortunately for evolution, the carefully and closely regarded fossil record has now proven to be a great disappointment indeed. Listen to this frank admission of Dr. David Raup, a notable evolutionary paleontologist from the University of Chicago. He writes, "Most people assume that fossils provide a very important part of the general argument made in favor of Darwinian interpretation of the history of life. Unfortunately, this is not strictly true."[25] In fact, the historical data produced by uncovered fossil remains is actually far more consistent with the Genesis record of creation and a universal flood.

The fossil record, which at one time was believed to be the most powerful proof supporting Darwin's evolutionary transition, has clearly failed to live up to the long anticipated saga of gradualism. Now, consider these words from an outstanding American biochemist and lecturer, Dr. Duane T. Gish, who writes, "It is our contention that the fossil record is much more in accord with the predictions based on creation rather than those based on the theory of evolution, and actually strongly contradicts evolution theory."[26] His basic argument continues with this description: "The fossil record, rather than being a record of transformation, is a record of mass destruction, death, and burial by water and its contained sediments."[27] According to the words of Dr. Henry M. Morris, a longtime authority on earth history, typical evolutionary claims are clearly not supported by evidence from the fossil record. Dr. Morris has described the serious problem this presents for evolution theory with the following conclusive statement. He strongly emphasizes that "the very existence of fossils in any significant size and number seems to require rapid processes of sedimentary deposition, burial, compaction, and lithification. Otherwise, normal decay processes would soon destroy and dissipate such organic remains. Furthermore, the fossil record does not show a continuous evolutionary progression at all as the theory requires. The same great gaps between the major kinds of plants and animals that exist in the present world are also found in the fossil world."[28]

This accurate assessment of the distinctive gaps that are typically found in the fossil record has also been openly confirmed and acknowledged by those in the evolutionist's camp. Consider this statement from evolutionary paleontologist Dr. David B. Kitts, who has served as the head curator of the Stoval Museum. "Despite the bright promise that paleontology provides a means of 'seeing' evolution, it has presented some nasty difficulties for evolutionists, the most notorious of which is the presence of 'gaps' in the fossil record. Evolution requires intermediate forms between species and paleontology does not provide them."[29] According to Harvard's Dr. Stephen J. Gould, "The fossil record caused Darwin more grief than joy. Nothing distressed him more than the 'Cambrian explosion,' the coincident appearance of almost all complex organic designs."[30]

Based upon a vast accumulation of scientific data from fossil remains that have been cataloged over the last two hundred years, Dr. Gould reports that the earth history of most fossil species, uncovered to date, presents two basic characteristics that are readily admitted to by modern evolutionists. Consider the following description of these features that are so highly incompatible with the evolutionary hypothesis of gradualism.

1. "Stasis: Most species exhibit no directional change during their tenure on the earth. They appear in the fossil record looking pretty much the same as when they disappear; morphological change is usually limited and directionless."

2. "Sudden Appearance: In any local area, a species does not arise gradually by the steady transformation of its ancestors; it appears all at once and 'fully formed.'"[31]

These clear statements made by the leading evolutionary voice of the twentieth century, tell us that species have appeared suddenly on the earth, are fully formed at their appearing, and have certainly not arrived on the scene by some gradual, steady transmutation of supposed ancestors. Evolutionary natural history, which unfortunately continues to be relentlessly expounded in American public schools and universities, would suggest to us that mankind and apes have descended from some common ancestor between thirty and seventy million years ago. In order to effectively deliver this mandatory educational training, many textbook publishers have included a variety of charts and suggestive drawings depicting some employed artist's strange notion of what a prehistoric transitional primate creature of the past might have looked like. Unfortunately, a great deal of biased speculation and guesswork goes into the construction of these primate models that are commonly presented to unwary students in public school classrooms. These crude models are usually based on embarrassingly few fossil fragments, and, sadly, represent pure conjecture, influenced of course by some strong evolutionary bias. The most obvious conclusion here is that evolutionists have made a very bold and calculated attempt to manipulate the occasional discovery of organic remains to fit neatly into their preconceived, extremely biased, and deeply entrenched ideology concerning the origin of mankind. Fraudulent pictures and bogus claims appearing in many middle-school and high-school textbooks have been used for years to successfully indoctrinate naive school children throughout recent generations. It now appears to be quite obvious that certain unscrupulous partial investigators, along with many thoroughly indoctrinated and methodically manipulated public educators, are known to present what they and others *believe* to be true whether the actual evidence confirms it or not.

An ancient creature of the marine world that has long been considered by evolution science as a genuine transitional link has now been proven to be a great disappointment. The Coelacanth is a rather primitive looking fish described by evolutionists as a transitional link to land animals; it is believed to having become extinct long before the dinosaurs appeared. According to twentieth-century naturalists, this stout-looking fish supposedly first appeared in the Devonian period some 350 million years ago, before it evolved into a four-footed land-dwelling animal of some kind. Imagine the embarrassment of many diehard evolutionists when this fossilized marine specimen, believed to be long extinct, was discovered alive off the coast of Africa, after being netted by fishermen in 1938. In 1952, a second specimen was captured, and since then underwater researchers investigating the depths of the Western Indian Ocean have successfully filmed more of the same. I actually had the opportunity to observe this for myself via a Fox News broadcast that was aired on November 17, 2009, which reported the newest discovery, and offered live video footage of researchers successfully filming the living Coelacanth in its own native habitat off the coast of Indonesia. Imagine this creature, which was believed to be an extinct transitional form that supposedly had died out one-hundred million years ago, being filmed alive with exactly the same features that appear in the fossil record uncovered from the distant past! These living Coelacanth marine specimens have provided us a great example of a living fossil, but this example is not unique to the fossil world.

There are many other examples of organisms that were thought to be ancient, long-extinct precursors to newer life-forms that have turned up alive in the present world with the exact same features that earth scientists have discovered in archived fossil records, supposedly dating from the ancient past. Contrary to over one-hundred-fifty years of evolutionary speculation, the basic kinds of plants and animals are clearly and distinctly represented in the fossil record. They are all found to be completely formed and fully developed with distinct and undeniable gaps separating each kind from all the others, as indicated by a very noticeable lack of any intermediate forms expected to be connecting them. When we begin digging for reliable fossil evidence from the past, what we find, in the words of creation scientist Gary Parker, are "billions of dead things buried in rock layers laid down by water all over the earth."[32] This succinct phrase speaks very clearly to us of sudden death, destruction, and massive devastation on a worldwide scale; it certainly does not speak well for a popular theory that projects, as its core premise, a continuous and very gradual improvement in living organisms that are somehow randomly advancing toward greater fitness and complexity over vast, unconfirmed, and extremely prolonged periods of time.

Did you know that fossils are the means by which rocks are assigned to a geological age? Index fossils are the particular specimens considered to be typical, abundant, and representative within a certain geological period, as laid out by the evolutionary model. If it can now be shown that fossils are not nearly as old as they have been claimed to be, the entire geologic-age timescale becomes useless speculation that is necessary only to prop up the rapidly declining philosophical view of "naturalism." Therefore, because fossils are used to assign geological ages, the entire geologic dating system that has become so deeply engrained in the public mind-set is found to be based entirely on the unproven assumption of evolution!

With regard to geological, fossil-bearing rock formations, creationists and evolutionists can both agree that the most ideal conditions for the deposition of fossil specimens in rock-forming layers were initiated by major flood devastation. The one thing many knowledgeable people understand is that the extreme conditions necessary to produce fossil and sedimentary rock formation can occur very rapidly, as the result of a catastrophic-type volcanic and flooding cataclysm. Such was the case in the explosive eruptions of Mount St. Helens beginning on May 18, 1980, in Washington State, USA, when an angry volcano blew off 1,300 feet of her upper north side, and left utter desolation and ruin over a wide remote area, while also claiming every life that was in her path. The initial explosion sent hot ash some eighty thousand feet into the upper atmosphere; and that ash, we have been told, proceeded to circle the entire earth twice before eventually coming to rest. Because I was living with my young family in Western Washington at the time, I was able to personally witness this devastating eruption from a vantage point some fifty miles away. Another major eruption, at the site, occurred in June of 1982, which triggered a massive mudflow with glacier run-off that spilled over the confines of Spirit Lake at the base of the mountain, carving out a 1/40-scale version of the Grand Canyon in just one afternoon. Imagine, if you will, a new geological formation, resulting from volcanic eruption and flooding devastation, that would certainly appear to have taken many millions of years to form by standard geological interpretation; and such a dramatic topological transformation was etched into this Western Washington landscape in only a matter of hours!

How scientific is a theory whose main evidence is based solely on the assumption that the theory itself is true? Since there are no dependable ways to accurately date geological formations, rocks are most generally dated by the fossils contained within them. And sadly enough, this unscientific dating method is based entirely upon the assumption of evolution. This is why the evolution advocates have constructed the geological-period timescale. It's hard to conceive of an entire earth-history dating system being based on belief in a theory that is dreadfully void of definitive and substantial physical evidence. Consequently, there remains a complete absence of proof that a vast evolutionary organic chain, and geologic-age dating system holds any validity whatsoever.

The concept of evolution must live or die by the fossil record, because it is entirely based on a previously accepted core belief that, somehow, transforming plant and animal remains were all gradually entombed within rock-forming sediments over millions, if not billions of years of earth history. The story told by various uncovered remains should demonstrate a very slow and gradual transformation of species from simple to complex without the presence of distinctive gaps separating them. In the expert opinion of paleontologist, evolutionist, and a longtime curator of the American Museum of Natural History, Dr. Niles Eldredge recently wrote, "[We modern] . . . paleontologists ever since Darwin have been searching . . . (largely in vain) . . . for the sequences of an insensibly graded series of fossils that would stand as examples of the sort of wholesale transformation of species that Darwin envisioned as the natural product of the evolutionary process. Few saw any reason to demur—though it is a startling fact that . . . most species remain recognizably themselves, virtually unchanged throughout their occurrence in geological sentiments of various ages."[33] And now, according to Dr. P. L. Fortey, "Many fossils have been collected since 1859, tons of them, yet the impact they have had on our understanding of the relationships between living organisms is barely perceptible . . . In fact, I do not think it unfair to say that fossils, or at least the traditional interpretation of fossils, have clouded rather than clarified our attempts to reconstruct phylogeny."[34]

Whenever anyone speaks about fossils, most people will automatically think of preserved evidence of organic remains in the crust of an ancient earth from perhaps millions of years ago. We have become conditioned, as the result of biased evolutionary indoctrination, to think of any fossils and especially dinosaur fossils in terms of vast ages of earth history. It's important to note that dinosaurs have always been a favorite subject of evolutionists because they tend to create a dilemma in the minds of young people. Because biased evolutionary interpretation has largely succeeded in convincing the public that dinosaurs lived some sixty to eighty million years ago, many people, and especially young people tend to conclude that this information disproves the genesis account of biblical history and therefore the Bible must be wrong and can't be trusted. After all, how could the dinosaurs have fit inside of Noah's ark?

Are fossils really that old? Dr. Mary Sweitzer, a noted paleontologist, is currently on staff at the campus of North Carolina State University. She is well known for leading a small research group that discovered the remnants of blood cells and later identified other soft tissue samples from the fossil remains of a Tyrannosaurus rex, which her research team had uncovered in the state of Montana. Formerly from Montana State University, she was the first researcher to identify and isolate what appeared to be dried red blood cells and other soft tissue remains recovered from a partially fossilized leg bone of a dinosaur specimen.

These startling tissue samples were isolated and classified from a T-rex skeleton, which had been dated at sixty-eight million years old. What is so absolutely remarkable about this discovery involves the prior established assertion by scientists that DNA cannot possibly remain intact much beyond ten thousand years. After first publishing her discovery in 1993, a huge storm of controversy ensued as devoted evolutionary biologists had scrambled from all directions to dispute the claim in an attempt to protect a geological time scale and fossil-dating methodology that has come under greater attack than ever before. The unique and very powerful ramifications of this recent discovery cannot be silenced, however, and the logical conclusion would be to assert that this set of bones, and perhaps many others like them, are not anywhere near the sixty to eighty-million-year target age that evolutionary scientists have typically assigned. Can you imagine a dinosaur that is claimed to be this ancient having leg bones that are not even completely fossilized, containing red blood cells and other soft tissue remnants? This unique discovery was particularly remarkable considering that the sediment layer where the T-rex skeleton was found would have contained copious amounts of water; the water would have been gradually absorbed into the porous bone matrix of the dinosaur carcass and, of course, would have thoroughly destroyed and mummified all existing soft tissue remains.

Researchers have also uncovered some very interesting specimens at other locations as well that have cast suspicion upon the accuracy of the fossil-dating methods that are currently in use. The Clarkia fossil beds of Idaho have produced many impressive specimens of some fossil leaves in exquisite condition. It is interesting to note that some of the specimens uncovered at this research site have contained partially fresh leaves; and in fact, some samples were not even fossilized at all and were actually found to retain their natural color. For example, a green magnolia leaf was discovered in these popular fossil-bearing formations that had been dated at twenty million years old according to evolutionary assumption; this leaf, however, retained its green color, was fresh looking, and even pliable. The scientists were also able to successfully extract DNA from this specimen, which has matched the

DNA of modern magnolia trees. Many scientists are now scratching their heads in amazement as to how this DNA could have survived intact for so long considering the fact that DNA has a limited shelf life when it comes into contact with moisture. Dr. Brian C. Sykes, an Oxford University professor of human genetics, has reported in the journal *Nature* that the rate at which DNA breaks down in the laboratory would suggest that after ten thousand years, no intact DNA should be found.[35] This would suggest that a magnolia leaf specimen, found within fossil-bearing strata, could not possibly be dated at twenty million years old. Therefore, if the vast geological timescale dating methodology conceived by and continually promoted by evolutionists is now found to be grossly inaccurate, as recent fossil discoveries would suggest, then this entire bizarre evolutionary scenario of naturalistic gradualism will ultimately collapse upon itself like a house of cards.

Why do we have such vast fossilized deposits that cover the entire earth, including many marine and shellfish deposits, which are commonly uncovered at very high elevations on many mountain ranges throughout the world? I can remember as a small boy having gone on a field trip to the Willapa hills outside of my childhood hometown of Raymond, Washington, where my male companions and I spent the afternoon extracting clamshell fossils from the side of a mountain. How can you possibly explain this in terms of local flood activity, as evolutionists will commonly claim, in support of gradual fossil deposition? As previously quoted by ardent evolutionist and well known atheist Carl Sagan, "Evolution is a fact amply demonstrated by the fossil record."[36] Unfortunately for modern evolution, Sagan's bold, although terribly inaccurate statement, is now known to be without credibility after being held up to scrutiny against a well-researched fossil record that denies evolutionary gradualism and is remarkably void of any seriously valid naturalistic support.

Now let us consider this direct and rather blunt remark from Dr. Steven M. Stanley, who served as a leading paleontologist at Johns Hopkins in the 1970s. "The known fossil record fails to document a single example of phyletic evolution accomplishing a major morphological transition."[37] Professor David Woodruff from UC San Diego has also added a similar conclusion to the admission by Stanley. "But fossil species remain unchanged throughout most of their history and the record fails to contain a single example of significant transition."[38] Oxford zoologist Mark Ridley has summarized this critical point by admitting to the obvious major lack of support within the fossil record. "In any case, no real evolutionists, whether gradualist or punctuationist, uses the fossil record as evidence in favor of the theory of evolution as opposed to special creation."[39] Because the current fossil record does not provide sufficient evidence to support the theory of evolution, we can be quite certain that there still remains insufficient evidence that life has ever evolved at any time during past earth history.

The loud voice of the fossil record has thus far spoken great volumes against traditional evolution; and without this convincing support, the theory no longer has any valid reason to identify itself in the scientific method at all; therefore, any teaching of evolution must now be properly relegated to the realm of faith. The formidable evidence of uncovered and cataloged earth history has proven to be a great disappointment to many mainstream naturalists, and, in fact, revealed data has actually aligned itself consistently with the Genesis record of creation, and a massive worldwide flood that occurred early on in human history.

Dr. Gary Parker, whose accomplished work includes expertise in both biology and paleontology, began his career as an atheist with great enthusiasm, believing he was ridding his students of outdated prescientific superstitions, such as Christianity. He became personally challenged to examine the real evidence, without preconceived bias, by a chemistry professor at the same university where he himself was teaching. He courteously accepted the challenge, and spent the next three years re-examining the evidence with a very open-minded approach. Eventually, as a result of this thorough investigation, he became compelled to renounce his deep-seated belief in evolution. He concluded, as so many other scientists have in recent years, that the biblical framework has offered the world a much more logical explanation for the existence of life based upon today's vast and ever-growing catalog of scientific discovery and observation. He has subsequently offered the following statements as a way to summarize the many problems one encounters when attempting to use the current fossil record as the evidence to defend evolution. "In most people's minds, fossils and evolution go hand in hand . . . In reality, fossils are a great embarrassment to evolutionary theory and offer strong support for the concept of creation . . . If evolution were true, we should find literally millions of fossils that show how one kind of life slowly and gradually changed into another kind of life . . . But missing links are the trade secret, in a sense, of paleontology . . . The point is, the links are still missing. What we really find are gaps that sharpen up the boundaries between kinds. It's those gaps, which provide us with the evidence of creation of separate kinds . . . As a matter of fact; there are gaps between each of the major kinds of plants and animals. Transition forms are missing by the millions. What we do find are separate and complex kinds, pointing to creation."[40] This particular anomaly alone has proven to be a devastating blow to an old, worn-out theory that has now reached the very brink of extinction. Evolution? The fossils say no!

Chapter 3

Case of the Missing Links

Where Are the Transformers?

In recent years Hollywood productions have glorified the imagined story of mechanized vehicles that are somehow able to magically transform themselves into phenomenal, robotic-looking, behemoth-like creatures, which then become focused on the drama of fierce fighting in an epic battle of good versus evil. Survival of these emotionally driven mechanical creatures seems to be linked to the degree to which they are able to generate the defense mechanisms and survival features that will make them superior to their formidable rivals of like kind and similar ability. Even though this popular story line has made for some interesting entertainment, the producers, of course, are dabbling in pure fantasy.

When we get back to the reality of change in the organic world and thoroughly examine the fossil record for evidence of any real-life transformation leading to transitional intermediates linking one species to another, we seem to come up empty. The superior transformers equipped with new defense mechanisms and survival features that are believed to having been achieved over millions of years through mutation and natural selection simply are not to be found. These imagined improvements that have supposedly led to the appearance of new and improved species over vast ages of time by some evolutionary process seem to be as rare and fantastic as those found in the imagination of Hollywood writers and producers today. Unfortunately for secular naturalists, the fossil record provides no reliable examples of macroevolution, which may seem surprising to many people who are accustomed to the strong public perception that the fossil record has provided the most powerful evidence for evolutionary change. In 1859, Darwin was unable to cite a single example of evolutionary transition from the fossil record; and today, more than 150 years later, in spite of intensive activity from the scientific discipline of paleontology, the mysterious absence of bona fide missing links still holds true. So where are the countless transformers of the organic world that are required to validate the long standing tradition of evolutionary gradualism that has been taught with such overwhelming enthusiasm in Western cultures over the last century? In what would appear to be another strange case of Dr. Jekyll and Mr. Hyde, contemporary paleontologists have proudly projected the public persona of a fossil record that clearly supports naturalistic evolution while privately admitting to themselves that any reliable evidence for a smooth transition in the fossil record is basically nonexistent. They are doing a great disservice to people by disseminating publicly a view that their work does not support privately. Based upon this disturbing scenario, John Lennox of Oxford asks the obvious question: "What conceivable reason could there be for members of an academic community to suppress what they know to be the truth—unless it were something which supported a worldview, which they had already decided was unacceptable?"[1]

Evolution theory teaches that microorganisms, over several billion years, have evolved into complex invertebrate life-forms such as clams, sponges, and jellyfish. These invertebrates, in turn, evolved into fish, fish into amphibians, amphibians into reptiles, reptiles into birds, and so on until apes appeared, which eventually evolved into man. Based on the record of empirical science, these claims certainly seem absurd considering that the fossil record has not produced a single, genuine intermediate link connecting any of these uniquely different and incredibly complex life-forms. In fact, current factual evidence strongly supports the biblical view of distinctly created plant and animal kinds with noticeably wide, insurmountable gaps between them. If the current concept of evolution were true, then what could we expect to observe in the plant and animal kingdoms today?

If all living organisms existed within a continuity of environment across the same world, having appeared alive completely by random chance through natural processes alone, then we could easily predict a vast continuum of related organisms living together without any sharp distinguishing gaps separating them. With evolution theory, the evidence of transitional intermediates between the various kinds of organisms should be clear and abundant in both the fossil world and within the world of living organisms as we observe them today. Since the present is a clear window to the past, what we observe today should give us an unmistakable view of the characteristics of living organisms as they appeared in the ancient world. However, what we observe today is a total absence of transitional intermediates of any kind. Therefore, it should not be surprising to us that the missing links are still missing. What is undeniably true about planet earth both presently and in the past is the existence of distinct kinds of complex life-forms without any transitional connections between them. Now, consider this rather bold assessment from Mr. Jerry Adler, who tells it the way nature has actually revealed it to us: "In the fossil record, missing links are the rule: the story of life is as disjointed as a silent newsreel, in which species succeed one another as abruptly as Balkan prime ministers. The more scientists have searched for the transitional forms that lie between species, the more they have been frustrated . . . Evidence from fossils now points overwhelmingly away from the classical Darwinism, which most Americans learned in high school: [that new species evolve out of existing ones by the gradual accumulation of small changes . . . each of which helps the organism survive and compete in the environment]."[2] This undeniable and universal absence of transitional forms in the organic world is perhaps the most devastating indictment ever spoken against evolutionary thought.

If evolution is true science, doesn't it seem odd that 150 years of historical research has not produced even one intermediate transitional link that can be fully verified? Paleontologists will even admit to this glaring void, and yet they have persisted in seeking some means by which to explain their way around this very disturbing flaw in their cherished theory. This virtually total absence of genuine, documented evolutionary transition still remains today the most monumental source of confusion and disappointment for modern evolutionists. Nevertheless, many contemporary naturalists simply assume these predicted intermediate links must have existed, in spite of the overwhelming evidence to the contrary, evidence that has been demonstrated by prudent observation of both living and fossilized specimens.

In November of 1980, *Newsweek* magazine reported on a scientific conference at the Chicago Field Museum of Natural History entitled "Macro Evolution." At this professional academic conference, many disillusioned paleontologists reported on their current findings. They reluctantly revealed that the fossil record does not and perhaps never will support the Darwinian scenario of a very smooth and continuous progression of ever-advancing life-forms that are seen graduating upward from very simple to complex. Instead, they were essentially forced to concede that our fossil deposits have shown a pervasive pattern of undeniable gaps between the various plant and animal kinds with many new life-forms appearing suddenly, and no transitional links leading to them. These abundant life-forms have simply appeared abruptly in the fossil record, followed by long periods of stability, during which they show very little or no change at all.[3]

If this noticeable frustration among modern naturalists resulting from the failed documentation of evolutionary transition within a vast array of fossilized animal remains was not discouraging enough, consider as well these rather startling comments from Professor Chester A. Arnold of the University of Michigan. Dr. Arnold is considered to be one of the most outstanding paleobotanists of modern time. In referencing the ascending progression of plant life from ancient time to the present by way of gradual transformation and adaptation, he has recorded the following remarkably profound statement: "It has long been hoped that extinct plants will ultimately reveal some of the stages through which existing groups have passed during the course of their development, but it must be freely admitted that this aspiration has been fulfilled to a very slight extent, even though paleobotanical research has been in progress for more than a hundred years. As yet, we have not been able to trace the phylogenetic history of a single group of modern plants from its beginning to the present."[4] Dr. Eldred Corner, a notable professor of botany from Britain's Cambridge University, has also summed up the vast fossilized evidence documenting ancient plant life with this point of view: "I still think that, to the unprejudiced, the fossil record of plants is in favor of special creation . . . Can you imagine how an orchid, a duckweed and a palm tree have come from the same ancestry, and have we any evidence for this assumption? . . . The evolutionist must be prepared with an answer, but I think that most would break down before an inquisition."[5]

Darwin's hope was that one day the fossil record would reveal the numerous intermediate forms (missing links) predicted by his theory. However, with modern scientific research making such terrific gains over the last half century, Darwin's initial claims appear to be more uncertain than ever due to the failed attempt to fill the wide gaps between species in the past; and these are the same wide gaps that we observe in the present. The truth is now crystal clear; the current fossil record reveals only distinct kinds of plants and animals with no evidence of transitional links connecting them; the detail of their physical anatomy is found to be virtually indistinguishable from modern life-forms of the same species observed in our present world. Paleontologist and evolutionary biologist Dr. Steven Stanley explains our vast, currently cataloged fossil documentation: "Species that were once thought to have turned into others have been found to overlap in time with these alleged descendants . . . In fact, the fossil record does not convincingly document a single transition from one species to another."[6] The well-known evolutionary biologist Douglas Futuyma of the University of Michigan and Stony Brook University has also verified the accuracy of this claim: "The majority of major groups appear suddenly in the rocks, with virtually no evidence of transition from their ancestors."[7] Continuous and extremely gradual change moving from the very simplest of life-forms progressing upward toward the more complex organisms, with a notable abundance of intermediate links connecting the various species at every stage of evolutionary transition, is absolutely not the case that is represented by today's vast catalog of research documentation.

Dr. Colin Patterson, the world-renowned senior paleontologist of the famous British Museum of Natural History, has offered the following remarks in response to a direct criticism he subsequently received for the noticeable lack of transitional forms illustrated in his recent book on evolution. He wrote, "I fully agree with your comments on the lack of direct illustration of evolutionary transitions in my book . . . If I knew of any, fossil or living, I would certainly have included them. You suggest that an artist should be used to visualize such transformations, but where would he get the information from? I could not, honestly, provide it . . . and if I were to leave it to artistic license, would that not mislead the reader? Yet Gould and the American Museum people are hard to contradict when they say there are no transitional fossils . . . As a paleontologist myself, I am much occupied with the philosophical problems of identifying ancestral forms in the fossil record. You say that I should at least 'show a photo of the fossil from which each type of organism was derived.' I will lay it on the line; there is not one such fossil for which one could make a watertight argument . . . The reason is that statements about ancestry and descent are not applicable to the fossil record."[8] This is most certainly an astonishing statement considering that it came from a highly respected, world-class evolutionary scientist of the twentieth century!

Even if transitional links had been discovered in the fossil record, how could we possibly ever believe that an intermediate between two different species would be fitter to survive than the parent organism it evolved from? If a good leg, for example, was to somehow slowly evolve into a wing, it would be a bad leg long before it became a good wing. Any such imagined transitional physiology would make that intermediate organism much less fit to survive and highly subject to predation. Any such makeshift creature would, undeniably, be wiped out by natural selection and would certainly add nothing to the ongoing advancement of evolution. Imagine if you will a small reptile in the process of evolving into a bird. Can you picture the elongated scales on the forelimb of a lizard, destined to become transitional feathers? Would this not impose a significant disadvantage for this poor critter that cannot yet take flight, neither can he run very well, having now been burdened with the added weight of this awkward transitional appendage. This imaginary trans-mutating intermediate would certainly have significantly impaired mobility, and, therefore, would be greatly disadvantaged in competing for necessary resources as well as eluding life-threatening predators. As such an easy target of prey, his kind would be routinely wiped out from the population long before any subsequent transitional modification could be randomly achieved that would make him adequately fit to compete and survive in a hostile, unforgiving world.

I believe evolution is a theory that has reached the breaking point! More than 150 years of rigorous, painstaking research, discovery, and observation since its modern public inception has brought us no closer to validating Darwin's claim. And instead our current, vast accumulation of documented evidence has strongly discredited his strange notion. The late German zoologist Dr. Albert Fleischmann explained the real problem evolution theory is still facing today: "The theory suffers from grave defects, which are becoming more and more apparent as time advances. It can no longer square with practical scientific knowledge, nor, does it suffice for our theoretical grasp of the facts; no one can demonstrate that the limits of species have ever been passed. These are the Rubicon's, which evolutionists cannot cross . . . Darwin ransacked other spheres of practical research work for ideas but his whole resulting scheme remains, to this day, foreign to scientifically established zoology, since actual changes of species by such means are still unknown."[9] Imagine a century and a half of fossil discoveries with impressive historical research uncovering a vast quantity of evidence from the crust of the earth, which has failed to produce a single valid transitional form linking one living species to another. As previously mentioned, this fact alone has been a devastating indictment against a so-called scientific theory that has, strangely enough, received worldwide acclaim.

Now, consider this remarkable statement from a gentleman that many consider America's leading twentieth-century proponent of evolution. The late Dr. Stephen J. Gould was a popular evolutionary biologist and a longtime professor of paleontology at Harvard University. He once offered this very frank analysis: "The absence of fossil evidence for intermediary stages between major transitions and organic design, indeed, our inability, even in our imagination, to construct functional intermediates, in many cases, has been a persistent and nagging problem for gradualistic accounts of evolution."[10] Since gradual change is essential for evolution theory, and apparently can only be found in the imagination of devoted loyalists, proponents of this hypothesis will just have to look somewhere other than the fossil record in order to find the convincing support and scientific validation they so desperately seek.

The Descent of Man

It has been over a century and a half since Darwin's classic work, *On the Origin of Species*, was first published. After carefully weighing the vast evidence revealed by the considerable accumulation of scientific discovery over that span of time, it is now quite safe to say that a well-documented fossil record overwhelmingly denies classical evolution; yet this bizarre concept has been taught as factual to most Americans through public education and mass media bias. The historical past of modern man is one area where evolutionists have painstakingly labored to fill in the blanks. I suppose that if they were able to accurately connect the dots, and to paint a clear picture of the emergence of modern man from his evolutionary past, all of their other claims about the evolutionary history of our planet earth would certainly seem that much more plausible. However, nowhere have we seen greater abuse of power, and more blatant deception, than in the highly calculated effort many evolutionists have made to establish a credible link between modern man and his supposed ape-like predecessors. Based upon embarrassingly few fossil specimens discovered by various research anthropologists at locations around the globe, evolutionists have proclaimed to the world, through a biased scientific community, the discovery of numerous intermediate transitions between man and his so-called primitive primate ancestors. Using a few jawbones, teeth, and other fossil remains, evolution-minded researchers have directed artists to carefully construct various models of life-sized primate figures, including some complete human-like specimens fashioned from only a single bone fragment. They have photographed, published, and have proudly displayed these imaginary models in support of an unproven, naturalistic-minded worldview. This is just another area where many people have been brainwashed into believing what essentially amounts to biased speculation, and, as you will soon discover, the resulting fallout has been very deceiving to the unsuspecting public.

A great deal of evolutionary guesswork goes into the construction of primate models, which are often based on, perhaps, only one or two fossil fragments. As you will quickly discover from the following material, it appears quite obvious that evolution-minded researchers have, to a large extent, made a consistent and bold attempt to interpret the occasional discovery of organic remains in a manner designed to conform to their preferred, preconceived ideology about the origin of man.

The presentation of pro-evolutionary material that is based on a biased interpretation of evidence is a deceptive practice that has clearly violated the integrity of truthful and honest scientific research. If any true transitional intermediate between man and apes really did exist, this would certainly be powerful evidence favoring the evolution model. However, as you will soon see from many revealed facts, the high level of faith evolutionists have placed in their cherished theory has ultimately made it necessary for them to steadfastly believe that a single jawbone, tooth, skullcap, or even a femur had belonged to some bizarre, brutish transitional creature__ a creature that allegedly roamed the earth millions of years ago, somewhere between the time of modern man and his historically imagined primate ancestors. As it turns out though, when the best available evidence has been carefully weighed and analyzed, following a thorough investigation by today's unbiased researchers utilizing the finest scientific methods available, modern science has discovered that many of these ancient bone fragments have told a deceptive tale.

Such fragments have typically belonged to the skeletal remains of some mammal or man, but never to some bizarre creature, described as transmutation between primate and human. Whenever a determined individual really wants to believe something is true, professional or otherwise, it ultimately requires very little evidence to confirm their belief. This most basic of human flaws has caused certain evolutionists to uncover, announce, and to widely publish findings that would certainly appear to support their cherished neo-Darwinian theory, even though such reputed evidence does not, and never has truthfully existed.

The initial published paper proclaiming an intermediate transitional humanoid, known as "Java man" (*Pithecanthropus*), came about when a Dutch geologist named Dr. Eugene Dubois discovered a human femur in the same general area where the skullcap of an ape was also found. While failing to report that he also found human skulls in the same area, Dubois proceeded to convince the scientific world that he had discovered a genuine missing link between ape and man. This so-called intermediate life-form was hailed for many years as a definitive connection between mankind and his primate ancestors. However, before his death, Dr. Dubois confessed that his Java man was nothing more than a large gibbon (ape).[11] It appears that in their great eagerness to produce the missing link, evolutionists have been found guilty of dishonesty and deception by making many false and erroneous claims. Unfortunately, however, the ultimate retraction of these hasty and overzealous reports never seems to receive sufficient publicity to effectively erase the initial impression that fraudulent claims have left upon the public mind-set.

With today's liberal media so terribly biased in favor of evolution theory, it is a common occurrence that people are not adequately informed when a retraction is made based on the eventual follow through producing the unbiased results of a more complete scientific investigation.

Another bizarre case involved bone specimens discovered in England, which resulted in the initial designation of the famous "Piltdown man." In 1912, a man named Charles Dawson, an amateur British archaeologist, came upon the fossil fragments of a jawbone and a skull in a gravel pit near Piltdown, England. Dawson, and the group of scientists with whom he consulted, soon became convinced that these fossil specimens represented a legitimate link to man's evolutionary past, a link that must have lived perhaps several million years ago. Top authorities from around the world became fascinated with Piltdown man, believing the discovery to be a genuine intermediate transition in the evolutionary ascent to modern man. Piltdown man was given the official name *Eoanthropus dawsoni* and was considered an actual subhuman ancestor of Homo sapiens. However, after many years of prime exposure from the scientific community, and top university educators alike, suddenly in 1953 Piltdown man was buried once again. In that particular year a more careful, independent investigation had proven this supposed intermediate to be a complete fraud! When the jawbone was tested to determine a relative age, it was discovered to be no fossil at all; researchers reported the sample to be only slightly older than the day it was found. When these unbiased investigators determined that someone had purposefully manipulated the jawbone of an ape and the skull of a modern human to create a deliberate deception, this bizarre pretense began to emerge. Further investigation had revealed that these specimens had been chemically treated to make them appear very old, and scratch marks on the teeth disclosed that they had actually been filed down. Apparently this was done to make them appear to be more humanlike. After planting these bones in a gravel pit apparently to enact what would appear to be a genuine ancient humanoid discovery, some trickster (perhaps Mr. Charles Dawson, himself) had actually succeeded in creating a colossal deception that has left a lasting impression upon the public mind-set for generations.

This finding turned out to be a complete hoax, but somehow it had, unfortunately, succeeded in deceiving many of the world's so-called experts, who apparently were eagerly waiting and ready to embrace and report any possible link to man's prehistoric past! Unfortunately, however, it was over forty years before this fraud was exposed; in the meantime, the widespread reporting of Piltdown man was to appear in public-school textbooks for some fifty years. In addition, over five hundred books and periodicals were published about this discovery.

Why did it take the experts so long to uncover the truth and to detect this premeditated forgery? And why did they not notice file marks on the teeth when these specimens were initially examined? Why were they unable to discover early on that the dark brown, ancient looking stain that coated the bones was only a thin outer layer? And why were they able to detect what they believed to be human characteristics in an ape's jawbone and apelike qualities in a human skull? The obvious answer would be because they saw in these bone specimens exactly what they were hoping for, and somehow failed to see the actual truth that was clearly unsupportive of their cherished theory.

The late biochemist Dr. Duane T. Gish has summed up this disgraceful fraud by stating, "The success of this monumental hoax serves to demonstrate that scientists, just like everyone else, are prone to find what they're looking for, whether it is there or not."[12]

In 1921 Dr. Davidson Black discovered two tooth molars near the village of Choukoutien, which is located in very close proximity to what is now modern-day Beijing, China. The original written report establishing "Peking man" (*Sinanthropus pekinensis*) as a possible link between humans and apes was, strangely enough, based only upon these tooth fragments. The Peking story had also made a big public impact; however, it, too, appears to have been based upon very careless and over anxious reporting with little regard to genuine scientific protocol.

In 1922, another tooth specimen was discovered, this time in Western Nebraska by a man named Harold Cook. The subsequent publication of this find resulted in the designation of an intermediate known as "Nebraska man" (*Hesperopithecus haroldcookii*), which has turned out to be very nearly as embarrassing as Piltdown man. Dr. Henry Fairfield Osborn, a science professor at Columbia University, who was one of America's foremost fossil experts at the time, was among the first to examine this new discovery. Amazingly enough, Dr. Osborn, along with his other colleagues in the growing field of fossil interpretation, all agreed that this tooth revealed characteristics of an intermediate link between ape and modern man, even though they knew absolutely nothing about the primary characteristics of any such intermediate. Once fully presented to the scientific world as real evidence for the evolution of modern humans, Nebraska man was to take his place in a line of the descending links believed to be connecting man to his former primate ancestors. In that same year, the *Illustrated London Newspaper* published the picture of a life-sized hybrid model someone had quickly constructed from this single tooth fragment. It's hard to imagine that a complete, full-size humanoid intermediate was actually created from the discovery of a single tooth! That's unbelievable! As it turns out though, in spite of the opinion of the so-called experts of that day, a few years after the find, additional bones were discovered at the original site, and the true identity of the mysterious creature was finally revealed. The infamous tooth of the world famous Nebraska Man had belonged to an extinct pig. What does this tell us about the blatantly overzealous and far-reaching effort of the world's so-called scientific experts of the twentieth century—experts who have painstakingly and misleadingly laid additional groundwork for a false and deceptive worldview adopted by millions today?

Around 1930, more jawbone fragments and a few teeth were discovered in India. Again, the experts declared the discovery of a transforming intermediate humanoid that was well on the way to becoming human. *Ramapithecus* was soon considered by experts to be an ancient link connecting man to his ape-like relatives, but was thought to walk upright like humans. This discovery, like so many others, was received with great enthusiasm in the scientific and educational communities, and with time it would become a household word among evolution proponents and the general public as well. However, after more thorough, unbiased investigative research was completed, *Ramapithecus* turned out to be very apelike for sure, but was certainly in no way related to humans. The experts were finally forced to admit that this supposed evolutionary transition was completely unrelated to man, having subsequently been identified as the primate mammal we know as an orangutan. Again, desperation ruled the day and once more false and misleading information was presented to the unwary public, adding more fuel to the mounting deception caused by other fraudulent reports.

By jumping so quickly to erroneous conclusions these investigators, like so many others, were found to be guilty of deception by prematurely publishing ambiguous information. They had failed to conduct a thorough and adequate investigation well before enthusiastically announcing their research findings to the public at large.

You will surely remember hearing of an intermediate hominid specimen known by the name of "Cro-Magnon man" (*Homo sapiens*). The famous Frenchman Mr. Louis Laret had discovered this popular fossilized skull specimen in 1868. This common terminology, no doubt, brings an image to everyone's mind of some brutish-looking forerunner to modern man that was reported publicly with such great exuberance by the scientific community. However, many experts today have agreed that this earnestly proclaimed link to man's evolutionary past was actually fully human, and for all practical purposes identical to today's modern European.

Around 1982, a skullcap was discovered in southern Spain, and declared by Spanish experts to be the oldest fossil link connected to modern man ever to be discovered on the European continent. Initially referred to as "Orce man," a reference to the village located near the discovery site, experts were again very determined to nominate another ancient specimen as a possible link in a long chain of ape-to-man evolutionary transition. However, Orce man did not amount to much. French experts, upon thoroughly examining the specimen in question, were ultimately able to determine that this particular skullcap had belonged to a four-month-old donkey! Embarrassed Spanish investigators quickly sent out five hundred letters canceling invitations to an international symposium scheduled for May of 1984 that would have announced the discovery to the scientific world of yet another intermediate link to man's evolutionary past. This was just another bizarre example of how anxious and overly enthusiastic investigators have been to uncover what they are so desperately hoping for and wanting to find.

In 1974, Dr. Donald Johanson, an American anthropologist, had discovered the remains of several human/ape-like specimens in the Afar Triangle region of Hadar, Ethiopia. Johanson believed this find to be the significant unveiling of a new hominid species to which he proceeded to assign the official name *Australopithecus afarensis*. One of the best-preserved fossil skeletons in the group was subsequently determined to be a small female, whom he affectionately named "Lucy". He reported a distinctively apelike creature who was thought to walk upright, and therefore was well on the way to becoming fully human. Lucy was subsequently dated at 3.2 million years old, and eager anthropologists the world over hailed this discovery as a definitive intermediate link connecting man to his primitive, prehistoric past. However, the story does not end there. Research on *Australopithecus* remains was conducted by Dr. Solly Zuckerman (Lord Zuckerman), a noted British zoologist and anatomist who had graduated from Yale University in the United States and had taught extensively at Oxford before becoming a professor of anatomy at Birmingham University in the UK. Along with a very select team of other well-qualified scientists, he carefully studied the fossil remains of *Australopithecus* for some fifteen years, using the most sophisticated methods of anatomical analysis available at the time. After many years of painstaking research, Lord Zuckerman's team of experts had finally concluded that the subjects of their long-term investigation were definitely not intermediate in transition between apes and man.[13] Although these *Australopithecus* remains were found to be somewhat different from today's modern apes, in the final analysis, this unbiased research, thoroughly conducted by a very qualified team of scientists, determined that these creatures were nothing more than another primitive ape species with no real confirmed human characteristics. Lord Zuckerman's final reports were carefully summarized and documented in a book he subsequently published, entitled *Beyond the Ivory Tower*.[14]

According to Solly Zuckerman, who does not profess to be a creationist per se, there is simply no reliable evidence revealed by the fossil record that adequately supports the very strange notion that man evolved from apelike ancestors. The African born, British paleoanthropologist Richard Leakey, director of the National Museums of Kenya, has offered his professional opinion in regard to the new Lucy controversy. He wrote, "Echoing the criticism made of his father's *habilis* skulls, he added that Lucy's skull was so incomplete that most of it was 'imagination made of plaster of Paris,' thus making it impossible to draw any firm conclusions about what species she belonged to."[15]

Dr. Charles Oxnard was a former student of Lord Zuckerman who became a professor of anatomy at the University of Chicago, USC, and the University of Western Australia. He subsequently studied in great detail the post-cranial skeletal remains of the controversial hominid specimen that was dubbed Australopithecus. Dr. Oxnard, who carefully employed the most sophisticated techniques in completing his thorough research, came to the determination that Lucy was neither human-like nor ape-like, but more closely resembled an orangutan in terms of physical characteristics. And even though he was also not known to be a creationist per se, the final outcome of his thorough investigation confirmed that these primate creatures did not walk primarily upright like humans, and were certainly not intermediate links between apes and man.[16] Still, the Lucy controversy continues with much disagreement yet today.

"Neanderthal man" (*Homo neanderthalensis*) was first discovered in Germany in the 1800s and is a very familiar example that we have heard much about as a link to man's evolutionary past. However, this specimen, like so many others, was also a profound misconception. These remains have stirred up a great deal of speculation over the years among ardent evolution researchers and educators. The famous German pathologist and anthropologist Dr. Rudolph Virchow, who had carefully examined Neanderthal remains over a century ago, confidently reported that the somewhat primitive-looking features he had thoroughly examined were not the result of Neanderthal's subhuman origin, but were due, in fact, to diseased pathological conditions, namely arthritis and rickets. For many years, determined evolutionists stubbornly refused to accept Dr. Virchow's expert finding until some other Neanderthal skeletons were thoroughly examined. These new discoveries finally confirmed Dr. Virchow's authoritative conclusion. Today, there is no longer any considerable doubt among professional researchers that the world famous Neanderthal man is, and always has been, fully human.

The notable American biochemist, Dr. Duane T. Gish, who was formerly with the Institute for Creation Research, has fully summarized for us the research findings about this popular, so-called human ancestor of the past. During his professional life Dr. Gish, who was well versed in the fossil record, offered this update on Neanderthal status: "It is now known that Neanderthal man was fully erect and in most details was indistinguishable from modern man, his cranial capacity even exceeding that of modern man."[17] It is now quite commonly believed that the stooped posture observed in the skeletal remains of Neanderthal man was, as Dr. Virchow had clearly suggested many years ago, the result of some crippling disease, probably arthritis, rickets, or both.

When you look closely at the fossil record to examine the history of *Homo sapiens*, the evidence and unbiased research findings clearly reveal the following facts: man has always been human, and apes have always been primate! They are clearly unrelated!

Dr. Timothy White, paleoanthropologist and professor of biology at UC Berkley, has offered some evidence of yet another bizarre incident involving wild speculation and overzealous reporting that has led researchers to further embarrassment in the scientific community. "A 5 million year old piece of bone that was thought to be a collar bone of a human-like creature was actually part of a dolphin rib, . . . He [Dr. T. White] puts the incident on a par with two other embarrassing faux pas by fossil hunters: *Hesperopithecus*, the fossil pig's tooth that was cited as evidence of very early man in North America, and *Eoanthropus* or 'Piltdown Man,' the jaw of an orangutan, and the skull of a modern human that were claimed to be the 'earliest Englishman.' The problem with a lot of anthropologists is that they want so much to find a hominid that any scrap of bone becomes a hominid bone."[18]

Listen to the comments of Dr. Greg Kirby, a senior lecturer and teaching professor of population biology at Flinders University in Australia, who is suggesting that some field scientists are tempted to interpret various bone fragments in a way that favors what they are hoping to find. He has offered this commentary: "Not being a paleontologist, I don't want to pour too much scorn on paleontologists, but if you were to spend your life picking up bones and finding little fragments of head and little fragments of jaw, there's a very strong desire to exaggerate the importance of these fragments."[19]

The fossil record has revealed very distinctive gaps with no conclusive evidence of intermediate or transitional links leading to modern man from apelike ancestors. Many of the well-publicized, so-called intermediate links, believed to be connecting modern man with animal primates, have been thoroughly discredited and discarded, one by one, as the result of unbiased scientific investigation and advancing technological research. It now appears virtually certain that the hypothetical common ancestor between ape and man is only a phantom figure. This is a creature created only in the minds of those who can conceive of no other explanation for the existence of human life in a modern world where naturalism dominates nearly all subject matter offered by our public institutions of academic study. Consider this frank admission from Harvard's Dr. Stephen J. Gould: "Most hominid fossils, even though they serve as a basis for endless speculation and elaborate storytelling, are fragments of jaws and scraps of skulls."[20] He was apparently not very impressed by the elaborate and grossly misleading speculation of those who insist on imposing their biased worldviews with endless storytelling based solely on unidentified or misunderstood bone fragments. The missing links in man's descent are really only imagined creatures that have been conceived in the minds of those who are determined to find any bit of evidence that may help to validate their determined reliance on evolution as the key to understanding the emergence of life on planet earth.

The renowned Dr. Henry M. Morris, who served as the acting director of the Institute for Creation Research for many years, has accurately summed up for us the current dismal state of evolution theory: "No one has ever seen anything evolve, no one knows how evolution works, the fossil record shows no evolutionary transition taking place, and the basic laws of science show it to be impossible; yet evolutionists insist that this is 'science' and should be taught as proven fact to school children."[21]

Recapitulation Theory

For many years, our science textbooks have taught that the early stages of human embryological development supported the theory of evolution. They point out that the human embryo has gill slits like a fish, thus proving common ancestry with aquatic life-forms from hundreds of millions of years ago. Innocent school children have often been taught that the growing human embryo goes through stages reflecting evolutionary transition from fish to reptile to ape and finally to man. Such supposed evidence for evolution was very popular during Darwin's time, and was actually proclaimed the world over as indisputable proof for an evolutionary pathway to human life (*Homo sapiens*). This false and terribly misleading information has, unfortunately, been taught in the schools of developing nations for well over one hundred years and still appears in many textbooks yet today.

About the time Darwin's theory was taking hold in England, a German scientist named Ernst Haeckel was working on, and would eventually publish, some biology drawings that he had carefully designed. These controversial drawings supposedly illustrated the many various stages through which a human embryo passes before becoming distinctly human. Haeckel's drawings received worldwide attention, were published extensively, and had introduced a concept referred to as the "biogenetic law." It was commonly believed that Haeckel had truly provided the proof for evolution that the scientific world of that day was eagerly anticipating, and was certainly ready to embrace. He used the slogan "ontogeny recapitulates phylogeny," which was just a fancy way to say that a developing human embryo passes through stages reflective of the previous major steps in evolutionary transition, moving from aquatic toward human life, suggesting common ancestry with lower life-forms.

As it turns out, however, the human embryo does not have these imagined gill slits. This was a very clever misrepresentation based on a serious deficit of knowledge at that time! Remembering back to my embryology class in college, I seem to recall a series of bars and grooves running along the neck region of the developing human embryo, which early evolutionists had mistaken for gill slits. In reality these are simple structures called "pharyngeal pouches." During gestation, these formations will eventually develop into the lower jaw, the middle ear, and certain glands over time. In 1875, it was reported that Ernst Haeckel had actually been convicted of fraud by a group of his peers! Apparently, he intentionally manipulated his biological drawings to make them appear to resemble the many evolutionary stages of human development he had so strongly believed in. Now, even though a nineteenth-century German biologist appears to have been rightfully discredited for his bogus and deceitful drawings, this publicly circulated misinformation left a powerful impression that would become deeply ingrained in the mind-set of many developing Western nations. The lasting, but terribly inaccurate and deceptive impression that was left by Ernst Haeckel's many controversial charts and drawings has, only in recent years, been exposed publicly for what it really is: a gross misrepresentation that has created a fraudulent impression on man's fragile understanding of a possible historical pathway to human life.

Today, modern embryologists no longer believe in any such thing as a recapitulation theory. In fact, some years ago, a well-known anthropologist Dr. Ashley Montague, who was once considered one of the world's foremost evolutionists of his time__ having taught and lectured often at Harvard, Princeton, and Rutgers__ publicly admitted that Haeckel's theory with regard to the early development of the human embryo had been thoroughly discredited, and therefore, it should no longer be cited to promote the evolution model. Unfortunately, however, these misleading and fraudulent illustrations remained in many of our public school textbooks long after Haeckel's deception was thoroughly exposed within the recognized scientific community. Unfortunately, this included material used extensively in the Western world during the most influential period for evolutionary propaganda—throughout the twentieth century.

What Are Vestigial Organs?

In regard to human anatomy and physiology, there is one more area that I would like to call to your attention where evolutionists have been guilty of reporting false and misleading information based upon presumption and a lack of accurate knowledge. For many years, evolutionists claimed that the presence of so-called vestigial organs in the human body proved that modern man evolved from lower life-forms. They have defined "vestigial organs" as the useless vestiges of various organs that were necessary at some previous stage in man's evolutionary history. Evolutionists had commonly claimed for many years that various structures and appendages are no longer useful within the human body, or at best may have a somewhat diminished purpose today when compared to their vital function at some previous stage of evolution. These structures were believed to be remnants that may have now become totally obsolete to modern man, but were quite essential at some time during his evolutionary past.

In 1893, a German anatomist by the name of Mr. Robert Wiedersheim published a list of 86 vestigial structures in man.[22] Through expanded interpretation, the original list was eventually enlarged to 180. Wiedersheim had picked up on the concept of "rudimentary" organs mentioned by Darwin in his second book, *The Descent of Man*. Zoology expert Horatio Newman formally testified, in a written statement that was read into evidence in the famous 1925 Scopes trial, explaining that "there are, according to Wiedersheim, no less than 180 vestigial structures in the human body, sufficient to make of a man a veritable museum of antiquities."[23] However, thanks to modern anatomical study and current advanced technological research into human physiology, that list has now been reduced to nearly zero. Many of the structures on the list are now known to be essential to human health, while some others support and enhance the body's function and structure in various ways. If you were to come across some object that was mysteriously unknown to you, and, therefore, decided to pronounce it of little or no value, this may simply mean that you are actually ignorant of its beneficial utility. It should be rather obvious to us that "the list" of 1893 actually represents an historical record of the physiological deficit-of-knowledge and misunderstanding of that day. Apparently ignorance ruled back when the godless teachers, philosophers, and scientists of the nineteenth and twentieth centuries were laying the foundation for the monstrous deception of evolution__ a deception that today has thoroughly permeated Western culture and has greatly influenced the worldviews of a thoroughly misinformed public.

It seems hard to imagine, but among some of the most essential organs and structures that were once claimed to be vestigial by overzealous evolutionists of the past are the pituitary gland, thymus gland, pineal gland, tonsils, appendix, and the coccyx (tailbone). Thoroughly modern and updated medical research has now declared vestigial organs to be one more example of how over one hundred years of blatant misinformation, lack of knowledge, and at times clearly dishonest reporting has left a dark cloud of deception over the most highly developed, and most powerful nations of the world. The highly bogus claim of these so-called vestigial organs, which were once considered to be unnecessary or of very little value to advanced human physiology, were used to propagandize millions of people toward embracing an evolutionary view in regard to the origin of human life. This type of very damaging misinformation, however, like so many other widely disseminated false and terribly misleading claims, has now been discarded on the trash heap of history by the advancing knowledge of modern scientific research and investigation. Current study into human anatomy has clearly identified the useful utility of many human organ systems and structures that were once very misunderstood.

Closing Thoughts

We live in an age where both empirical science and theoretical science are discussed and regarded in great detail. However, to be accurate, scientific theories that are born out of repeated observation and experimentation should always carry more weight and authority than hypotheses that are not. There is always the impending danger that biased presupposition may tempt man to endow weak hypotheses with the same authority as empirically proven scientific revelation. Sadly enough, this has certainly been the case with evolution theory__ a highly speculative accumulation of hypothetical ideas that, over time, have strongly permeated every facet of Western culture, resulting in unwarranted factual overtones.

Many scientists bring with them preconceived notions and worldviews that, no doubt, influence their decision-making experience in every situation they encounter. In spite of such overwhelming evidence and the growing number of expert opinions that strongly oppose naturalism, the massive impression left by evolution theory on today's Western societies has been rather overpowering. Even some of the more conservative, creation-minded scientists of the twentieth century have often felt somewhat inclined to bow before the relentless pressure to compromise their worldview thinking in order to accommodate the currently accepted scientific paradigm by embracing some evolutionary thought. Some scientists have even attempted to determine a way of introducing "naturalism" into the biblical narrative of creation.

This clear denial of scriptural integrity has led to much confusion, doubt, and even dissent in the Christian community__ and to a false perception of God's magnificent power displayed in his creative works. Creation scientist Dr. Henry M. Morris, who has been a longtime advocate of intelligent cause, has spoken out boldly about the acceptance of evolution that is now being observed in some of today's most liberal church organizations: "The evolutionary scenario with its billion-year spectacle of random variation, evolutionary meandering, struggle for existence, suffering and death and extinction, utterly contradicts not only the plain teaching of Scripture, but also the very nature of God. Evolution is the most cruel and inefficient process that could be devised for populating a world and creating man, and God should not be held responsible for any such system!"[24]

One sure lesson we have all learned in life is that every finite effect requires an sufficient cause, and no effect can ever be greater than its cause. A house requires a builder, a watch requires a watchmaker, and a painting requires an artist. It is, therefore, highly illogical to assume that our vast and remarkable universe including such a beautiful planet as earth teeming with abundant life and complex design, could somehow be adequately explained by an infinite number of purely non-intelligent, randomly occurring, chance events. Evolution theory makes no real sense from a logical standpoint as expressed openly by Dr. Wolfgang Smith: "And the salient fact is this: if by evolution, we mean macro-evolution (as we henceforth shall), then it can be said with the utmost rigor that the doctrine is totally bereft of scientific sanction . . . Now, to be sure, given the multitude of extravagant claims about evolution promulgated by evolutionists within an air of scientific infallibility, this may indeed sound strange . . . And yet the fact remains that there exists to this day not a shred of bona fide scientific evidence in support of the thesis that macro-evolutionary transformations have ever occurred."[25] This consideration alone should cause us to abandon the evolution model and forsake the thought of "materialistic naturalism" in favor of a more reasonable belief system__ a historical system that relies primarily upon an adequate initial intelligent cause for a vast, remarkable universe. In his outstanding work, *The Battle for Truth,* the philosopher, religious leader, and writer Mr. David A. Noebel clearly states what should now be obvious to all of us who are determined to follow the evidence wherever it leads. After logically examining a great volume of evidence, he wrote, "Reason requires the biologist to abandon evolution and to embrace the more rational explanation (for life): Creation! Of course, creationism is untenable for all atheists; therefore, even if the atheist recognizes the irrationality of traditional evolutionary theory, he must postulate an equally indefensible theory to circumvent the notion of God."[26]

Before moving along to the next chapter, we will pause here to consider a personal confession offered by the atheist-turned-Christian, legal expert, writer, and speaker Mr. Lee Strobel. Strobel is the author of a powerful book entitled *The Case for Christ,* which became a full-length feature film that was released in public theaters in the spring of 2017. As an atheist, Strobel was always very skeptical of the strange idea that genuine faith in an unseen God was a position that could, in fact, provide him with intellectual satisfaction and fulfillment. However, after thoroughly examining the evidence as a trained investigative journalist, he discovered that he could not refute the claim for the historical life of Jesus Christ, the fact of his brutal death by crucifixion at the hand of the Romans, and the monumental truth of his confirmed resurrection from the grave several days after the burial. In the following candid remarks, Mr. Stroble speaks openly about a common philosophical worldview that is upheld by so many today who continue to believe in an unproven theory, and are convinced that it has offered them the freedom to live a self-directed life in whatever manner they would so choose. "I was more than happy to latch onto Darwinism as an excuse to jettison the idea of God, so I could unabashedly pursue my own agenda in life without moral constraints . . . And try as I might, I couldn't turn my back on nagging inconsistencies that were undermining the foundation of Darwin's theory."[27]

Chapter 4

NOT BY CHANCE

Probability Analysis

One example of a new frontier in science and mathematics is a discipline known as "probability analysis." This field is currently allowing today's scientists to analyze the mathematical probability that certain events could occur solely on the basis of blind, random chance alone without the aid or guidance of any outside influence. When we consider the evidence of a probability analysis, the unlikelihood of random chance as a factually sound model to explain the appearance of biological systems becomes very clear to us. When evolutionists speak in terms of billions or millions of years, the average, uninformed person is inclined, by virtue of inexperience and lack of knowledge, to accept the word of the so-called experts. After all, who would dare to question the scientific opinion of the university PhD, wearing a white coat? The average person will simply conclude that *the experts must know what they are talking about__ after all, haven't they studied this subject matter all of their lives?* However, we need to know just how accurate the dogmatic opinions of these self-proclaimed experts really are. Could it possibly be that an erroneous, outdated worldview has led many of the so-called experts to the wrong conclusions? Is it then possible to be a misinformed and misguided "expert" because of preconceived bias?

We owe it to ourselves and to our impressionable children and grandchildren to seriously consider whether or not evolution is really a logical, evidence-based concept that is strongly supported by science and history. Is this theory worthy of our personal trust, confidence, and allegiance? Should a naturalistic explanation of life be the guiding principle that undergirds the shaping of our own personal worldview?

All complex biological systems are composed of billions of highly complicated proteins, which are specialized molecules interacting with each other to direct organic function within living cells. Proteins are made up of long chains of amino acids in some very specific arrangements as directed by the DNA genetic code. In each case, the sequential order of amino acids must be exact to produce a functioning organic unit. Each one must be able to network with other proteins to perform a vast array of cellular functions. You might say that these amino acids are the building blocks of life. If evolution were true, the basic theory would predict that thousands of very complex protein molecules have been generated purely by random chance. A major problem for evolution is the fact that many thousands of complex proteins would have had to appear all at the same time just to assemble the basic structures comprising the intricate molecular machinery required to maintain the vital functioning of a single living cell.

We should also keep in mind that of the many amino acids found in nature, only a select twenty of them are included as the essential components comprising the physiology of organic proteins. These twenty essential amino acid molecules must occur in a very precise linear sequence in order to generate a functioning protein compound called a "polypeptide." As we will soon discover, this basic requirement makes the prospect of spontaneous, self-generated polypeptides, having the correct sequence of amino acids, entirely impossible, and completely unsupported by probability science. Now, we certainly must keep in mind that in nature, amino acids occur in mirror-image pairs called "isomers" (in chemistry we call it a "racemic mixture"). For the sake of this study, however, we will simply think of amino acids as having right-handed and left-handed organic configuration.

The utilization of these amino acids to produce proteins creates an even bigger problem for evolution, because we discover that only the left-handed isomers are found in organic cellular polypeptides. Since amino acids are the building blocks of all biologically active molecules within living cells, for evolution to work, the purely random forces of nature would not only have to select the correct twenty amino acids, while placing them in the exact required sequential order, but would also have to accurately differentiate between all the right and left-handed ones at the same time. For the sake of argument, however, let's assume that the many unguided, randomly occurring events of nature were somehow accidentally able to select only the organically approved, left-hand configured amino acids (a big stretch indeed) to spontaneously generate a functioning biological protein. Let us also assume that nature is building a protein with a very small structure of one hundred amino acids (the average protein is about three hundred to four hundred amino acids in length).

The unfathomable odds against nature accidentally assembling, by blind chance alone, even a single, biologically active, one-hundred-amino-acid polypeptide, based on the mathematical law of probability, has been scientifically established at one chance in 10^{130} (1 followed by 130 zeros). Allow me to explain further. The minutely remote chance of getting all one hundred amino acids to appear in the L-form is 1 chance in 10^{30}.

When a biologically active protein is produced, its folded shape will always appear in a precise three-dimensional geometric configuration upon which specific biochemical activity depends. This folding will allow the host cell to recognize the exact purpose for each protein, and where exactly it fits into the grand scheme of cellular physiology (somewhat like a lock and a key). In order for a precise sequence of amino acids to appear in the required three-dimensional shape, each acid base must be linked together in what are called "peptide bonds." However, the purely random, undirected binding of amino acids will produce the required peptide bond at only a 50 percent rate. Because of this, there is only a 1 in 2 chance probability of forming a peptide bond between every two chemically linked amino acids. Again, this leaves us with a probability for peptide bonds in all one hundred amino acids at 1 chance in 10^{30}. Thus, in order to randomly achieve a series of one hundred levoform amino acids that are all strung together with peptide bonds, we have an initial probability of only 1 chance in 10^{60}.[1] This remote scenario alone, by chance, is considered to be an impossible occurrence based on probability science.

In every known life-form, the generation of functional protein polypeptides proceeds with uncanny accuracy because the mandatory chirality and peptide bonding of the amino acids is controlled and maintained by every cell's DNA and it's genetically coded guidance. These difficulties for random chance, however, are minor compared to the mandatory chronological sequence in which these one hundred amino acids must be linked. In other words, the most critical feature in the basic formation of any given organic protein molecule is the precise sequential order in which each and every amino acid component must appear; this is because protein molecules will exhibit a very high level of molecular sensitivity. Even one single misplaced amino acid would likely result in catastrophic failure. Now, of the many different amino acids found in nature, only the essential twenty have been utilized in producing organic proteins. Therefore, randomly selecting one hundred such molecules in the correct order from this pool of twenty amino acids would generate a chance probability of 1 in 20^{100}, which equates to 1 in 10^{130}.[2] If we combine this figure with our initial chirality and bonding probability of 1 in 10^{60}, there is absolutely no question that it would be considered as scientifically irrational to believe that nature could form an operational one hundred amino acid polypeptide by random chance processes alone. Scientists are currently concluding that any accidental, random chance occurrence of an event with a probability exceeding 1 in 10^{50} is considered to be scientifically impossible, if not completely irrational.

In reference to our simple protein and considering the precise sequential order of amino acids alone, let us now consider the following scenario. If there were only twenty letters in the alphabet and they were all mixed together then placed in a hat, what would happen if the letters were selected randomly, one at a time, by a blindfolded man until a total of one hundred selections have been made? By placing the letters in the exact sequential order in which they were selected, what is the remote chance, for example, of correctly spelling out a predetermined sentence that requires one hundred letters in length? Could we possibly expect to accidentally spell, with exact precision, the following short sentence by random chance alone: "We hold these truths to be self-evident, that all men are created equal, that they are endowed by their Creator with rights!" Now, all one hundred characters in this simple statement must be arranged in a very precise sequential order; otherwise the resulting message would be left partially unintelligible.

The same is true in all biological systems; when any required proteins are generated within cellular physiology, the sequence of amino acids must be very precise for the cell to recognize the intended purpose of a given polypeptide molecule. Even if our simple experiment of randomly generating a short intelligible message, by blind chance alone, was to be repeated twenty billion times, do you really think this precise sentence could ever be spelled out correctly? If you believe this to be impossible, as I do, let us now consider why.

Without exception, any written message or coded communication, which would be highly intelligible to an interested observer, will always require a mind to construct. You can be certain that each and every written word in this book was methodically selected for a very specific purpose by a mindful process__ none of which are the result of an accidental explosion in the printing shop! For anyone to successfully combine the given letters of a formal alphabet in such a precise manner as to produce an understandable, coherent, and intelligible message is highly inconceivable apart from intelligent activity.

Dr. Gerald Schroeder is a Jewish physicist who graduated from MIT, receiving his PhD in nuclear physics, along with earth and planetary science in 1965. He has subsequently completed significant work involving the scientific discipline of probability analysis, by which he has refuted the idea that life arose by chance in a godless universe. By utilizing the example offered by a group of monkeys banging away at a computer keyboard, Schroeder has shrewdly demonstrated the futility of attempting to explain the emergence of life as a colossal super accident. In a very bold experiment conducted by the British National Council of Arts computers were placed inside of a cage with a small group of monkeys to demonstrate the possibility of creating any meaningful words by random chance. Dr. Schroeder has reported that after one month of hammering away on the keyboards (along with using them for a urinal) six monkeys had produced fifty typed pages, but not a single word—not even a simple one-letter word such as "a" or "I" was found in the recorded material. According to Dr. Schroeder, the likelihood of producing, by accident, even a single one-letter word using this primate investigational tool would be one chance out of twenty-seven-thousand. Using the science of probability analysis, Dr. Schroeder has also calculated the extremely remote chance that a monkey could accidentally produce a complete Shakespearean sonnet (14 lines totaling 488 letters) at only one chance in 10^{690}. He has subsequently compared this completely incomprehensible figure with the total number of physical particles in the known universe ("particles" meaning protons, electrons, and neutrons), which has been estimated to be 10^{80}. Gerald Schroeder's final authoritative conclusion is that you could never produce a Shakespearean sonnet by chance alone, even if the entire universe was completely filled with computer chips that were randomly producing letters at the rate of one million per second from the beginning of time until now.

I am also quite certain that natural, random chance, accidental events acting totally independent of any significant guiding influence or intelligence, would never be able to provide an adequate means by which to explain the basic production of complex cellular polypeptide design, and therefore, would fail the test each and every time.

Microbiologist Dr. Michael Behe has compared the random chance probability of linking just one hundred amino acids in exactly the correct sequential order (forming a rather small protein molecule) to a blindfolded man locating a single marked grain of sand somewhere in the vastness of the Sahara Desert, and doing it, not just once, but three times.[3] With this thought in mind, to give the reader just a very small perspective of the incomprehensible chance of the incredible number (1 in 10^{130}) that has arbitrarily resulted from the insurmountable odds of randomly self-generating this tiny, seemingly insignificant protein, consider the fact that thirty billion years is the equivalent of only 10^{18} seconds. As I have already mentioned, it is now commonly reported that probability scientists will no longer even acknowledge any chance-generated event with odds exceeding 1 in 10^{50}, but will simply consider the event to be out of the question.

In his informative book entitled *Darwin Was Wrong*, I. L. Cohen confirms this common practice: "Mathematicians agree that any requisite number beyond 10^{50} has, statistically, a zero probability of occurrence."[4] In other words, it is considered to be mathematically impossible to form even a very simple protein molecule through random chance processes alone, even if all the correct amino acids are available, and each one has appeared in the mandatory left-handed configuration. This is why so many serious researchers are beginning to abandon any chance-based approach to explaining life's origin.

Keep in mind that the unique chemistry of a single cell is now known to be vastly more complex than this very simple polypeptide example might suggest. And in fact, generating all the necessary material for a complete living cell would require the spontaneous generation of thousands of specialized proteins, each averaging perhaps three hundred to four hundred amino acids, and all coming together randomly at the same time by pure chance. These uniquely complex polypeptide organic molecules would also have to be accompanied by the accidental appearance of DNA and RNA (the most complex chemical polymer structures ever found in organic systems), followed very closely by the necessary energy required to produce biologically active material.

The famous British astrophysicist Sir Frederick Hoyle has made a very colorful comparison by equating the odds of the random chance generation of the most basic chemistry of life with this very interesting remark: "The chance that higher life-forms might have emerged in this way is comparable to the chance that 'a tornado sweeping through a junkyard might assemble a Boeing 747 from the materials therein.'"[5] Hoyle then goes on to explain his position from a personal point of view that is based on a lifetime of science as he understood it: "A common sense interpretation of the facts suggests that 'a super intellect' has monkeyed with physics, as well as with chemistry and biology . . . the likelihood of the formation of life from inanimate matter is one to a number of 10, with 40,000 naughts [zeros] after it. It is enough to bury Darwin and the whole theory of Evolution . . . There was no primeval soup, neither on this planet, nor on any other . . . and if the beginnings of life were not random, they must therefore have been the product of a purposeful intelligence."[6] The brilliant, Nobel Prize-winning cellular biochemist Christian de Duve has also aptly described the enormous improbability of the chance generation of a living cell (the most basic unit of life) with the following straightforward and concise remarks: "If you equate the probability of the birth of a bacterial cell to chance assembly of its atoms, eternity will not suffice to produce one . . . faced with the enormous sum of lucky draws behind the success of the 'evolutionary game,' one may legitimately wonder to what extent this success is actually written the fabric of the universe."[7] As an educator and conference speaker Kenneth Ham, the founding director of Answers in Genesis, has also commented about the vast complexity of living cells. He wrote, "Life is built upon information . . . In fact, in just one of the trillions of cells that make up the human body, the amount of information in its genes has been estimated to fill at least 1,000 books of 500 pages of typewritten information."[8] In other words, logically thinking people today are forced to admit that the random, spontaneous generation of even the basic proteins required for organic life is now known, by impartial and genuinely rational scientists, to be mathematically and scientifically incomprehensible—no matter how many billions of years are claimed to have been available to randomly generate and empower this unbelievably complex organic design.

This undeniable scientific conclusion, which unbiased investigators have now accurately confirmed after so many years of exhaustive cellular research, also became a personal reality to a retired Apollo 14 astronaut by the name of Edgar Mitchell. Commander Mitchell has commented quite openly about a vivid revelation and a personal experience that had impressed him so greatly on his heroic flight into outer space: "When I went to the moon, I was a pragmatic test pilot. But when I saw the planet Earth floating in the vastness of space, the presence of divinity became almost palpable, and I knew that life in the universe was not just an accident."[9]

DNA: The Language of Life

Francis Crick and his colleague James Watson shared the Nobel Prize for their discovery of the double helix structure of DNA, which seems to resemble a spiral ladder, and is composed of very long continuous chains of sugar-based molecules called "nucleotides." The rungs of the ladder are formed by the base-pair bonding of four specific organic components: adenine, thymine, cytosine, and guanine (ATCG). The precise chemical sequence of rungs on the spiral DNA ladder carries specific, detailed instructions encoded with this four-letter chemical alphabet. A gene consists of a grouping of these bonded chemical letters, specifying the production of certain protein molecules. The "genome" of an organism includes a complete set of genes encoded within the DNA matrix. Within each organic cell is found all the information that is necessary to build and to maintain a given organism. The remarkable human genome, which is neatly compressed within the nucleus of every one of our twenty trillion cells, comprises a remarkable information-bearing text containing over 3.5 billion chemical letters of coded detail, enough information to fill an entire library. The complete human DNA complex is so long and detailed that it must be tightly coiled within the nucleus of each living cell. Stretching it out in a straight line would require approximately two meters (about six feet) in length.

DNA (deoxyribonucleic acid) is clearly the most complex molecule known to mankind. The genetic material within each living cell is a blueprint for life that precisely spells out the characteristics of every living organism. DNA is classified as an organic "polymer," which just means it is composed of many smaller molecular compounds. Each molecular link (nucleotide) is distinguished from all the others by the base-pair chemicals attached to it. The order or sequencing of the base pairs attached to the DNA skeleton is the way that a hereditary blueprint is stored for each organism. This repeating sequence of chemical bases comprises a genetic master plan that codes for all organic design and activity.

According to Dr. Francis Collins, who served as the acting director of the Human Genome Project, "A live reading of that code at a rate of three letters per second would take 31 years, even if reading continued day and night. Printing these letters out in regular font size on normal bond paper and binding them together would result in a tower the height of the Washington Monument."[10] The entire human genome genetic manuscript is duplicated with every cellular division resulting in a perfect copy of the information-bearing content within the complex DNA polymer, which comprises the foundational chemistry for all activity related to human organic design.

The DNA instructs organic cells in the complex art of manufacturing proteins. As previously stated, polypeptide proteins are composed of amino acids, of which there are twenty specific ones that make up all such molecules in living things. The order of the specific amino acids in each polypeptide molecule determines its role and purpose in overall organic design. The required sequence of these amino acids must be exact in each and every case: this sequence bonding is what gives every protein molecule the correct three-dimensional shape allowing the host cell to recognize its particular function within the cellular chemistry. Protein molecules are often referred to as enzymes, which actually describe their function as a catalyst in biochemical reactions. During the cell's process of DNA replication, in order to reduce unwanted copying errors, cellular physiology is equipped with a proofreading system that detects and corrects any mistakes in the duplication process. Because of this very highly specialized cellular proofreading, the copying-error rate can be as low as one single mistake per every one hundred billion bits of information. This incredible accuracy rate could be compared to only one misplaced letter in fifty million typed pages of transcript.

Remember, of the trillions of cells that comprise complex organisms, only a mutation appearing in the germ cell (sex cells, egg or sperm, for example) can ever be passed to future generations. Multiple millions of genes composed of these base pair segments are organized into what you and I know as "chromosomes." All human cells contain forty-six chromosomes (twenty-three pairs) with offspring having received twenty-three chromosomes from each parent host. The different species vary quite significantly in the number of chromosomes that make up the genome of a particular organism.

The chromosomes are simply nature's way of packaging DNA within the cell's nucleus, and the number of chromosomes of a given species is certainly not a good indicator of the complexity of the organism. A dog, for example, has thirty-nine pairs of chromosomes, and a carp has a whopping fifty-two pairs. A specific DNA polymer may consist of several hundred thousand to as many as several billion links or subunits connected to each other. Each nucleotide subunit (sugar-link) encodes for specific genetic information that is necessary for the unique growth, development and functioning of each living organism.

You might think of the magnificent DNA molecule as a long spiral ladder upon which are written many organic symbols recording detailed instructions that are spelled out by nature's own unique four-character chemical alphabet. The sequence of recorded chemical letters in the DNA polymer comprises the coding commands that instruct cells in the specific art of making proteins. With the work of another genetic polymer called RNA (ribonucleic acid) the information content of each single gene is transcribed giving instruction to the cell on how to manufacture a vast array of essential protein molecules. Those scientists who are committed exclusively to a purely materialistic view of life have insisted that the information-bearing properties of the DNA polymer and the transcribing properties of RNA must have emerged randomly from raw, inanimate matter by some mindless, unguided process. With a complete genetic blueprint residing within the nucleus of every living cell, from bacteria to humans, the vast amount of information found in DNA and transcribed by RNA is the same common chemical apparatus of genetically mediated guidance that is now known to be universally active in all living organisms. Yes, complexity reigns in all cellular chemistry from an amoeba to man. Perhaps God designed it this way so that our elementary understanding of His grand design would inevitably point us back to Him.

According to eminent scholar and evolutionary biologist Richard Dawkins, "What has happened is that genetics has become a branch of information technology . . . the genetic code is truly digital in exactly the same sense as computer codes. This is not some vague analogy, it is the literal truth."[11]

Do you suppose that it takes intelligence to write computer code? Of course it does! This is surely something every one of us agrees on. The chemical, computer-like code found in DNA spells out each detail of every biological function, structural design, and molecular activity in controlling every facet of organic chemistry within the host organism. As aptly stated by educator Nancy Pearcey, a senior fellow at the Discovery Institute, "We can now explain why all experiments to create life in a test tube have failed—because we have tried to build life from the bottom up, by assembling the right materials to form a DNA molecule. But life is not about matter, it's about information."[12] Her same basic thought continues with this rather obvious fact: "Information does not arise from natural forces within matter, but it has to be imposed upon matter from outside by an intelligent agent."[13]

When we have personally observed a good example of a unique codified communication, or written, language-based message, it would be irrational to think of its origin in terms of some random chance process. As we have discussed in detail here, the DNA code comprised of these unique base-pair links, which are connected to each other and bonded to a nucleotide segment in a very precise way, will then transmit the specific information required to initiate all living processes. Similar to computer code, these bonds spell out many unique details with a particular digital message, making each biological function and all structural differentiation possible. This very remarkable genetic chemistry within living cellular design is an extremely complex mechanism that has caused many great men of science to conclude that the evolution model is totally useless when it comes to explaining how it came about.

According to the well-known geneticist Dr. Francis Collins, former director of the National Human Genome Research Institute, DNA chemically transmits instructions in live cells similar to the way one might program a cellphone to beep for specific reasons. He explains, "DNA is a three-billion-lettered program telling the cell to act in a certain way. It is a full instruction manual."[14] In a clear reference to the enormous progress that has been made in ongoing DNA research, Dr. Collins has also commented, "We have caught the first glimpses of our instruction book, previously known only to God."[15] How can we possibly account for a remarkably unique language within living cells, if not by intelligent design? Consider these powerful remarks from a famous Australian microbiologist, Dr. Michael Denton, who informs us that "the capacity of DNA to store information vastly exceeds that of any other known system; it is so efficient that all the information needed to specify an organism as complex as a man weighs less than a few thousand millionths of a gram. The information necessary to specify the design of all the species of organisms which have ever existed on the planet . . . could be held in a teaspoon . . . and there would still be room left over for all the information in every book ever written . . ."[16]

In his popular book entitled *In the Beginning Was Information*, Dr. Werner Gitt, who has formerly served as director and an acting professor at the famous German Institute of Physics and Technology, has made a specific claim that it is scientifically impossible for intelligible information to arise from disorder by chance. His science explains that "a code system is always the result of a mental process (it requires an intelligent origin or inventor) . . . It should be emphasized that matter, as such, is unable to generate any code . . . All experiences indicate that a thinking being voluntarily exercising his free will, cognition, and creativity is required."[17] He continues by explaining, "There is no known natural law through which matter can give rise to information, neither is there any physical process or material phenomenon known to do this."[18] Whenever any information is traced backward to its cause, it always leads to an intelligent source.

Information is the one central characteristic of all living things, and the information they contain, which regulates all of life's processes, can ultimately be traced back to an intelligent cause, an inventive mind. The storage medium for the vast amount of critical information-bearing code contained in living organisms is DNA. For any and every means of direct intelligible communication, by virtue of a code-driven language system, intelligence is clearly an essential element of its origin.

According to Microsoft founder Mr. Bill Gates, "DNA is like a computer program, but far, far more advanced than any software we've ever created."[19] The obvious question that so many researchers have asked themselves after carefully examining the evidence is, how in the world did the DNA genetic coding system and its translation apparatus originate? The following facts we know for certain:

1. All living things require a complex DNA database incorporating a chemically mediated language system, which constitutes a complete blueprint for life.
2. The only logical source of this language-based complexity requires the input of intelligence.
3. Every result demonstrated to date through probability science agrees that unguided chance and necessity are entirely incapable of generating such complexity.

If generating DNA without intelligent guidance sounds unlikely, consider this: the special chemical supervision that is required to assemble complex proteins comes from the DNA present in every living cell. The obvious question then is, where did DNA come from? DNA/RNA science presents a massive problem for evolution theory, because these molecules are vastly more complicated than other organic substances. The sheer mathematical odds against assembling the right material for DNA, simply by random chance, are so absolutely astronomical that very few researchers today even bother to think in these terms. We must also keep in mind that about twenty different protein enzymes are required in the manufacture and copying of DNA (replication). DNA controls RNA synthesis by which the information encoded therein is transcribed (transcription). RNA in turn controls all protein synthesis as directed by the genetic information within DNA (translation). This unique process constitutes a perfect example of the irreducible complexity previously referenced, in which the proteins are required to produce DNA. DNA is required to produce RNA, while RNA is required to produce the proteins that are essential to the production DNA. This critical circle-of-life cell chemistry can never be disrupted without certain death as the outcome. Because each of these critical phases of genetic physiology has required the others in a continuous process since the beginning of all carbon-based life, the unspeakably impossible chance that each single component of this irreducibly complex manufacturing system appeared spontaneously, all at the same time, is unthinkable.

If, for example, we were to consider the single DNA marker that code for blood clotting factor VIII, it might help to illustrate just how complex and unique genetic chemistry really is. This particular gene is comprised of about 186,000 nucleotides linked together in a complex molecular chain, which tells the human body how to produce blood clotting factor VIII, a very specialized protein of about 2,400 amino acids in length. Without this important organic protein, human blood clots very poorly, thus resulting in a serious genetic defect called hemophilia. During reproduction, DNA molecular structures in the germ cells are duplicated, thus making an exact copy of the parent host's genetic blueprint. If, for instance, when cellular RNA is engaged in transcribing the chemical sequence coded for blood clotting, and a reproductive cell was somehow able to accidentally insert just one defective nucleotide bond among the 186,000 that are required to produce factor VIII, with the offspring inheriting the defective gene, that child would be incapable of producing this essential blood clotting protein. He or she would then be facing the grave reality of a disadvantaged life as a hemophiliac. This rare mistake or mutation would create a unique problem, and would greatly affect that person's quality of life. In all of my study and research, everything I have learned to date about the controversial subject of mutations tells me that, almost without exception, they produce lethal, harmful, or useless outcomes. The Achilles heel of evolution theory must surely be seen in its absolute dependence upon what has now become only the phantom existence of multitudes of so-called *beneficial mutations*, an important topic I have already elaborated on in great detail in chapter 2.

Therefore, as you can see, the unique and amazingly complex DNA polymer, providing genetic instruction within every living cell is absolutely critical in directing all of life's physical processes, yet the theory of evolution is completely powerless to explain how it came to be. Some scientists are now routinely suggesting that genetic DNA chemistry may actually be the physical world's most powerful indicator of designed purpose in living things, and among the most devastating evidence that could ever be presented to countermand the evolution theory.

Notable American engineer and young-earth creationist Dr. Walter T. Brown has offered to us a fascinating indication as to why this sound and scientifically logical reasoning may in fact be true. He has reminded us that "DNA can only be produced with the help of at least twenty different proteins, but these proteins can only be produced at the direction of DNA. Since each requires the other, a satisfactory explanation of the origin of one must also explain the origin of the other . . . Apparently, this entire manufacturing system came into existence simultaneously. This implies creation!"[20]

DNA chemistry has also presented yet another extremely devastating problem for evolution theory: chirality![21] In chemistry, chirality refers to a molecular structure that has, or which produces, a non-superimposable mirror image of itself. In nature, chiral compounds typically appear equally in both right- and left-handed configurations called "optical isomers." The simplest example of chirality is found in the human hands. The right hand cannot be superimposed on top of the left hand. However, when the palms of the right and left hand are facing each other, they appear to be identical; they are perfect mirror images of each other. Now, in organic systems, chirality is a term that is applied to a biological requirement with regard to DNA and protein synthesis that occurs in every living cell.

The DNA molecules are formed by very long sequences of nucleotides (sugars) that must be of a certain molecular orientation to produce useful function. As we have previously discussed, in nature all amino acids occur randomly in a racemic mixture (equal numbers of right- and left-handed forms). Remember, however, that only the left-handed (levoform) amino acids are used in the construction of cellular proteins in organic systems; not a single defective component is allowed to appear or the entire manufacturing process fails. Again, the chiral requirement for protein synthesis must be met in every case. Now, just as amino acids must be of the left-handed orientation to produce functioning biological polypeptides, the nucleotides (also occurring naturally as a racemic mixture), which are required in the synthesis of complex DNA, are useable only if they appear in a specific right-handed configuration (dextroform). Can you begin to imagine the obstacle this presents for the random process of evolution?

Because DNA is made of only right-handed nucleotides, and organic proteins are produced with only left-handed amino acids, a major problem for evolutionary thinking is the revelation that any specific chemical reactions that produce either nucleotides or amino acids would always result in an equal racemic mixture of both right-handed and left-handed versions of each. For example, in a small DNA segment composed of one hundred thousand nucleotides, this means that all one hundred thousand sugars would have to appear at the very same time, and every last one of them with the right-handed configuration in order to produce biologically active gene. Our finite minds cannot even begin to grasp the monumental odds against any such random, spontaneous generation of a complex DNA molecule; these astronomical odds would be absolutely incomprehensible. However, just to give you a little perspective of the chirality requirement alone, please consider the following: for us to get all of the required sugars to show up in the right-handed configuration by random chance, in order to construct this DNA sequence, would be the same odds as flipping a coin one hundred thousand times, while correctly guessing heads each and every time. This fact alone presents a colossal problem for evolutionary theory, wouldn't you agree?

Abiogenesis (the spontaneous generation of life from nonliving material) means that the very first living cell required the perfect combination of all necessary right-handed nucleotides and left-handed amino acids, in the perfect design sequence in order to produce the many thousands of proteins, in addition to a complete complement of chromosomes composed of DNA and RNA, all at the same time. Again, trust me when I tell you that the infinitely impossible odds against accidentally producing these outrageously complex cellular structures belong light-years beyond the comprehension of mortal man, and are not even worth considering, no matter how many billions of years might be spent waiting for this to happen by chance.

In regard to the chance formation of complex DNA from isolated chemical elements in a primeval universe, Dr. Francis Collins of the Human Genome Research Project had this to say: "How could a self-replicating information-carrying molecule assemble spontaneously from these compounds? DNA with its phosphate-sugar backbone, and intricately arranged organic bases, stacked neatly on top of one another, and paired together at each rung of the twisted double helix, seems an utterly improbable molecule to have 'just happened.'"[22] With this in mind, the only reasonable conclusion we can draw from today's extremely detailed research into molecular biochemistry is that the magnificent biological machinery found to be present within the living cell is the unique and marvelous design of an ingenious, purpose-driven Intelligence with a superb imagination and a very complex mind.

There's No Room for Error

When American astronauts first walked upon the moon, nobody was claiming that this outstanding and dramatic feat had resulted from a long series of remarkable accidents. Thousands of scientists, along with gifted mathematicians and engineers worked diligently for many years to plan and prepare for this world-changing event. Complicated inventions of mechanical genius were conceived, planned, designed, constructed, and tested, resulting in millions of components that were integrated together with extreme precision to produce a working plan that would accomplish the goal of landing a man on the moon. Why were we successful in our effort to place man on the moon? There can be only one reason—because absolutely nothing was left to chance! The greatest engineering achievement of the twentieth century was attributed to the effective utilization of meticulous design and planning. And yet, by comparison, the simplest living cell (thanks to modern bio-molecular technological achievement) is now understood to be vastly more complicated and intricate than any spacecraft or machinery ever designed and built by human engineering. Still, however, many evolutionists refuse to entertain the possibility of supernatural intelligence, and yet they do not even hesitate to explain the alarming complexity of living things in the simplest terms of blind chance. You and I are purely accidental by their way of thinking, leaving them to conclude that our lives have no more value or purpose than a snail or a slug.

This strange logic requires an incredible leap of faith on the part of the evolution proponents, but this ideology will never be considered *reasonable* faith. These diehard intellectuals have essentially backed themselves into the blind corner because of their continual refusal to believe that a wise master design engineer is required to explain a vast, virtually incomprehensible universe. Over the last couple hundred years, worldwide scientific research and investigation has uncovered immeasurably more data regarding the physical universe than could ever have been remotely imagined by our ancestors. The great Hubble telescope, for example, has revealed that there are at least one hundred billion or more galaxies in the known universe, with, perhaps, one hundred billion or more stars per galaxy. It certainly seems to me an act of great pride, and perhaps presumptuous human arrogance, to explain away the need for a sovereign creator God in the light of such a vast, and virtually unknowable, physical macrocosm.

Research Says "Abandon Ship"

Can we really trust in spontaneous generation as the correct model to explain the origin of biological systems? As we consider where the evidence is taking us in our search for the truth about the origin of life, let us examine an authoritative statement made by molecular biologist Dr. Michael Denton, who has authored the book *Evolution: A Theory in Crisis*. Speaking from many years of professional research experience in the field of cellular physiology, Dr. Denton has provided us with yet another commanding assessment in light of the extreme complexity of the living cell: "Although the tiniest bacterial cells are incredibly small, weighing less than 10 (-12) grams [10 to the minus 12], each is in fact, a veritable micro-miniaturized factory containing thousands of exquisitely designed pieces of intricate molecular machinery, made up altogether of 100,000 million atoms, far more complicated than any machinery ever built by man, and absolutely without parallel in the nonliving world."[23] The study of bacterial cells through modern bio molecular research has revealed a complexity of design that is unparalleled in the nonorganic world, and yet these tiny, although extremely multifaceted organisms are so minute that you could fit a trillion of them in a single teaspoon.

Many of the casual proponents of evolution still insist on random chance to explain the unique complexities of life and the complicated physiology within the living cell. However, today's most sophisticated scientists, conducting up-to-date origin-of-life research, are, by virtue of the latest scientific findings, now rapidly abandoning and discarding all chance-based theories. Imagine every living cell in the human body containing much more information than the world's most advanced computer hard drive. Then try to imagine all this information-bearing physiology coming together by random chance, all at the same time. As I have already emphasized, molecular DNA chemistry alone demonstrates the monumental futility of scientists who would insist on explaining the origin of life in the terms of simple, natural processes. Many believe it is now time to look seriously at a supernatural explanation for the origin of life!

Eminent scientist Dr. Walter L. Bradley has explained it this way: "What I've found is absolutely overwhelming evidence that points toward an intelligent designer."[24] Because of the fair and honest research that is currently underway, the evidence is indeed compelling great men of science to look beyond nature for the answers they seek. Even the highly revered evolutionist and Oxford biologist Richard Dawkins was compelled to concede on this point when he stated that "the more statistically improbable a thing is, the less can we believe that it just happened by blind chance. Superficially, the obvious alternative to chance is an Intelligent Designer."[25]

In the early part of the twentieth century, evolutionists were forced to admit that Darwin's theory was beginning to appear rather inadequate in the light of advancing new scientific achievement, which was identifying insurmountable problems his outdated theory could never overcome. This had prompted a transformation in evolutionary thought over the next forty years culminating in what is now commonly referred to as the "neo-Darwinian theory." Also known by the term "modern evolutionary synthesis," Neo-Darwinism has combined Darwin's theory of evolution by natural selection with ideas from the field of population genetics that were initially championed by Gregor Mendel. This remodel placed greater emphasis on random mutations as the sole source of evolutionary variation, suggesting that the accumulation of any small genetic changes over time has eventually led to so-called species variation. Although the newest concepts in evolution theory further explained adaptive change and microevolution (variation of physical traits within a kind as originally written into the genetic code), the updated theory still fails to adequately address the two most important complaints about evolutionary thought that were presented by Darwin's early critics: *spontaneous generation and macroevolution.*

No credible evidence has ever been presented to confirm that life arose spontaneously from nonliving material, nor has any data ever explained how new information can be added to the genetic composition of any living organism. These revisions in Darwin's theory were a desperate attempt to answer the many difficulties that new discoveries had presented. This bold effort has sought to answer Darwin's critics by proposing changes that would align themselves more closely with updated scientific data. However, not long after these few new modifications in the theory were adopted, the advance of scientific knowledge began to accelerate at light speed, and has continued to move forward at a blistering pace for the last seventy years. The desperate attempt to satisfy the early critics of naturalism has now fallen on hard times as well, and can no longer square itself with current scientific data. The biggest problem facing evolution today, even if the infinitely impossible assumption of spontaneous generation was considered a given, is the sure fact that multiple, mutation-driven alterations would have had to occur at the same time and become complementary to one another for major improvements in any given species to occur.

For example, suppose an animal experienced a very rare mutation resulting in longer lower leg bones. Unfortunately, this single mutation would result in diminished fitness, and greater vulnerability, unless this extremely rare anomaly was accompanied by a series of additional, complementary mutations. This creature would also require longer upper leg bones (for balance—equal distribution of weight); larger joints; longer muscles, tendons, and ligaments; along with more skin. These vital changes all working together could possibly allow for more explosive land speed in pursuing prey and evading predators. Yet without these other coincidental and complementary mutations, no physically adaptive advantage would ever be achieved.

We are reminded, however, that the vast majority of mutations are injurious, if not lethal. Regrettably for naturalism, the evolutionary hypothesis must rely upon the hope of multiple "beneficial mutations" occurring together, resulting in a cumulative advantage. Without such occurrence, this disadvantaged creature would be quickly wiped out by natural selection. The impossible odds of a rapid succession of favorable mutations occurring within the germ cells of the same organism at the same time creates an infinitesimally remote probability that is far too outrageous to be given serious consideration. These so-called minor beneficial mutations would each have to contribute a very small amount of information to the genetic blueprint. The extreme degree of desperation that is found in this kind of wishful thinking has never been adequately confirmed by any documented observations within natural science.

Darwinism, new or old, has never revealed an adequate, practical mechanism that could explain how the genome of a particular organism could have accumulated vast amounts of information in its genetic programming, and the extremely remote and exceptionally rare occurrence of occasional copying errors in germ cells during DNA replication has been a major obstacle for neo-Darwinian theory.

Stephen C. Meyer, who holds a PhD in history and the philosophy of science from Cambridge University, states, "While many outside origin-of-life biology may still invoke chance as a causal explanation for the origin of biological information, few serious researchers still do."[26] In an ever-increasing trend, today's most serious investigators in various scientific disciplines such as biology, biochemistry, genetics, geology, and even cosmology are beginning to raise serious objections to the hypothesis of evolution, claiming that its implications are often based on incomplete and flawed data.

Upon a much closer examination, many of the so-called factual elements of the theory now appear to be unraveling in light of current research findings. These recent discoveries have prompted numerous knowledge-seeking scientists to concede that an intelligent designer must have been at work in the initial appearance of the earth's complex living creatures. Dr. Michael Behe, of Lehigh University, has spoken out very clearly on this matter. He wrote, "The conclusion of intelligent design flows naturally from the data itself—not from sacred books or sectarian beliefs . . . The reluctance of science to embrace the conclusion of intelligent design . . . has no justifiable foundation . . . Many people, including many important and well-respected scientists, just don't want there to be anything beyond nature."[27] Dr. Michael Denton offered us yet another reflective insight when he wrote, "[Evolutionary theory] is still, as it was in Darwin's time, a highly speculative hypothesis entirely without direct factual support, and very far from the self-evident axiom some of its more aggressive advocates would have us believe."[28]

The highly technological world of modern scientific research has shown a bright and revealing light upon the evolution model, exposing numerous problems that, many are convinced, cannot be overcome. As a consequence, the most cherished hypotheses of neo-naturalism are beginning to unravel in the light of continuing scientific investigation. Michael Denton sums it up for us, with a very serious accusation against evolutionary thought, by stating, "Nowhere was Darwin able to point to one bona fide case of natural selection having actually generated evolutionary change in nature . . . ultimately, the Darwinian theory of evolution is no more nor less than the great cosmogenic myth of the 20th century."[29] Because of abundant and glaring flaws, when compared with what are now known and observable facts, many of today's most renowned scientists and researchers are beginning to abandon ship, and who can blame them? When you examine the worldviews of today's top-notch scientists, you will discover very few atheists among them. Why is this? It is because they have experienced firsthand the futility of attempting to explain natural phenomena, and especially organic life in terms of blind chance. Today, the world's most devoted atheists, who are still clinging desperately to the rotting corpse of naturalism, are much more likely to be found among educators in the darkened hallways of liberal ivory-tower universities where they can be found instructing their students in the social sciences and humanities.

Life in the Primordial Soup

There are two immutable truths in the field of biology that have never changed. No real evidence discovered through serious empirical scientific research has ever come remotely close to contradicting these fundamental laws of nature. I would strongly challenge anyone to show sufficient evidence to the contrary.

1. Only the living can give rise to new life! Dead things cannot produce life. Raw chemicals and the basic elements found in the crust of the earth cannot produce life in and of themselves. Life comes forth only through the reproductive mechanism that was designed for this purpose within the world's vast array of complex living organisms.
2. Plants and animals can only reproduce after their own kind! This rather obvious fact has never been violated. However, a wide variation of traits has clearly been written into the genetic code of every living kind; this has allowed for an extensive variety of complementary features within each basic plant and animal group. Even with the many known variations we observe and enjoy within the basic kinds, we can be certain that dogs will always reproduce dogs, and corn will always reproduce corn.

According to genetic biochemist Dr. Michael Denton, the incomprehensibly drastic jump from the nonliving material world to the living, breathing world of organic design "represents the most dramatic and fundamental of all the discontinuities of nature. Between a living cell and the most highly ordered non-biological systems, such as a natural crystal or a snowflake, there is a chasm as vast and absolute as it is possible to conceive."[30] Denton has further explained that "molecular biology has also shown us that the basic design of the cell system is essentially the same in all living systems on the Earth, from bacteria to mammals. In all organisms, the roles of DNA, RNA, and proteins are identical. The meaning of the genetic code is also virtually identical in all cells . . . In terms of their basic biochemical design, therefore, no living system can be thought of as being primitive or ancestral with respect to any other system, nor is there the slightest empirical hint of an evolutionary sequence among all the incredibly diverse cells on Earth."[31] The 1965 Nobel Prize-winning biochemist Dr. Jacques Monod concurs, "We have no idea what the structure of a primitive cell might have been. The simplest living system known to us, the bacterial cell . . . in its overall chemical plan is the same as that of all other living beings. It employs the same genetic code and the same mechanism of translation as do, for example, human cells. Thus, the simplest cells available to us for study have nothing 'primitive' about them . . . No vestiges of truly primitive structures are discernible."[32] Therefore, we certainly must never underestimate the vast complexity of a living cell, no matter what organism it comes from.

The intricate interlocking physiology within all viable cells are abounding with irreducibly complex molecular machinery that operates with sophisticated, precision-coordinated moving parts capable of manufacturing protein polypeptides with uncanny accuracy and stunning efficiency. Within the outer membrane of living cells are contained thousands of complex protein molecules that comprise highly specified components generated by the genetic software encoded in their DNA, and yet these cells are so tiny that several hundred of them could be placed on the period at the end of this sentence. According to prominent biochemist Dr. Michael Behe, flagella (the complex propeller-like structure that enables a bacterium to swim) are so miniscule that if you laid thirty-five thousand of them end to end their total length would occupy approximately 1 millimeter of space (0.04 inch).[33] Dr. Behe has argued that the existence of irreducibly complex, micro molecular machinery within the living cell can only point, unmistakably, toward the intelligent design of these complex organic features. He once wrote, "To a person who does not feel obliged to restrict his search to unintelligent causes, the straightforward conclusion is that many biochemical systems were designed. They were designed, not by the laws of nature, nor by chance and necessity; rather, they were planned . . . The designer knew what the systems would look like when they were completed, then took steps to bring the systems about. Life on earth at its most fundamental level, in its most critical components, is the product of intelligent activity."[34]

With this in mind, it must be firmly emphasized that no team of scientists anywhere in the world has ever been capable of creating something even remotely close to organic life from nonliving chemicals. However, many evolutionists still remain convinced that what cannot be accomplished by specially trained scientists with the most up-to-date equipment in the artificially controlled environment of a modern laboratory, somehow occurred randomly, through blind chance several billion years ago; and it happened without any intelligence directing the event. Men and women who persist in tenaciously clinging to this scenario have invested their complete faith in a protracted series of mathematically impossible biological accidents, which contemporary mankind with his most sophisticated and technologically advanced surroundings, has not even come remotely close to reproducing today.

In 1864, Dr. Louis Pasteur addressed a major university in Paris where he predicted that the idea of the "spontaneous generation" of a living cell from dead lifeless chemicals in some ancient primordial state would never sufficiently recover from the lethal blow that was inflicted upon it by his various painstaking experiments and observations. Those profound words have indeed stood the test of time as science continues to struggle in providing a reliable answer to explain the original emergence of carbon-based life. Consider this rather dramatic commentary written by the famous British physicist and notable astronomer Sir Fredrick Hoyle. He states, "If there were a principle of matter, which somehow drove organic systems toward life . . . its existence should easily be demonstrable in the laboratory . . . One could, for instance, take a swimming bath to represent the primordial soup. Fill it with any chemicals of a non-biological nature you please. Pump any gases over it, or through it, you please, and shine any kind of radiation on it that takes your fancy. Let the experiment proceed for a year and see how many of the 2,000 enzymes [proteins produced by living cells] have appeared in the bath . . . I will give you the answer, and so save the time and trouble and expense of actually doing the experiment. You would find nothing at all, except possibly for a tarry sludge, composed of amino acids, and other simple organic chemicals. How can I be so confident of this statement? . . .Well, if it were otherwise, the experiment would long since have been done and would be well known and famous throughout the world. The cost of it would be trivial compared to the cost of landing a man on the moon; in short, there is not one shred of objective evidence to support the hypothesis that life began in an organic soup here on the Earth."[35]

Imagine, if you will, the determined belief in a naturalistic view of the origin of organic life against insurmountable odds, with a serious absence of any hard evidence to support such an outrageous claim. Even though evolution has been taught as factual in America and elsewhere, the evidence simply does not support this hypothetical conclusion. Dr. Wolfgang Smith is a very well-respected mathematician, physicist, and philosopher of science, who has taught at MIT, UCLA, and Oregon State University. Dr. Smith has cordially offered the following professional assessment from his thorough understanding of the current trends in science: "Today, 128 years after it was first promulgated, the Darwinian theory of evolution stands under attack as never before . . . the fact is that in recent times there has been increasing dissent on the issue within academic and professional ranks, and that a growing number of respectable scientists are defecting from the evolutionist camp. It is interesting, moreover, that for the most part these 'experts' have abandoned Darwinism, not on the basis of religious faith or biblical persuasions, but on strictly scientific grounds, and in some instances, regretfully, as one could say . . . We are told dogmatically that evolution is an established fact; but we are never told who has established it, and by what means. We are told, often enough, that the 'doctrine' is founded upon evidence, and that indeed this evidence 'is henceforward, above all verification, as well as being immune from any subsequent contradiction by experience'; but we are left entirely in the dark on the crucial question wherein, precisely, this evidence consists."[36]

As it turns out, Charles Darwin's own personal letters have revealed to us a very troubled soul whose confidence had become quite shaken toward the direction his life took him in. "Often a cold shudder has run through me, and I have asked myself whether I may have not devoted myself to a fantasy."[37] Darwin was forced to recognize that evidence from the fossil record did not and perhaps never would support his theory, and for this, along with other reasons, he remained very skeptical of his own conclusions. If he was having such disturbing second thoughts during his lifetime, imagine what he would be thinking now after more than a century of modern-day scientific research, which has revealed countless technological breakthroughs that have noticeably shaken his worn-out theory to its very core. The unique proposal that a primitive hypothesis modeled in the early 1800s could possibly account for the origin of every organic structure in the vast, irreducibly complex world of molecular microbiology is laughable. The outdated theory of evolution has become a religious dogma so deeply ingrained in its adherents that they have become totally oblivious to its many absurdities.

The past several decades of cellular research have dramatically widened the broad gulf that currently separates the realities of empirical science from the growing myth of Neo-Darwinism, a proud theory that is hopelessly riddled with unfounded assumptions. Therefore, if Charles Darwin were alive today, I would not be surprised if, based on the last one hundred-fifty years of revealed facts that have strongly denied his claims, he were to join the thousands of other scientists, philosophers, and educators who have now wisely abandoned an obsolete theory.

Apart from direct divine intervention in the pre-organic world, impossible events can be divided into two very specific categories:

fundamentally impossible and statistically impossible. A fundamentally impossible event would leave absolutely no room for human logic or reasoning of any kind. An example of this type of event would include the bodily resurrection of Christ from the dead. The statistically impossible idea of the spontaneous generation of organic life from some random chance interaction of raw chemicals in the commonly referenced primordial soup is revealed to us in the following powerful statement from a Russian-born, Belgian chemist by the name of Ilya Prigogine. The late and very highly decorated Dr. Prigogine, who was awarded the Nobel Prize for chemistry in 1977, offered the following rather blunt statement when he was questioned about the probability of the chance generation of carbon-based life being solely dependent on a purely random, unguided series of millions of lucky, coincidental chemical accidents. He said, "The statistical probability that organic structures, and the most precisely harmonized reactions that typify living organisms, would be generated by accident is zero!"[38]

Beyond Reason—Strange Logic

Logic alone teaches us that every design requires a designer. This logic would also suggest that the creation requires a creator. It is really quite elementary to recognize when something has been created. Everything that has been created required intelligent planning, designed purpose, and deliberate intent. Consider, if you will, the stark appearance of a magnificent arrowhead as compared to a crude piece of black obsidian, or perhaps Mount Rushmore seated next to a rough granite mountaintop; do these vivid images speak to us of design? How about a sandcastle along the seashore, a beautiful painting, a massive skyscraper, or even the construction of a simple paper airplane? Intelligent design is always employed when some basic raw materials are assembled into something that is useful, intelligible, or in some way pleasurable to the senses. Design always requires a designer!

We may observe the majestic grandeur of a snowcapped peak, or walk slowly along the seashore as powerful wave's pound forcefully against the sand; and perhaps we have observed a myriad of stars on a moonless night. To say that these remarkable sights are the product of random blind chance is a clear departure from sound reason. Every effect demands an adequate cause. This truth has been alluded to time and time again by a notable contemporary physicist Paul Davies who declares, "Every advance in fundamental physics seems to uncover yet another facet of order."[39] His personal impression continues with this statement: "The laws [of physics] . . . seem to be the product of exceedingly ingenious design. The universe must have a purpose."[40] These authoritative statements are coming from a world-class, non-Christian scientist, and are certainly a tremendous blow to the materialistic view of blind chance.

Therefore, it remains entirely unreasonable to believe that the unique complexity and order we have observed in the universe is merely the product of freakish, random events. Creation, on the other hand, refers us to the planned and purposeful acts by which God, through his unlimited power, brought into existence time, space, matter, energy, and organic physiology, all interacting in a perfect world that was designed specifically around his plan and purpose for mankind. Everything we humans have presently learned from origin-of-life science tells us, without question, that the universe had a beginning. This suggests to us that someone or something is responsible as the first cause; to believe otherwise is to infer that time, space, and matter have always existed, or have created themselves, which is clearly irrational.

However strange it may sound, when you break it all down to the basic hypothesis, the argument for evolution really amounts to this bizarre and highly unreasonable scenario: no one (no God) plus nothing (no matter) times blind chance (freak accidents) equals everything (the entire universe). Do you actually have enough faith to believe such a strange and fantastic ideology as this? I certainly do not!

As a devoted student of both science and history for over thirty years, and one who has carefully and continually examined the question of origins during that time, I have personally come to a most logical conclusion__ that the thoroughly and aggressively promoted concept of evolution is complete and utter nonsense. It's designed to exalt man and to diminish the need for faith in a physical universe that is, at best, barely comprehended by the combined historical achievements of a fragile human race! So why would so many people insist on clinging to a dying philosophy that cannot stand up to the basic scrutiny imposed on it by today's modern, highly technological world of scientific research? The answer can only be found in man's free volition__ that vital freedom to exercise one's will in attempting to control the circumstances related to personal choice and lifestyle decision-making. Once people have made a firm commitment to a philosophical point of view that they strongly believe in, very little evidence is then required to confirm what they already consider to be true. It's simply a matter of choice! Consider the following statement from the world-class evolutionist Richard Dawkins, who states, "Even if there were no actual evidence in favor of the Darwinian theory . . . we should still be justified in preferring it to all rival theories."[41] As a respected man within the scientific community and a top-notch educator, how can Mr. Dawkins possibly justify making such a bold and controversial statement? The answer to this can only be because he has long since ruled out any and every option that does not conform with naturalism, and naturalism, to the unaided human mind and self-centered human heart, seems to sit much easier on the post-modern intellectual mind than a commitment of believing faith in what may seem to many as the mysteriously unexplained supernatural. There are those who believe that religion, and especially the Christian worldview has significantly impeded the progress of science. Is it true? Have faith systems actually hindered the acquisition of scientific knowledge as many naturalist proponents are claiming? A closer look at the historical footprint of Western civilization would seem to indicate otherwise. I would be inclined to remind them once again to re-examine the historical roots of the scientific revolution__ for it was Christianity and nothing less that gave rise to the advent of modern science as nearly all the early scientific pioneers held a Christian worldview. Perhaps, then, it is atheism, and not religious faith, that is hindering the progress of science.

How can we explain the common-place reluctance of secular science to accept the idea of a creator when the evidence for a designer is simply overwhelming? Some four hundred years ago a courageous innovator named Galileo set about to seek after knowledge and understanding of the physical world based solely upon the evidence derived by experimentation and subsequent observation. These were the key elements he believed to be required to accurately establish empirical scientific knowledge. Galileo's objective approach to scientific inquiry began at a time when the general public and even the Roman Catholic Church maintained that scientific facts were better understood when based on the philosophy and tradition embraced by Aristotle and the classical philosophers. However, in spite of great opposition and even imprisonment by the mainstream establishment of his day, the perseverance of Galileo and his contemporaries successfully altered the scientific paradigm, and ushered in an age of enlightenment resulting in a new scientific revolution. Men became scientists because they believed in the laws of nature, and they believed in the laws of nature because they believed in a "lawgiver." This unbiased, fact-seeking method used to achieve empirical scientific knowledge and understanding was commonly based on a firm belief in a Creator God, and the goal of such investigative inquiry was to discover a small measure of His supernatural plan in designing a physical world that has generated so much irresistible curiosity.

Because the advent of evolution theory has fanned the flames of "naturalism" in modern cultures the world over, many within scientific circles have sought to redefine science in a manner that conforms with materialistic views and excludes any mention or acknowledgment of supernatural causation for a remarkable universe. With such a biased, short-sided point of view becoming common-place within the scientific community for generations, it is easy to understand why so many scientific minds would view religion as an obstacle and a hindrance to the advancement of modern science. If, however, evolution theory represents a false view of the world as the evidence has overwhelmingly suggested, then it is this theory, pointing toward a strictly materialistic worldview, that has now become the greatest obstacle to a deeper understanding of the world around us by limiting the advance of truthful and accurate scientific achievement based on the observed results of unbiased investigation.

We may hear secular scientists referring to the "god of the gaps." This is the kind of god atheists say that religious people believe in. To those who would deny any mention of deity in the grand scheme of things this is a type of god that is only created out of necessity and because of ignorance. The thinking goes something like this: if I cannot understand it, then god did it. For example, early human cultures did not understand thunder and lightning. In Greek culture, this physical phenomenon was attributed to the deity Zeus (the god of the sky). A single class in atmospheric science today and the god Zeus quickly disappears. The many gods of Greek mythology were imagined by those could not explain or understand certain characteristics of the natural world. In this kind of scenario an unknown god is only given credit as author to that which we do not understand. As soon as science is able to explain a given phenomenon and provide enlightenment in the public discourse, this god disappears. If this were true, then of course you would have to choose between god and science. The so-called god of the gaps is not, however, the God of the Bible. The God of the Bible is the author of the whole show, regardless of whether we do or do not understand a given physical phenomenon from a scientific point of view. Science exists because there is a sovereign creator God, and we have endeavored to study his grand design by utilizing the intellectual capacity and curiosity he has so graciously entrusted to us.

Many of the humanist-oriented philosophers have sadly devoted themselves to a complete and utter disregard of the vast factual evidence that clearly points to a creator. A similar argument to that of Mr. Dawkins had once appeared in the modern scientific literature courtesy of a Kansas State University professor, which was subsequently printed in the journal *Nature*. He commented with this: "Even if all the data point to an intelligent designer, such an hypothesis is excluded from science, because it is not naturalistic."[42] Even though this educator and well-known biology professor Richard Dawkins have both clearly made an unwavering commitment to materialism, Dawkins's personal statements would still seem to reflect a strong temptation to concede the vast implications of such exquisite design in nature. He once stated, "Biology is the study of complicated things that give the appearance of having been designed for a purpose."[43] Many, who have desperately feared the controversial implications suggested by design, just keep running right into them. The persistent determination of naturalists, who consistently hold on so firmly to their prior commitment to materialism, was clearly expressed by another Nobel Prize winner in medicine and physiology. Dr. George Wald explains it this way: "There are only two possibilities as to how life arose. One is spontaneous generation arising to evolution; the other is a supernatural creative act of God . . . There is no third possibility. Spontaneous generation, that life arose from nonliving matter, was scientifically disproved 120 years ago by Louis Pasteur, and others . . . That leaves us with the only possible conclusion—that life arose as a supernatural creative act of God. I will not accept that philosophically, because I do not want to believe in God. Therefore, I choose to believe in that which I know is scientifically impossible; spontaneous generation arising to evolution."[44] Amazing! Because of their strictly devoted commitment to a worldview that excludes God and their passionate disdain for the concept of the supernatural, the proponents of evolution theory are forced to interpret the evidence in a way that conforms with their emotionally and intellectually preferred philosophical point of view, even though the known scientific facts clearly dictate otherwise.

Prominent geneticist and evolutionary biologist Theodosius Dobyhansky has offered a strange remark that seems to explain for us why so many scientists have willingly ignored valid empirical evidence and continue to cling ever so tightly to their preferred worldview. "No evidence is powerful enough to force acceptance of the conclusion that is emotionally distasteful."[45]

We should pause here to briefly consider what these scientists are actually saying. The noted writer and educator Nancy Pearcey has aptly summed up for us these rather foolish conclusions with the following: "Even if there is no evidence in favor of Darwinism, and all the evidence favors intelligent design, still we are not allowed to consider that in science. Clearly, the issue is not fundamentally a matter of evidence at all, but of a prior philosophical commitment."[46] Many other people have simply avoided the creation-evolution controversy altogether, having fallen victim to a modern-day secular culture that is moving further and further away from belief in a personal loving God. Perhaps they are no longer interested in where the evidence is leading science, but are simply content with the ideology that an increasingly secularized culture is demanding. Many of these individuals will continue to maintain the following unfortunate disclaimer: *My mind is made up—don't confuse me with the facts*!

Chapter 5

Beyond the Ivory Tower

Old Mother Earth?

How old is the earth? Do we have any idea? Is there any information that can help us determine our planet's relative age? Scientists love to invoke the magic of colossal numbers. The mystique generated by outrageous dating makes it sound as though anything is possible, even if it is not. Many scientists have insisted that our planet is approximately 5.3 billion years old, if not older. If we take their word for it, we are buying into a statistic that is based entirely on the false assumption of evolution. We are also told that life appeared spontaneously on this planet in a primordial soup of chemicals about 3 billion years ago, and that modern man began to emerge from his long evolutionary past at least 1 million years ago. Since literally billions of years are required to accommodate the evolution model (if it were even possible), the relative age of planet earth has, therefore, become an important factor that deserves some thoughtful consideration. Consequently, we should examine some of the physical evidence ourselves__ evidence that, perhaps, may offer another perspective by which the age of the earth may be considered.

The real question we need to address is whether the earth is relatively young or extremely old as measured by thousands, millions, or billions of years. Because an extremely ancient earth is absolutely critical to the plausibility of the standard evolution model, perhaps we can learn something interesting and informative by examining this question in some detail. Here, again, we discover that the modern evolutionist is relying heavily upon speculation and guesswork rather than factual data that can be observed and verified. The truth is that we cannot determine an accurate age for planet earth; however, what we can do is point to verifiable physical evidence that may indicate to us whether our planet is relatively young or exceedingly old. Perhaps this valuable information will provide some assistance as we continue to shine the light of truth in our search for understanding about the origin of life on this planet. Actually the earth could be relatively young, and it would still very easily accommodate the biblical view of creation, as recorded in the venerated Genesis account.

There are many problems that are associated with radiometric dating methods, which actually make them highly unreliable for use in dating geological formations.[1] Therefore, we have seen that the dating of rock strata has now become primarily dependent on a fossil record that is interpreted within the wide framework of evolution theory. Evolutionists rely upon a dating method that is dependent on what are called index fossils. Index fossils (as I mentioned in chapter 2) are those that appear in great abundance during a particular geological age as assigned within the evolutionary scenario. Their relative ages have been predetermined, and are based entirely on speculation within the evolution model. This unscientific technique relies on "circular reasoning" (the dating of rocks by the fossils they contain, and the dating of fossils by the rocks they are found in), and by employing this technique, evolutionists have opportunely assigned what they believe to be relatively accurate dates to both fossil and rock formations. Consider, however, this very frank admission from geology expert Robert H. Rastall of Cambridge University: "It cannot be denied that from a strictly philosophical standpoint, geologists are here arguing in a circle. The succession of organisms has been determined by the study of their remains embedded in the rocks, and the relative ages of the rocks are determined by the remains of the organisms they contain."[2] Many have considered such dates to be both reliable and scientific, even though their dating method is totally dependent on a theory that is bankrupt of evidential support. As a teaching professor of paleobiology at Kansas State University, Dr. Ronald R. West has also commented on the rather unscientific practice of circular reasoning that is so prevalent in evolutionary thinking: "Contrary to what most scientists write, the fossil record does not support the Darwinian theory of evolution because it is this theory which we use to interpret the fossil record. By doing so, we are guilty of circular reasoning if we then say the fossil record supports this theory."[3] Paleo-evolutionist and American Museum curator Dr. Niles Eldredge has confirmed this obvious weakness in evolutionary thinking with the following conciliatory statement: "Paleontologists cannot operate this way. There is simply no way to look at a fossil and say how old it is unless you know the age of the rocks it comes from. And this poses something of a problem: if we date the rocks by their fossils, how can we then turn around and talk about the patterns of evolutionary time in the fossil record?"[4] With this said, it is obvious that there is not, in reality, any reliable justification by which one could validate the vast geological timescale as proposed by the evolution model, when man is considering the relative age of fossils and or geological formations. Consider this expert opinion from a world-renowned organic chemist, Dr. A. E. Wilder-Smith, who is widely known to be highly critical of current fossil dating methodology: "So firmly does the modern geologist believe in evolution, up from simple organisms to complex ones over huge time spans, that he is perfectly willing to use the theory of evolution to prove the theory of evolution . . . applying the theory of evolution to prove the correctness of evolution. For we are assuming that the oldest formations contain only the most primitive and least complex organisms, which is the base assumption of Darwinism . . . If we now assume that only simple organisms will occur in old formations, we are assuming the basic premise of Darwinism to be correct. To use, therefore, for dating purposes, the assumption that only simple organisms will be present in old formations is to thoroughly beg the whole question. It is arguing in a circle."[5]

I am always amazed when pondering the number of intelligent people who believe that evolution is a valid scientific reality and, as a result, how few objections are raised when it comes to the poor dating methods that are used to support the theory. The only evidence in favor of evolution is the assumption that it is true, based on the overwhelming degree of indoctrination modern cultures have expounded on its behalf. When considering the age of the earth, we will soon discover that the primary evidence for an extremely ancient earth history turns out to be its absolute necessity to validate the proposed evolution model; but even if evolution had the definitive support of a very old earth (which is highly speculative), it is still sadly lacking in unbiased evidential support.

It turns out that a consistent drumbeat of "billions of years" is simply necessary to create the false impression required to attract the unwary public to a theory that cannot possibly rely upon the known facts of true science. No valid scientific methodology could ever confirm the conclusion of a 5.3 billion-year-old earth, a number that is based solely on unscientific assumption. In fact, when we take a look at the data that can and has been measured, we see a very different story entirely.

For example, according to Dr. Stuart Nevins, a reliable expert in the scientific discipline of geology who has carefully studied and documented the rate of sedimentary deposition within the ocean basins, approximately 27.5 billion tons of sediment is currently being washed into the oceans by river systems every year. Therefore, he has concluded, based upon the present rate of sedimentary erosion over the surface of the planet, that all the earth's continents would have been completely reduced to sea level in about 14 million years.[6] How could one possibly explain the current rate of sedimentary erosion in terms of a 5.3 *billion-year-old* earth?

According to evolution theory, comets are believed to be the same age as our solar system, yet each time they orbit near the sun large amounts of debris is lost. This rather rapid disintegration of the comets within our solar system is very telling, and according to Dr. Henry Morris, the comets are burning up at a significant rate suggesting that they are only thousands and not billions of years old, as evolutionists have claimed.[7]

Also consider that decay-rate data from measuring the earth's magnetic field may also be an indicator of our planet's age, at least with regard to its ability to support life. Scientific research has indicated that the earth's magnetism is decaying at a rate of approximately five percent every one hundred years. If we can assume the rate of decay of our planet's magnetism has been constant throughout the historical past, then, by going back around ten thousand years we would soon discover that the earth's magnetic field was 128 times stronger than it is today.[8] The great amount of heat generated by a magnetic field of that intensity would have prevented life's existence on the earth at that time. Dr. Thomas G. Barnes, a former professor of physics at the University of Texas in El Paso, has aptly pointed out that the strength of our planet's magnetism has been studied, and carefully measured with empirical data recorded for over 130 years. He has reported a current rate of decay in the magnetic field, which equates to a half-life of 1,400 years. This means that every 1,400 years the strength of the earth's magnetism has diminished by one-half. At such a rapid rate of decay, according to Dr. Barnes, it is inconceivable that a starting point for the earth's magnetism could produce a life supporting planet with an age greater than ten thousand to twenty thousand years. This data amounts to powerful evidence in support of an earth that could be younger than the so-called experts have insisted upon!

Every day an influx of metallic dust is settling to the planet's surface resulting from what is called "fine particle cosmic drift," as debris from outer space is constantly entering the earth's atmosphere. The best possible measurements of this vast accumulation of particulate matter that is continually inbound from outer space were made by the notable German mathematician Hans Pettersson.[9] He has carefully calculated that cosmic debris is reaching the earth's surface at a consistent rate of over 14 million tons per year. If we were to multiply this large number by 5 billion years (a conservative age of the earth by evolutionary standards), according to Pettersson, we could estimate an enormous stockpile of cosmic dust at a current level of 182 feet in depth covering the entire earth. However, there is absolutely no indication of this predictable accumulation of cosmic debris covering the planet. Even erosion and/or dilution fail to account for the noticeable absence of this predicted massive buildup of foreign dust that should be present for us to observe. This truth has been confirmed because the "missing" cosmic debris is known to have a composition that is very distinctive and quite different from the native raw material found in the earth's crust, especially with regard to its comparably high content of nickel and iron. The current concentration of these minerals in the earth's oceans does not even come close to identifying the enormous influx of space particles that should be accounted for with a 5.3 billion-year-old earth. Now, since the presence of nickel is relatively uncommon as a naturally occurring metallic element upon the earth, and therefore, the mineral's existence is largely due to the vast accumulation of cosmic dust, it is very interesting to note that researchers are reporting a very small amount of nickel concentration found within ocean basins as a result of the river-wash deposition of space debris. According to earth scientist Dr. Henry Morris, considering today's current level of nickel concentration found in the oceans, this measurement, due to river-fed seawater accumulation, can only account for about nine thousand years of earth history.[10] This data is certainly very fascinating, but it is not something you are likely to read about in a morning newspaper, or hear reported to the public on a national television broadcast.

What about the current salt concentration within the oceans of the earth? Could this also become a measurement that might indicate a relative age of the earth? The water cycle is well established with rain consistently falling from the clouds, running off the dry land back into the sea, only to evaporate once again by radiation from the sun to form new clouds. If this water cycle has existed on earth for billions of years as evolution would suggest, the oceans should be much saltier than they actually are today. The common water cycle causes many mineral salts to be deposited in the ocean basins, constantly adding to the saltiness of seawater. A significant portion of the earth's precipitation that falls from the clouds around the globe eventually returns to the sea. The river water that eventually reaches the oceans has leached minerals salts from exposed soil and river basins, which are then deposited into the seawater. Evaporation from solar radiation removes fresh water from the oceans, leaving the accumulation of mineral salts behind. Because of this, the oceans are gaining salt content every day. Wikipedia reports that seawater is estimated to have a current salt concentration of about 3.5 percent. By using predictable rates of mineral deposition in seawater, it has been calculated that the oceans could have become noticeably salty within only about five thousand years.

What about population dynamics? If modern man first appeared on the earth approximately a million years ago, doesn't it seem strange that overpopulation has only been discussed in recent years? It is now estimated that the world's population is growing at a rate of two percent per year. If we can assume that man has been populating the earth for up to one million years, we can easily calculate the reproduction rate that would be necessary to produce today's population of around six to seven billion people. We would soon discover this growth rate to be only 0.002 percent.[11] This means that the world's current population growth rate is one thousand times greater than would be necessary to validate evolutionary teaching about the emergence and occupation of human life on this planet. On the other hand, if the population growth began with eight people, some five thousand years ago as the Bible teaches, we find ourselves well within range of the world's current population. If, for example, we are to consider a very modest family size of say 2.5 children (a very conservative estimate on a worldwide scale), this would produce a population of about 3.5 billion people in only four thousand years. If we apply this growth rate to the typical evolution model using one million years as the beginning of mankind's reproductive occupation of the planet, would it then make sense that twenty-five thousand generations of human history could only produce a population size of six to seven billion?

The obvious reality is that 2.5 children per family over twenty-five thousand generations of human reproductive life would produce a worldwide population so enormous that it would be far beyond the realm of reason. In fact, this utterly impossible number would result in a world that could not possibly sustain its own human population.[12] If you and I could somehow imagine the number of people that would have lived and died throughout twenty-five thousand generations of human history—another question we would have to ask ourselves is—where are all the bones? The whole earth could not contain the enormous pile of bones that you and I would be living on top of.

Many years ago, a Canadian professor named Dr. Harold Armstrong conducted a very interesting study on human population dynamics in which he determined that the average ethnic group would double in number every 150 to 175 years. With this statistic in mind, Dr. Armstrong began his study with the current worldwide population. Then, by reversing the data projection, his research was able to estimate the starting point for the earth's initial population growth at around 4,800 years ago, which coincides very closely with the worldwide flood account at the time of Noah as recorded in the book of Genesis. This definitely gives you and I ample food for thought. Now I am certainly not suggesting that we know for certain the earth is relatively young, nor would I ever insist that we must rely heavily upon these few statistical indicators that I have presented for your consideration. I am, however, suggesting that this information is significant, and even though we will never be able to determine an accurate age for the earth, much of the evidence available today, based upon an ever-increasing catalog of research data, would strongly suggest to us an earth age vastly younger than that which evolution theory requires to make its claims appear somewhat credible.

Is It Science or Religion?

Even though he remained a committed evolutionist receiving worldwide acclaim, paleontologist Colin Patterson has offered a caution that must be considered when he wrote, "Karl Popper warns of a danger: 'a theory, even a scientific theory, may become an intellectual fashion, a substitute for religion, an entrenched dogma.' This has certainly been true of evolutionary theory."[13] We find this to be true in America and around the world—that the teaching of evolution has become deeply ingrained in the education process among many teachers and professors, who may or may not have garnered first-hand knowledge through research experience, but have adopted a philosophy of life thought to be consistent with the intellectual demands of a culture that has increasingly excluded God from the mainstream of public life. Many have earnestly embraced this godless worldview because it fits quite neatly into their own personal disdain for the idea of moral absolutes. They have convinced themselves that evolution is scientific, and that it adequately explains the emergence of life on planet earth without the need for a supernatural agent, which they do not believe in. Listen to this interesting remark from British zoologist L.H. Matthews: "The fact of evolution is the backbone of biology, and biology is thus in the peculiar position of being a science founded on an unproven theory. Is it then a science or a faith? Belief in the theory of evolution is thus exactly parallel to belief in special creation. Both are concepts, which the believers know to be true, but neither, up to the present, has been capable of proof."[14]

People can only believe evolution to be factual by virtue of its remarkable prevalence in our culture. Therefore, this unproven and ungodly philosophy of life has been offered as truth to young American students through every subject in the learning process, and especially in the many disciplines of science. No other explanation for the existence of carbon-based organic life is considered or even tolerated in modern academia's relentless effort to influence the emerging worldview of today's eager young minds. Nevertheless, world-renowned French zoologist Pierre-Paul Grasse openly ridiculed Neo-Darwinism as a religious philosophy, and nothing more, when he wrote, "Directed by all-powerful (natural) selection, 'chance' becomes a sort of 'providence,' which, under the cover of atheism, is not named but which is secretly worshiped."[15] Cal. State University history professor and noted author Dr. Theodore Roszak became best known for his 1969 publication *The Making of a Counter Culture*, in which he thoroughly chronicled and publicized a drastic shift in Western culture during the 1960s. He subsequently offered this very disturbing insight regarding the profound effect of evolution theory on the American mind-set: "The irony is devastating. The main purpose of Darwinism was to drive every last trace of an incredible God from biology . . . but the 'theory' replaces God with an even more incredible deity—omnipotent chance."[16] On the other hand, the high degree of biased evolutionary indoctrination within academia today is not what we discover when we finally get beyond the ivory tower.

Very serious and highly credible research conducted with the modern world's most sophisticated technology has all but cast the evolution theory onto the scrap heap of history. Today, many notably impartial and open-minded scientists have determined, not only that evolutionary theory is completely barren of any factually based support, but also, given what we now know, the basic tenets of the entire theory would be mathematically impossible. For this, and so many other compelling reasons, unbiased researchers, actively armed with today's first-hand scientific knowledge, are now rapidly discarding any chance-based theories, and are beginning to look well beyond nature for the answers they seek.

Dr. Dean Kenyon, professor emeritus of biology at San Francisco State University, after weighing all the facts from many years of diligent study in his chosen field, has come to the following conclusion: "When all the relevant lines of evidence are taken into account and all the problems squarely faced, I think we must conclude that life owes its inception to a source outside of nature."[17] Scientists can speculate about the past and even guess about the future, but they can only *observe* the present.

The study of origins, whether it pertains to creation or evolution, is therefore outside of the scope of science because direct observation of either model at work is impossible. Both of these philosophical positions are belief systems that have utilized different scientific methods with some vastly different interpretations of the physical evidence provided for mankind through ongoing research. However, when it comes to matters of faith, what we need is faith that is consistent with reason, and not in conflict with it. We need a faith that is grounded in reality and supported by evidence, not one that is contrary to it. The extremely remote possibility of macroevolution can only be embraced and believed as factual by those who have sufficient faith to steadfastly deny the possibility of any supernatural power at work behind the forces of nature. Science has never observed evolution theory at work, and there is no indication of a remarkable series of improvement-bearing mutations leading to an abundance of transitional forms in the fossil record. Since no one has ever observed this bizarre process at work in nature, we are forced to conclude by the obvious lack of evidence that the strange notion of evolution does not qualify as a valid scientific theory. Listen once again to the experienced and expert judgment of Dr. Wolfgang Smith, who comments, "I am convinced, moreover, that Darwinism, in whatever form, is not in fact a scientific theory, but a pseudo-metaphysical hypothesis, decked out in scientific garb. In reality, the theory derives its support, not from empirical data or logical deductions of a scientific kind, but from the circumstance that it happens to be the only doctrine of biological origins that can be conceived with the constricted worldview to which a majority of scientists, no doubt subscribe."[18]

Any proposed theory that is thought to be scientific must first be tested against the known physical laws of nature. When the creation model is held up against all the natural laws of science and physics, we soon discover that it stands up very well to such scrutiny, and continually bears out the truth of what is recorded about the physical world in the Word of God. Evolution theory, on the other hand, requires its devoted adherents to imagine some things that are clearly against the laws of science, against logical human reasoning, and even against vast historical knowledge. Evolution, therefore, repeatedly fails the rigorous testing that it must be constantly subjected to. Many people are now concluding, and rightfully so, that the creation model is actually more scientific than evolution theory. Evolution certainly is not empirical science, but perhaps it would qualify as science fiction! Speaking of fiction, please consider this definition of the term, which may help us to understand what we are up against with evolution theory. The word fiction constitutes a deliberate or unintentional fantasy without any basis in reality . . . an imagined creation or pretense, without a solid factual basis . . . something (an idea, concept, or bit of information) accepted as factual, but without any adequate justification, and believed merely for the sake of preference or convenience. Webster's New World Dictionary divines the word fiction as a counterfeit . . . something made up or imagined . . . something that is accepted as fact for the sake of convenience, although not necessarily true. Evolution theory is certainly a very convenient ideology among those who choose to reject the concept of a supernatural creator. Since the loyal adherents of naturalism cannot rely upon documented physical evidence to support their cause, they can only hold fast to this ideology as their preferential worldview in order to satisfy intellectual demands for a humanly gratifying "natural" explanation of life that ultimately supports certain preferred lifestyle choices.

The basic position of the modern evolutionist begins and ends with the premise of, *there is no God*! This narrow view has left them with only one possibility—that random, blind chance events are all that is necessary to explain the complexity and diversity of life, as we know it. Consequently, this has left evolution theory in a very precarious position indeed. Why? Because its adherents are unable to provide relevant evidence that would somehow establish a reasonable degree of credibility to their core belief (that there is no God, and therefore chance and necessity is all that is needed to explain life's existence).

This glaring lack of evidence makes evolution extremely religious in nature and not very scientific at all, because it is not based on verifiable facts, but on unproven, fundamental beliefs that require great faith for one to maintain. Consider this insightful remark written by Mr. Louis T. More: "The more one studies paleontology, the more certain one becomes that evolution is based on faith alone; exactly the same sort of faith which is necessary to have when one encounters the great mysteries of religion."[19]

The truth (based on the evidence) reveals to us that evolution is nothing more than a philosophical dogma. Just like any other creed, evolution requires serious and exceptional faith. As a highly religious ideology, it must be accepted by personal choice apart from any direct empirical scientific support. The nonexistence of God is certainly an impossible concept for mankind to prove, but it still remains the centerpiece of the neo-Darwinian worldview as we know it today.

Unfortunately, adherence to evolution is the founding principal of a dangerous and widely emerging religious philosophy called "secular humanism." Hitler, Stalin, Pol Pot, and Mao Tse-tung were the ruthless leaders of the most ungodly and violent political regimes in human history. Each one of these twentieth century political figures possessed an evolutionary driven humanistic view of life that led to the sadistic extermination of multiple millions of innocent lives. Listen to a description of humanism by the well-known atheist Julian Huxley, who was himself absolutely convinced that mankind controls his own personal destiny and answers to no authority greater than himself: "I used the word 'humanist' to mean someone who believes that man is just as much a natural phenomenon as an animal or plant; that his body, mind, and soul were not supernaturally created, but are products of evolution, and that he is not under the control or guidance of any supernatural being or beings, but has to rely on himself and his own powers."[20]

Our federal government is supposed to be strictly limited by the First Amendment with regard to actively promoting any religious philosophy over another. Consider the ruling of Supreme Court Justice Abe Fortas: "Government in our democracy, state and federal, must be neutral in matters of religious theory. It may not foster or promote one religious theory as against another."[21] This is clearly not the case in America today, where the religious ideology of evolutionary humanism is so often publicly endorsed, by government authority, at taxpayers' expense. Evolution is a strange worldview that people have adopted out of choice, not because the evidence favors this particular ideology, but because it has become a very popular, high-profiled, media and education-driven philosophy with favorable public and didactic support. The theory is easy to accept by those who are not interested enough to examine the real evidence for themselves. Belief in evolution is widely accepted among the populace who are opposed to the idea of a just and moral God interfering with their personal lifestyle choices and decision making. The secular humanistic approach in regard to explaining life's origin has always demanded a natural explanation for every observed phenomenon, and it strongly and passionately objects to any suggestion of divine origination, authority, and judgment. As a result, the intelligent design model is often openly ridiculed and rejected because it infers the existence of a divine, supernatural power or deity that the intellectual mind of man alone cannot rationalize, understand, or possibly begin to comprehend.

The mistake that so many people have made in their search for understanding is in attempting to examine the truth about life using only human intellect, while refusing to consider what their hearts are telling them, based on the evidence. Therefore, they have steadfastly rejected the sure concept that faith and science can and do coexist quite naturally. Western culture has now become fully saturated with the strange notion that science alone can provide all the answers we need to explain the many mysteries of life. However, based on the evidence that is available to us now, it is becoming more apparent than ever that the most incredible hoax of the twentieth century has been the remarkably common misconception that biological evolution is a reliable scientific fact. Obviously, neither popular philosophical position on the origin of life can actually be tested, demonstrated, or repeated before the watchful eyes of qualified witnesses, and therefore must remain within the belief system of the individual. What we can and must do, however, is to examine all the best available evidence we can gather and determine, as accurately as possible, which philosophical worldview is most strongly upheld by known, verifiably facts.

According to American author and philosopher Mr. David A. Noebel, "The belief that God created all things, including man in his own image, requires faith. But evolution requires more faith, because it runs very much contrary to reason, science, and history. Still, many people hold on desperately to this so-called theory, simply because it is the only explanation of origins that excludes God."[22] After much soul-searching about the true nature of the evolutionary hypothesis, science philosopher Michael Ruse of Florida State University has openly admitted that "evolution came into being as a kind of secular ideology, an explicit substitute for Christianity; even today, it is promulgated as an ideology, a secular religion—a full-fledged alternative to Christianity with meaning and morality."[23] Still a passionate evolutionist who maintains an unwavering commitment to naturalism; Ruse was forced to yield the following point in response to the argument of well-known creationist Dr. Duane T. Gish: "I must admit that in this one complaint . . . the (biblical) literalists are absolutely right. Evolution is a religion. It was true of evolution in the beginning, and it is true of evolution still today."[24] This powerful statement is an extremely serious admission coming from an evolutionist, and should be the cause of great concern for many of today's parents, whose children are now being systematically indoctrinated into a religious worldview at public expense.

Consider the words of Mr. R. Kirk published in National Review in 1983: "Darwinism is a creed not only with scientists committed to document the all-purpose role of 'natural selection.' It is a creed with masses of people who have, at best, a vague notion of the mechanism of evolution theory as proposed by Darwin, let alone, as further complicated by his successors . . . Clearly, the appeal cannot be that of a scientific truth, but of a philosophical belief, which is not difficult to identify. Darwinism is the belief in the meaninglessness of existence."[25] This popular evolutionary creed is clearly a religious dogma that, ultimately, enables people to believe they can justify a lifestyle that is in conflict with traditional moral values. They may sense a greater measure of confidence in discarding God's firmly established moral laws, which then allows man to decide for himself what is right and wrong. With no divine authority to govern his decision making, human morality will vacillate with the norms of society, as determined by popular public opinion__ opinion that is often swayed by intellectual bullying. Since it has now become clear that evolutionary thought is simply a nonscientific religious dogma, and nothing more, promoting this ideology as factual actually amounts to proselytizing for the religion of secular humanism, which crowns man supreme, and stubbornly denies that he was created in the image of a personal, loving God.

To offer the reader evidence of just how far evolutionary thinking has driven modern man away from his traditional moral framework, please keep in mind that Adolf Hitler's hateful extermination of over six million Jews was somehow justified in his evolution-driven mind. His bizarre hatred coupled with a desire to annihilate a whole race of people was ultimately conceived out of some twisted, self-righteous delusion leading him to believe that his actions were actually speeding up the evolutionary process—a process that strongly favored his Aryan race. The widespread dissemination of evolutionary thought throughout the world has led to very disastrous and destructive consequences like that of Joseph Stalin in communist Russia. The Soviets adamantly believed they could reject God and retain value and dignity for human life, but they are now admitting that they were terribly wrong and this mistake cost the lives multiple millions of precious human souls.

Consider as well the wide influence of the American eugenicist Margaret Sanger, the founder of Planned Parenthood__ the leading advocate and provider of abortions in America today. Sanger was profoundly influenced by Darwinism, which ultimately led her to conclude that by controlling the human population through eugenics, achieving a superior race of humanity was possible. Eugenics to Margaret Sanger was the idea of advancing human evolution by discouraging reproduction among the "less fit" or "inferior races." This concept led to profound racism, as she believed that inferior races included Negroes, Jews, and Italians among others. She believed the brain capacity of the Australian Aborigine was only slightly more developed than a chimpanzee. Sanger was the leading advocate for birth control distribution in the twentieth century and strongly encouraged its use in populations she considered to be inferior. However, in her sick desire to control population and reproduction, she also became a strong advocate of euthanasia, abortion, and human sterilization for those who should not be allowed to procreate. In addition to this, her books encouraged sex outside of marriage and were instrumental in the sexual revolution that has radically changed our culture over recent generations, leading to rampant sexual immorality, sexually transmitted disease and a rate of unwed pregnancy that remains out of control. This is another direction evolutionary thinking has led mankind over the last one hundred years.

It certainly has proven to be a very dangerous and destructive philosophy that is leading to disastrous consequences in our world.

The Great Debate Rages On

The proponents of evolution theory have been hiding behind the cloak of science for over 150 years, but now that false perception has been clearly exposed. Consider this statement from Dr. Marjorie Grene on the philosophy of science: "Today the tables have turned. The modified, but still characteristically Darwinian theory, has itself become an orthodoxy, preached by its adherents with religious fervor, and doubted, they feel, only by a few muddlers imperfect in scientific faith."[26] Many anatomical structures examined in public school biology labs are typically interpreted based solely upon the misleading claims of evolution, as thousands of unwary students are being indoctrinated by polished professors who hold on tightly to their preconceived bias, in spite of where all the evidence is now leading us. NASA senior systems analyst and computer specialist David Coppedge has remarked about this unfortunate reality. "Darwin is liked by evolutionists, because he liberated science from the straitjacket of observation and opened the door to storytellers. This gave professional evolutionists job security so that they can wander through biology labs as if they belong there."[27] As an interesting side note Mr. Coppedge, who had a very successful career with the Jet Propulsion Laboratory, became the victim of severe persecution. He was fired from NASA for his personal views on intelligent design. His case, and that of many others who have been blackballed in their careers, demonstrates once again that freedom of speech and thought in the public domain regarding evidence favoring intelligent design remains under severe attack and persecution by the rigid advocates of scientific materialism. Paleontologist Dr. Colin Patterson reflects on the numerous storytellers associated with evolution theory. He has commented that "it is easy enough to make up stories of how one form gave rise to another, and to find reasons why the stages should be favored by natural selection. But such stories are not part of science, for there is no way of putting them to the test."[28]

Although much arduous disagreement still exists among evolutionists today, those who remain in the mainstream all agree that life on planet Earth came about through blind, random chance events with no divine architect to guide it. On the other hand, Christians generally agree that the known universe and everything in it is the marvelous creative handiwork of an unseen, personal God. At the very heart of this debate over origins is the one question of whether an "intelligent agent" actually exists. Was a living God at work in preparing the design and complexity of the vast and profoundly diverse world that we observe around us? This is an important topic we will cover in much greater detail in the next chapter. Unfortunately, many Western societies have been thoroughly saturated with a bogus theory, which lies in stark contrast to many revealed facts of science__ facts that have been observed in the present and also painstakingly uncovered from the past. Why then is this unproven philosophy so prevalent in American society and elsewhere? I will tell you why I believe this is so.

Evolution theory is the central issue in a genuine cultural war between two diametrically opposed philosophical worldviews that can be best described as biblical Christianity and secular humanism. Evolution is simply a religious philosophy cleverly disguised as science, and taught as factual to naive school children with government sanction. It comprises the foundational principle establishing a secular, state-funded and media-driven religion that is taught, preached, and promoted from our public-school classrooms, instead of a pulpit. Humanism routinely seeks to indoctrinate people (especially young people) with the false claim that man has descended from simple life-forms by way of apelike ancestors millions of years ago. However, it is certain that the evolution theory is not just about fish becoming frogs and monkeys turning into humans. This popular ideology is clearly a profoundly religion-based philosophy that simply tries to explain everything in the cosmos without God.

Many of the most dedicated evolutionists, however, tend to make a grave mistake, believing that all creationists are ignorant, unenlightened and gullible dupes, who believe in myths, legends, and fanciful stories. Such evolutionists maintain that scriptures penned several millennia ago should bear little or no relevance and have a very limited influence upon the scientifically enlightened men and women of the twenty-first century. By continually mocking the Word of God, what they have failed to understand is that creationists do not live in blind faith, as they do. The hard, factual evidence actually supports and repeatedly validates the traditional Judeo-Christian worldview.

Dr. Richard Bliss, a former professor who taught biological science at Christian Heritage College, has commented in this way: "The miracles required to make evolution feasible are far greater in number and far harder to believe in than the miracle of creation."[29] If it requires miracles either way, it seems most logical for man to believe in a miracle-worker who commands the intelligence and power to create with purpose in mind, than to trust in blind chance events with no guiding hand to direct them. Consider the sheer frustration of evolution-based researchers, who have sought to explain life without even a hint of supernatural influence. Esteemed biochemist Dr. Klaus Dose has provided us with some additional insight into the many difficulties and immense challenges these determined researchers are up against. He once commented that "more than thirty years of experimentation on the origin of life in the fields of chemical and molecular evolution have led to a better perception of the 'immensity of the problem' of the origin of life on earth rather than its solution . . . At present, all discussions on principle theories and experiments in the field either end in stalemate, or in a confession of ignorance."[30] As a popular belief system, one that is based entirely upon pure materialism, evolution elevates humanity itself as supreme, and seeks to eliminate any accountability to divine authority. The cultural battle for hearts and minds, in the war over the souls of men, basically comes down to these all important questions: is there a supreme creator God behind the scenes who is responsible for the appearance of life, as well as the existence of a material world that we are all privileged to observe and experience? The obvious companion question to this one would be, if there is a supreme God working out his purpose through the physical reality, how then are we expected to relate to or respond to him as the subjects of his creative power and authority?

The answers to these two basic questions are critical enough that they should be viewed as a matter of life and death. For this reason, it is essential to embrace a sincere search for the truth! There is so very much at stake regarding this crucial deliberation, and you and I certainly cannot afford to underestimate the importance of these fundamental questions; and neither can we simply ignore the issue altogether, because the answer to these questions comprise the most significant and life-changing knowledge that humankind will ever hope to comprehend.

If evolution is, indeed, a false and erroneous claim offered by naturalists to explain the diversity of life, then we have been handed the most colossal deception the world may have ever known—a real deception that will carry eternal consequences for literally millions, if not billions, of human souls. Humanists remain defiantly dogmatic in their determination to explain life without God. Many have preferred to actually bury their proverbial heads in the sand, and to ignore a great body of evidence, which strongly opposes their deeply entrenched philosophy. Some have simply dismissed the evidence as inconclusive, while still others have tried to change the theory to accommodate current revealed facts.

Dr. Walter L. Bradley, a renowned scientist, author, and noteworthy professor from America's Baylor University, made the following revealing remarks based upon the current state of research investigating how life emerged. He wrote, "There isn't any doubt that science, for the moment at least, is at a dead end. The optimism of the 1950s is gone. The mood at the 1999 international conference on the origin-of-life was described as grim—full of frustration, pessimism, and desperation. Nobody pretends that any alternative provides a reasonable path of how life went unguided from simple chemicals to proteins to basic life-forms."[31] Ultimately, these determined men and women have effectively offered the modern world yet another religious alternative to biblical Christianity, so that they and others like them might continue the pursuit of personal lifestyle choices thought to be free of objectionable moral constraints, personal accountability, and, ultimately, judgment.

Many years ago, when he was asked in a television interview why the scientific community had so unexpectedly engaged in the opportunity of embracing Darwin's ideas, evolutionist Julian Huxley offered this response: "I suppose the reason why we leapt at the *Origin of Species* was that the idea of God interfered with our sexual mores."[32] At least he offered the world an honest and I believe accurate response; the truth is that God is oftentimes viewed as an unwelcome intruder in regard to the moral choices and lifestyle decision making of carnal man.

In Defining Science, the Stakes Are High

Considering everything at stake in the great debate, it is now reported that even after a century of persistent indoctrination into the ideology of naturalism, most people still refuse to fall prey to this deceiving philosophy. In the American population it has been estimated that, even today, well into the twenty-first century, those who support and believe in the traditional creation worldview still outnumber those who believe in evolution by a wide margin—nearly two to one. However, many humanist-thinking philosophers have attempted to change the rules in an effort to generate greater compliance with their anti-God sentiment. Nancy Pearcey has astutely reminded us that "historically speaking, it was Darwinism, more than anything else that barred the door on any consideration of Christianity as objective truth."[33] Even so, as we have seen from current evidence, Darwin's ideas now hold little, if any, real credibility in light of today's highly technical, research-minded, scientific revolution. The ever-advancing progression of empirical science has now found his ideas, and his philosophy to be highly impractical, if not completely impossible. By attempting to redefine true science in the broad terms of naturalism, atheist-minded evolutionists have conveniently excluded any and every view that does not comply with their materialistic definition. The commonly held philosophy of scientific skepticism is clearly evident based in the following statements, spoken by Harvard evolutionary biologist Dr. Richard Lewontin: "Our willingness to accept scientific claims that are against common sense is the key to an understanding of the real struggle between science and the supernatural. We take the side of science in spite of the patent absurdity of some of its constructs . . . in spite of its failure to fulfill many of its extravagant promises of health and life . . . in spite of the tolerance of the scientific community for unsubstantiated . . . 'just so stories,' because we have a prior commitment, a commitment to materialism. . . It is not that the methods and institutions of science somehow compel us to accept a material explanation for the phenomenal world, but, on the contrary, that we are forced by our priori adherence to material causes to create an apparatus of investigation, and a set of concepts that produces material explanations, no matter how counterintuitive, no matter how mystifying to the uninitiated. Moreover, that materialism is absolute, for we cannot allow a Divine foot in the door."[34] Dr. Lewontin has basically admitted that a determined commitment to materialism and a complete denial of the supernatural has forced evolutionists to believe in strange hypotheses that are scientifically flimsy at best and completely nonsensical at worst.

A common concern for today's diehard evolutionists is that a widespread invasion of supernaturalism into the world of modern science, as they have conveniently defined it, would eventually provide a firm foundation for the entire orthodoxy within the Christian worldview, complete with its vast theology and biblical moral absolutes. However, in the final analysis, people shouldn't allow themselves to become indoctrinated by elite scholars, even if their strange ideology is convincingly supported by mass media bias. If we fail to thoroughly examine legitimate, unbiased evidence that is readily available today, we are essentially permitting the so-called *enlightened elite*, whom you and I will never personally know, to systematically shape within us our own personal worldview. And they are doing this without ever being subjected to any accountability that requires providing adequate evidence and valid support to verify and authenticate their materialistic claims.

Whatever happened to the open-minded men of true science who would allow the actual evidence to point them down the right path? With heads firmly buried in the sand, many have, in fact, attempted to redefine science so that it fits quite nicely into their preferred philosophical point of view. As previously quoted, Mr. Julian Huxley made this very clear when he said, "Modern science must rule out special creation or divine guidance."[35] One thing is certainly true, as was pointed out by creation scientist and former atheist Dr. Gary Parker: "If evolutionists had to prove their case in court, evolution would be thrown out for lack of evidence."[36] This idea stands as the professional judgment of two well-known attorneys, Norman Macbeth[37] (author of *Darwin Retired*) and Philip Johnson[38] (author of *Darwin on Trial*)__ neither of whom are specifically arguing in favor of the Bible, but are simply writing their legal opinions from years of experience as experts in the rules of evidence and logic.

After arguing his point of view, Macbeth concluded that "this does not mean that the profession is about to abandon Darwin forever or endorse my views publicly. The situation remains much as it was: the inner circles are full of doubt, but the public utterances are confident. The doubts may be greater now and the confidence less serene, but it will be a long time before the public is given the full dark picture . . . There is still need for a dissenting voice, a devil's advocate, a skeptical whistle-blower."[39] All of the determined attempts to somehow manipulate the real evidence and to shroud the history of science in a cloak of theoretical jargon are, in my opinion, doomed to certain failure. When we have thoroughly considered and examined an historical appraisal of man's great search for knowledge and understanding, it soon becomes clear that modern science, as we know it today, sprang forth from a Christian cradle. The compelling drive of sixteenth century mankind to understand the planned design and purpose of the Creator was the initial spark that ignited a major scientific revolution__ a revolution that exploded on the scene in Western Europe out of a commonly held biblical worldview. Even the aggressively driven opponents of contemporary Christian faith, including Richard Dawkins, are now admitting this is true. You might even say that modern science was a gift to the world courtesy of the Judeo-Christian heritage. The early Christian pioneers who engaged in the scientific endeavor were compelled by a great desire to understand just why their Creator had designed things as they are. Up to the present day, modern science has done nothing at all to diminish the impression that the universe is not self-existing but was caused. The reason that a modern scientific revolution sprang forth out of Western culture was because these people held in common the unifying concept of a Creator, and they set out to discover what the Creator had done in establishing the governing laws of nature. Men loved science because they believed in the laws of nature, and they firmly believed in the laws of nature because they believed in a lawgiver. Many of the world's most remarkable historical figures such as—Galileo, Kepler, Maxwell, Boyle, Faraday, and Newton, along with a great number of their early contemporaries, all believed in a living eternal God, Creator of heaven and earth. The great early mathematician and astronomer Johannes Kepler had once declared that "the chief aim of all investigations of the external world should be to discover the rational order and harmony, which has been imposed on it by God, and which he revealed to us in the language of mathematics."[40] Unlike Lewontin's earlier claim that godless materialism was needed to develop an apparatus of investigation in order to disallow a divine foot in the door, these men understood that they were investigating the master plan of a divine architect, and they never questioned his existence and authority as the creator. The famous physicist Galileo Galilei added a thought very similar to Kepler's when he once wrote, "The laws of nature are written by the hand of God in the language of mathematics."[41] Sixteenth-century scientist Sir Francis Bacon, a notable founder of the scientific method, had spoken of two books from which he received inspiration into scientific inquiry. He spoke of the book of nature and the book of God. Sir Isaac Newton, a brilliant mind and yet another major architect of the scientific revolution, expressed openly that the more he would discover about God's magnificent design, the greater became his genuine commitment to and belief in the Grand Designer, who had lovingly created the extraordinary surroundings and beauty that caused his life such great pleasure and irresistible fascination.

This scientific/pioneer spirit, modeled by early experimental inquiry, is still often found in some of today's most brilliant minds—men who have essentially allowed the evidence to speak on behalf of the Creator.

Keith Ward is a philosopher, theologian, and scholar, who, as a well-respected member of the British Academy, has often spoken of the mathematical connection between the physical universe and the mind of God. He wrote, "The continuing conformity of physical particles to precise mathematical relationships is something that is much more likely to exist if there is an ordering cosmic mathematician who sets up the correlation in the requisite way. The existence of laws of physics strongly implies that there is a God who formulates such laws and ensures that the physical realm conforms to them."[42] Consider as well the following words of Dr. Henry F. Schaefer, a professor and a director of the Center of Computational Quantum Chemistry at the University of Georgia: "The significance and joy of my science comes in those occasional moments of discovering something new and saying to myself 'so that's how God did it' . . . My goal is to understand a little corner of God's plan."[43] Dr. Kurt Godel was a brilliant Austrian mathematician, logician, and scientific philosopher who has greatly impacted the recently revived *theistic revolution* that began in the latter part of the twentieth century. His unique mind and professional career won him the Albert Einstein Award in 1951. After thoroughly examining the evidence using his unique expertise in logic and mathematics, Godel finally concluded that "the order of the world reflects the order of the supreme mind governing it."[44]

The strange idea that religion is at war with science, and has been for hundreds of years, is nothing but a disturbing psychological myth! We certainly should never have to make a choice between God and science; faith and knowledge are not mutually exclusive concepts by any means. Science has truly had remarkable success at probing the nature of a physical reality and discovering many of the mechanisms by which the physical elements operate, but, ultimately, science has done a very poor job at explaining *why* those elements exist. We must, therefore, always distinguish the difference between mechanism and agency. When Sir Isaac Newton discovered the universal law of gravitation, allowing us to account for planetary motion in the solar system, he was wise enough to understand that this law existed because of a lawgiver. Through his diligent investigation of how this law operates, Newton became overwhelmed with great admiration for the magnificent, intelligent designer who created it that way. In an outstanding publication entitled *God's Undertaker . . . Has Science Buried God?* British mathematician John Lennox of Oxford University thoroughly discusses the effect that science has had on the concept of faith in God in a world that is governed by the fundamental laws of physics. Dr. Lennox has subsequently remarked that "far from science abolishing God, it would seem that there is a substantial case for asserting that it is the existence of a Creator that gives to science its fundamental intellectual justification."[45]

Dr. Lennox has also added this thought in regard to the current rigid view of materialism: "The world of strict naturalism in which clever mathematical laws all by themselves bring the universe and life into existence, is pure fiction . . . Theories and laws simply do not bring anything into existence."[46] I like the argument he will often use when addressing a common complaint proposed by atheists with regard to a perceived war on science. Professor Lennox has been known to offer the following illustration to help solidify his rebuttal: "To say that God is competing with science as an explanation for life is like saying Mr. Henry Ford was competing with the laws of the internal combustion and mechanical engineering as a sound explanation for the extraordinary innovation of the Ford Motor car."[47] Mr. Henry Ford was the designer of the mechanized motor vehicle developed for everyday use by the common man; he was the innovative mind behind this historical achievement. However, in order to produce a truly functioning automobile, it was necessary that Ford understood the physical laws of internal combustion, and was able to utilize the basic principles of mechanical engineering. For modern mankind to arrive at such a remarkable end point, we needed both the creative mind and the physical mechanism. To deify science, claiming it to be the only way to discover the truth about life is, in my view, terribly misleading and also intellectually dishonest, not to mention being absolutely untrue. Astrophysicist Stephen Hawking, who held the academic chair at Cambridge that once belonged to the famous Sir Isaac Newton, but who does not share Newton's devoted Christian faith, once admitted in a television interview: "It is difficult to discuss the beginning of the universe without mentioning the concept of God. My work on the origin of the universe is on the borderline between science and religion, but I try to stay on the scientific side of the border. It is quite possible that God acts in ways that cannot be described by scientific laws."[48]

Long before the classical Greek philosophers, ancient Hebrews recorded that time was linear, and expressed a strong belief that the physical elements had their beginning at the time of God's creative masterpiece. This profound worldview held a powerful allegiance, strongly dominating the civilized world's intellectual landscape for many centuries. The conviction that the universe had a beginning is once again the predominant viewpoint of scientists in the contemporary world, where we now see a remarkable consensus of opinion favoring this position. Many, however, still object to the idea of an original beginning, probably due to the fact that it implies a first cause, which points, philosophically, toward a Creator. As we gain greater insight into our world, the hypothesis of a creator God, who designed the universe with great purpose in mind, is now gaining stronger credibility as the most rational explanation for why we exist.

According to the Nobel Prize winner Dr. Arno Penzias, "Some people are uncomfortable with the purposefully created world. To come up with things that contradict purpose, they tend to speculate about things they haven't seen."[49] As an American Nobel Prize winner for physics in 1964, notable physicist and educator Charles Townes said this: "In my view, the question of origins seems to be left unanswered if we explore it from a scientific point of view. Thus, I believe there is a need for some religious or metaphysical explanation . . . I believe in the concept of God and in his existence."[50] No matter what evidence or testimony is presented that has denied the claims of evolution, a firm commitment by many in scientific circles has already been made. According to their view, only theories that rely solely upon naturalism, to the exclusion of God, will be considered worthy of discussion by virtue of their revised definition of what constitutes science. Sadly enough, though, this contemporary redefinition of science has gone basically unchallenged throughout the American public school system, and has been strongly impressed upon the minds, and thoroughly engrained in the lives of young students__ individuals who lack the knowledge, maturity, and boldness to challenge it.

Teaching Children: "Age of Enlightenment"

The basic goal of humanism has always been to capture the minds of our young people at an early age; this is why humanists have pressed so hard to take over the public education system with their narrow-minded, anti-God philosophy. Let us consider once again another rather aggressive statement by the late, well-known atheist and evolutionist Julian Huxley, who writes, "It is essential for evolution to become the central core of any education system, because it is evolution, in the broad sense, that links inorganic nature with life, and the stars with Earth, and matter with mind, and animals with man. Human history is a continuation of biological evolution in a different form."[51] Unfortunately, ideas from Mr. Huxley, and other very determined atheists like John Dewey, have been aggressively infiltrating the American public education system for decades with a blatant anti-God philosophy. Sadly, these early devoted humanists have apparently had their way with the education methods that are now used in America to the great peril of millions of unsuspecting and naive young people, who, without knowing it, have now become thoroughly indoctrinated in a religious worldview that denies God. I truly did not know how invasive evolutionary teaching had become in our American public schools until recently, when I came across a junior-high-school science textbook first published in 1968.[52] In this widely used publication, distributed to impressionable young students so soon after the tidal wave of evolutionary thought swept through our nation, two entire chapters are devoted to expounding on the evolutionary history of planet Earth and its diverse life-forms. The text offers no evidence whatsoever to verify the many claims that are made, but simply proceeds in a narrative that would suggest to the reader that the elements of evolutionary thought are undisputed scientific facts.

Consider this sample quotation from a typical high-school textbook demonstrating once again the extreme bias that favors a secular religious philosophy—a philosophy that for many generations has been actively promoted in public schools throughout the land: "Many people believe that a supernatural force or deity created life. That explanation is not within the scope of science."[53] Now, think about this statement from yet another American high-school textbook: "By attributing the diversity of life to natural causes, rather than to supernatural creation, Darwin gave biology a sound scientific basis."[54] How about this narrow-minded view that was published in a college-level textbook: "Biological phenomena, including those seemingly designed, can be explained by . . . 'purely material causes,' rather than by divine creation."[55] Consider as well the following bold statement from a university textbook on evolution, by Monroe Strickberger (Museum of Vertebrate Zoology, Berkeley, California): "The fear that Darwinism was an attempt to displace God in the sphere of creation was therefore justified. To the question: is there a divine purpose for the creation of humans?—Evolution answers No . . . According to evolution, the adaptations of species, and the adaptations of humans come from natural selection and not from design."[56] In yet another textbook entitled *Evolutionary Biology*, Dr. Douglas Futuyma strongly concurs with this remark, "By coupling undirected, purposeless variation to the blind uncaring process of natural selection, Darwin made theological or spiritual explanations of the life processes superfluous."[57] Harvard evolutionary biologist and geneticist Richard Lewontin adds this confident statement about evolutionary thought: "It is time . . . to state clearly that evolution is fact, not theory . . . birds arose from nonbirds and humans from nonhumans. No person who pretends to any understanding of the natural world can deny these facts any more than he or she can deny that the Earth is round, rotates on its axis, and revolves around the sun."[58]

This is the indoctrination that is being directed at our children! Imagine the impression these bold claims have left upon their eager young minds. And worst of all, no valid evidence is ever presented to back them up. The profound influence of men like Dr. Richard Lewontin have led to a commonly held impression among many university professors, students, and others that evolution theory has buried God under an avalanche of widespread scientific and didactically delivered revelation on the topic of origins, making him appear obsolete and irrelevant. Many people have now become convinced that a designer is unnecessary when mindless, unguided evolutionary processes are able to explain the emergence of life in the physical dimension. It is no stretch of the imagination to consider that the theory of evolution has had the devastating impact of a tsunami upon the human quest for meaning and significance in a vast, virtually unknowable universe.

However, if we should choose to observe the real evidence, a different story quickly emerges. We find lurking behind the cloak of science a sinister dogma whose implications have led to a drastic cultural shift in American life. Therefore, we might say that, for all practical purposes, the public doctrine of secular humanism, firmly founded upon evolutionary teaching, has become an American state-sponsored religion that is systematically forced on children and young adults in our public schools, colleges, and universities throughout the land. In public life we have all but forsaken the God of our fathers, and have replaced him with a new redefined brand of pseudoscience birthed in the darkened halls of academia across this nation. Education in America used to be about teaching our children the real facts concerning the world they were growing up in; but now it has become increasingly more about the spreading of a religious-type, philosophical worldview that does not even enjoy any sound factual basis supported by reliable evidence and historically accurate data. Children are being routinely deprived of many newly discovered scientific facts and verifiable historical details all for the purpose of propping up a theory that cannot stand on its own merit. Our schools are teaching religion today more than ever, but the religion being taught amounts to simple, blind faith in random chance, naturalistic processes that are not only illogical, but enjoy no true scientific or historical support whatsoever.

What very few people have known is that many humanist leaders are surprisingly open about using the public schools as the principal means by which to proselytize their godless religion. I was initially shocked when I read the following statement that first appeared in a copy of *The Humanist* magazine in 1983. This rather frightening public scenario is what the twentieth-century humanist movement has secretly planned and thoroughly implemented throughout America for many decades with minimal resistance in keeping with their determined goal to fundamentally transform Western culture from the inside out. This very ambitious effort to reshape our nation into a fully secularized society has been underway now for well over seventy years, as many of us have stood idly by and watched it happen. Imagine the implications of the following horrific quotation, which, I am now convinced, should be carefully read and very prayerfully considered by every conservative parent of school-age children throughout the land. This humanist writer, who represents the anti-God secular revolution sweeping America, has boldly declared, "I am convinced that the battle for humankind's future must be waged and won in the public school classroom by teachers who correctly perceive their role as the proselytizers of a new faith: a religion of humanity that recognizes and respects the spark of what theologians call divinity in every human being. These teachers must embody the same selfless dedication as the most rabid fundamentalist preachers, for they will be ministers of another sort, utilizing a classroom instead of a pulpit to convey humanist values in whatever subject they teach, regardless of the educational level—preschool, day care, or large state university. The classroom must and will become an arena of conflict between the old and the new—the rotting corpse of Christianity, together with all its adjacent evils and misery, and the . . . new faith of humanism . . . it will undoubtedly be a long, arduous, painful struggle replete with much sorrow and many tears, but humanism will emerge triumphant. It must, if the family of humankind is to survive."[59]

This deliberate anti-God religious campaign, which has been deceptively masquerading for years as fundamental modern science while proselytizing a blatantly materialistic view of life and the cosmos, has been specifically designed to divest students of any conceptual knowledge of a Creator. Humanists have essentially declared war on Christian values, concepts, principles, and theology, while falsely believing that religious faith is the greatest obstacle to human progress.

Evolution, by the way, did not come about primarily from men of science. Not even one of the men who laid the foundation for modern evolution was technically a man of science in a strictly professional sense. Charles Darwin was actually a divinity school dropout who had taken an interest in becoming a naturalist. Charles Lyell was a notable British lawyer. James Hutton served as a trained physician and agriculturalist. Robert Chambers was a noted Scottish journalist and book publisher who had, ultimately, pursued an interest in becoming an evolutionary thinker. Evolution is a man-made ideology that has been cleverly disguised as science and works to convince the unwary public that the philosophical tendencies of man require no special guidance from some unknown, unseen, and mysterious deity.

Chapter 6

THE BATTLE FOR TRUTH

Expelled—No Intelligence Allowed

The religion of humanism, firmly rooted in evolution theory, is carefully guarded in the public domain as teachers and professors who dare to question or challenge this sacred cow of intellectual ideology are swiftly reprimanded and severely reproved with extremely harsh measures. In a very successful documentary film entitled *Expelled*, hosted by Mr. Ben Stein, the current tragic loss of academic freedom in America is thoroughly exposed.[1] In an open country that has always prided itself on academic excellence and freedom, sadly enough, American instructors of higher education are now being consistently denied the opportunity to openly teach what we know to be true, whenever it conflicts with the established, entrenched views on evolution. We have seen this unfortunate reality appear over and over again, especially in the many disciplines of science where college and university students are often deprived of various factual disclosures and reliable research findings, only because this knowledge fails to support the cause of naturalism.

A professional critique of American biology textbooks commonly used has revealed the following conspicuous details about the origin-of-life documentation contained therein: "It should be apparent that the errors, overstatements, and omissions that we have noted in these biological texts . . . all tend to enhance the plausibility of hypotheses that are presented. More importantly, the inclusion of outdated material and erroneous discussions is not trivial. The items noted mislead students and impede their acquisition of critical thinking skills. If we fail to teach students to examine data critically, looking for points both favoring an opposing hypotheses, we are selling our youth short and mortgaging the future of scientific inquiry itself."[2]

A great deal of important scientific evidence is now being censored and distorted for the purpose of promoting an obsolete theory that simply doesn't fit the known facts. Evidence for the radical claim that all species developed from a single life-form on a primeval earth is completely lacking, and unbiased scientists, doing hands-on origin-of-life research, have made this reality abundantly clear. It appears that educators in today's modern, highly compromised world of academia (the ivory tower) are forcing their worldview upon unwary students at government expense. Consider this powerful statement from writer Timothy Lahaye: "Long before the 55 million children in our American school system are old enough to understand or examine humanism for themselves, already they are convinced it is scientific . . . Until educators in the public school system awaken to the fraud they are perpetrating, humanists will continue to dominate them and force them to disseminate unsupported and unscientific dogma."[3] Our science education in America has all but destroyed the freedom of thought and inquiry of today's eager young minds as it pertains to the origin of life and the material world. At the same time, we often see that brave, honest educators in many public institutions, who would actually dare to suggest the rather obvious conclusion of design and purpose in nature, are browbeaten and stifled at every turn. On most public college and university campuses, any professors who bravely admit to having serious doubts about the factual nature of the evolution theory are typically laughed off their college campus and out of a job. Those who will not be silenced by unrelenting humanist demands risk losing tenure, or being fired and totally blackballed from the educational system.

I recently became aware of yet another blatant example of how university administrators will often deal with any teacher or professor whose personal philosophical view of life is perceived as a threat to the closely guarded academic position on evolutionary thought. This case involved Mr. Mark Armitage, a research scientist from California State University Northridge. In May of 2012, Mr. Armitage was working at a research site called the Hell Creek formation in the state of Montana. While he was unearthing fossil remains at this location, his team came upon the largest triceratops horn specimen that has been uncovered in North America to date. The Hell Creek, Montana, location boasts a formation that has become legendary for fossil-bearing rock strata, which have produced a variety of well-preserved dinosaur remains. With this fascinating discovery in hand, Mr. Armitage returned to his laboratory in Los Angeles at the CSUN campus to complete a thorough examination of the specimen. He typically would use a high-powered microscope to examine the fossil remains in minute detail, and then proceed to thoroughly record his observations. To his surprise, the material inside this triceratops horn revealed something that remains a shock the scientific community and even threatens to alter a widely protected, academic view on paleontology. Mark Armitage was amazed to discover preserved layers of soft tissue that were actually pliable to the touch inside this ancient specimen. Now based upon previous laboratory experiments, conventional wisdom suggests that soft tissue and possibly DNA could remain intact, it has been estimated, for up to eight thousand to ten thousand years at most, but certainly not for millions of years.

Elite members of the scientific community were stunned by this finding, which again suggests that dinosaurs are most likely only thousands, and not millions, of years old. You and I have been told that dinosaurs roamed the earth sixty to one hundred million years ago before becoming extinct. Taken only at face value, aside from evolutionary bias, it would seem as though this Hell Creek discovery casts serious doubt upon the vast eons of time that are constantly spoken of in the dating methodology that is so prevalent in today's evolutionary thought. It must be strongly emphasized here that in this particularly interesting case, which has received a great deal of public scrutiny, evolutionists and biased ivory-tower educators are not dealing with a novice or some fly-by-night rookie who had set out to make a name for himself. Mr. Mark Armitage is a very well-educated specialist in his field (a recent doctoral candidate of Liberty University). His work includes an appearance on the cover of scientific journals eleven different times, and is a well-published researcher whose work spans over thirty years.

As he has done on many other occasions, Armitage again published a scientific review revealing his professional observations of the Hell Creek discovery. His investigative research appeared in a peer-reviewed journal called *Acta Histochemica* that was published in February 2013.[4] This is a scientific journal that typically reports on cell and tissue research. Armitage's article was peer-reviewed by Mary Schweitzer, a paleontologist at North Carolina State University (the same woman who discovered soft tissue in the leg bone of a Montana T-rex) and was found to be professionally done without making any unwarranted religious claims related to the discovery. Mark Armitage simply stated the facts of what he had observed through a careful scientific analysis of the material specimen that became available to him.

Two weeks after this scientific article was made public, the CSUN officials abruptly pulled back the funding for his laboratory research, silenced the evidence, and immediately terminated Mr. Armitage from employment with the university, where he had successfully managed the biology department's electron and confocal microscopy suite for a number of years. Later, an angry university official even made it clear to him why they were letting him go when he said, "We are not going to tolerate your religion in this department!"

At the time of this writing, an ensuing legal battle against the university was still progressing on behalf of Mr. Armitage in his effort to win reinstatement of his position with the university, where, by all accounts, he was doing an outstanding job. An attorney representing him soon issued a statement in which he explained that the act of terminating an employee because of his or her religious views is most definitely illegal. He further explained that the termination of an employee in an attempt to silence or censor scientific evidence, thus preserving the university's position on the evolutionary dating of fossil remains, is even more alarming. The attorney went on to suggest that this incident should be a wake-up call to the entire academic world as it has become a blatant example of how evolutionary thought and ideals are closely guarded and protected by public academic institutions even to the point of violating the law to do so.

It should be stated here that the soft tissue deposits revealed by this triceratops horn is not a unique discovery without complimentary evidence from others dinosaur remains. We have already considered the evidence of soft tissue found and documented within the leg bone of a T-rex by paleontologist Mary Schweitzer. Now, Dr. Kevin Anderson, a molecular biologist and the director of the Van Andel Creation Research Center in Arizona has reported that soft tissue has been discovered in numerous dinosaur fossil remains, including a rib bone and a theropod claw that had sat on a museum shelf for one hundred years before these specimens were examined and subsequently revealed the existence of soft tissue.

This stressful incident involving Mr. Armitage is not unique either. There have been numerous cases of honest researchers and professors being blackballed from the education system because they dared to report on findings that do not support long-standing academic traditions on evolutionary thought. This was the compelling point made by the *Expelled* documentary—that scientific inquiry and curiosity at the university level is welcome and even encouraged as long as any revealed evidence from such inquiry does not conflict with established academic traditions, and are not supportive of intelligent design. The actions taken by CSUN officials appear to be censorship of physical evidence found to be in conflict with the protected view of "naturalism" that is expounded consistently by the majority of today's academic institutions. This incident offers a perfect example of how today's eager young students are denied the presentation of valid, empirically derived scientific evidence, so that universities may continue to shape their fragile understanding in favor of a long-held evolutionary view of life. Today, however, more than ever before, we are finding that many bold and courageous research scientists are beginning to publicly admit what they have, in fact, known privately for many years—that the concept of evolution theory that is routinely disseminated within America's public school textbooks is based mostly on speculation, guesswork, and human imagination, and believing in such requires an act of profound faith.

The misguided educational authorities who have so blatantly authorized the deceiving misinformation commonly found in public education are hopelessly biased by their unwavering devotion to and belief in a rapidly dying and outdated theory. They seem to be convinced, against sound reason, that this strange ideology adequately explains how all living systems came to be. Evolutionary thought has actually, and I should add erroneously, concluded that noble humankind is nothing but a highly advanced form of animal life. However, we do know that many undeniable differences exist between humans and animals, which are really quite remarkable, especially with regard to man's free volition, as well as the ability to use language, reason, logic, and even to express religious faith. Let's never forget the very unique and profound complexity seen in human emotional responses, along with a very strong sense of moral truth and accountability, governed by our conscience. And let's not forget the many negative emotions and behaviors that are very unique to mankind resulting, or course, from the free will instilled in us by the Creator. For example, have you ever observed behaviors in animals that would exhibit hatred, greed, lust, bigotry, prejudice, deceit, and a host of other negative responses directed at another member of their own? Of course not, these are strictly human behaviors made possible by the fact that man was created in God's image with the freedom to express both good and bad behaviors.

Why should you and I willingly submit to a blatant, ill-conceived form of evolutionary indoctrination without putting forth any resistance whatsoever? Even our nation's highest courts have recognized this as a significant abuse of intellectual power: "To promote one faith in the public school system at public expense, while banning the other, is an example of viewpoint discrimination, which the Supreme Court has declared unconstitutional in its variety of cases."[5]

The Media Monster Reigns

During these days of high-tech, modern communication, the public media has had a profound impact upon all of our lives. Television and radio, magazines, books, and newspapers are presenting ideas that strongly influence the thoughts and opinions of the young and old alike. Now, high-speed internet comes directly into our homes and is influencing us with many new thoughts, ideas, and even lifestyles that we were rarely exposed to only a short time ago. It is indeed unfortunate that the mass media outlets of our world have, to a large extent, succeeded in establishing the concept of evolution as a widely accepted scientific reality in the minds of the general public. Nothing, however, could be further from the truth!

Mass-media bias continually offers evolution as the only possible explanation for the origin of life as we know it. Today's standard textbooks, magazines, newspapers, and nearly every nature documentary recorded in our generation have offered this ideology as factual by direct, bold statements, or through various means of indirect, subtle inference. As defined for us in Webster's II New Riverside University Dictionary, a fact is something presented as having an objective reality. In other words, a genuine fact can be historically or experimentally verified, or perhaps corroborated by eye witnesses. Dictionary.com defines a fact as a truth known by actual experience or observation__ something that is actually known to be true. Webster's New World Dictionary describes a fact as the state of things as they really are as distinct from fantasy. Since the strange concept of evolution has never been proven by any objectively real observation, and the evidence to support it is still very much nonexistent, we can and must quickly eliminate it from the category of scientific fact. It is apparent, however, that the people who control the media are, by and large, evolutionist in their thinking. We know this because the public rarely sees any objective material supportive of another point of view, and strict censorship is constantly employed to aggressively filter out any adversarial ideas.

The vast majority of public observers in today's Western culture will generally accept the unverified statements and misinformation disseminated through the media without question or challenge. Since our media outlets have had such a powerful influence upon all our lives, we owe it to ourselves, and to our children, to be careful and very vigilant before accepting suspicious-sounding reports that are delivered to us as factual. Someone once said that if you tell a lie publicly often enough and long enough, the people would begin to believe it. I think this is true; it's called brainwashing! It's a technique that was used and perfected by none other than Adolf Hitler.

There are some very questionable and certainly unproven ideas that have been consistently presented to the public over the years through media channels and public education. Unfortunately, these ideas have received wide public acceptance even though their validity has seldom been seriously challenged. For example, geologists tell us that the earth is at least 5.3 billion years old. We are expected to believe that the beginning of life occurred when mindless elements in some kind of ancient primordial soup accidentally assembled themselves by some unguided process to randomly form the complex array of chemical bonds creating proteins required to produce and sustain a living organism. Anthropologists report that the dinosaurs became extinct after roaming the earth 60 to 100 million years ago. Many evolution-minded scientists state that humans began to evolve from primate ancestors no less than one million years ago. They also claim to have some reliable scientific methods of determining the age of fossils, and even that of massive geological formations. These so-called experts have also led us to believe that our vast oil deposits resulted from the decay of prehistoric life-forms over multiple millions of years of earth's history, long before humankind appeared. We are also informed that the discovery of organic-life fossilization within the earth's crust has given us a very clear historical record of early life-forms, which, we are told, have largely substantiated the claims of the evolutionary model. However, all these claims are currently being refuted by a vast accumulation of past and current scientific knowledge.

The evolutionist is always the first to deny the idea of a worldwide flood as recorded in the biblical record of Genesis. We are often led to believe that Charles Darwin was confident in the accuracy of his conclusions. By the age-long process of mutation and natural selection, we are even expected to believe that somehow one species successfully evolved into another in an endless progression of ever-advancing life-forms from very simple to very complex. Finally, the strange notion of evolution is presented to us as a scientific fact, while the Holy Bible is consistently ridiculed as merely mythological. These strange concepts are continually embellished before us within the public domain as undisputed scientific reality in magazines, newspapers, television broadcasts, textbooks, and even over the internet.

Many people today accept these naturalistic claims with little hesitation because of biased reporting that constantly censors any claims to the contrary. To give you an impression of just how biased most media channels have become in recent years, consider this: in 1982, the highly regarded Institute for Creation Research requested that *Reader's Digest* (a popular magazine that has been known to give an occasional "nod to God"), publish at least one short research article from their organization defending creationism. This simple request seemed to be only fair considering the highly scientific work that has been done by this remarkable organization. Listen here, if you will, to the very rigid reply they received in response from the publishers of *Reader's Digest*: "Because predominant scientific thinking considers evolution as a solid basis for further research, *Digest* articles focusing on man's origin will continue to refer to evolution as a virtual certainty."[6] The blatantly biased teaching and reporting expounded so consistently before the public provides us with all the more reason to believe that modern evolution theory constitutes a dangerous and deceiving philosophical worldview.

If we continually allow ourselves to become fully indoctrinated by the popular opinions of the so-called experts, without challenging the ideas they present, then perhaps we do not deserve the freedom of intellectual thought so cherished as an American ideal. Evolutionary theory is all about placing man's opinion above God's Word, resulting in rejection of his authority and his supreme power! The theory of evolution is religious in nature, somewhat like believing in the biblical record. Why? Because it takes enormous faith to believe that matter, energy, and living organisms came to be accidentally, totally out of chaos, without God. This very cleverly disguised religious philosophy has consistently overwhelmed the public by the sheer magnitude of the mass-media bias and didactic support it has received.

Those who instead have favored the traditional creation model of origins have apparently not become influential enough to generate a substantial public impact through media channels. However, it would be clearly in our best interest to fully consider the evidence available to us through many years of diligent and reliable research, so that we may truly understand, for ourselves and our families, how it is that life on this earth actually began.

Now that we better understand the true nature of evolutionary thought, we must now consider which origin-of-life model makes the most sense from an objective point of view. Which involves reasonable faith supported by scientific and historical evidence, and which one is a leap of blind faith, designed to exalt man and, ultimately, to protect him from moral absolutes that are often viewed as too restrictive with regard to personal lifestyle choices?

This critical question is so very important because what each person comes to believe about the origin of the material world and the living creatures that inhabit it will lead the way in shaping his or her entire worldview. And sooner or later, that personal worldview will serve to govern each individual's chosen lifestyle and perceived purpose, along with shaping his or her entire future destiny. Many modern-day evolutionists, who are vehemently attacking their creationist opponents as nothing but unenlightened religious fanatics, are actually themselves promoting a significantly religious philosophical view that, ultimately, relies upon faith alone.

War of the Worldviews

The long-standing dispute between creation and evolution is really a battle between two differing philosophies of life. Biblical Christianity and secular humanism are the two mutually incompatible worldviews that have framed this debate for the last century; and now the argument has become more heated than ever. This we see in light of current revealed evidence, and many recently discovered facts, which so strongly favor the biblical framework, and have, subsequently, threatened the core principles of evolutionary thought. These two controversial worldviews, at war in our world, form the basis for a wide cultural divide that is deeply rooted in the question of origins. The ongoing debate holds the key to determining which philosophy of life a person will choose, and, ultimately, their decision making as to this crucial question will serve to shape the very standards and principles by which they will live.

The false and unwarranted public perception that evolution is true science has given highly educated naturalists an undeserved advantage when it comes to explaining the origin of life. Many people tend to think that anyone who has a PhD after his or her name must have all the right answers. However, when the underpinnings of their shortsighted perception begins with the firm conviction that there is no God, the PhD must become adept at formulating biased responses, by interpreting any new data to conform with their predetermined worldview. Sadly enough, this deeply engrained philosophy of life has proven to be highly incompatible with many reliable, known facts when they are taken at face value.

Tenured educators at many of our very best public colleges and universities are often thought of as completely unbiased, objective, and open-minded when just the opposite is often the case. However, even in spite of the uncompromising, inherent prejudice among many of today's top educators, there is a new trend and a rather remarkable redirection taking place among many objective-minded scientists and professors, some of whom have finally become open to the idea of allowing recently revealed evidence to guide them in a very new direction. Creationist, aerospace engineer and notable author Dr. Luther D. Sunderland has commented on the numerous contemporary viewpoint transformations that have taken place on university campuses over the recent years. "Hundreds of scientists who once taught their university students that the bottom line on origins had been figured out and settled are today confessing that they were completely wrong. They have discovered that their previous conclusions, once held so fervently, were based on very fragile evidences and suppositions which have since been refuted by new discoveries . . .This has necessitated a change in their basic philosophical position on origins. Others are admitting great weaknesses in evolution theory."[7]

The greatest objection to the view of creationism by the many proponents of evolution is the idea of miraculous, supernatural events in history, which cannot possibly be accounted for on the basis of the dependable natural laws of physical science. The laws of nature are universally valid and apply equally to both living things and nonliving substances. These laws are immutable, having never changed, based on all known human observations. However, the sovereign Deity who dwells outside of the time-space physical reality (the One who initiated and established these laws) is also able to circumvent them at will whenever it pleases him to do so. As the Creator of the laws of physics, God is not subject to them. The miracles described in the Bible are extra-ordinary events in which the effects of natural laws were either partially or completely suspended for a given period time in a certain place, which resulted in a unique purpose at God's discretion. A miracle would be defined as a mysterious event that cannot be explained by the physical laws of nature, and therefore must be considered an inexplicable occurrence resulting from unimpeded supernatural power. For the committed materialist, who subscribes to naturalism in explaining life's origin, absolutely no allowance can be made for the possibility of the miraculous.

However, if the Creator were truly all-powerful, as he has proclaimed himself to be, then for him to circumvent natural laws that he himself established would be a small thing indeed. As our Creator, the miracle-working God who dwells in the spiritual realm outside of time and space is never limited by natural laws, which he has set into motion to govern the physical world. According to Dr. Henry M. Morris, "If God is the creator and sustainer of all natural processes, then he can surely change those processes when and as he wills. Thus, to say that miracles are impossible is simply to deny God."[8]

When it comes to the sensitive matter of miracles or supernatural events, the question is not "Are they possible?" but "Have they occurred?" If the known weight of scientific and historical evidence suggests that many supernatural events have occurred in the past, events that cannot be accounted for by natural laws, then we would be ill-advised to insist on rejecting the idea of a supernatural intelligence only because we do not understand how or why the miraculous occurs. I recently attended the Yuma Air Show in my home state of Arizona. At this show, I became especially impressed by the performance of one particular airplane, which was entertaining the audience by drawing an enormous design in the clear blue sky as it cast a stream of smoke in a giant circular pattern above our heads. As I gazed at this giant circle in the brilliant afternoon sky, a peculiar thought occurred to me that if the vast space inside this giant circle represented to us everything there is to know about the physical universe, I believe that the combined total of mankind's accumulated knowledge including every generation until now, could be represented inside that circle as a tiny dot the size of a pinhead. Would it then be remotely possible that a sovereign, omniscient God could reign supreme within the immense area of that huge circle that is so mysteriously unknown to man? I remain continually amazed at the profound arrogance of so many well-educated men and women who continually act as though they are far too intelligent, and thoroughly enlightened, to need the help and the grand wisdom of an omniscient Creator.

Years ago Dr. Albert Einstein, who won the coveted Nobel Prize for physics in 1921, had reflected a similar thought when he made the following statement: "I'm not an atheist, but I don't think I can call myself a pantheist. We are in a position of a little child entering a huge library filled with books in many languages. The child knows that someone must have written those books. It does not know how . . . It does not understand the languages in which they are written. The child dimly suspects a mysterious order in the books, but does not know what it is . . . That, it seems to me, is the attitude of even the most intelligent human being toward God."[9] Dr. Antony Flew was an award-winning British philosopher and well-known atheist whose final major publication was a book with the title *There Is a God: How the World's Most Notorious Atheist Changed His Mind.* Long before the well-known professor Richard Dawkins of Oxford became popular as a contemporary proponent of neo-Darwinian evolution, world-class philosopher Antony Flew was widely considered to be perhaps the most celebrated atheist of the academic world during his generation. Prior to his recent death, however, Dr. Flew renounced atheism, and turned his heart, as well as his brilliant mind toward a firm, and profound belief in a creator God. He explained to his critics how modern science had recently uncovered a level of complexity in design that Darwin's theory has utterly failed to account for. As a lifelong observer of modern scientific research and discovery, the late Antony Flew offered this direct insight from his own personal experience with modern scientific discovery: "It now seems to me that the findings of more than fifty years of DNA research have provided materials for a new and enormously powerful argument for design."[10] Immigrant and German-born rocket scientist, the late Dr. Wernher von Braun, who eventually became a NASA aerospace engineer, also offered up a very profound commentary when he publicly announced his view. "I find it as difficult to understand a scientist who does not acknowledge the presence of a superior rationality behind the existence of the universe, as it is to comprehend a theologian who would deny the advances of science."[11] "Nature does not know extinction; all it knows is transformation . . . Everything science has taught me and continues to teach me strengthens my belief in the continuity of our spiritual existence after death. Nothing disappears without a trace!"[12]

Are those of us living in America, Europe, and other developed nations really so full of ourselves as to dare think that, somehow, given our insignificant and insecure level of intelligence, knowledge, and understanding, that we require no special help or guidance in a vast, virtually unknowable universe? In order for anyone to exercise faith in the God of the Bible, one must truly believe in miracles. This we know to be true because supernatural acts that are unexplained by natural laws or human reasoning are known to be commonly characteristic of the God whom the Bible declares to be the Creator of all things. The Bible declares to mankind that "for the invisible things of him from the creation of the world are clearly seen, being understood by the things that are made, even his eternal power and Godhead; so that they are without excuse" (Romans 1:20 KJV). In other words, the Bible says that if we deny God as the creator of the physical world, we will have no valid excuse when, on one future day, we stand before him in judgment. This is because he has revealed to us everything we need to know in order to exercise our faith in him. It's not that we can't believe. Believing in a creator God is clearly the most reasonable option. The truth is that many people simply refuse to believe, in spite of the overwhelming evidence that so strongly favors a "theistic" universe. As it turns out, however, it is often our own foolish human pride and moral depravity that causes many of us to deny him.

Evolutionary theory has been designed to give self-centered man a glimmer of hope that, perhaps, he will never be required to stand before a Holy God in personal judgment. You do not have to visibly see the Creator, or observe firsthand his powerful acts, to recognize the evidence of design all around you. What need is there for anyone to prove that an artist lives or has lived in the past? There is no need, for his fine works of art are surely all that is required to validate his existence. When we take an honest and sincere look at the hard, factual evidence available in our world today, what we observe clearly and consistently lends commanding support to the traditional, and time-tested, creation worldview.

Creationist, conference speaker and Christian leader Mr. Kenneth Ham, the founder and director of *Answers in Genesis* and a powerful voice in the creation movement, describes it this way: "Only the Bible explains why there is beauty and ugliness; why there is life and death; why there is health and disease; why there is love and hate. Only the Bible gives the true and reliable account of the origin of all basic entities of life and the entire universe."[13]

As we have previously discussed, an immutable principle of biology is the fact that life always comes forth only from existing life. If you or I could somehow artificially assemble all of the indispensable chemistry needed with all the proteins and other required structural features to form a perfect, complete organism, and nothing was missing, you would still not have life because a "life force" must also be imposed on the physical elements by a source outside of this material world. The Lord God created Adam from the raw material in the dust of the earth, and then he fashioned his new body with every chemical structure and physical feature necessary for life. Perhaps, you will recall from your childhood Sunday school class years ago that the first human on the earth did not become a living, breathing, and viable creation until *after* "God . . . breathed into his nostrils the breath of life"(Genesis 2:7 KJV). Then, and only then, did man become a living being. It is very important for us to thoroughly understand that perfect chemical structure and complete physical form, in and of itself, could never produce life.

Life can only come from existing life! The life we see on planet earth could only have come from an existing, living Supreme Being, who alone possesses the very unique capacity to impose "the breath of life" on the physical elements, which he himself has created. This concept explains why all attempts to create life in the laboratory are doomed to certain failure. You and I are reminded of the absolute futility of relying upon the evolution theory with the penetrating words of Dr. Albert Fleischmann, who said, "The Darwinian theory of descent has not a single fact to confirm it in the realm of nature. It is not the result of scientific research, but purely the product of imagination."[14]

If your belief system is based on what might seem intellectually sound, according to the word of so-called experts and the idea of naturalism appeals to your mind, then the concept of evolution is likely to capture your allegiance. If, however, you are actually more interested in where the physical evidence is leading, then you should come to the conclusion that life on planet earth cannot be rooted exclusively in materialism. And you and I will be forced, if we are intellectually honest with ourselves, to consider a worldview that could never be arrived at by merely drawing expedient conclusions that are grounded in biased assumption based on the mounting secular propaganda within our culture. Can we afford to trust our eternal souls to the insecure wisdom and will of man, whose very logic and opinions are often an insult to the Creator? Or, will we trust our lives and future to the wisdom of the revealed Word of God?

The truth is this—the sovereign eternal God of the Bible has created everything existing in both the physical and spiritual realm. He has purposefully designed a magnificent universe, and also lovingly fashioned our beautiful home (earth), when He carefully planned the perfect dwelling place for mankind. No single flaw or imperfection existed in the perfect world the Most High God had deliberately created. However, man chose to disobey his Maker, and subsequently, fell into sin. Because of this willful sin and rebellion, a drastic change came over the perfect world of God's original creation. Man's sinful, selfish act invited the curse of death, sorrow, disease, pain, and suffering with no one to blame except himself. "Therefore, just as through one man sin entered the world, and death through sin, and thus death spread to all men, because all have sinned" (Romans 5:12). You and I are required to live out our days with sin, corruption, greed, lust, and disease all around us. This was certainly not God's original plan! But make no mistake about it, as the Creator, God retains absolute authority over his creative works! We, as human beings, who were created in the image of Almighty God, are under complete obligation and total accountability to the one and only sovereign Lord of the universe. As the Eternal God, the only one with infinite power and authority, he most certainly has the right, and the utmost responsibility to establish and maintain the basic moral standards that will continually define human behavior. Therefore, it is in our best interest to reverently acknowledge and humbly fear the divine authority God has lovingly placed over our lives as the focal point and centerpiece of his creation.

Secular humanists strongly oppose such a worldview and, consequently, they cannot afford to allow the possibility of "God" any credibility in the public discourse. They have cleverly deceived the public into thinking that by eliminating Christian views from public schools, they have simply left our children in a neutral position with regard to religious faith. This is absolutely not the truth! All they have really succeeded in doing, which should be of the utmost concern for every responsible parent in America, is eliminating Christianity from the public schools in favor of the anti-God religion of secular humanism.

Make no mistake about it—the seemingly innocent views of children are radically shaped through public education and public policy. The bottom line here is that humanists refuse to accept Christianity because they deplore the idea of a creator God, by whom they will be judged. They claim that evolution theory is scientific fact, but they cannot offer valid evidence to support this claim, and this is, of course, because there is none! Dr. Henry Morris explains their troubling and rather difficult dilemma in the following remarks: "No one in all human history has ever observed one species evolve into a more complex and better adapted species by natural selection or any other mechanism . . . No one has seen evidence of any mechanism that would make evolution work. In the fossil record of the past, with billions of fossils preserved in the Earth's sedimentary crust, no one has ever found any fossils showing incipient or transitional structures, leading to the evolution of more complex species."[15] He continues: "All the hard data in these life sciences show that evolution is not occurring today, all the real data in the earth sciences show that it did not occur in the past and all the genuine data in the physical sciences show that it is not possible at all. Nevertheless, evolution is almost universally accepted as a fact in all the natural sciences . . . all of the real data of these sciences can be understood much better in the context of creationism . . . It is the evolutionary framework in which they are taught and the evolutionary premises upon which they are built that ought to be rejected."[16]

The fundamental basis for the far-reaching philosophy of evolution decrees that God does not exist. Therefore, at least to some degree, our vast and extremely influential public education institutions have now become indoctrination centers for the promotion of atheism. If we are determined to examine the physical evidence at face value, then we must seriously consider the implications of where that crucial information is directing us. The former atheist and MIT graduate Dr. Frank Tipler is a mathematical physicist and a brilliant cosmologist who converted to Christianity after many years of researching the deep secrets of the universe. Dr. Tipler is currently serving a joint professorship in the

Department of Mathematics and Physics at Tulane University. Tipler now offers what he has come to believe as the most rational approach to facing the problem of origins when examining abundant physical evidence based upon scientific observation alone. "My approach to reality is different. I believe that we have to accept the implications of physical law whatever those implications are. If they imply the existence of God, well, then God exists."[17] We should all applaud this courageous professor for his bravery and intellectual honesty, which is so rare today in the vastly liberal ivory-tower world of modern academia.

For anyone who has willingly spent the time to investigate it, the evidence is overwhelming that evolution theory is dead wrong! This bizarre and grossly inadequate theory actually amounts to nothing less than the most monumental deception the world has ever known. In spite of a devastating lack of evidence, many loyal proponents of "the theory" are simply not ready to throw in the towel. These are people who dreadfully fear any connection between God and science! Unfortunately, the staunchest and most dogmatic defenders of naturalism are often seated in places of great influence and power, having been elevated to lofty positions as professors, scientists, and journalistic editors. In addition, they have received the unequivocal backing of the most influential media distribution network in the world. In spite of this, however, the truth about the physical reality is being disseminated more widely today than ever before by every possible means to those who are willing to investigate with an open mind.

Once these facts are thoroughly understood, it becomes evident that the theory of evolution is long overdue for the scrap heap of history. Like so many species of animals in the past, evolution is destined for extinction. A long-time professional molecular scientist recently told me that he believes within two generations neo-Darwinian evolution will be only a passing memory. As you have thus far experienced in the pages of this book, many of today's well-respected scientists, who have openly allowed the true facts to speak for themselves, are now rapidly defecting from the evolutionist camp in record setting numbers. The only other tactic that is really left to the most ardent proponents of evolution theory is to ridicule their philosophical opponents as uninformed simpletons who really do not understand how the theory actually works. Before we move along here, let me just affirm that I wholeheartedly approve of genuine open-minded education, but I must say I adamantly deplore the way in which liberal educators have conveniently and consistently censored the facts, and are hiding legitimate scientific truth for the purpose of proselytizing a worldview that continually mocks God and casts stones at his eternal Word.

True Confessions

There is a war against God that is being waged throughout every civilized culture in the world. This radical warfare has been orchestrated against the Almighty One by many skeptical men and women who falsely believe they are speaking in the name of science. However, just because a scientist speaks does not mean that what he or she says is scientific or that it should not be questioned, scrutinized and put to the test. The German philosopher Friedrich Nietzsche once declared that "God is dead," inferring that science had buried him under an avalanche of modern intellectual enlightenment. It seems as though Nietzsche's philosophy has now fallen on hard times indeed in a world that is no longer satisfied with wild speculation, biased rhetoric and unfounded assumptions.

In the popular 2014 full-length feature film entitled *God's Not Dead* by Pure Flix Entertainment, we witnessed the not-untypical saga of an atheist college professor whose goal was to coerce his students into denying the existence of God. In doing so, he believed himself a hero who was ultimately doing his unsophisticated students a great service by freeing their minds from the shackles of religious superstition to an understanding of their world from the standpoint of intellectual reason and enlightenment. As the story begins to unfold, we observe each character becoming more seriously challenged by the difficult circumstances affecting human lives in a broken world. Each one will ultimately face their desperate need for a "divine presence" that would enable them to make sense of the very challenging and difficult life experiences over which they have no control. This outstanding and compelling production provides the audience with the understanding that logic, evidence, and human emotional need will ultimately drive every open-minded human soul toward a very personal creator God who loves us. We have today plenty of naturalist thinkers who are telling us that modern science has systematically eliminated the need for God. However, at the same time, we also have a growing number of influential, theist-minded intellectuals who are testifying that it was science that ultimately confirmed their faith and belief in a higher power, whose authority is far more superior and benevolent to that of feeble mankind.

After more than one hundred years of constant evolutionary propaganda broadcast via the public airwaves and taught with religious zeal in modern public institutions, secular societies have increasingly demanded, throughout municipal and academic circles, that science and religion can peacefully coexist but only if religion remains private and does not infiltrate the public domain.

With this said, allow me to update you on a new phenomenon taking place in the remarkable world of science. I would like to call to your attention a current encouraging transformation that is taking place in the evolution camp. The revelation of scientific knowledge that has been observed and documented over the past seventy years or so has now cast a dark shadow of uncertainty over evolutionary claims that were previously thought, by many, to be indisputable facts. However, this new evidence is now leading us down a much different path than most scientists could have ever imagined. Those who currently reside within the scientific ranks are generally responding in one of three different ways to the new direction scientific research is now taking us. Some have dug in their heels and remain determined to find a way of explaining life without God, even if it means making up a new theory to somehow circumvent the notion of deity. In their rigid refusal to acknowledge where the weight of evidence is now directing us, many still insist on maintaining a drumbeat litany that boldly proclaims, "We know evolution is true, even though we do not know how it works and have never seen it happen." The second wave of conviction suggests that

Darwin's theory is all but finished in the minds of those who are open-minded enough to let the evidence lead wherever it wants to take them. Still these stalwart intellectuals, who are nearly ready to admit Darwin's demise, will often persist by simply stating, "We just don't know; so we will simply have to keep right on looking for a way to explain the physical realm and the remarkable emergence of organic life." And finally we see brave souls who are genuinely ready to acknowledge what the actual evidence is teaching us about life in the physical realm. These reformers are quite willing to embrace whatever understanding our vast accumulation of evidence has revealed about a remarkable universe, even if it means to openly and honestly recognize that it is impossible (based upon current scientific knowledge) to explain life without a certain reliance on some principle means of intelligent oversight.

In spite of how you and I were raised, or what prejudices toward Christianity we may have come to know, we must not be dissuaded from examining the valuable information that is readily available to us, as we honestly consider where new revelation is leading our hearts and minds. Nothing is really worth believing, unless there is a reasonable degree of reliable evidence supporting it! William Paley, the eighteenth-century Christian apologist and philosopher, wrote the original framework for the following compelling statement: "There is a principle, which is a bar against all information, which gives proof against all argument, and which cannot fail to keep any man in everlasting ignorance. The principle is contempt prior to examination!"[18] This simple and yet very profound thought reminds us that when a person's mind is already firmly made up, any and all evidence is to him of little significance. When considering the very important question of origins, many good people, including many well-educated intellectuals, have remained extremely guarded about what they believe, and will often see any attempt to persuade them otherwise as a threat against their intelligence, as though someone were attacking their religion. No surprise there, because we now understand that this is exactly what belief in evolution is—a religion!

When I was a young boy growing up in Washington state, it may have been my father who once explained to me that it is often quite difficult to persuade someone to change their mind about certain well-established personal views, even if you were to present a reasonable argument as to why they should consider a change of heart. This basic admonition says, "A man persuaded against his will is of the same opinion still!" This firmly engrained posture is commonly observed when we are considering creation versus evolution. However, after more than one hundred-fifty years of revealed facts that have flatly denied Darwin's claims, the scientific tables are beginning to turn. And we are now witnessing a newfound resurgence of the traditional Judeo-Christian worldview. This trend is not necessarily because of religious philosophy or biblical persuasion, but instead it seems based upon the sure laws of physics and the evidence of design.

Allow me to offer a few of the revised opinions, conclusions, and honest statements that some of today's evolutionists are now inclined to share publicly because of their admitted frustration over the fact that science has not been kind to their preferred naturalistic worldview. Paleoevolutionist Dr. Niles Eldredge is a curator with the American Museum of Natural History. As such, he has seen and evaluated a wide and vast array of fossil evidence over the years, and now, he is publicly revealing the dark secrets of paleontology. He wrote, "We have proffered a collective tacit acceptance of the story of gradual adaptive change, a story that strengthened and became even more entrenched as the synthesis took hold. We paleontologists have said that the history of life supports that interpretation, all the while really knowing that it does not."[19] How about this acknowledgement by Scottish anthropologist Sir Arthur Keith who has said, "Evolution is unproved and unprovable . . . We believe it only because the only alternative is 'special creation,' which is unthinkable."[20] When the famous molecular biologist Francis Crick, along with his colleague James Watson, discovered the remarkable double helix structure of the DNA polymer and both were subsequently awarded the Nobel Prize in 1962, their work popularized DNA research as never before. Later, as a research professor at the Salk Institute for Biological Studies in La Jolla, California, Francis Crick remained on the cutting edge of molecular biological research for many years. After a lifetime of devoted research at the molecular level, Dr. Francis Crick ultimately came to the following conclusion: "An honest man, armed with all the knowledge available to us now, could only state that, in some sense, the origin of life appears, at the moment, to be almost a miracle . . . so many are the conditions which would have had to have been satisfied to get it going."[21] The ever-so-troubling frustrations of many of today's ardent naturalists are expressed quite clearly in the following powerful statement from evolutionist Roger Haines Jr. who has openly confessed, "The arguments for macroevolution fail at every significant level when confronted by the facts."[22] Again and again, we see more startling admissions coming forth from the evolutionist camp. Professor Edmund J. Ambrose of the University of London has offered this insightful comment: "At the present stage of geological research, we have to admit that there is nothing in the geological records that runs contrary to the view of conservative creationists, that God created every species separately, presumably from the dust of the earth."[23] Now, consider another rather remarkable confession by the evolutionary paleontologist Mark Czarnecki as he highlights a difficult obstacle for naturalism: "A major problem in proving the theory (of evolution) has been the fossil record; the imprints of vanished species preserved in the Earth's geological formations. This record has never revealed traces of Darwin's hypothetical intermediate variants; instead species appear and disappear abruptly, and this anomaly has fueled the creationist argument that each species was created by God."[24] Gifted astronomer, physicist, and highly regarded cosmologist Dr. Robert Jastrow explains the current dilemma that many scientists are now facing: "Scientists have no proof that life was not the result of an act of creation, but they are driven by the nature of their profession to seek explanations for the origin of life that lie within the boundaries of natural law. They asked themselves, 'how did life arise out of inanimate matter? And what is the probability of that happening?' . . . And to their chagrin, they have no clear-cut answer, because chemists have never succeeded in reproducing nature's experiments on the creation of life out of nonliving matter"[25] Harvard's Dr. Stephen J. Gould, a famous American paleontologist and evolutionary biologist who was undoubtedly the leading evolutionary voice in America during the late twentieth century, has now offered the following comments regarding the incompleteness of the fossil record: "The extreme rarity of transitional forms in the fossil record persists as the trade secret of paleontology. The evolutionary trees that adorn our textbooks have data only at the tips and nodes of their branches; . . . the rest is inference, however reasonable, not the evidence of fossils . . . We fancy ourselves as the only true students of life's history; yet to preserve our favored account of evolution by natural selection, we view our data as so bad that we never see the very process we profess to study."[26] The multiple award-winning astronomer Dr. Allan Sandage, who is widely regarded as the modern world's greatest living cosmologist, made this candid remark after having explored the many mysteries of astronomy for a lifetime: "I find it quite improbable that such order came out of chaos. There has to be some organizing principle. God to me is a mystery, but is the explanation for the miracle of existence, why there is something instead of nothing."[27] H. J. Lipson, a professor of physics asks the question that is on the minds of so many evolutionists today who have repeatedly failed to discovered what they so earnestly expected to find. Lipson has commented, "In fact [subsequent to the publication of Darwin's book, *Origin of Species*], evolution became, in a sense, a scientific religion; almost all scientists have accepted it, and many are prepared to bend their observations to fit with it . . . To my mind the 'theory' does not stand up at all . . . If living matter is not, then, caused by the interplay of atoms, natural forces and radiation, how has it come into being? . . . I think, however, that we must go further than this and admit that the only acceptable explanation is creation . . .I know that this is anathema to physicists, as indeed it is to me . . . but we must not reject a theory that we do not like if the experimental evidence supports it."[28] Now, let's consider the lamenting remarks of a lifelong physicist and notable mathematician Dr. Wolfgang Smith: "A growing number of respectable scientists are defecting from the evolutionist camp . . . moreover, for the most part, these 'experts' have abandoned Darwinism, not on the basis of religious faith or biblical persuasions, but on scientific grounds, and in some cases, regretfully."[29] It is now very easy to understand why esteemed, world-class figures like Sir Frederick

Hoyle, Antony Flew, and many others have altered their philosophical worldview in recent years.

Many of these open-minded seekers of truth and knowledge have recently come around to agree that the majestic universe, as we know it, could never reasonably be explained as a colossal cosmic accident. The well-known and highly regarded science historian Frederick B. Burnham, who appeared briefly on ABC's *Nightline* with Ted Koppel, has publicly confirmed the current openness of modern science to the intelligent design model with this remark: "The scientific community is prepared to consider the idea that 'God created the universe' a more respectable hypothesis today than at any time in the last 100 years."[30] Established science does not have the faintest idea how life began on planet Earth, and this admission should be confessed openly and honestly throughout the scientific community__ and to the public at large. Because of this well-established truth, influential scientists and biased professors must refrain from cluttering and confusing the minds of students with statements and ideas that are based solely on philosophical beliefs and nothing more. The last seventy years of scientific inquiry has clearly denied the traditional evolutionary model, and men of science are beginning to consider, and in many cases accept, the only alternative: that a powerful, intelligent being must be acknowledged and revered as the chief architect who purposefully fashioned a remarkable universe to include a beautiful planet such as earth. This innovator created many unusual and fascinating life-forms to populate the waters and the expansive terrain, and, ultimately, made mankind in his own image to become the caretaker of his vast and magnificently created earthly works.

Final Thoughts

The decorated Canadian geologist Sir William Dawson has also helped to bring additional clarity to the argument when he summarized for us the plight of evolution theory. "This evolutionist doctrine is itself one of the strangest phenomena of humanity—a system destitute of any shadow of proof, and supported merely by vague analogies and figures of speech . . . Now, no one pretends that they rest on facts actually observed, for no one has ever observed the production of even one species . . . let the reader take up either of Darwin's great books, or Spencer's *Biology*, and merely ask himself . . . as he reads each paragraph, 'What is assumed here and what is proved?' . . . and he will find the whole fabric melt away like a vision . . . We thus see that evolution as an hypothesis has no basis in experience or in scientific fact, and that its imagined series of transmutations has breaks which cannot be filled."[31]

After many years of study and research into the question of origins, the vast amount of material I have encountered has thoroughly convinced me that the catalog of physical evidence, derived from both the modern world of science and the past world of natural history, lends much greater credibility to the creation model of origins than to any evolutionary account. After five hundred years of scientific inquiry and investigation, it has now become increasingly safe to say that the vast preponderance of evidence gathered throughout the scientific age most strongly favors theism as opposed to naturalism; so many are the unexplained anomalies that have greatly strained the fragile integrity of supposedly objective scientists. Some were even willing to manipulate revealed evidence in order to promote a naturalistic worldview, which they have so desperately believed in against such insurmountable odds. Today's evolutionists have a very serious problem on their hands, however, because they have been forced into the uncomfortable position of having to logically account for the remarkably complex designs found in nature without the creative power of any intelligent influence behind them. Subsequently, they insist that our children should be taught such things in school as if they were undeniable facts. There was a time in America when observable facts were used to identify truth and knowledge, but I suppose that time was long before the current modern age of humanistic pretense, political correctness, and overwhelmingly biased media indoctrination. The current cultural climate has compelled the American public to embrace and believe in outlandish ideas that are actually grounded far more in guesswork and wishful thinking than true empirical, observable, and testable scientific methodology.

Many aspects of the vast physical domain in which we live cannot be understood at all when God is excluded from the equation. The one basic flaw we find in all the evolutionary views of life has been the obvious inability to explain where the information came from that is essential for life to exist. It is quite certain that the critical information contained in DNA could only have been produced by the cognitive mental process of a very ingenious mind. Therefore, evolutionary thought is bound by the unthinkable scenario in which the vast information needed for spelling out life required no intelligence whatsoever, but simply owes its miraculous existence to a mindless, unguided process. Consider these remarks from Dr. Henry Morris, who was perhaps one of the greatest scientific philosophers and educators of the twentieth century. This dedicated man devoted his entire adult life to the interpretation of observed and applied science in the present world, as well as to the historical world of the past. He has presented the following expert analysis with regard to the major cultural and intellectual battle that we are all facing in America today. "The modern creation/evolution conflict is more than a mere scientific controversy, or even a battle between science and religion, as many evolutionists pretend. It is nothing less than a new and critical phase in the age-long conflict between the only two basic worldviews . . . One is centered on the creator of the world, and his redemptive work on behalf of that lost world; the other is centered in the creatures of that world, not only man in his self-oriented goals, but also the devil himself, who is ultimately behind all rebellion against God."[32]

German-born, British biochemist Ernst Chain was among the recipients of the 1945 Nobel Prize for physiology and medicine. After the remarkable discovery of the drug penicillin by Alexander Fleming, Dr. Ernst Chain worked with both Fleming and Howard Florey on penicillin research for which they all shared the Nobel Prize. Dr. Chain became successful in identifying the structure of penicillin, and was able to isolate the active substance in his laboratory research. For this effort he has been considered as one of the founding pioneers of the modern medical field of antibiotic therapy. In regard to his personal views on Darwin's theory of evolution, Dr. Chain found the theory to be "only a very feeble attempt to explain the origin of species based on presumptions so flimsy that it can hardly be called a theory." He had viewed the evolution model's absolute reliance on chance mutations as a "hypothesis based on no evidence and irreconcilable with the facts." He wrote, "These classic evolutionary theories are a gross oversimplification of an immensely complex and intricate mass of facts, and it amazes me that they were swallowed so uncritically and readily, and for such a long time, by so many scientists without a murmur of protest."[33] Dr. Chain finally came to the conclusion that he "would rather believe in fairies than in such wild speculation" as Darwinism. These statements are the powerful personal reflections of a world-class, Nobel-Prize-winning scientist whose dazzling research successfully pioneered a new scientific field of research and investigation by altering the future of medicine with groundbreaking discoveries.

Consider also the words of Dr. Robert Jastrow, the decorated astronomer, physicist, and cosmologist, who eventually became the founding director of NASA's Goddard Institute for Space Studies in 1961. He has offered another interesting perspective. Although a self-proclaimed agnostic, Dr. Jastrow has provided a very revealing conclusion after finally reaching the end point of scientific limitation where he, along with many other investigators, ultimately made a very startling discovery. Please consider, if you will, the serious implications suggested by his profound observations: "A sound explanation may exist for the explosive birth of our universe; but if it does, science cannot find out what the explanation is. The scientist's pursuit of the past ends in the moment of creation . . . This is an exceedingly strange development, unexpected by all but the theologians. They have always accepted the word of the Bible: In the beginning God created heaven and earth . . . At this moment it seems as though science will never be able to raise the curtain on the mystery of creation. For the scientist who has lived by his faith in the power of reason, the story ends like a bad dream. He has scaled the mountains of ignorance; he is about to conquer the highest peak; as he pulls himself over the final rock, he is greeted by a band of theologians who have been sitting there for centuries."[34]

In 1929, astronomer Edwin Hubble discovered that the galaxies are receding from one another as the universe appeared to be continually expanding. This observation eventually lead to a firm conclusion by the vast majority of physicists and cosmologists that our universe began at a single moment of time__ a profound concept that is now commonly referred to as the "big bang." Physicists are now virtually all in agreement that the present universe began as an infinitely dense and unexplainably dimensionless point of pure concentrated energy. The modern scientific concept of a big bang explosion of energy "in the beginning" is currently being considered by many to be perfectly compatible with the Judeo-Christian tradition as stated in the opening words of Genesis, "In the beginning God . . .Then God said: Let there be light; and there was light" (Genesis 1:1, 3). The brilliant Dr. Arno Penzias, who won a Nobel Prize for physics in 1978, has come to a remarkably similar conclusion based on a lifetime of study: "The best data we have [concerning the big bang] are exactly what I would have predicted, had I nothing to go on but the five books of Moses, the Psalms, and the Bible as a whole."[35] Even though many of today's well-trained scientists claim to have discovered some answers that would circumvent what theologians have believed for centuries, their bold and often dogmatic claims have not always turned out as they expected. The hard, proven scientific facts gathered from many years of disciplined technical research continue to refute such claims. The Bible is not in conflict with science, as evolutionists would have us believe. In fact, it can be stated, categorically, that not even a single known contradiction exists between the biblical record and any proven or otherwise observed fact of science.

The notable Swedish embryologist and biochemist Dr. Soren Lovtrup has taken a parting shot at the evolution model that I believe may still be reverberating throughout the scientific community. "Micro-mutations do occur, but the theory that these alone can account for evolutionary change is either falsified, or else it is an un-falsified, hence meta-physical theory. I suppose that nobody will deny that it is a great misfortune if an entire branch of science becomes addicted to a false theory . . . But this is what has happened in biology . . . I believe that one day the Darwinian myth will be ranked the greatest deceit in the history of science . . . When this happens, many people will pose the question: How did this ever happen?"[36] The more extensive and advanced the revelation of man's knowledge becomes, the more evident it appears that creation is the correct explanation for the origin of life on planet earth. Certainly, the amazing degree of complexity and order that we have thus far discovered in our universe is not merely the product of blind chance events. Since today's scientific observation and research clearly supports the Genesis account, it is most unfortunate that so many good, intelligent people are still clinging to the unproven and historically repudiated philosophy of evolution. Dr. Louis Bounoure is a former biology professor at the University of Strasbourg and served as the director of the Strasbourg Zoological Museum. He put it rather bluntly when he said, "Evolutionism is a fairy tale for grownups. This theory has helped nothing in the progress of science. It is useless!"[37] Dr. T. N. Tahmisian of the U.S. Atomic Energy Commission elaborates further: "Scientists who go about teaching that evolution is a fact of life are great con-men, and the story they are telling may be the greatest hoax ever . . . In explaining evolution, we do not have one iota of fact."[38]

Ultimately, belief in evolution leads mankind to a form of self-worship or humanism. This false belief tenaciously maintains that there is not and never has been any intelligent power greater than man. The Bible refers to this type of ideology in Romans chapter 1, and beginning with verse 22, where we read this powerful reproof: "Professing themselves to be wise, they became fools, and changed the glory of the un-corruptible God into an image made like corruptible man . . .who exchanged the truth of God for the lie [evolutionary humanism] and worshipped and served the creature rather than the Creator . . . and even as they did not like to retain God in their knowledge, God gave them over to a debased mind" (Romans 1:22, 25, 28).

Many people are eager to accept the philosophy of evolution because it allows them, at least within their own minds, to somehow justify a self-directed lifestyle by offering to mankind the imagined hope of never having to face personal accountability and judgment. Unfortunately, however, evolution has provided its followers with only a false sense of security—suggesting that at the end of life, they will have no one to answer to except themselves. This false hope is the ultimate lie of evolution! It is truly a monumental deception wrought with deadly consequences. The greatest and most significant danger of evolution theory is that it ultimately leads mankind to a rejection of the authority of the Bible, resulting in the failure to appropriate the promises therein, leading to salvation and eternal life. It is certain that the Creator has had definite purpose in his undeniable works of creation, and it appears very evident that his purpose was centered primarily in man. There is, therefore, no legitimate reason for any one of us to deny the Creator, or even question his divine power and authority. "Who are you to reply against God? Will the thing formed say to him who forms it, 'why have you made me like this'? Does not the potter have power over the clay?" (Romans 9:20, 21).

When it finally comes down to the origin of life and the universe with all of its broad claims and life-altering ramifications, I believe we can now separate the truth from fantasy. Evolution theory is the consummation of man's stubborn refusal to submit his personal will to a powerful intelligence greater than himself__ a submission that, once offered, will prove to be truly life-altering toward the prideful independence and arrogance of the self-centered human heart.

Now is the right time to answer the ultimate question; in which direction is scientific discovery pointing us? Which existed first, mind or matter? Was eternal intelligence existing before the vast physical domain came to be? Do we owe our existence to sovereign power greater than random chance? After all these arguments have been thoroughly examined, either we are the accidental outcome of billions of random events in an impersonal universe, or there is a living God in heaven that has planned for us to be here. As Professor John Lennox has aptly stated, "Either human intelligence ultimately owes its origin to mindless matter; or there is a Creator."[39] In spite of over one hundred years of evolutionary propaganda, the Judeo-Christian tradition remains remarkably strong in light of the powerful evidence mankind has discovered, as revealed by the many expert testimonies we have encountered here. The great preponderance of evidence confirms the following:

1. The physical elements are clearly not eternal but had a beginning.
2. The universe has had its beginning through an initial cause.
3. The causal agent is the God of the Bible, Creator of heaven and earth.
4. God is eternal; he existed long before the universe was created and is entirely independent of it.
5. The physical dimension was designed and created with humanity in mind.
6. Eternal God has thoroughly revealed himself to his creation!

Materialistic naturalism has been exhaustively weighed in the balance and found wanting! Therefore, now that evolution theory has been thoroughly discredited and exposed for the monstrous deception that it is how will you and your loved ones respond to the overwhelmingly powerful evidence that strongly supports a theistic universe and the creation worldview? Will you and the people that you love remain reluctant, unconcerned, and even indifferent toward judging a very dangerous ideology that is perhaps the most colossal fabrication ever imposed upon human lives? Now that we have discovered the truth, you and I have a great responsibility to those who have not, because, only the truth will set them free!

"And you shall know the truth, and the truth shall make you free." (John 8:32)

"But without faith it is impossible to please Him; for he who comes to God must believe that he is [that he exists], and that he is the rewarder of those who diligently seek Him." (Hebrews 11:6)

"In the beginning, O Lord, you laid the foundations of the earth, and the heavens are the work of your hands." (Hebrews 1:10 NIV)

"I have made the Earth, and created man upon it: I, even my hands, have stretched out the heavens, and all their host have I commanded." (Isaiah 45:12 KJV)

"The god of this age has blinded the minds of unbelievers, so that they cannot see the light of the Gospel of the glory of Christ, who is the image of God." (2 Corinthians 4:4 NIV)

"For thus saith the Lord that created the heavens; God himself that formed the Earth and made it; he hath established it, he created it not in vain, he formed it to be in the inhabited: I am the Lord; and there is none else." (Isaiah 45:18 KJV)

It has been said that around the beginning of the twentieth century an unknown scientist of that time had discovered and subsequently reported what he sincerely believed to be the five basic properties defining physical reality. These five essential properties of the physical dimension were subsequently identified as time, force, action, space, and matter. I would submit to you that this early-twentieth-century scientific thinker, whoever he was, had simply stumbled upon what was only the most basic knowledge that a sovereign creator God had revealed to his creation thousands of years before! "In the beginning [time] God [force] created [action] the heaven [space] and the earth [matter]" (Genesis 1:1 KJV, [with amendments]). The jury is back on the question of scientific skepticism and a verdict has been reached. To the intellectually honest seeker of truth, divine providence cannot be denied.

So let him, the only sovereign God of all creation and the supreme Lord and Ruler of the universe, who alone is found to be worthy of our worship, praise, and devoted allegiance, be glorified by the thoughts we are thinking, the lives we are living, and the God-ordained posterity we are producing!

Chapter 7

ALMIGHTY OR ALL MYSTERY

The All-Important Question

On the one hundredth anniversary of Mr. Darwin's profound revelation to the academic and scientific worlds, the atheist Julian Huxley said this, "In the evolutionary scheme of thought there is no longer either need or room for the supernatural. The Earth was not created, it evolved. So did all the animals and plants that inhabit it, including our human selves, mind and soul as well as brain and body. . . ."[1] Mr. Huxley was certainly living proof that atheism is the logical outcome and ultimate consequence of evolutionary thinking, even though his many bold, dogmatic, and very provocative statements are now proven to be totally baseless and without vindication. I hope you will now agree that the material from the previous chapters is more than enough and should convince any seriously interested person that the existence of the universe and everything in it had nothing to do with unguided, random chance events, as expressed in the rapidly declining ideology of naturalism.

You and I have already discovered the evolution model to be terribly lacking and grossly inadequate as a sound means by which to explain the remarkable diversity and complexity of life on planet Earth. Therefore, the most logical conclusion we can come to, based on the evidence, is the stark realization that there has to be a living intelligence with great power and infinite knowledge, who is responsible for the incredibly unique beauty and design that surrounds us. In this chapter, we will examine, even more closely, the various evidence for a purposeful God behind the scenes__ the one who planned, designed, created, and sustains the universe in which you and I are privileged to live. There remain, however, many good people who are skeptical about the possibility of a creator God. Therefore, let us carefully examine some very compelling thoughts that offer sound evidence, which will point us to the rational conclusion that God does, indeed, exist.

We must now consider the most basic question that can ever be answered during our lifetime. Does there exist a personal, powerful creator God to whom we will all, ultimately, be held accountable? By answering this one critical question, we should find that all of the other deeply philosophical mysteries about life will become much easier for us to understand. Consequently, we will be left with an accurate worldview, a view that will prepare us for the challenges we are facing in the present, those that are yet to come, and, of course, the ultimate prospect of leaving this physical world behind for good when we finally cross over that hallowed threshold into eternity. How do we know if there is a divine, unseen force governing this universe? Since we cannot detect the unseen God directly through our physical senses, we can only experience him through faith based on what we are able to observe, and in what he has been willing to reveal to us. Who is this Almighty God of the spirit world that desires our attention, devotion, and allegiance? What is his divine claim as the chief architect of the material world? Has he adequately revealed himself through his creation? Has he taken satisfactory measures to make himself personally known to us? In this important chapter, I will offer the reader what I believe will be sufficient reason to accept the reality of God's eternal existence; and I am quite certain that discovering the truth about him is not nearly as difficult as many people would like to believe.

If there truly is a sovereign God beyond time and space, in a reality scarcely understood by mortal man, then it is entirely up to this living Lord of the universe to reveal himself to us. He would certainly have to do this in a way that will adequately satisfy the deep longing within humanity for knowledge and understanding about our Maker. You and I can only view reality from the very remote perspective of a mundane three-dimensional world. This leaves us with only two basic ways by which we can discover the truth about God, if we are looking for him with an objective, open heart and mind. The first method is certainly found through "observation": we can infer what is true about God by observing the many physical features on display in our world and, also, in the vast universe that surrounds us with all of its fascinating complexity and design. The second means of discovering the truth about God can be found through what is called "revelation": we can know more specifically many details about God and his nature only if he is willing to reveal them to us. The real truth about God and his undeniable role in designing the vast physical reality is certainly of the utmost importance in our quest to fully understand "the mystery of life." How could a powerful, just, and loving God, who dwells beyond time and space, reveal himself and his character to finite man in such a way as to address the question about his eternal existence, as well as his great love and undeniable devotion for those he has created in his own image? Now, we will proceed to carefully and sincerely examine some reliable evidence as we begin a thorough investigation into numerous, compelling reasons for believing in the existence of the Almighty.

Observation: The Anthropic Principle

Through much investigative research and discovery, we can detect that both secular and Christian scientists have reported detailed data about the sensitive physical characteristics of planet Earth in what is now often referred to as the "anthropic principle." They report that it appears the earth's most delicate parameters have been finely tuned and perfectly balanced for the very purpose of allowing organic life to exist. This reveals to us that many features of our planet, with respect to the solar system and the galaxies, are uniquely and precisely set to exactly where they must be to support life. According to author and conference speaker Nancy R. Pearcey, a senior fellow at the Discovery Institute, when you examine the unique physical characteristics of the universe with so many primary constants carefully dialed in with such amazing precision: "What you discover is that each of the thousands of dials just happen to be set to exactly the right value for life to exist. Even the slightest tweak of one of the cosmic knobs would produce a universe where life was impossible."[2] We have been informed that the slightest variation in one of these critical physical parameters would result in our rapid demise. Evolutionist and world-renowned scientist Stephen Hawking, the famous British astrophysicist and a strong advocate for scientific research and discovery, seeks the knowledge that has thus far eluded us—for when we find it he states, "Then we shall be able to take part in the discussion of the question of why it is that we and the universe exist . . . If we find the answer to that, it would be the ultimate triumph of human reason—for then we would know the mind of God."[3]

Many believe that current evidence points us directly to only one possible conclusion. Contemporary, world-famous astrophysicist Dr. Paul Davies explains it like this: "Why is nature so ingeniously, one might even say suspiciously, friendly to life? . . . It's almost as if a Grand Designer had it all figured out."[4] "Everywhere we look," says Davies, "from the far-flung galaxies to the deepest recesses of the atom, we encounter regularity and intricate organization . . . moreover, the behavior of physical systems is not haphazard, but lawful and systematic."[5] He then continues with this interesting remark based on many years of intense hands-on research into the laws of physics: "The equations of physics have in them incredible simplicity, elegance, and beauty. That in itself is sufficient to prove to me that there must be a God who is responsible for these laws and responsible for the universe."[6] Let's consider a similar compelling thought from NASA planetary scientist Mr. John O'Keefe, who writes, "We are, by astronomical standards, a pampered, cosseted, cherished group of creatures . . . If the universe had not been made with the most exacting precision, we could never have come into existence . . . It is my view that these circumstances indicate the universe was created for man to live in."[7]

Listen as well to the words of Cambridge University physicist John Polkinghorne who adds, "When you realize that the laws of nature must be incredibly finely tuned to produce the universe we see, that conspires to plant the idea that the universe did not just happen, but that there must be a purpose behind it."[8] British astronomer and world-renowned mathematician Sir Frederick Hoyle has also described this fascinating pattern of life supporting parameters with these carefully chosen words: "Such properties seem to run through the fabric of the natural world like a thread of happy coincidences. But there are so many odd coincidences essential to life that some explanation seems required to account for them."[9]

As I see it, we have two choices to pick from, faith in a living creator God or faith in the accidental, spontaneous generation of all living and nonliving matter in an impersonal, godless universe. Can we really believe that a physical reality was accidental, or, perhaps more wisely, should we consider it the masterful work of a divine architect__ one who planned and lovingly prepared a perfect world intended specifically for his most prized and noble creation, mankind? Here is another rather bold statement we can each reflect on. The following thoughts offer the view of American theoretical physicist Dr. Steven Weinberg, the esteemed winner of the Nobel Prize for high-energy physics in 1979. He has remarked, "How surprising it is that the laws of nature and the initial conditions of the universe should allow for the existence of beings who could observe it. Life as we know it would be impossible, if any one of several physical quantities had slightly different values."[10] The short list below includes only a few of the many measurable physical constants about our planet that if varied only slightly could impose rather dire consequences on the existence of life. Please thoughtfully consider these extremely fine-tuned and exceptionally dependable physical characteristics of the planet we are privileged to call home.

1. Our planet is the ideal size for the atmosphere we need to survive. We know of no other planet with an atmosphere containing the perfect mixture of gases uniquely suited to support plant, animal, and human populations.

2. The earth is perfectly positioned within our solar system; it is exactly where it needs to be in regard to its distance from the sun and other planets. If positioned closer to the sun, we could never survive the heat; if farther from the sun, life would succumb to the frigid temperatures. Even the slightest variation in this critical parameter would be disastrous for all life-forms.

3. The exact speed of the earth's rotation, and its precise orbit around the sun, are perfectly suited to allow for an even warming and cooling of the continents, creating an excellent environment for living organisms. This makes it quite possible for a great variety of unique life-forms to flourish and thrive. A slowdown of our planet's velocity would result in temperature fluctuations between day and night that would be far too extreme to support life. An increase in rotational speed would produce disastrous and devastating wind velocities.

4. The moon is the perfect size and distance from the earth; this has provided the gravitational pull that allows for critical tides and currents. This feature alone keeps the oceans from becoming stagnant, and maintains a healthy environment for the aquatic marine life so important to our food supply.

5. The abundant amount of water on the earth is necessary for the critical hydration cycle; precipitation provides essential moisture offering life-giving support to all living organisms on the planet; nothing can survive without it.

6. The earth's essential gravitational constant is finely tuned to support life, as well.

7. The ratio of electrons to protons in the physical world cannot vary by more than one part in 10^{37}. Otherwise, the electromagnetic interactions that are so crucial for life would prevent essential chemical reactions in nature from occurring.

8. The earth's magnetism is finely tuned, having been purposely designed to support and sustain the planet's abundant variety of life-forms.

9. The ozone layer above us is a critical characteristic of our planet that protects us from a dangerous overexposure to ultraviolet

light, which would be lethal if not adequately deflected away from us in the earth's upper atmosphere.

10. The crust of the earth is exactly the thickness it needs to be to support life.

11. The carbon dioxide-to-oxygen ratio is dialed in exactly where it needs to be.

12. The earth's reflectivity of sunlight is also perfectly fine-tuned for life support.

The slightest variation in many of these primary constants of physics would cause life, as we know it, to cease. Does this sort of evidence point to the existence of God? British-born cosmologist Edward Harrison certainly seems to believe that it does. He once wrote, "Here is the cosmological proof of the existence of God—the design argument of William Paley updated and refurbished. The fine-tuning of the universe provides *prima facie* evidence of deistic design."[11] Another American astronomer, George Greenstein, would seem to concur, "As we survey all the evidence, the thought insistently arises that some supernatural agency, or rather 'Agency,' must be involved. Is it possible that suddenly, without intending to, we have stumbled upon scientific proof for the existence of a Supreme Being?"[12]

And now, we find even non-Christian scientists have reported that the earth appears to be specifically designed as a suitable home for mankind, which, by the way, is also how the Word of God has described it. "The heaven, even the heavens, are the Lord's; but the Earth has he given to the children of men" (Psalm 115:16). Consider this remark from a famous Soviet mathematician, Alexander Polyakov: "We know that nature is described by the best of all possible mathematics, because God created it."[13] That the universe must be finely tuned to make carbon-based life possible is a universal concept in science today. A powerful example of what is meant by this fine-tuning was presented for our consideration by Oxford mathematician Professor John Lennox, who has aptly stated, "The ratio of the electromagnetic force to gravity in the early universe had to be accurate to about one part in 10^{40} in order to have the chemistry of the universe as we now see it."[14] Just to give you some perspective of the precision commanded by this incredibly huge number, world-class physicist Paul Davies has compared it to the odds of hitting a one-inch target on the opposite side of the universe, some twenty billion light-years away. Also, with regard to these elaborate fine-tuning arguments, mathematician John Lennox has offered this candid comment: "The remarkable picture that is gradually emerging from modern physics and cosmology is one of a universe whose fundamental forces are amazingly, intricately, and delicately balanced or fine-tuned in order for the universe to be able to sustain life . . . 'the fundamental constants of nature' . . . Change any of them just a little, and the universe would become hostile to life and incapable of supporting it. These constants are precision-tuned, and it is this fine-tuning that many scientists (and others) think demands an explanation . . . fine-tuning has established itself as an aspect of the universe that merits very serious consideration."[15] The precision-tuning argument has now led many qualified scientists to conclude that the earth and its unique life-supporting parameters were intended with us in mind—we did not just accidentally show up in a world that has randomly turned out to be perfectly designed and exceptionally well suited for us.

The highly esteemed physics Nobel Prize winner Dr. Arno Penzias has described the anthropic principle in this manner: "Astronomy leads us to a unique event, a universe which was created out of nothing, one with the very delicate balance needed to provide exactly the conditions required to permit life . . . and one which has an underlying (one might say supernatural) plan."[16] Consider, as well, this very interesting quotation from Henry Schaefer, a physical scientist who ultimately became a five-time nominee for the Noble Prize: "It is relatively unusual that a physical scientist is truly an atheist. Why is this true? . . . Some point to the anthropic constraints, the remarkable fine-tuning of the universe. For example, Freeman Dyson, a Princeton faculty member, made this observation: 'Nature has been kinder to us than we had any right to expect.'"[17] The impressive anthropic evidence now suggests that someone designed, and carefully dialed in planet earth's most delicate physical parameters in order to provide the perfect world where so many plant, animal, and human populations could flourish and thrive, in keen balance and harmony with nature.

Observation: Law of Cause and Affect

Someone or something eternal was the cause of everything that exists in the material world. If there is a God, why do so many intelligent people remain unconvinced of this truth? The law of causality does not predict that everything requires a cause, but that every finite thing requires a cause. Every effect in the physical world must have a sufficient cause, but by definition, an infinite being does not require a cause. Since we know the universe is finite, we understand that it has had an initial cause. Therefore, we know that someone or something (a necessary being or entity) had to be uncaused (infinite and eternally existing) and would, therefore, qualify as the initial causal agent of the material reality that you and I are so fortunate to observe and experience.

Everyone we know agrees with the scientific principle of "cause and affect". However, in Europe, the Americas, and other highly advanced cultures the world over, many people have educated themselves to the point of arrogance, and to the degree that God is no longer necessary in their personal lives. These modern societies have built education systems that subscribe to cause and affect for sure, but only if the cause conforms to naturalism, and, of course, does not invoke supernatural agency. By beginning with the narrow-minded premise of *no divine cause allowed,* educators the world over have generated a rather hardened worldview that excludes any and all reference to a divine power and authority greater than man. In doing this, they have actually educated faith out of the hearts and minds of young people. Thus, they have attempted to enlist students, by way of biased indoctrination, into the current and fashionable view of atheism. A person is never born an atheist. Atheism occurs when people no longer have a use or need for God, resulting from a variety of secular influences within a modern, contemporary culture. The problem is not that there remains an insufficient amount of evidence to convince rational individuals of God's existence, but many intelligent and highly influential people (especially the elite, powerful, and well educated) have often held a natural antipathy toward the idea of God in spite of the abundant evidence favoring a theistic universe. The notion of God, perhaps, feels threatening to their autonomy. The very idea of a divine presence may antagonize man's self-directed nature (that compelling desire within the human heart to live life on one's own terms and without moral constraint). This may explain why many decidedly intelligent people remain unconvinced of the reality of God; they have willingly chosen to firmly embrace an unyielding worldview that can accept only a purely natural explanation for every observed effect. This may also explain why evolution teaching has had such a powerful influence on the most advanced cultures throughout the civilized world. Evolution theory has given self-centered man what he considers to be sufficient reason to deny God as the designing influence over all things.

Some will say that belief in God is old-fashioned, and, therefore, no longer fits into the scientific thinking of today's modern, intellectual world. For this reason, many believe that allowing the concept of God any credibility or consideration in the final equation of life would somehow diminish today's advanced world of enlightenment through science and education. But perhaps some minds would be challenged and ultimately transformed by taking the time to evaluate and carefully compare modern science with the biblical record. The truth remains that the Bible is, and always has been, in perfect harmony with all known facts of science; and, in fact, the ancient Hebrew text has always been far out ahead of science with its accurately recorded truth about the physical dimension—truth that has taken man thousands of years to verify. This undeniable reality has been confirmed over and over again by the understanding that so much of what the Bible records about the physical world was not even discovered and validated by mankind's inquisitive search for knowledge until only the last couple of centuries.

These documented discoveries have amounted to powerful evidence favoring the existence of God, considering that so many known details regarding the physical laws of science were accurately recorded in Scripture thousands of years ago. Sadly, however, many of today's most elite scholars and educators are determined to rid their students of "outdated religious superstition" by persuading them to believe that evolution is truly scientific. However, nothing could be further from the truth! Genuine empirical science deals only with observable and repeatable events in the present, not with wild conjecture and speculation about numerous unrepeatable, unproven events from the past, which will ultimately lead toward a philosophical dogma that is, of course, highly religious in nature.

Imagine, if you will, a closed empty room with no doors or windows, and it's finished with a smooth, level concrete floor. We will consider this room to be completely isolated from any outside influence. In the middle of the room, hanging by a rope from the ceiling, is a very large bag of marbles. Eventually, due to the constant strain of gravitational force over the passage of time, the great weight of its content causes the heavy bag to burst wide open, spilling thousands of marbles onto the polished concrete floor below where they scatter about everywhere in a totally random pattern, to remain indefinitely. Now, even if ten billion years of time were to pass, the marbles in this completely closed-off system, totally isolated from any and all outside influence, would by no means become highly organized into a very specific and orderly configuration. To rearrange the marbles (like setting up dominos) in a specifically designed pattern would definitely require force, energy, effort, planning, and will. This chaotic mess of marbles would remain in a maximum state of randomness forever, unless or until an organizing agent from outside the room was eventually enabled to impose willful design upon them.

Likewise, all the dead, lifeless matter in a closed universe would never have become spontaneously organized or even somehow intricately arranged without willful intelligent intervention! This cause-driven phenomenon could only have happened in an open universe that would allow for the action of a powerful, intelligent being that could, by personal choice, impose his willful design and purpose upon the random physical chaos. For science to suggest that all matter was concentrated in an isolated space before it randomly exploded to produce the entire universe in what has become known as the big bang theory, would still not sufficiently explain a closed universe. The problem is that someone had to hang the big bag of marbles to begin with! An honest atheist, maintaining a vigilant view of materialism, must constantly maintain that all matter and energy is self-existing and not created, otherwise he or she ceases to be an atheist. If matter had a beginning, as nearly all scientists now believe, yet was not created, this leaves the atheist in a position of having to imagine that the material/physical dimension has appeared randomly, out of nothing, and completely without any intelligent cause. Could such an idea be a highly irrational way of thinking? Logic would certainly suggest to us that whoever was initially responsible for the existence of the marbles (stars, planets, galaxies, etc.), which have become highly ordered and extremely organized with such incredible mathematical precision, would also have to possess the supernatural power, creativity, and willful intent of a highly intelligent and inventive mind.

In no way am I suggesting that this is how God created the universe, but I am suggesting that in order to think logically, we must understand that every known material outcome in the finite physical realm demands a sufficient initial cause. Since all atheists remain strictly bound to a prior commitment with naturalism, they are unable to explain life without a firm reliance upon many freakish, random events that have somehow altered the basic raw-material (elements), whose existence they cannot account for. Those who still insist on maintaining that truly purposeful, supernatural events have never occurred are sadly confined to a belief system that cannot be adequately confirmed. For any one of us to be actually open-minded, and, therefore, willing to follow the evidence wherever it leads, we would surely have to seriously consider the logical possibility that intentional design has been creatively imposed on the vast material existence of the magnificent universe that you and I are privileged to know.

When we consider the workmanship of a magnificent handmade clock, or the finely detailed painting of a skilled artist, how is one to believe that the universe with all of its amazing detail and complexity could have come into existence merely by chance. The mathematical order in the movement of the stars is so accurate and consistent that we set our clocks by it!

Who set the earth at precisely the right distance from the sun? Who set the moon in orbit around the earth? Who caused the earth to revolve around the sun while spinning on its own axis? Who divided the night and the day? The waters of the oceans evaporate to form great clouds, which are pushed by winds across the dry land where they pour out their life giving moisture upon the ground. The melted snow and rain rushes down the mountains to form great rivers, which make their way onward toward the sea, only to be caught up and efficiently delivered across the thirsty dry land once again, providing life-sustaining strength to all the plants, animals, and people of the earth. We observe a very complex world around us, yet everything is in careful balance and harmony, as though it was all diligently planned. We view the majestic splendor of the mountain peaks covered with snow. Many have pondered the bold grandeur of world's restless seas as their wave's pound forcefully against the sand. We marvel at the fragile beauty of a spring flower, and the magnificent perfection of a single snowflake. We experience four unique seasons as they each come and go consistently without ceasing. Standing beneath a star-filled sky on a moonless night, we wonder in amazement at the awe-inspiring scene before our very eyes. With the electron microscope we gaze into a single cell, only to find an amazing world about which we know so very little. We are confronted every day with the miracle of life and the mystery of death, and yet the keen balance of nature continues uninterrupted. We may endeavor to explain the many mysteries of life with modern science, but still there remains so much we do not even begin to understand about the incredible universe that surrounds us.

The atom is the building block of all material substance, yet with our limited knowledge, we do not fully understand this mysterious force that holds the nucleus of the atom together. The nucleus of the atom contains neutrons and protons. The neutrons have no electrical charge, while the protons carry a positive charge. In any electrical system, it is commonly known that like charges repel one another, and unlike charges attract. According to our electrical laws relating to the activity of like and unlike charges, positively charged protons in the nucleus of the atom should repel one another and scatter into space. However, there is a mysterious nuclear force that holds the atom together, maintaining the integrity of the material world. Although we are still learning about this nuclear atomic force, without it everything would vaporize instantly into heat energy. It is certain that we still have much yet to discover about the magnificently designed physical forces that surround us.

There is one thing we know for sure: every observed effect has had a definite cause, and the cause is always greater than the effect. If atheists are right, "nothing" was the initial cause; therefore, matter has come to be without a source greater than itself, which clearly defies reason. For the atheist to maintain that physical reality had a spontaneous, unexplainable cause, they have simply created a religion of the much-maligned theory of evolution. The true scientific principle of cause and affect would flatly deny this conclusion. It is more logical to suggest that the first cause had to come from beyond the realm of the natural world. This is the only conclusion that makes rational sense. The new atheist logic is hard to understand, because they have come to believe that "no one, plus nothing, times blind chance, equals everything." Since there remains today no real evidence to validate the far-reaching claims of evolution theory, people must choose to believe this ideology because they cannot accept the alternative: that there was a creator God at work, initiating the appearance of the physical universe.

Would you not agree that something (a physical substance) could never come from nothing without cause, and this revelation requires that someone very powerful has to be eternal (outside the constraints of time and space)? This implies God! The initial cause of the physical reality could not have been part of the time-space, material world, because this providential agent has caused that dimension to initially appear. Listen once again to the previously cited words of the highly decorated American astronomer Alan Sandage, who has offered this candid remark: "I find it quite improbable that such order came out of chaos. There has to be some organizing principle . . . God to me is a mystery, but is the explanation for the miracle of existence, why there is something instead of nothing."[18]

The ultimate first cause had to be both infinitely powerful and eternally existing! The actual scientific principle of cause and affect, or any other established natural law, for that matter, would clearly place no limitation on a God that exists outside the wide constraints of the material, time-space reality. Why is it so hard for people to acknowledge life as the work of a divine architect? People have become so eager to explain away the magnificent complexity and amazing diversity of life with what, ultimately, amounts to an unproven philosophical dogma. The atheist movement within today's modern Western culture has, no doubt, resulted from a wide variety of circumstances affecting the life of each individual influenced by it. Consider this revealing quotation from a well-known architect of evolution theory who certainly had many years to think about the logical practicality of randomly occurring blind chance: "Reason tells me of the extreme difficulty or rather impossibility of conceiving this immense and wonderful universe, including man and his capability of looking far backward and far into futurity, as a result of blind chance or necessity . . . When thus reflecting, I feel compelled to look to a 'First Cause' having an intelligent mind in some degree analogous to that of man; and I deserve to be called a Theist."[19] These compelling words were penned by Mr. Charles Darwin himself after having had plenty of time to fully appreciate the ramifications of the direction his professional life had taken him. His tone here seems to reflect the thoughts of a troubled soul who was clearly unable to find solace in a strange theory that had eventually found itself in direct conflict with a vast array of empirical physical evidence.

"By the Word of the Lord the heavens were made and all the host of them by the breath of his mouth" (Psalm 33:6). The compelling argument of cause and affect requires and even demands a truly adequate initial cause for the entire physical dimension, and that first cause must have been the unseen, sovereign God of the Universe, who has clearly revealed himself to humankind in a variety of ways. This sound argument points toward a very powerful and intelligent being

THE MYSTERY OF LIFE

that a very high percentage of humankind holds in great reverence as the Eternal God.

Observation: Principle of Logic and Design

Can you really have remarkable design without a designer? Perhaps you have seen and considered the magnificent sculptural masterpiece upon Mount Rushmore. Could any rational person conclude that the four faces of our great former presidents, carved into a mountainside in South Dakota, are the result of millions of years of wind and water erosion? Of course not! That would be ludicrous! So in response to this astounding work of artistic genius, our minds should immediately begin to marvel at the astonishing creativity and skillful perseverance of a great professional artisan. Because of the determined efforts of Danish-American sculptor Gutzon Borglum and his son Lincoln, who began construction on this iconic scene in 1927 and ended it in 1941, the world is now able to enjoy one of the most extraordinary man-made landmarks of all time. This famous American attraction serves to remind us all of the fact that design requires a designer. William Paley made this compelling argument so many years ago, when he suggested that a watch requires a watchmaker.[20] This is a fact that no one who thinks rationally could possibly deny. However, even though no reasonable person is likely to argue against the need for a watchmaker, a painter, or a sculptor, when the results of their work are so clearly seen, yet the most complex design ever known, the human body, has been continually relegated to the imagined world of blind chance, with no "design engineer" given well-deserved credit. Consider this interesting thought from Dr. Isaac Asimov, who was a former professor of biochemistry at the Boston University School of Medicine, He said, "And in man is a three-pound brain, which, as far as we know, is the most complex and orderly arrangement of matter in the universe."[21] For us to declare that the human brain is the end product of a mindless, unguided process in a godless universe seems to me quite absurd. This kind of thinking makes no rational sense; it defies reason, denying the need for intelligent planning behind the most complex organization of organic chemistry ever realized in the physical realm. The truth is that human physiology is an exquisite design of pure genius, and God alone deserves the glory as the chief architect and master design engineer.

The psalmist David declared the wondrous nature of the human body when he wrote this: "For you formed my inward parts; you covered me in my mother's womb. I will praise you for I am fearfully and wonderfully made; marvelous are your works, and that my soul knows very well" (Psalm 139:13, 14).

It is not up to God to prove he is our maker. It is up to us to disprove it if we can. You would not say to an artist, "I don't believe you painted this. You must prove it to me." Of course not! It would be up to you to prove him to be a fraud. Perhaps the greatest evidence for intelligent design in living organisms is cellular DNA. As we have already discussed in a previous chapter, this highly organized and extremely complex composition of genetic chemistry, that is an essential feature in all living things, contains a unique instructional, chemical code-transmitting system. This exceptional cipher conveys intelligent information very much like computer code. The human genome contains around 3.5 billion "chemical letters" in every one of our 10 to 20 trillion cells. Every cell contains the blueprint for life (a complete instruction manual) spelled out very precisely using a four-letter chemical alphabet attached at specific locations on the DNA polymer. How is it possible for one to believe that the remarkable DNA-laden human genome came about because of random chance through the unconscious blind forces of nature?

DNA provides incredibly unique biological signals—the information that accurately directs the complete physiology, biochemistry, and the cell differentiation of all carbon-based life-forms, resulting in the distinctive physical characteristics of all living things. Never have we discovered any source of information-transmitting code that has appeared without the meticulous effort of an innovative master design engineer. Our DNA is no exception; it also requires a code-maker in the exact same way that a written manuscript requires an author. This amazing cellular DNA information-storage mechanism has pointed numerous unbiased researchers directly toward a master design engineer, an inventive mind with supreme intelligence, who had demonstrated purposeful intent and ingenious planning when he carefully orchestrated his most remarkable design of all—human physiology.

Naturalism, which relies on random chance processes alone, is powerless to explain how programmed information code could be found in the composition of cellular genetic chemistry. Nowhere on this earth are we able to locate a single example of written language or code without an intelligent source behind it. When someone carefully records a detailed instruction manual, they obviously have done so with a very definite purpose in mind. The very complex chemistry of DNA genetic code acts as a complete instruction manual for each and every life-form on the planet. Can you imagine every cell in your body containing much more information than the world's largest supercomputer hard drive? Chemical letters provide instruction for every physical feature and every biological function. With such a vast number of these chemical signals in every cell, human physiology instructs in a detailed way exactly how the body will develop, grow, and function. Dr. Antony Flew, whose entire life was forever altered by the sheer magnitude of complexity he discovered and the rational implications presented through DNA research, said this: "The genetic message in DNA is duplicated in replication, and then copied from DNA to RNA in transcription . . . following this, there is translation, whereby the message from RNA is conveyed to the amino acids, and finally the amino acids are assembled into proteins."[22] As aptly described by world-class physicist Paul Davies, a gene is nothing but a set of coded instructions with a precise recipe for manufacturing proteins. How foolish it would be to deny God simply because man's finite mind cannot comprehend his infinite power and incomprehensible creativity.

The science of mankind cannot possibly understand unexplainable, supernatural events; therefore, many have concluded there is no creator, when the truth is that any open-minded observer should be able to recognize the many divine fingerprints that have been revealed throughout the universe. This world operates by the basic, uniform, natural laws—why is this? Why is the entire cosmos so orderly and dependable? There is certainly no logical necessity for you and me to expect a smart universe that consistently obeys defined laws, and especially the highly dependable laws of physics and mathematics. American theoretical physicist Dr. Richard Feynman, who won the coveted Nobel Prize in 1965 for his work in the field of quantum electrodynamics, has commented in this way: "Why nature is mathematical is a mystery; the fact that there are rules at all is a kind of miracle."[23]

The Holy Bible makes some very remarkable statements referring to scientific principles that are consistently at work in nature. As I have previously noted, many of these references pertain to natural processes that were not even verified by human discovery until the last century or two. Now, even though the biblical record was not written to address natural laws per se, it's clear statements about the many powerful forces that are at work in nature have been fully verified, and are found to be completely accurate as revealed by the ongoing advancement of empirical science.

Aside from the astonishing design and complexity found in nature, evolution is also quite powerless to explain the appearance of the remarkable functionality and necessity of two opposite sexes in many organic life-forms. We might also consider the ability of humans to make logical decisions based on reason, not to mention a vast array of complex emotional responses that includes romantic love, our universal need for interpersonal relationships, a strong drive to create music and beautiful works of art, and the desire to help and support friends and neighbors during life's most difficult times of personal crises. Naturally, most people have an overwhelming desire to find purpose and meaning for their daily lives, as well as sure hope for the future. The ideology of naturalism will leave people unfulfilled by not offering them the personal assurance of something to hope for beyond this life. I would submit that the remarkable design, order, and exceptional beauty found in nature required the purposeful intelligence, and the deliberate planning of an ingenious, inventive mind.

By utilizing many resources such as power, intelligence, creativity, and knowledge, a project engineer is able to formulate and construct a given design concept. However, another commanding force must be constantly at work to maintain, to preserve, and to sustain functional design once it has been thoroughly planned and constructed to its completion. When we consider the unlimited complexity of organic life, and all of the necessary chemical interactions that comprise multifaceted living organisms, it is hard to imagine how these chemical bonds could come together, all at the same time, simply by random chance alone apart from intelligent oversight. In addition to this design complexity, another indispensable force was essential to enable these elements to function as a viable living entity, and to maintain this complex order once the created design was successfully performing in the way that was intended. "You alone are the Lord; you have made heaven, the heaven of heavens with all their host, the earth and everything on it, the seas and all that is in them, and you *preserve* them all" (Nehemiah 9:6).

Believing in the unseen God is not a proposition of blind faith; it is logical faith, well supported by many known facts and finite details witnessed all around us. While the atheist will often invoke his or her own view of science as a reason to deny God, many open-minded scientists have related to us a much different story altogether. Having been thoroughly bombarded, for many years, by the compelling evidence of logic and design, as observed through current research findings, many of today's top-notch research scientists have initiated a radical shift in their own personal worldview, having finally reached a dead end with evolution theory.

The atheist has no reliable way of explaining the existence of an orderly universe. If he or she argues that matter is eternal, without cause, factual science would surely deny this claim based on the highly dependable laws of thermodynamics. These vital laws teach us that the universe had a beginning, and is gradually running down, like a giant toy that was tightly wound up. On the other hand, though, if the atheist acknowledges the fact that the universe indeed had a beginning, then his or her belief system must adequately account for an initial cause. In the final analysis, even though atheism strenuously objects to the existence of God, this belief system is unable to provide reliable answers regarding a logical explanation for the existence of human life.

The noted atheist Julian Huxley once said, "We are as much a product of blind forces as is the falling of a stone to the earth, or the ebb and flow of the tides. We have just happened, and man was made flesh by a long series of singularly beneficial accidents."[24] If you are inclined to reject Mr. Huxley's bold claim as I am, then I would submit instead that the current revealed evidence encourages us to embrace the idea that we are the purposeful and thoughtful intent of a supremely wise and benevolent designer.

Even the liberal writers of *Time* magazine have now been forced to admit that modern naturalism has often failed to adequately explain the emergence of the physical reality that surrounds us. We read, "In the quiet revolution in thought and argument that hardly anyone would have foreseen only two decades ago, God is making a comeback. Most intriguingly, this is happening . . . In the crisp intellectual circles of academic philosophers."[25] Buoyed by the powerful influence of Darwinism, scientific thought in the late nineteenth and early twentieth centuries certainly appeared to be leading mankind down the road of naturalism. In the perceived wisdom of the academic and scientific communities, public opinion alleged that the "god of the gaps" was finding himself in a niche that was becoming more and more narrow. Now, however, in the late twentieth and early twenty-first century, true science is now leading mankind in a completely new direction, a direction that is clearly pointing, once again, toward the more logical conclusion of design and purpose in the natural world. The current paradigm shift toward *theistic design* has been gaining momentum because of the unveiling of new data, which is now beginning to require that reluctant men and women must once again consider an explanation involving intelligence, an admission that science does not deal with very well.

As a result of many recent findings that strongly support special creation, numerous scientists finally admit to expressing a genuine belief in a creator God. Consider an especially revealing quotation penned by a staff writer from the *Wall Street Journal* in December of 1997. The journalist offered this startling remark after contemplating the degree to which science is now pointing its brightest minds in a very new and different direction. "I was reminded of this a few months ago when I saw a survey in the journal *Nature*. It revealed that 40 percent of American physicists, biologists, and mathematicians believe in God—and not just some metaphysical abstraction, but a deity, who takes an active interest in our affairs and hears our prayers: . . . The God of Abraham, Isaac, and Jacob."[26] This surprising, emerging new trend toward multiple worldview transformations within the scientific community serves to remind all of us that the more we discover about life and the universe, the more clearly we are pointed in the direction of a magnificent, loving God. As we follow the evidence wherever it would naturally lead us, the truth about the material world comes more and more sharply into focus. The remarkable degree to which the major constants of physics must match razor-sharp criteria in order to adequately explain our physical existence is causing great numbers of previously agnostic scientists to finally conclude that there has to be some sort of supernatural plan or Agency at work.

"God created everything by number, weight, and measure . . . In the absence of any other proof, the thumb alone would convince me of God's existence."[27] This is the conclusion of an iconic figure in the fascinating world of science by the name of Sir Isaac Newton, who is arguably the greatest scientist of all time. Now, let us consider a more contemporary, modern-day impression: "There is for me powerful evidence that there is something going on behind it all . . . It seems as though somebody has fine-tuned nature's numbers to make the universe . . . The impression of design is overwhelming."[28] This very influential statement comes to us once again from a present-day world-class scientist. British-born cosmologist Dr. Paul Davies is highly regarded as one of the greatest living physicists of our time; he was the winner of the 2002 Faraday Prize issued by the Royal Society and the 1995 winner of the Templeton Prize.

Consider, as well, these remarkably compelling statements from two other leading scientists of the twentieth century, both of whom are Nobel Prize winners. "Both religion and science require a belief in God. For believers, God is in the beginning, and for physicists he is at the end of all considerations. To the former he is the foundation, to the latter, the crown of the edifice of every generalized worldview."[29] This powerful statement comes from the German theoretical physicist Dr. Max Planck, who originated quantum theory, a discovery that won him the Nobel Prize for physics in 1918. Quantum theory has now revolutionized man's understanding of atomic and subatomic processes in the way Albert Einstein's theory of relativity greatly enhanced our understanding of space and time. Now commonly regarded as one of the most outstanding physicists of the last century, Dr. Planck is telling us that when arriving at the current apex of man's knowledge and understanding, we are ultimately forced to conclude that a very powerful unseen intelligence was actively at work in creating, empowering, and sustaining the physical universe. Dr. Antony Hewish is a British scientist and radio astronomer who was awarded the Nobel Prize for physics in 1974. Here is what he wrote about his personal inclination to believe in the powerful works of God: "The ghostly presence of virtual particles defies rational common sense, and is non-intuitive for those unacquainted with physics. Religious belief in God, and Christian belief that God became Man around two thousand years ago, may seem strange to common-sense thinking . . . But when the most elementary physical things behave in this way, we should be prepared to accept that the deepest aspects of our existence go beyond our common-sense intuitions."[30]

I believe that many honest men of science would like to express the need to look beyond nature for the answers they are seeking, if only constant peer pressure were not right there, holding them back. Consider this refreshing, whimsical comment from another American physicist, Dr. Tony Rothman: "When confronted with the order and beauty of the universe, and the strange coincidences of nature, it's very tempting to take the leap of faith from science into religion. I am sure many physicists want to. I only wish they would admit it."[31] The deeper we look into the marvelous mysteries of the natural world, the more convinced we are becoming that the signature of God is very clearly written in the remarkable complexity of living things__ a complexity that the greatest minds of history are unable to explain or even begin to comprehend.

The discipline of cosmology on an unimaginably colossal scale and the study of elementary particle physics on an inconceivably minute scale have methodically opened our finite minds to the spectacular splendor and astonishing precision of the remarkable universe in which we live. As what would seem to be insignificant specks of dust in a vast unknowable universe, how does one determine the value of a single human soul? By viewing our lives through the lens of creationism and a biblical worldview, we recognize that God sees every living soul as having infinite redeeming value. Many scientists, like Dr. Paul Davies, have now rejected the idea that we are unplanned and insignificant in the grand scheme of things. Davies once wrote, "I cannot believe that our existence in this universe is a mere quirk of fate, an accident of history, an incidental blip in the great cosmic drama. Our involvement is too intimate . . . We are truly meant to be here."[32] The rational intelligibility of the universe points us toward a transcendent and supernatural being that is responsible for creating and sustaining these uniquely complex physical elements. With this being said, and after civilized mankind has carefully investigated and thoroughly examined many of the unique phenomena observed in his vast and complex surroundings for so long, those who are sincerely seeking after the truth must now be willing to consider that the goal of true empirical science is essentially to discover what we can about God's grand design, and also determine, to some degree, how it works.

Observation: Religion and Morality

If evolution is true, how can we possibly account for the common-place expression religious faith? Many careful observers of human behavior have pointed to the fact that in nearly every human culture the world over is found a significantly religious element in terms of human expression. This spectacle demonstrates the innate tendency of man to worship and serve an intelligent power considered greater than, or at least more worthy than, himself. This common trend is found throughout the world, and only a few people have a real problem acknowledging a divine presence of some kind. What causes man to seek strength and wisdom from a source outside of him or herself? In cultures the world over, people are passionately religious. The evolution model certainly has no way of explaining this universal worldwide phenomenon. Just because this mortal life is all many of us know, doesn't mean that this is all there is.

People the world over are still asking the following questions: Who am I? Where did I come from? Why am I here? And where am I going? What I find very interesting is that atheism is rather uncommon in the underdeveloped nations of the world. This fact seems to be compelling evidence that no one was born an atheist. People must learn how to deny God's existence; it is not in human nature to lean this way naturally. Clearly, it has been the most highly developed nations that have conscientiously worked at promoting the anti-God theory of evolution through their education systems, and other public works programs that have been unknowingly designed to indoctrinate the masses. When we fully consider the powerful evidence demonstrated by the widespread reality of religion, faith, and worship, we can easily discern three major commonalities among people who practice such spiritual endeavor.

1. Everyone, with the exception of atheists and possibly agnostics, is inclined to practice some form of religion, worship, or to demonstrate some level of faith in an intelligence that they consider to be greater than themselves, or at least most worthy of their devotion and allegiance.
2. People tend to have a strong sense of morality, which helps to govern the way they act and the way they treat others; this stark reality consists of a predetermined set of moral values that they have often been unable to live up to.
3. Many of us are to some degree psychologically unsatisfied. The obvious unhappiness that some people experience is, perhaps, because they have hinged their sense of fulfillment on the wrong set of objectives. Aside from and in addition to their obvious emotional, physical, and material needs, humans have

a pressing hunger and a compelling desire for a genuine spiritual connection that will give lasting purpose and meaning to their lives. They want to know and in some way relate to the spiritual power they believe to be guiding their uncertain steps through an often difficult existence.

The reality of worldwide religious expression is strong evidence for the existence of the supernatural. There has become a movement among the so-called new atheists to label all religions as dangerous, evil, and immoral. I suspect this to be a knee-jerk reaction to the tragic events of September 11, 2001. Many have sought to universally discredit the exceptional worth of religious practice based upon the extremist views and actions of a few terribly deranged fanatics, who have wreaked havoc, terror and death upon innocent lives without remorse. To make such a broad negative judgment about all religions is a classic example of the desperation seen in today's determined atheists who have lost their footing in the great debate, and are left with only this sad overreach. To use an old cliché, these new atheists have "thrown the baby out with the bathwater"!

In spite of its flaws in times past when men of violence mistakenly believed they were fulfilling the will of God, an honest observer of history would have to admit that Christianity, in its true sense, is the very bedrock upon which Western civilization rests. It has also become a dependable foundation for the genuine cause of freedom and democracy in a very dangerous and hostile world that is forever plagued with religious persecution, extreme hatred, and unbelievable violence.

Another big problem for evolution is morality, which is difficult to make sense of in a world without God. The problem is that science has a difficult time when it comes to explaining why morality exists. For example, science can tell you that if you laced someone's food with cyanide, it would kill them. However, science cannot tell you if it is morally right or wrong to poison your spouse in order to collect the life insurance money. This would constitute an ethical question that is beyond the reach of science to consider. This is not to say that secular society does not observe moral values, which of course would not be true. However, you can't measure morality in a test tube. The atheist philosopher Mr. Bertrand Russell once wrote, "Whatever knowledge is attainable, must be attained by scientific methods; and what science cannot discover, man cannot know."[33] This strange statement is far from accurate in my view. There are many crucial questions that scientific inquiry cannot answer, or even begin to explore, and therefore, an outside source of information is required__ information such as revelation from God. Somebody had to set the standard for acceptable, as well as unacceptable, human behavior. Because of his self-serving goals, man is clearly not qualified to do that. This ethical insight must be provided by someone who is moral in nature and who is not self-seeking, but has extreme concern and devotion for the happiness and welfare of others. God is the one most qualified to define the proper ethical guidelines for humanity. He clearly represents the perfect standard of moral restraint and selfless generosity. If the evolution theory were true, where then did morality come from? Is morality something that is found in humanity because of the mindless work of natural selection? If all men were created in the image of the same eternal God, and all men were given a conscience to help govern life with respect to right and wrong, then this could explain why ethical values are largely universal within the human family, even among those who deny that God exists. How is man possibly able to consistently distinguish between what is right and what is wrong? With evolution, there is no one to set the ethical standards that define objective moral values. Atheism, as we understand it, could never provide man with a sound basis for determining what is good and what is evil, and, therefore, the theory cannot account for the ability all humans have to distinguish between good and bad behaviors. Apart from the very existence of Almighty God, who is the moral lawgiver and the perfect standard of absolute good, atheism can offer no rational explanation as to why moral values exist at all. Therefore, without God, there is no sure reference point for judging something to be good or evil. And there is very little doubt that certain well-defined moral principles exist in all human cultures.

Throughout history, in every human society that has ever been studied, researchers in the field of anthropology have found a deep and consistent understanding that certain selfish behaviors are deemed to be morally offensive, and thus, are determined to be damaging to human lives. They have found that hatred, lying, cheating, stealing, murder, rape, adultery, incest, and other harmful, self-centered actions are consistently seen as morally wrong in human cultures throughout the world. From where did this universal sense of right and wrong behavior come, if not from God? If man evolved from the apes as evolutionists have claimed, morality within the heart of man makes no sense; therefore, evolution is found powerless to explain why moral convictions are consistently found in every human culture. The only real explanation that makes any logical sense is that moral laws were given to mankind by a moral lawgiver. Guilt, shame, and remorse are the feelings we experience when we violate one of these moral laws. Why is this? This is because everyone has been given a moral conscience to help govern their lives with respect to what is right and wrong. When we choose to stubbornly disregard the clear warnings of our conscience, by ignoring that inner voice and acting upon our selfish impulses, the result is usually feelings of guilt and condemnation. These feelings are a stark reminder that we have violated a moral law established by a moral lawgiver to whom we are ultimately accountable. Evolution has no answer as to why we possess a moral conscience at all. Why do the people long for true justice and fairness and decency? Could it be because they were all created in the image of a just, fair, and decent God, who is extremely moral in character, and has created mankind in his own likeness? This, I believe, is the only sensible way to explain the very strong reluctance of man to recklessly engage in certain universally condemned behaviors.

I would say, without hesitation, that most of the people I have met would certainly agree that having sexual relations with another man's wife is morally reprehensible. Why? Could it be because the Holy Bible says, "Thou shall not commit adultery"? We feel violated when someone wrongs us in a way that is emotionally or physically painful; we feel the sting, because a moral law has been breached. Basic logic would suggest that there could be no moral law without a moral lawgiver. If evolution is true, and humankind is simply a higher form of animal life, human nature would surely be motivated solely by survival instinct (survival of the fittest), and there would be nothing to prevent you and me from acts of assault, theft, and even murder, if it improved our chance of survival. The well-known Oxford professor John Lennox, who has traveled and lectured extensively throughout the former Soviet Union, reports that the famous Russian writer and intellectual Fyodor Dostoyevsky is known to have said, "If God does not exist, everything is permissible!"[34]

Evolution can provide no moral reason to restrain from rape, robbery, or incest. I would even submit that objective moral values would be completely foreign in a nontheistic universe, and they certainly are difficult to explain in any other way. To say that as highly evolved primates, we have developed a sense of morality through an evolutionary process is a desperate stretch of sound reason. I remember recently watching a nature program on television that featured the nesting habits of a certain breed of penguins. The male penguins were observed gathering rocks to prepare a nesting area for the female, much like you would gather rocks to prepare a fire pit. I was very interested to observe that while some penguins were searching for more rocks to complete the nesting area, a few tuxedoed rascals would be stealing rocks that were previously gathered by others instead of finding their own. We know that penguins do not understand this behavior to be morally wrong. They are simply acting out their inborn survival instinct, and whatever it takes to survive is fair play to them. Not so with humans who must answer to each other and also to a higher power for the moral choices they have made.

When animals reproduce, the strong instinct for the survival of a species can be seen in the fact that nesting mothers will sometimes abandon or destroy one of their own offspring if it appears too small, weak, or infirm to some degree. In this way, the most hardy and robust-looking newborns, which would have the greatest chance for survival, are preserved. Aside from isolated historical events that have led to the sacrifice of infant children through very bizarre religious mandate, this is generally not the case with humans, who tend to possess a moral obligation to care for and preserve every life and will go to great lengths and great expense to do so. (Tragically, however, many humans have decided that it is somehow okay to destroy life prior to birth if they should determine the unborn to be inconvenient, unwanted, or defective!) This human morality, to a large extent, cannot be determined solely by the individual, or by the culture, because certain behaviors are objectively wrong in all cultures at all times. In the mind of Oxford professor John Lennox, "Everyone would agree that torturing babies is ethically and morally wrong." According to Professor Lennox, "Ethics involves top-down causation, and cannot be deduced from a bottom-up system of arguments."[35] In other words, having a clear sense of moral responsibility requires the input from an outside influence greater than man, and cannot logically be generated from the accidental manipulation of simple chemical elements in a closed universe. This is because the sovereign, eternal God, who has created mankind, has also provided for us the moral laws intended to govern our ethical behavior in a fallen world, and to keep us safe!

The human conscience is the active restraining force in the life of every individual. The atheist certainly can be moral, and do good, without question. At the same time, certain religious people can and sometimes are very immoral and corrupt. However, the actions of some, who are defiant, rebellious or perhaps fanatical, certainly do not negate the value of religious faith in those who are consistently faithful and extremely devout. Everyone has the capacity for good, because we were all created in the image of the same God, and we all possess a truly moral consciousness within. Even Richard Dawkins has agreed that "it is pretty hard to define absolute morals on anything other than religious grounds." However, he is also quick to add that "DNA is neither good nor bad; it just is, and we danced to its music."[36] If we are simply dancing to the direction of our DNA, when we do harm to others, how then, can we be considered evil? I would submit that our DNA has no control over our moral choices when we exercise free volition by imposing our selfish will upon others, at their expense. We must take the responsibility for our actions, and not attempt to blame them on something like "natural selection."

If we repeatedly violate and disregard the voice of conscience, we will eventually lose that healthy conviction toward certain behaviors that God has defined as morally offensive. Because of God's convicting moral laws, man is forced to face up to the problem of sin and to acknowledge that only God is in a position to do something about it. The crucifixion of Jesus is a definite fact of history that raises a very profound question—a question that each of us must eventually come to grips with: what was God doing on a Roman cross? The famous Russian dissident Alexander Solzhenitsyn explained it like this: "The line dividing good and evil cuts through every human heart including me. The cross of Jesus Christ not only gives me hope that evil will one day be conquered, it shows me that God loves me enough to deal radically with the guilt of my own heart, to forgive me, and give me a living relationship with him."[37] You and I will forever be challenged in our thinking by the starry heavens above us, as we grapple with the moral law within us. And our own moral consciousness toward right and wrong is neither subjective nor is it relative; moral truth within us far transcends the individual and his culture. This conviction within every human soul has a common source—a transcendent, moral lawgiver!

There are many liberal professors teaching at prestigious universities throughout America, and other nations, who are instructing their students to believe that there are no moral absolutes. I would submit that this flawed thinking is reckless, and a dangerous pattern of intimidation! The idea that morality is a subjective concept (open to personal interpretation) that should be custom fit to meet the desire of each individual has led to disastrous consequences, as we have witnessed throughout human history, and as we continue to observe in our world today. When a culture discards or begins to diminish and minimize the need for moral absolutes, that civilization is on a path of ethical decline that will lead to moral chaos and, if the trend goes unchecked, can eventually result in the loss of cultural identity. The existence of conscience, morality, and universally held values represents strong evidence for the reality of a morally righteous God, who created man to live under the powerful conviction of moral law. Without God, men become a law unto themselves, and who can say which person's set of values are the right ones.

Through the misguided teaching of evolution, man has created a god in his own image, a god that does not require moral accountability. This truth explains why evolution has been widely embraced by recent generations. Many have chosen to serve a man-made god, so their personal desires and private impulses are not subjected to moral restraint. We have a clearly defined legal system to help govern our society; but the truth of the matter is that our entire legal structure is based upon the moral standards that were given to us by the sovereign God of the Bible. If atheism is true, there will never be a single victim of moral terrorism who will ultimately have the satisfaction of seeing true justice prevail. Adolph Hitler, Joseph Stalin, Pol Pot, and Mao Tse-tung will have all gotten away with their heinous, repulsive acts of pure carnage against humanity! On the other hand, the Judeo-Christian heritage, which, in the course of time gave birth to civilized Western society, teaches us that justice will eventually prevail at the end of days, when humankind will finally face his eternal maker, and the scales of divine justice are ultimately balanced. I am convinced that without God-given values and sound, morally based principles there could never have become any sophisticated, civilized society.

In the early part of his distinguished career, Oxford mathematician John Lennox felt a compulsion to learn both Russian and German, and ultimately he would travel and lecture extensively in both of these influential countries. Dr. Lennox has reported some striking thoughts from a very prominent German philosopher by the name of Jurgen Habermas, whom he has quoted as making the following powerful statement about modern Western culture. "Christianity, and nothing else, is the 'ultimate foundation' of liberty, conscience, human rights, and democracy, the benchmarks of Western civilization."[38] This is certainly a remarkable confirmation of the extraordinarily positive influence that has been so clearly provided to the world by the historical footprint of Christian faith, in which a solitary figure in history provided the primary foundational influence upon which all of Western civilization rests.

When considering the question of morality, the atheist will often point directly at the existence of evil as a reason to deny God. After all, how could a moral God allow suffering and evil to exist in a world that he supposedly cares about? And why does there exist in people the uncanny ability to discern good from evil? Those who deny the very existence of God, and yet fail to adequately explain how humans can consistently make moral judgments, demonstrate the illogical nature of the atheist's belief system. Let's consider the following statement from business learning specialist Rolaant L. McKenzie, who explains, "It is impossible to tell the difference between good and evil in the absence of some reference point that is absolutely good. One cannot determine 3 inches from 4 inches without using a ruler as an absolute reference. One cannot determine actions to be good or evil, without an absolute moral standard. The very presence of evil actually demonstrates the existence of God rather than disproves it."[39] And therefore, we can confidently say that it is the very presence of any evil that fully illuminates for us the presence of goodness. The true atheist may also argue in this manner: if God exists, God is good, and he is all-powerful, then why does he not purge the world of evil? Atheists are so quick to reject the idea of God because of the presence of evil, pain, and suffering in the world. Rejecting God, however, is a very poor way of dealing with the tough problem of evil, pain and suffering, because it removes all hope, and still leaves the pain and suffering. With atheism, death is the end, no matter what you make of the pain and suffering that causes the innocent to die. Atheism removes the hope of a world without pain and death. It denies that the scales of divine justice will, ultimately, be balanced in the life to come.

Certainly all of us have experienced terrible pain, sorrow, suffering, and injustice at some time. It has touched every life, and will continue to impact our world until the end of this age. Instead of blaming God for all that is wrong in the world, we should actually stop to consider just why pain, death, and suffering are a part of the human story. Consider this quotation from the late C.S. Lewis, the British novelist, literary critic, and Christian apologist, who became famous for his fictional series of novels called the *Chronicles of Narnia*. "God created things with a free will—that means creatures, which can go either wrong or right. Some people think they can imagine a creature, which was free, but had no possibility of going wrong; I cannot! If a thing is free to be good, it is also free to be bad, and free will, though it makes evil possible, is also the only thing that makes possible any love or goodness or joy worth having."[40] When we, then, have considered all that God has done in creating mankind, at the emotional and moral levels, we must all agree that you could never have genuine love in a robotic universe. True, authentic love requires freedom of choice! God chose to make us, creating us in His image, and also empowering us as free moral agents. He did this because he wanted to experience a relationship with man that was based upon mutual love and respect. Yes, life is chocked full of jagged edges, with raw, inexplicable pain and suffering. This world is filled with broken bodies, broken hearts, and broken dreams, and unfortunately that's the reality of the earthly human experience. How could I ever explain to my adult son why his beautiful thirty-three-year-old wife, Amy, was tragically taken from him very suddenly by a brain aneurysm, leaving him with their infant son to raise alone? Nobody can offer an adequately comforting explanation to soften the blow from such an unexpected and devastating loss.

Some things in this life we cannot possibly explain, and obviously, we will never fully understand many of the *why* questions on this side of eternity; however, we can know for sure that our Heavenly Father is still in control, and His deep love for us will never change. We can and must, therefore, give an answer in response to the argument presented by the question of pain and evil in this world. If God were to abolish all evil in a single act, a major part of humanity would be instantly wiped out. Why is this? The answer can be found in our fallen nature, because we all possess within ourselves a compelling inclination to occasionally engage in behaviors that are morally wrong and very offensive toward God; these acts would include many self-centered behaviors that have also proven to be offensive toward one another. Therefore, man is and always has been the cause of evil in this world, and is solely responsible for the sad state of affairs that ill-advised and immoral choices have created all around us.

By contrast, evolutionists view humans as basically good and suggest that the inclinations of the human spirit should not be stifled by moral restraint. The Bible clearly teaches otherwise___ revealing that man was born with a sinful nature that often gravitates toward evil. In Ephesians 2:3, the Bible explains that by nature, we humans are the "children of wrath." Isaiah 64:6 has even compared the righteousness of man to "filthy rags" when measured against the perfect standard of a Holy God. Also, Jesus himself acknowledged the sinful nature of man when he said, "If you then, *being evil*, know how to give good gifts to your children, how much more will your Father who is in heaven give good things to those who ask Him! (Matthew 7:11). At first glance, most people would appear to be basically good, especially when their personal lives are measured strictly by broad human standards. However, when weighed against the absolute standard of a morally righteous and Holy God, we are not! And yes, God has adequately dealt with the problem of evil, pain and suffering, but He did it in a loving and merciful way that did not require the annihilation of unredeemed humanity.

Why are people so quick to blame God when things go terribly wrong? I suppose that is because they believe he has the power to change everything for the better, and they are right, he does! However, we seem never to be satisfied unless we receive instant gratification in response to our most urgent and pressing needs. But this is not usually how God works. The difficulties of life can result in bitterness toward Him in some people, but they can also lead us toward dependence on God in those things over which we have absolutely no control. It's all in a matter of how we choose to respond to the difficult challenges life will inevitably throw our way. Perhaps God wants to teach us something valuable, lasting and eternal through the many trials and burdensome obstacles we face on life's journey, like learning to depend upon his eternal Word, giving lasting purpose and meaning to our lives.

God's original creation was perfect in every way! Sin (man's selfish choice to rebel against God's authority) has, unfortunately, destroyed that original perfect world designed to be our eternal home. However, because of God's unspeakable love and compassion for humanity, he has already faithfully prepared and thoroughly carried out a flawless plan by which to restore unto mankind everything that was lost and forfeited through sin. By virtue of his own sacrificial death, Jesus has made the way for a complete restoration that will culminate in the fulfillment of God's divine plan and purpose for the ages.

For many years, researchers have observed and carefully studied human populations throughout the world; from these prudent observations, it has become quite clear that mankind possesses an inward awareness of an intelligent power greater than himself. We have reflected on the fact that some form of religion is found everywhere in the world. The universal belief in God, or some divine, unseen force or power, serves to demonstrate man's instinctive awareness of a supreme and majestic being that is able to elevate him above his pitiful circumstances. We have often seen this belief exhibited in young children, who naturally display an innate perception of God when they express words and actions of simple faith, thus demonstrating a unique awareness of his undeniable presence. The amazing ease with which small children are able grasp the concept of God suggests that the reality of his existence has been instilled in their innocent young lives from birth. "But God shows his anger from heaven against all sinful, evil men who push away the truth from them. For the truth about God is known to them *instinctively*; God has put this knowledge in their hearts" (Romans 1:18, 19 TLB).

We have also discussed the universal existence of the moral laws, values and principles that have served to govern the ethical behavior of people in all cultures. In a well-attended debate with Antony Flew in 1998, William Lane Craig, an American philosopher and a very capable Christian apologist, calmly proposed five powerful arguments for the existence of God. When he eloquently presented the obvious fact of the moral nature of man, he also offered this conclusion as related to objective moral values: "If God does not exist, then objective moral values do not exist."[41] As his argument continued, he explained that observations the world over clearly reveal that there are objective moral values, which are apparent in all human cultures—"therefore, a moral God exists!" The final conclusion we can and must draw (from evidence that clearly reveals morality in all human cultures) is that the religious nature and moral character that has been universally confirmed by the expressive behavior of humanity clearly serves to represent powerful evidence for the handiwork of a personal, unseen, sovereign God.

Observation of the physical world and the nature of man have given us a clear invitation to consider the reality of the unseen eternal God who created the universe and governs it with his sovereign power and divine authority. However, this has given us only a partial revelation of the super intelligence that has authored life in the physical dimension. In the following chapter, we will take a close look at the way in which a powerful creator God has personally revealed himself to his creation in specific ways that cannot be denied.

Chapter 8

THE REVELATION OF GOD

Revelation: Israel—Miracle Nation

Anyone who is aware of the unique history of the Jewish people will understand that God intervened in miraculous ways to establish, protect, and preserve this peculiar nation, whom he chose for a very special purpose. The story of the Hebrew nation is unlike the story of any other people that ever existed. The truth is that most of us living today cannot even remember a time when there wasn't a recognized state of Israel. However, before 1948 for nearly 1,900 years there was no such nation. A brief review of the history of the Jewish people will help us to understand just how God revealed himself to the world through this tiny miracle nation.

Through the great patriarchs Abraham, Isaac, and Jacob, God had established a divine covenant that would bring about great blessing to the whole earth and provided a plan by which he could restore fallen humanity to a right relationship with himself. The seed of the Jewish nation was planted in the heart of Abraham whom God chose, and through whom God had promised to fulfill covenant blessing in which Abraham's seed would become as the stars of heaven in number, and the land to which God was taking him would be given to his direct descendants through a divine promise. This irrevocable covenant of divine blessing was passed on to Abraham's miracle son Isaac who in turn bore two sons Jacob and Esau. The covenant blessing was passed to Jacob whose family included twelve sons. Through Jacob's sons God would ultimately establish the twelve tribes of Israel. Now, while Jacob was dwelling with his family in the land of Canaan, which God had promised to his descendants through Abraham and Isaac, by divine providence a severe famine came into the land and eventually forced the chosen ones to flee into Egypt where food provisions were still plentiful. The abundance of food in Egypt was due in large part to God's divine intervention in the life of Jacob's son Joseph, who had been sold into slavery in a cruel act of jealousy by his brothers and became an Egyptian captive. What was meant for harm in the life of Joseph, however, God ultimately meant for good in a commanding way that was to preserve many lives, who would have otherwise faced sure starvation. In Egypt, Jacob's tiny tribe became a strong nation of ambitious and energetic people. However, in the course of time, after many generations had passed, successive ruling pharaohs found themselves threatened by the strength and number of this new, emerging nationality within their borders. This fear resulted in the harsh captivity and oppression of God's people, as Israel became enslaved under the heavy hand of Egyptian rule. Eventually, however, after centuries of bondage, God sent Moses to deliver Israel from their oppression. They were eventually able to escape the cruel hand of pharaoh by a series of miraculous events God displayed through Moses.

By these many miraculous signs and wonders, God profoundly demonstrated his power to preserve and protect his chosen people. The decisive blow became the death of the first born of Egypt, which, at last, released the cruel grip of pharaoh upon the Jewish captives. With Moses leading them, the Hebrew nation escaped the land of Egypt, and a miraculous parting of the Red Sea into which the fearsome army of pharaoh was completely destroyed, had finally broken the power of Egypt over the fleeing refugees. Israel proceeded as one nation across the barren desert wilderness toward the land that had already been promised to them by God through their patriarchal father Abraham.

In their difficult migration across the hot desert, this Hebrew band was miraculously led by a cloud during the daytime and a pillar of fire at night, as they made their way through the harsh, dry, empty land. The powerful hand of God upon their lives was unmistakable, as by heavenly intervention divine providence afforded one miracle after another during their long, arduous journey through the bleak and barren wilderness. These miraculous signs offered safety, protection, and provision for the wandering Jewish refugees. Almighty God was preparing this tiny nation to be the instrument through which he would reveal himself in great detail to the whole earth. They were fed manna from heaven, drank fresh water that sprang from the rocks, and their clothes and sandals did not wear out during the long, grueling trek across the empty wasteland. God's law, delivered to them through his faithful servant Moses, would eventually shape the character of this people, making them into his great messenger of hope to a fallen world. After forty years of wandering in the desert during which God was preparing his chosen people, they were finally allowed to enter the Promised Land where God gave them great victories over the heathen nations who were opposing them. These adversaries, whom they were able to defeat by a firm reliance upon a miracle-working God, had comprised the nationalities that occupied Israel's inheritance during their prolonged and difficult captivity in the land of Egypt. In the centuries that followed, God gave his people many prophets and judges and kings. He blessed them when they obeyed him, and he disciplined them when they refused. And unto them alone were entrusted the oracles of God (the biblical revelation), as this tiny Hebrew nation began to faithfully receive, record, maintain, and meticulously preserve God's written revelation comprising his eternal message of hope and promise to humanity. This was truly a message of divine origin intended as a priceless gift of knowledge and understanding to be shared abroad throughout the entire world for the beneficence of all humankind.

Finally, in the fulfillment of God's promise to Abraham, the Messiah, Jesus, was miraculously born into the world to deliver the people from their sins. These sins were the cause of the terrible curse of death that had brought sorrow, grief, and despair upon the whole earth, and had alienated man from a personal relationship with his Creator as in the beginning of God's original plan for humanity.

For the most part, the Jewish people rejected Jesus as their promised Messiah, and for this they paid a dreadful price. God would ultimately bring severe judgment upon them at the hand of their enemies when the brutal Roman legions proceeded to thoroughly destroy and remove their sacred temple, the Jewish commonwealth, and a very dynamic civilization that had long endured since the days of Moses. They were all scattered throughout the world in the Great Diaspora that lasted almost two millennia. However, on May 14, 1948, a remnant of Hebrew nationals would once again declare their sovereign independence after being restored to their beloved homeland (the land promised to their forefathers by God himself). The Jews had finally become a self-governing and independent nation once again. Never before in the entire history of planet earth, has any single nationality of people been so thoroughly demoralized, devastated, and utterly forsaken as Israel was. Yet somehow, through all their traumatic turmoil, which culminated in the dreadful Holocaust, they were miraculously able to maintain their national identity as a unique people who never stopped longing to return to their promised inheritance. The Hebrew tongue became a discarded language but, astonishingly, it has been revived once again and restored to the Jewish people against insurmountable odds. The nation Israel, whom the Almighty had divinely chosen to bring the whole earth back to the worship of the one true God, was and still is a miracle nation. The unique and very fascinating history of Israel (the Jewish people) was orchestrated and sustained by the miraculous power of the true and living God and demonstrates unmistakable, and very compelling evidence for the existence of a powerful supreme being, a divine presence who has very unpredictably, but quite thoroughly, revealed himself to a skeptical and unbelieving world.

Revelation: What about the Bible?

Man cannot understand a supreme intelligence that dwells outside the physical realm, unless that intelligence has chosen to reveal himself. It would certainly be necessary for man to discover greater detail about a personal God than he can possibly know by observation of the natural, created world alone. We understand that because of man's exalted position in God's eternal plan, the Creator has gone to great lengths to make himself personally known. We have understood this only in a general sense by observing the amazing works of his creative power. In order to relate to a personal God in the way it was originally intended, we need much more than just a general revelation of who the Creator is. The very basic knowledge of God, which we are able to glean from our personal observation of the created world, tells us nothing about the depths of his love, grace, mercy, compassion, and forgiveness, for example. Therefore, God has clearly chosen to disclose a much greater revelation of himself through a personal written record, including detailed information about his plan and purpose for humanity throughout the dispensations of time that include the past, present, and future.

For an infinite God to reveal himself adequately to feeble mankind, he would surely have to say and do things that are completely foreign to the normal, mundane experiences of human life. This he most certainly accomplished when he openly performed many miracles, fulfilled countless ancient prophecies written centuries before his miraculous incarnation, and publicly unveiled to first-century witnesses the greatest miracle in recorded human history—when Jesus of Nazareth became the central figure in the most monumental event ever chronicled in the annals of mankind—the resurrection.

The Holy Bible, which was once and for all time delivered to us through the miracle nation Israel, has provided humanity with a very profound understanding of who the living God of heaven really is, and what he has done for all of us through his love without limit for mankind. In these inspired writings, the Holy Spirit has revealed to us much more detail and knowledge regarding the character and nature of the sovereign Creator of the universe.

Among other things, the biblical record serves as God's autobiography. It has offered us a thorough accounting of his divine personality and character, including everything he has provided for humankind and many important details about his plan and purpose for the ages. Let us consider, for just a moment, those uniquely divine attributes that have been so clearly revealed to us in the biblical text, which all serve to represent God's great transcending nature as the eternal sovereign of the universe—the One who has set the laws of nature into motion, but has never been limited or restricted in any way by those laws. The Bible clearly credits the God of Israel with having eight fundamental qualities or divine attributes that are known to no other being in existence in either the physical or spiritual realm.

1. God is omnipotent (all powerful) (Revelation 19:6).
2. God is omniscient (all knowing) (Hebrews 4:13).
3. God is omnipresent (everywhere present) (Proverbs 15:3).
4. God is infinite (without beginning or ending) (Psalm 90:2).
5. God is perfect (without character flaw) (Matthew 5:48).
6. God is immutable (not subject to change) (Malachi 3:6).
7. God is holy (unable to look upon sin with approval) (Leviticus 19:2).
8. God is sovereign (without equal and supreme in authority) (Exodus 8:10).

God is life, energy, and personality, having unlimited authority over his vast creative works. He is the ultimate judge to whom all of humankind remains accountable. Men and women would be wise if they were to humbly reverence and fear him, instead of trying to explain away the reality of his existence with some irrational theory that is actually designed to exalt man and to advocate for the supremacy of mankind. We know that no mortal man will ever fully comprehend the magnificence of the Creator. The remarkable ingenuity, creativity, and resourcefulness of Almighty God is far beyond the comprehension of the most brilliant of the world greatest minds, even if they are open to his truth, although many are not. The message of the Bible is so often found to be counterintuitive to the way man is inclined to think and act. For example, we are admonished to "love our enemy," to "turn the other cheek," to "walk by faith and not by sight," We are encouraged to "give and it will be given unto you." Man has always been inclined to believe that an all-powerful God should simply rid the world of evil and everything will be just fine. However, God has always been more interested in ridding our self-centered hearts of sin than in taking away our freedom of choice (the very thing that ultimately led to a sinful, corrupt and dying world). As C. S. Lewis famously suggested__ choice allows for both good and evil, but without it there could never be anything remotely resembling the kind of love worth having. "For my thoughts are not your thoughts, neither are your ways my ways, says the Lord. For as the heavens are higher than the earth, so are my ways higher than your ways, and my thoughts than your thoughts" (Isaiah 55:8, 9).

Although most people are sensible enough to refrain from denying the existence of God, it is apparent that our meager knowledge and understanding of him is limited by what he has chosen to reveal to us about himself. "God's ways are as mysterious as the pathway of the wind, and as the manner in which a human spirit is infused into the little body of a baby, while it is yet in its mother's womb" (Ecclesiastes 11:5 TLB). "The secret things belong unto the lord our God; but those things which are revealed belong to us and to our children forever . . ." (Deuteronomy 29:29). Of course, we cannot understand the great miracles of God that have defied the laws of nature! However, if the God of the Bible is the true author of the physical laws that govern the universe, then why would it seem so odd to us if he should choose to transcend those laws, which he himself has ordained?

In addition to his many unique attributes of deity, the sovereign God of heaven also possesses many noble characteristics that are found to be common to mankind as well. These character qualities of God Almighty were infused into humankind when Adam was created in the image and likeness of his Maker. Characteristics that are common

227

to both God and man would include the personal attributes found in the expression of emotional feelings and relational behaviors like love, compassion, mercy, forgiveness, grace, joy, generosity, sorrow, sympathy, kindness, hope, and trust. These and many other distinctively human character traits were given by divine authority and are found to be generally nonexistent, or at least drastically limited, in the aggressive and instinctively driven world of the animal kingdom, to which evolutionists have mistakenly assigned humanity.

We find that some worldviews would suggest there are many sovereign gods inhabiting realms of authority in the universe or possibly another universe. The God of the Bible would flatly deny this erroneous claim! "I am the Lord, and there is no other, there is no God besides me: I will gird you, though you have not known me" (Isaiah 45:5). "Remember the former things of old, for I am God and there is no other; I am God, and there is none like me" (Isaiah 46:9).

"You are my witnesses, says the Lord, and my servant whom I have chosen, that you may know and believe me, and understand that I am He. Before me there was no God formed, nor shall there be after me" (Isaiah 43:10). The true God of the Bible is a jealous God who will never share his Glory with any imagined, superficial, or false deity. Now, we observe that most of the world's religions advocate some form of written documentation to direct their devoted followers, but the Holy Bible is uniquely different from all others and it stands apart as the complete, inspired, inerrant revelation that the Holy Spirit of God has faithfully addressed to all humankind. Only the Bible demonstrates abundant evidence that it stands alone as the Word of God, and is able to back this claim for many valid and undeniable reasons.

It was certainly not dropped from the sky like some falling object, but God-breathed and thoroughly infused with divine power, knowledge, and purpose as he has painstakingly communicated his thoughts and intentions to human writers who have faithfully recorded and preserved them. The amazing and very powerful evidence that strongly supports the Bible alone as the eternal Word of a personal, loving God will be more thoroughly addressed in the book's epilogue section. However, we should consider here that a book with such a diverse and unique history, which is able to demonstrate an amazing unity throughout its many pages, can only be adequately described as the sovereign work of a powerful, purposeful God who was determined to reveal life transforming truth to his crowning creation.

The Holy Bible has presented to man a unified, internally consistent message proclaiming one grand central theme: *redemption*! Redemption has revealed God's love for mankind and the amazing lengths to which he was willing to go to demonstrate that love! It was compiled over 1,600 years by forty different writers in three languages and penned by a diverse group of faithful men on three separate continents, most of whom did not even know one another. And yet the Bible demonstrates remarkable unity and astonishing continuity throughout its many compiled books, suggesting that one single guiding influence orchestrated all of it. Feeble mankind could never have compiled such a book through personal will and intention. This stark reality will become much more evident to the reader at the end of this book, where many of the divine characteristics revealed in Scriptures will be more thoroughly explored. The Holy Scriptures certainly represent to mankind a very unique and compelling proof of our Creator's existence!

No other written material that was penned on this earth can be defined by such remarkable, prophetic details that were written many hundreds of years before the events they describe were so clearly and decisively fulfilled. Only the sovereign, omnipotent, and all-knowing God of heaven could make that happen. How else can we possibly explain thousands of detailed facts of history that have been recorded so far in advance of the events they have unmistakably described?

As opposed to evolutionary assumption, which relies primarily on blind faith in unguided processes, the Bible maintains that the physical elements came into existence out of nothing—but at the command of intelligent cause. Earlier, I alluded to the fact that some well-intended authorities and investigators have now attempted to incorporate evolutionary teaching into the biblical narrative. This effort is the result of a determined attempt to satisfy everyone, and to somehow quell an imagined conflict between science and religion. This accommodation has required a very loose interpretation of Scripture where anyone is free to determine what was intended as allegory and what is literal truth. This compromising position on the part of well-meaning scientists, philosophers, and educators certainly does not constitute an accurate discernment of Scripture and should be widely condemned and rejected.

We must be careful not to misinterpret the intended meaning of scripture. The biblical narrative was meant to be interpreted just like any other written document; in which case, the basic rules of literary interpretation and grammar will require us to accept the biblical framework as literal and factual, unless obvious symbolism was intended. For example, Jesus said, "I am the door." This short phrase is clearly a metaphor, but it represents something very real about his role as it relates to you and me. In the Psalms we find these words: "the earth shall not be moved." This does not mean that the earth is stationary in space, but that the earth is stable and consistent in its rotation and movement through the solar system. Therefore, we should be reminded once again that we dare not accept multiple millions of years of death and struggle, and add it to the Bible without destroying the message of the cross. The biblical record clearly states that death has come upon this planet as a consequence of man's sin. "Therefore, just as through one man sin entered the world and death through sin, and thus death spread to all men, because all (have) sinned" (Romans 5:12). The true message of the cross is that the ravages of death and decay will ultimately be reversed, and not only for those who have placed their hope in the atonement resulting from Christ's sacrifice, but for all of nature and the entire whole of creation as well. "For the creation was subjected to futility . . . because [of Jesus Christ] the creation itself also will be delivered from the *bondage of corruption* into the glorious liberty of the children of God" (Romans 8:20, 21). You and I must, therefore, get back to accepting the literal authority of the Word of God as the primary basis for our thinking if we are to have any hope of ever fully understanding the magnificent "mystery of life".

Many puzzling questions have been considered in man's effort to fully comprehend the mysterious nature of God; and certain aspects of God's divine character and willful purpose, as revealed in the Bible, will no doubt run contrary to human logic and basic reasoning. As a consequence, the strange paradox of God's mysterious character is often used as a reason to deny him, when it is actually very strong evidence affirming the reality of his existence. We must ask ourselves again, how could God be superior to men if mankind was able to fully comprehend every aspect of his divine nature? If the Bible reveals something about the Creator we cannot grasp with our intellect or perhaps something that we object to on moral grounds, we should accept it by faith, rather than attempting to explain it away or to deny God altogether, based on some weak-minded human reasoning. For example, we hear many people complain that the Old Testament narrative of the Bible records human carnage on an unprecedented scale and that God condoned the violence. Many people find it hard to get past this, so they judge God as evil and hateful. I believe these people fail to understand the big picture of what God was attempting to accomplish through the nation Israel. We must keep in mind that God's ultimate goal for the human souls he created in his own image was to reveal his love to them in providing a means of redemption so that fallen humanity could ultimately return to a right-standing relationship with him and become a part of his eternal family. Because of man's free volition, he has always had the capacity to choose either good or evil. All men are morally culpable before their Maker. Now, because real love and relationship requires free choice, God knew that evil was not only possible but inevitable as a consequence of poor choices. In fact, the choices of mankind became so evil in the Old Testament that on one occasion God destroyed everything he had made save Noah's family. "The Lord saw that the wickedness of man was great in the earth, and that every intent of the thoughts of his heart was only evil continually. And the Lord was sorry that He had made man on the earth, and He was grieved in His heart" (Genesis 6: 5, 6).

To establish a chosen nationality through whom God could reveal himself to the whole world, it was critical that Israel become a separated people unto God who would not become polluted by the heathen practices of many other ancient tribes around them. The wickedness and idolatrous practices in the land of Canaan had become so depraved that God could not allow this terrible evil to infect the children of Israel or His plan to redeem humanity would be thwarted. The depravity of sexual immorality in Sodom and Gomorrah, for example, had become so corrupt that God chose to destroy those cities with fire from heaven because the inhabitants refused to repent of their evil deeds. The Canaanite tribes, who occupied Israel's inheritance during their long captivity in Egypt, had become so depraved that they commonly practiced bestiality, incest, and even child sacrifice to their gods of stone. Deviant sexual behaviors became the norm in heathen cultures that had become so defiled that God said, "The land vomits out its inhabitants" (Leviticus 18:25). These vile abominations had even approached the level of depravity that caused God to send the universal flood to destroy mankind in the days of Noah. If you go to a doctor who discovers that you have cancer, the doctor will say we must remove it or you could die. Are you going to have the doctor remove all of the cancer or just most part of it? There was a cancer in the land of Canaan when the children of Israel returned from captivity and God instructed them to remove it lest they should become like the heathen nations that surrounded them, which would bring failure in their national calling to represent the true character of God to a sick and dying world. The Canaanite tribes were given over four hundred years to repent of their wickedness, and they refused. Therefore, God used the ensuing conquest of Canaan to generate the historical context and religious climate that would allow him to ultimately introduce the promised Messiah to the whole world, offering salvation to all men, including Israel's enemies. Therefore, God our Creator has revealed to us everything that our feeble minds can possibly comprehend, and it's more than enough to find fulfillment in this life and the next through a satisfying personal and ongoing relationship with him.

The Holy Spirit of God has wisely revealed to our inquisitive minds that "we can see and understand only a little about God now, as if we were peering at his reflection in a poor mirror; but one day we are going to see him in his completeness, face to face. Now, all that I know is hazy and blurred, but then, I will see everything clearly, just as clearly as God sees into my heart right now" (1 Corinthians 13:12 TLB). The many supernatural aspects of the biblical text make it very obvious to me that a supremely intelligent and benevolent Creator has intentionally revealed himself to fallen humanity. Yes, you and I can be absolutely certain that the powerful evidence revealed in God's written revelation of the Bible clearly confirms and validates the reality of his eternal existence. There is no other way to explain the remarkable supernatural material of the biblical text, which is far beyond the intellectual capacity of man to knowingly record in and of his own willful intent. The extraordinary reality of the biblical revelation must be considered a most impressive and overwhelming evidence for the existence of the personal, all-powerful, and loving God who created us! Please refer to the epilogue section for more thorough detail regarding the reasons we can trust the authenticity of the Bible as the revealed Word of God.

Revelation: The Incarnation

We know that God has instilled in man an awareness of himself. He has made himself known by the beauty and splendor of nature and the extremely complex design of the universe. He provided mankind with a healthy conscience to govern his response to established moral laws intended to protect him from choices that would do harm to himself and those around him. The sovereign Lord of creation has made himself well known in all the earth through the impressive historical record of his chosen people, Israel. The God of creation has also revealed himself in great detail through the divinely inspired pages of the Holy Bible. And finally, and most amazing of all, God has completed the revelation of himself through the person of his Son, Jesus Christ.

To many people, the Word of God has remained systematically vague. It's only when we look at the person of Jesus Christ that we find God's Word coming into clear focus and making perfect sense. The most astonishing revelation God has ever given to us of himself was the day he stepped out of eternity, passing through the veil between heaven and earth, to clothe himself in human flesh, becoming one of us. In so doing, he subjected himself to all the pain, sorrow, suffering, and grief commonly faced by humanity. By this single world-altering event, God has faithfully demonstrated a love without limits for his *crowning creation*. He had truly withheld nothing when he subjected his Son to public humiliation, and the most horrible death imaginable on a cruel Roman cross—to finally prove once and for all time that the *redemption of mankind* was and is the compelling motivation that drives the heart of God.

Jesus Christ, the Son of God, was much more than a great moral teacher or prophet. He said many things that would be considered totally outrageous if they were not true, and then he backed up his words with miraculous signs, proving his divine nature to all those willing to follow him. He basically said to his followers, "If you do not want to believe what I'm telling you (that I am the way, that I and the Father are one), then you should at least believe me based on the many miracles you have seen" (John 14:11, paraphrase). When God took the form of man, faced the hardships, trials, and temptations we all face, and ultimately accepted, by his humiliating death on the cross, the punishment that was due for our transgressions, he proved beyond any doubt his unspeakable love for humanity.

This passionate love for image-bearing mankind is something that we can barely comprehend! And of all the many religions throughout world history, only in Christianity, through the life and work of Jesus Christ, do we see God reaching out to man, and providing a sure way for us to be reconciled to a right relationship with our Creator. We can be entirely certain that God will never force us to believe in him, but it must be understood that he has provided us with more than enough proof to validate his existence. He has also given us an understanding of the unselfish motivation that led to his voluntary and sacrificial death. The great hope of God Almighty is that those, whom he has lovingly created in his own image, would ultimately recognize the unspeakable sacrifice (his atonement for sin) that was once and for all time offered on their behalf, and that they would willingly accept and gladly embrace this conciliatory and overwhelming demonstration of unconditional love.

The so-called new atheists have quite often professed to be genuinely interested in what the current scientific evidence has revealed, but their follow-through on any major commitment suggests a different story altogether. Richard Dawkins, Christopher Hitchens, and others have believed and have taught that the historical evidence for the life of Jesus Christ is still in dispute. This unwarranted attack on the very core doctrine of Christian theology has been decisively and unequivocally refuted. The eminent British archaeologist and ancient-literature specialist Sir Grahame Clark, who was a longtime professor at the University of Cambridge, has written this definitive statement: "Frankly, I know of no ancient historian, who would have a twinge of doubt about the existence of Jesus Christ—the documentary evidence is simply overwhelming."[1] And according to Dr. Gary Habermas, author of *The Historical Jesus*, there are no less than twenty different non-Christian written sources that have documented important details of the life of Christ. When these details are all put together, they provide enough information to give us a reasonable outline of the life of Jesus without ever touching the New Testament.

The Bible claims Jesus to be God on numerous occasions. "In the beginning was the Word, and the Word was with God, and the Word was God . . . and the Word became flesh and dwelt among us . . . (John 1:1, 14). Jesus proclaimed, "He who has seen me has seen the Father" (John 14:9). "I and My Father are one" (John 10:30). And, "Before Abraham was, I Am" (John 8:58). The fact that so many of his unbelieving listeners wanted to kill him was proof of their understanding that Jesus was claiming to be God. By fulfilling hundreds of prophecies concerning the coming messiah, as well as always backing his genealogy with miraculous signs and wonders, he has offered us the perfect credentials to support his claim of deity. Jesus was God in human flesh. There is no question about it! Everything he said and did strongly support the fact! He has faithfully provided everything we need to know about God and he has withheld nothing, including his own life. Jesus Christ was and is the ultimate proof of God's existence!

In addition to the powerful evidence I have already cited, we are compelled to consider, with great reverence, the grand finale in God's historical revelation of himself to mankind. This occurred when Jesus Christ rose from the grave triumphant over death as he promised he would. How can we possibly explain a death-defying miracle like the resurrection using human logic and reasoning? One thing we know for sure is that the God of heaven is not a prisoner of his own established physical laws of nature. The many miracles recorded in Scripture are certainly not a matter of science, but simply a matter of the ancient historical record that was faithfully documented and passed down to each generation. Since an all-powerful creator God would never be limited by the various laws he himself ordained to govern the physical realm, he can also choose to supersede those established laws and to interject divine power into the human experience whenever he chooses to do so. The great resurrection miracle required a colossal input of divine power as characterized by a deliberate overriding of natural law by a purpose-driven, omnipotent Creator. This single event in human history was the absolute and, ultimately, the God-given guarantee offered to humanity as evidence to validate the Christian faith. The literal bodily resurrection of Jesus is the final victory over death, and represents the most compelling proof that could ever be cited to confirm God's existence! This indisputably verifiable fact of history provides us all with the greatest confirmation yet that we live in a natural world that is continually subject to remarkable supernatural events at God's discretion, and in response to human need. The resurrection of Jesus Christ represents the ultimate wonder of Christian faith and theology. Without this single, miraculous, and very well-documented historical event, there would never have been a faith-filled Christian community as we now observe it throughout the world. Christianity has forever won its place in history by virtue of the sheer weight of evidence confirming that Jesus had actually risen from the dead in a world-altering event.

Scientific research and investigation cannot tell us if the resurrection of Christ was possible, but the revealed evidence complied over the centuries can and has established whether this event actually took place in recorded human history. The resurrection of the Lord Jesus Christ is a well-established event in the historical record, which has been judicially proven and quite thoroughly confirmed, far beyond any reasonable doubt, resulting in widespread religious zeal the world over.

When the apostle Paul wrote to the Corinthian church regarding the resurrection, he said, "If Christ is not risen, your faith is futile; you are still in your sins" (1 Corinthians 15:17). This astonishing miracle, which offers the entire world the central evidence to validate Christianity, has subsequently led to the committed and uncompromising faith of many millions worldwide. When Jesus entered into the time-space-material dimension, he showed us exactly who God is and he opened wide for us the doorway to heaven, so that all of us might have the opportunity to live with, and relate to our Creator forever in the kind of mutual love relationship God had originally intended.

If a person came into the lives of ordinary people, like you and I, claiming to be the Son of God and the Savior of the world, how could this person convince mankind of his true identity? What could this individual possibly do that would set him apart from every other self-proclaimed messiah that the world has ever known?

1. Perhaps he could say incredible things, such as the words spoken in the Sermon on the Mount, which would generate a large public following.

2. Perhaps he could perform many breath-taking miracles in the presence of eyewitnesses—incredibly mystifying supernatural acts such as healing the sick, casting out demons, walking on water, and the most fascinating supernatural feat of all, raising the dead.

3. Perhaps he could accurately fulfill hundreds of ancient prophecies that were recorded centuries before his appearance— detailed predictions that would clearly serve to identify the true messiah spoken of and meticulously documented by the great prophets of the Old Testament.

4. Perhaps he could accurately read the hearts and minds of those whom he was attempting to reach in his effort to reveal the will of God.

5. Perhaps he could predict the future as a genuine prophet in his own right.

6. Perhaps he could demonstrate an unconditional love and compassion for mankind that would be unprecedented in all of recorded human history.

7. Perhaps he could reveal many astounding things about the true nature and character of his Father in heaven with whom he communed daily.

8. Perhaps he could set aside his own personal interests and choose instead to go the distance in fulfilling the purpose of his Father by willingly laying down his pure and innocent life for the salvation of others.

9. Perhaps he could rise up from the dead and actually appear before his followers and other eye witnesses on multiple occasions, demonstrating that he came from beyond this world, that what he said was true, and that death could not hold back his life-giving power.

10. Perhaps he could ascend up into heaven in the presence of his disciples, thus offering the final confirmation of who he was, and establishing for all time the reality of his divine nature.

Every one of these credentials was demonstrated in the life of one solitary figure. Jesus drastically set himself apart from all other men in a shortened lifetime, when he lived and moved among the occupants of ancient Israel during the first century. And without the massive communication system that is now in place by virtue of mankind's ongoing scientific and technological achievement, Jesus left a powerful impression on human lives that has literally transformed the course of human history. What this single man said and did, in three short years of public ministry, has served to alter forever the direction and course of humanity by drastically transforming the civilized world.

I ask you to consider the following question very carefully: what else could a personal, loving creator God possibly do for humanity that would better reveal his existence to a mundane, three-dimensional, material world and, while doing so, fully demonstrate his intense compassion and unconditional love for fallen humanity? Jesus was and is God! He has loved every member of the sinful human race. And he proved this by his miraculous birth. He proved it by his history-altering life, and ultimately, he proved it by a brutal, voluntary, sacrificial death, followed by an astonishing and world-transforming resurrection.

Leaders of some major religious movements throughout human history__ like Buddha, Mohammed, and Confucius__ have all identified themselves as merely teachers or prophets. Only Jesus claimed to be God! When we seriously examine his history-altering life, take a hard look at his precise fulfillment of messianic prophecy, and honestly consider his earth-shaking resurrection from the dead, it becomes obvious that he had the necessary credentials to back that claim. Jesus never said to his audience that they must follow a set of rules or guidelines to find the truth. He said, "Follow me" (Matthew 9:9). "I am the light of the world, he who follows me will not walk in darkness" (John 8:12). "I am the way, the *truth*, and the life. No one comes to the Father except through me" (John 14:6). By these statements he inferred that in following him one would find the strength, motivation and conviction necessary to obey the laws of God, such as those established in the long revered Ten Commandments.

Jesus did what no other man ever could have done. He performed many astonishing miracles to verify his claim of deity. He fulfilled hundreds of prophecies recorded many centuries before by the inspired writers of the Old Testament. And he was miraculously resurrected from the dead, proving to everyone that even the physical laws of nature could not hold back his divine, life-giving power. Jesus was the total embodiment of deity, who voluntarily left the spirit world behind to fully reveal the heart of his Father to fallen humanity. "For in Him dwells all the fullness of the Godhead bodily" (Colossians 2:9). "No one has seen God at any time. The only begotten Son, who is in the bosom of the Father, He has declared Him" (John 1:18).

Humanity has been inclined to worship this Jesus of Nazareth. Why is this? I believe it is because, in him, we find the complete revelation of the very God of Israel, the sovereign Creator of the universe, the purpose-driven Savior of the world, and the One who promised that some future day he would return in glory to forever be with those who love him.

When God the Father sent his only Son into the world, he was revealing himself to humanity in the most personal way possible. By doing so, he left no doubt whatsoever that the intent of his heart was to fully and forever redeem the fallen ones. God's passionate and deliberate plan to become affectionately and intimately known to his *crowning creation* was the driving force leading to the crucifixion that personally demonstrated the unrelenting and everlasting love he has for each and every human soul.

Revelation: The Church of God

The worldwide Christian community is very powerful evidence that God did not remain distant from human suffering, but became part of it to an extent that we can never fully understand. The message of the church is that God loves us beyond human comprehension, and he has demonstrated that love by providing a means (the atonement) by which the penalty for sin could be forgiven for each individual who ultimately places his or her faith in the completed work of the cross (the decisive reason why God became a man). Those who have believed in what God did for humanity to address the problem of sin have subsequently entered into a personal relationship with their Creator, a relationship that enables them to spend eternity with the sovereign Lord of the universe, and not because they deserve it, but only because of God's grace and unfailing love. It is that personal experience with God, through this genuine heartfelt relationship, that has given millions of people the world over hope for a new and unimaginable life beyond this one, far transcending any optimism of carnal human expectation. Therefore, another overpowering and very note-worthy evidence for the existence of God can be found manifest in the simple lives of ordinary people who have responded in believing faith to the words of Jesus, when he declared, "I say to you, he who hears My word and believes in Him who sent Me has everlasting life, and shall not come into judgment, but has passed from death into life" (John 5:24). This big wide world is full of people who have believed in their hearts that Jesus was eternal God in human flesh, and that what he said was and is divine truth. They have believed in the many promises of God as revealed in his eternal Word, have repented of their sins, and have ultimately received the certain forgiveness that was made available to them by the death of Jesus Christ on a cruel Roman cross. Subsequent to the final atonement for sin on the cross, humanity received the absolute confirmation of his divine mission to rescue mankind when Christ rose up triumphantly from the grave three days later in a well-documented, supernatural event that has never been refuted. In believing this truth, many millions of lives have been remarkably transformed from the inside out, changing them into the people God created them to be.

The world-famous Reverend Billy Graham served his generation as a world-renowned author and preacher who is certain to be remembered as the greatest evangelist of the twentieth century. His monumental effort and devotion to a divine calling of building and strengthening the church of God in America and around the world is recognized everywhere that Christian influence is acknowledged. After more than seventy years in public ministry, at the age of ninety-five he has recorded these profound words in his most recent book, *The Reason for My Hope*. "If I did not believe that Christ overcame death on the cross and bodily rose from the grave, I would have quit preaching years ago. I am absolutely convinced that Jesus is living at this moment at the right hand of God the Father and reigns in my heart. I believe it by faith, and I believe it by evidence found in the Scriptures."[2]

Perhaps you have had the opportunity to know some Christian men or women before they made the decision to accept and declare their faith in Jesus Christ as their personal Lord and Savior. If so, then you have no doubt witnessed the remarkable transformation that comes over a life that has become sincerely submitted to the gospel truth. The outstanding character of God's people as found in those who have been supernaturally born of his Spirit (having entered into His eternal kingdom by faith alone), is very powerful evidence of a personal creator God who works in the simple lives of ordinary people. Those who have proclaimed the name of Jesus Christ, and have willingly submitted to his eternal truth and divine authority, have become members of the worldwide church of God. The transformed lives of these believing men, women, boys, and girls, has provided incontrovertible evidence to confirm the powerful working of a merciful Savior, who actively seeks to restore unto himself and to fully redeem a broken relationship with each and every member of the fallen human race.

Purpose-Driven God

In the words of the well-known creation scientist Dr. Henry Morris, we are reminded that "the evidences of intelligent design and special creation abound everywhere in nature, and there is no real excuse for anyone to believe in naturalistic evolution, for which there is no legitimate scientific or historical evidence whatever."[3] When we have carefully examined the remarkably compelling evidence for the existence of God, it becomes obvious to us that people who are set on denying him will refuse to believe no matter what convincing proof is offered to them. These determined individuals have created for themselves a very comfortable worldview—one that requires no divine accountability and opens the doorway to any and every kind of personal gratification at the expense of God's commands. Many people will stubbornly refuse to allow their self-gratifying lifestyle to become disrupted by even the most compelling evidence available today. These strong-minded souls may find themselves beyond the reach of a loving, purpose-driven God by their own choosing. However, there are surely many others in this troubled world who will remain open to the exciting possibility of a powerful, merciful creator God reaching out to them in a very personal way, a way that demonstrates a gentle and compassionate touch tempered by unconditional love. The God of heaven will surely help all who seek to begin the fulfilling experience of a life governed by saving faith. "Come unto me all you who labor and are heavy laden (by sin) and I will give you rest" (Matthew 11:28).

God has wisely revealed a great deal to us about who he is and what he has done. However, those who insist on a complete disclosure of God will never be adequately satisfied, no matter what persuasive evidence is presented to them. If God gave us full disclosure of himself, there would certainly be no need for faith. I believe the person who has no room for faith would also have no room for God because the Bible says, "But without faith it is impossible to please Him" (Hebrews 11:6). The Lord our God will never submit to the stubborn insistence of anyone to make himself fully and completely known to the absolute satisfaction of the intellectual mind. He has already revealed to us everything we need to know about him; anything more, we will simply have to accept on the basis of faith. The Bible tells us in Romans 1:17 that "the just shall live by faith"! It also teaches clearly that "he who comes to God must believe that He is (that He exists) and that He is a rewarder of those who diligently seek Him" (Hebrews 11:6). "By faith we understand that the worlds were framed by the Word of God (spoken forth), so that the things which are seen were not made of things which are visible" (Hebrews 11:3).

Without divine revelation unveiled to the finite human mind by supernatural means, the creator God of heaven would remain a mystery to all of us. He would always be essentially unknowable by virtue of the infinite knowledge that exists throughout the entire realm of his creative works. The mystery and wonder of the creator will continue to amaze us, and for finite man it will always be that way on this side of eternity. Because of our vastly limited understanding of divine providence, and the absolute requirement to exercise faith in the matter of our own relationship with God, we are left with only two choices. We can accept God on the basis of what we observe and what he has faithfully revealed to us, or we can reject him outright because of human pride by insisting that we will live life on our own terms as we stubbornly refuse to submit to divine authority. If, by a personal act of our own free volition, we should choose the latter, we will be risking everything when we pass over from this life, and ultimately face the consequences of our choices and actions in the next.

All of the powerful and truly compelling evidence, which verifies for us the reality of God, leaves modern man in a very serious predicament. As the certainty of death approaches for each of us, upon what possible ground does any man have to stand if he ignores the evidence, rejects

God, and continues to deny repeatedly that the atonement was required to address his sinful nature? Therefore, all men and women who seek to comprehend observed and revealed truth must understand that to acknowledge the reality of the God of heaven, and to believe that he is our Creator, is to recognize a divine authority to whom we will ultimately be held personally accountable. We must fear the living God, but at the same time, we must understand that his undying, purpose-driven love for humanity was personally intended to address the fallen condition of every human heart.

Is God really there? In the final analysis, everyone will have to answer that question for themselves. It is obvious that I cannot begin to prove the existence of God, in the scientific sense, any more than I can possibly prove that my wife loves me. However, even though you and I cannot detect the Creator with our physical senses, the true existence and the awesome power of God is actually something that few people are willing to deny. Have you ever heard anyone question the existence of the wind, because they cannot see it? I sure haven't! Who among us could possibly deny the reality of this invisible force, when its profound effects are so clearly seen? In the same way, we must ask ourselves, does our universe, and the human story played out on earth, exhibit the creative work of an unseen force? Do we see credible evidence to verify a world that was carefully planned and purposefully designed? Has observation and revelation provided us with sufficient confirmation, thus enabling man to make a confident, intellectual choice to acknowledge the reality of his Creator? If men were to be truly honest and sincere after having personally examined so many infallible proofs while considering the mystery of life, the final slogan on every heart should read, "God cannot be denied"! "Woe to the man who fights with his Creator. Does the pot argue with its maker? Does the clay dispute with him who forms it?" (Isaiah 45:9 TLB).

Even though the evidence for an infinite superior mind is overwhelming, many people choose to deny the existence of God because they cannot deal emotionally with anticipation of the accountability a just God would require for sin. For many years the wisdom of man has dominated the cultural institutions within Western societies. Education, politics, science, communication, and the entertainment industry have made it very difficult to make a rational judgment about the meaning of life. Listen to the words of British columnist Peter Hitchens, former atheist, and the brother of Christopher Hitchens (who became known for a rigid public stance opposing faith in God). As a prize-winning journalist and noted author, Peter Hitchens has publicly challenged the famed British Broadcasting Corporation (BBC) about their liberal stance of maintaining a mocking approach toward Christian faith. He wrote, "The BBC teased religious leaders by asking them if they believe in the literal truth of the great Bible stories . . . I would like to ask BBC chiefs, and the rest of our secular establishment if they believe in the literal truth of evolution. Evolution is an unproven theory. If what its fundamentalist supporters believe is true, fishes decided to grow lungs and legs and walk up on the beach. The idea is so comically daft that only one thing explains its survival—that lonely, frightened people wanted to expel God from the universe, because they found the idea that He exists profoundly uncomfortable."[4]

The Lord Almighty is pursuing us, drawing us, and asking each one of us to seriously consider the mystery of life, because he wants to be known by each one of us in a personal way, and he desperately wants all of us to be living in right relationship with him when we ultimately cross over into life after death. A lasting relationship of mutual love with his image-bearing sons and daughters was God's plan and divine purpose for mankind from the very beginning. The great and awesome God of heaven has always passionately desired to have a family—children that he could love and have fellowship with, who would also love him in return.

Allow me to paraphrase some inspiring words of senior pastor Rick Warren of the world-renowned Saddleback Church of Southern California: "You were planned and created for God's own pleasure; you were formed and designed with the intention of becoming a part of His eternal family."[5] Pastor Rick wrote a powerful book some years ago entitled *The Purpose-Driven Life*. Today, we are told that this book has sold more copies worldwide than any book other than the Bible. How is this possible? I would submit to you that it is possible because people desperately want to believe there is some actual purpose for their lives; they want to know they are here for a reason! The evolutionary theory has left mankind without any real reason for existing. Therefore, we continue to have the crucial issue of God's existence squarely before us, and we will never be rid of it in this lifetime, because he desperately wants us to believe in him, trust in him, and know that he created us with a very significant purpose in mind.

C. S. Lewis, Josh McDowell, and Lee Strobel are only a very few of the many men who initially set out to disprove, discredit, and discard Christianity and the Bible. However, after being confronted with the genuine evidence, each of them was forced to seriously reconsider his views. Ultimately, all of them abandoned a self-directed lifestyle that consistently denied divine purpose. At the end of their search for truth, all of these men opened their hearts and submitted their will to a new found faith in God that was so clearly confirmed by the evidence, and they all began a new and very exciting chapter in their lives by pursuing a personal relationship with the sovereign God they had originally sought to discredit and deny. I believe the only reason for anyone to stubbornly maintain that human life is merely a freakish product of blind chance, with no intended purpose, is because of willful choice. In fact, the bible says that there would come a time when, in spite of the evidence, men will chose to be willingly ignorant__ scoffing at the promises of God and his so-called love for humanity. ". . . There shall come in the last days scoffers, walking after their own lusts. . . And saying, where is the promise of his coming? . . . For this (God's existence, His creation, promised return, and divine judgment), they willingly are ignorant of . . . (2 Peter 3: 3-5) KJV. This type of personal choice constitutes a prideful reluctance on the part of humankind to seriously examine the evidence, and to honestly attempt to comprehend the truth about God, as well as the remarkable self-revelation he has clearly offered to a fallen and rebellious world as confirmation of his existence. The message of humanistic evolution is that you and I are completely insignificant in the grand scheme of things. No wonder so many people live like there is no tomorrow. No wonder sexual perversion and unwanted aggression toward women is so pervasive in our culture.

If man has no divine purpose, then why not take whatever you want in this life at the emotional expense of others. On the other hand, the message of the bible is that you and I are so valued and treasured that the God of creation was willing to die in order to purchase and preserve a relationship with each one of us.

If there really is a personal, purpose-driven God who thoroughly loves sinful mankind, and seriously desires intimate, personal fellowship with each and every one of us, then it would certainly be his sole responsibility to reveal himself to those he loves. Man needs to understand God's true nature, and the specifically designed plan he has ordained for the infinitely valued human lives that he has lovingly and purposefully created in his own image.

What is this plan? What is God's will for mankind? The bottom line is that God wants each one of us to become part of his eternal family. Unlike so many of us, God sees man as sinful and separated from him. This is why Christ had to die—to make a way for us to get back into a right relationship with our Maker. He is "not willing that any should perish but that all should come to repentance" (2 Peter 3:9).

How would a transcendent God go about the difficult task of relating, in a personal way, to a fallen, material world? Perhaps he could design exceptional beauty and complexity in nature to an extent that it would demand the acknowledgment of a designer—a chief architect of great intellectual capacity and ingenious creativity. Maybe he could instill within mankind an innate awareness of himself. Perhaps he could give humanity a moral conscience bringing true conviction to his thoughts and actions, and thus making his crowning creation aware of the difference between right and wrong. Possibly, he could use a nation of imperfect people, such as Israel, to record his very thoughts and actions in a divinely inspired Holy book, a book containing vast information and knowledge that could only have been known to a sovereign, omniscient God. Perhaps the most astonishing action he could possibly take would be to set aside his divine majesty (the magnificent glory of his heavenly domain) leaving the spirit world behind, and, at the will of God the Father, to clothe himself in human flesh becoming one of us; thus, in humility he became poor in order to personally walk among his creation and demonstrate for us the true nature of God. "For you know the grace of our Lord Jesus Christ, that though He was rich, yet for your sakes He became poor, that you through His poverty might become rich" (2 Corinthians 7:9). In doing this, he would surely reveal God's undying love for humanity in the most compassionate way conceivable. Then, perhaps, in his final act of love and devotion, he could humble himself and take the place of sinners by dying the cruelest and most agonizing death a criminal could ever face, for the purpose of paying that terrible price to redeem mankind, and to balance, for all time, the scales of divine justice. Then, in one final action of ultimate triumph and victory, he could rise up again from the dead, as he promised he would, proving to all mankind his divine nature. Surely, this would demonstrate God's endless love for humanity whom he considers to have great redeeming value and unspeakable eternal worth. I will ask once again, what else could He have done?

The Reality of God

When each one of my four children were born, I was forced to come to grips with the possibility that perhaps in exercising their free volition, they could grow up one day and choose to hate and reject me. Because of man's free moral agency, God does not have control over the choices people make any more than I had control over the choices my growing children would one day make. Years ago in Olympia, Washington, I remember speaking to a homeless young man on the street outside of a grocery store. I asked him why he found himself in these dire circumstances at such a young age. He related to me that his father was well off financially, but that he had come to despise his father's authority over him after a family dispute. As a result of these unfortunate circumstances, this young man was no longer willing to submit himself to the earthly authority that God had placed over his life. Guess what was keeping him from returning home, and repenting of his foolish rebellion. Pride! Isn't this exactly what all of us have done to our heavenly Father? We have each despised his authority, gone our own way, and have often allowed our foolish pride to keep us from returning back to him. The Bible says that each one of us have sinned against our Creator, and, in some way, we have all rejected his commandments, and have broken his laws. We have not wanted to admit that our sin and rebellion separates us from him, and that foolish pride has kept us from acknowledging our need to repent. Just as pride was keeping the homeless man in material poverty, pride is what keeps many people today in the hopelessness of spiritual poverty.

I chose to have children, because it was well worth the risk in order to have a relationship with them based on mutual love and respect. God also knew that man could choose to rebel against him, reject his authority, disregard his word, and even attempt to explain away his very existence in order to justify a self-directed lifestyle that often refuses to submit to moral restraint. God was taking a big risk when he created mankind with personal volition, but it was worth the risk, so that he might have the opportunity to enjoy each one of us as part of his own family.

It was not God's fault that Hitler, Stalin, Pol Pot, and Mao made the awful choice to exterminate millions of their own people. It's so easy to blame God for the cruelty and hatred that people display toward each other, when the truth is that mankind has often exercised his personal free will to commit horrendous acts of carnage against his fellow man. And none of the blame rests with God! Yes, there is a terrible curse on this world that has, sadly, resulted in horrifying disease, pain, suffering, and death. However, God warned us in Genesis 2 that this would happen if we chose to rebel against his authority. We have no one to blame for this fallen world except ourselves! God's original creation was completely perfect in every respect, but we had to have things our way, and now we are suffering from the awful consequences of sin. Keep in mind that we still have free will, which means we can choose to repent of our selfish acts and return, in faith, to a merciful, loving God, who offers us much more than we deserve. One thousand years before Christ, the psalmist King David asked God a question with these searching words: "When I consider your heavens, the work of your fingers, the moon and the stars, which you have ordained, what is man that you are mindful of him?" (Psalm 8:3, 4). This is a valid question that is still troubling the minds of many today—why does God care so much about humankind? It would seem rather hard to think of ourselves as special when you consider that we are merely a minute smidgeon of protoplasm, inhabiting a tiny speck of a planet, orbiting a very undistinguished and ordinary star, on the outer arm of a spiral galaxy that is populated by billions of similar stars, most of which are far greater in splendor and more magnificent than our sun. Mankind's home, which is located in a rather small galaxy called the Milky Way, would seem to be lost in space considering that our galaxy is only one of multiple billions of galaxies that have been distributed throughout the unimaginable vastness of the cosmos.

As strange as it sounds, God knows exactly where we are and He created us in His image to become a vital part of his eternal family. He did not create us because he needed us! He created us only because he wanted us! And that's why I love him and want to be his friend, because out of unconditional love, and the desire for mutual relationship, he first chose me, and delighted in my personal association with him. Without God, it is very difficult to even begin to understand the humanitarian concept of unconditional love. I do not place conditions upon the God I serve, such as "I will love you and serve you if you will do this or that for me." No! I love him because he has first loved me, and I worship him because he is worthy! This brings me, once again, to a compelling consideration of the core issue of Christian faith.

The heart of Christianity is the cross! Our eternal Creator, who found himself in a broken relationship with mankind because of humanity's rebellious use of free volition, wanted to set things right so badly that he was more than willing to place himself under the curse of fallen humanity. He has walked in our shoes, has suffered the many trials of human experience, and has withheld nothing from us, including his own life, by dying in our place, taking upon himself the penalty due for our selfish transgressions.

The most astonishing and truly incomprehensible thing about the creator God of the universe is his tremendous personal sacrifice on our behalf because of his passionate love for humanity. Our Creator, ultimately, became our Redeemer! There is certainly no greater love than this!

In the 1990s, a poll commissioned by the Pew Research Center had reported that 71percent of the respondents say they never doubt the existence of God. In this same poll, 61percent of Americans said they believe miracles come from the power of God, and 53 percent said prayer was important in their daily lives. Some people refuse to believe in creation because they argue that you cannot prove God is real. Apparently, these people are confused about what is meant by the concept of *evidential proof.* There are two basic ways to prove something is factual. The first method is, of course, a scientific one that is based on visual observation. If, for example, I wanted to prove to you that a bar of Ivory soap floats, all I would have to do is to prepare a basin of water and toss the bar of soap into it, in your presence. The fact of the matter would be confirmed by your personal observation. The second method of proof is at times called judicial or evidential; this is also referred to as the legal-historical method. The legal-historical method of proof is used in courtrooms throughout America every day. Judicial proof must rely upon a collection of all available physical evidence, eyewitness accounts, and expert opinions in order to reach a verdict that is considered "beyond reasonable doubt." This, of course, is the method we must consider as we render an opinion about the existence of God, and the validity of the Christian faith. Certainly, I cannot prove the existence of God in a strictly scientific sense. And for that matter, I cannot prove that my wife loves me, but I would stake my life on it because of the overwhelming weight of evidence that would confirm this fact to anyone who is at all interested to know.

Now, suppose I were to tell you that there is a tall man standing on the other side of my front door at this very moment. Perhaps you would question me as to how I could possibly know this to be factual. This prediction would certainly not be outside the remote realm of possibility. However, I would be a fool to stake my life on it. Why? Because I would have absolutely no reliable evidence to confirm that this is in fact true. The atheist likewise is foolish. Why? Because he has no reliable evidence, and yet he appears to be wagering his eternal soul on the singular belief that God does not in fact exist. Blind faith in an unproven theory that places all hope in pure chance and the imagination of man is a poor way to invest in the future. I believe we must always ask ourselves, what does the evidence teach us, and where is it leading? If we will just stick to the evidence, we will never be seriously misled! More so than ever before, intellectually truthful and open-minded scientists are honestly considering the current volume and reliability of scientific evidence, and are following the path where it would naturally lead them.

Consider if you will, the bold remarks of Dr. Frank Tipler, a professor of physics and cosmology at Tulane University: "When I began my career as a cosmologist some 20 years ago, I was a convinced atheist. I never in my wildest dreams imagined that one day I would be writing a book purporting to show that the central claims of Judeo-Christian theology are in fact true, that these claims are straightforward deductions of the laws of physics, as we now understand them. I have been forced into these conclusions by the inexorable logic of my own special branch of physics."[6] In his book entitled *The Physics of Christianity*, Dr. Tipler makes this remarkably prudent assertion: "From the perspective of the latest physical theories, Christianity is not a mere religion, but an experimentally testable science."[7] Another complementary conclusion is offered to us by Dr. Arthur L. Schawlow, who was a former professor of physics at Stanford University, and the esteemed winner of the 1981 Nobel Prize for his remarkable work in developing laser spectroscopy. "It seems to me that when confronted with the marvels of life and the universe, one must ask why and not just how. The only possible answers are religious . . . I find a need for God in the universe and in my own life."[8] He also added that "we are fortunate to have the Bible and especially the New Testament, which tells us so much about God in widely accessible human terms."[9]

Christian faith is by no means blind faith! The confirming evidence to honestly validate faith in God is overwhelming, and it appears rebellious for anyone to deny his existence when the evidence for this reality remains so abundantly clear. It is obvious to me that those who deny God, and reject the reality his existence, simply do not want him to be real. In general, it can truly be stated that genuine faith in anything is only as valid as the evidence that can be offered to back it up! The basic truth about the Christian gospel remains valid because of a massive weight of physical and historical evidence, reliable testimony, and multiple eyewitness accounts that can and have been verified to validate the personal historical claims of Jesus Christ. Among this evidence, we learn of his most remarkable life as a Jewish carpenter and an itinerant preacher, prophet, and healer of the first century. We would certainly all be foolish to believe in a living Messiah if there wasn't any valid evidence to back his claim of deity. A firm faith in historically valid Christian theology is a serious commitment made by the individual__ a commitment that is based on volumes of reliable evidence and well-documented eyewitness accounts.

The New Testament record is chocked full of historically accurate truth upon which one can justify a rich and full life of evidence-based faith. Thousands of men and women have made it their life's work to study and to document the compelling evidence pointing to the reality of a Judeo-Christian God and his redemptive work on behalf of fallen humanity.

Now, let's also consider the direct words of internationally known, Indian-born Christian apologist and evangelist Dr. Ravi Zacharias, who has personally concluded that "a man rejects God, neither because of intellectual demands nor because of scarcity of evidence. A man rejects God because of a moral resistance that refuses to admit his need of God."[10] Dr. Zacharias has wrapped up the issue with the following comment: "God has put enough into the world to make faith in him a most reasonable thing, and he is left enough out to make it impossible to live by sheer reason and observation alone."[11]

The world famous twentieth century philosopher Antony Flew was arguably Mr. Richard Dawkins predecessor as the world's most notorious atheist. Near the end of his life, however, Flew was given the opportunity to explain to Professor John Lennox of Oxford University exactly why he chose to abandon his decades long worldview of atheism. He graciously explained his newfound, updated worldview by pointing out that the study of DNA had shown an almost "unbelievable complexity" of the arrangements that were needed to produce life. Flew, therefore, concluded that an intelligent agent must have been involved. Many people who find themselves on the cutting edge of ever-advancing scientific research are concluding, as Antony Flew did, that the complexity of the universe points directly to the existence of a benevolent Creator. When all of the abundant evidence is carefully weighed in the balance, atheism can be seen as little more than an escape mechanism utilized in retreating from personal responsibility for ones choices and actions in a self-centered world, where people commonly reject moral absolutes.

Declaring a personal worldview should never be considered a choice between God and science. We must have both! God is the active agent who designed and created the universe. He is the brainpower behind the incomprehensible mechanism that spells out life. God is to life and the physical world what Henry Ford was to the mechanized motor vehicle.

The new atheists have confused the issue between mechanism and agency. They will say life can be explained by mechanism alone (natural selection) without agency (Creator). This is like saying, we can enjoy the modern motor vehicle only because of the principle of internal combustion (mechanism), and, therefore, we have no need of Henry Ford (agency). We need both the causing agent and the science to explain the diversity of life in this world! God is the innovator, but he is also the brilliant mind behind the many mechanisms (laws) by which everything operates with such amazing regularity in the physical world. The pursuit of true science actually comprises man's compelling ambition for the knowledge that attempts to comprehend what a sovereign God has created. The new atheists have fabricated the idea of a war between science and God, but this attempt is not working, because the more we learn about the physical universe, through the ongoing quest of modern empirical science, the more recognizable it is becoming that a design agent was required to conceive of and initiate the complexities of a remarkable world. Consider the following remarks from Dr. Albert Einstein, winner of the Nobel Prize for physics in 1921 for his groundbreaking theory of relativity. It is now commonly believed that Einstein possessed the most brilliant analytical mind of the twentieth century. Many scholars suggest that Albert Einstein was an agnostic, if not a full-fledged atheist. I beg to differ with them! This most fascinating man was certainly very well aware that a powerful presence far beyond nature is required to explain the physical universe, and the remarkable complexities of organic life on this earth. Albert Einstein once wrote this: "Everyone who is seriously engaged in the pursuit of science becomes convinced that the laws of nature manifest the existence of a spirit vastly superior to that of men, and one in the face of which we, with our modest powers, must feel humble."[12] His personal line of thought continued with, "My religiosity consists of a humble admiration of the 'infinitely superior spirit' who reveals himself in the slight details we are able to perceive with our frail and feeble minds. That deeply emotional conviction of the presence of a 'superior reasoning power,' which is revealed in the incomprehensible universe, forms my idea of God."[13] "Human beings, vegetables, or cosmic dust— we all dance to a mysterious tune, intoned in the distance by an invisible piper."[14] I think by now we should know who that mysterious, invisible piper really is!

I am convinced that God designed our remote world with such extraordinary beauty and complexity because he foreknew that (human nature being what it is) investigative knowledge would have a very tempting tendency to lead man into believing that there is no need for divine intelligence to explain the physical universe and the magnificent diversity of life on planet Earth. In fact, he has actually made it so complex that the more we study and learn about our physical surroundings, the more we are inclined to acknowledge that in a material world that operates according to the mathematical laws of physics, it would appear absolutely unimaginable for proteins and planets to generate themselves by pure chance. Nevertheless, if some strong-minded people are determined to wager their eternal soul on an infinitely impossible biological accident, they certainly have every right to do so. However, knowing what I have discovered in a lifelong search for the truth and meaning, as revealed through empirical science, history and logic, I am compelled to do everything in my power to persuade them otherwise if I possibly can, because the consequence of this choice will prove to be eternally devastating! When we are presented so many known facts and offered such a compelling weight of evidence, it would seem very foolish to conclude that there is no God! These are not my words, but words that certainly should ring loud and clear in the hearts and minds of those who refuse to acknowledge their Creator. These profound words were recorded not once but twice by the psalmist King David nearly three thousand years ago, and they are still reverberating today: "The fool has said in his heart, 'there is no God'" (Psalm 14:1, 53:1).

When God repeats himself in the Scriptures, he does this to generate a particularly strong emphasis upon the impressionable minds of the human audience he is attempting to reach. This presents another question that demands very serious consideration. Why is it so utterly foolish to deny God? The answer can only be because the genuinely persuasive and compelling evidence pointing toward God's eternal existence is rock solid. Therefore, the terrifying reality that should be keeping the atheists and agnostics of this world awake at night is the fact that they will not escape the divine judgment of Almighty God__ a judgment that will inevitably come upon their lives, and upon their posterity some future day whether they have believed in a theistic universe or not. "Why does the wicked man revile God? Why does he say to himself, He won't call me to account (for my sins)?" (Psalm 10:13 NIV).

"Professing themselves to be wise, they became fools, and changed the glory of the incorruptible God into an image made like corruptible man" (Romans 1:22, 23).

Don't be a fool! Believe in him! Acknowledge and trust Him, the sovereign God of creation who set the universe into motion by his awesome creative power. You and I have absolutely everything to gain and nothing to lose. If we choose to believe, we are well on your way to discovering the whole truth about *the mystery of life*.

Many are beginning to recognize that current evolutionary thought has become like a ball and chain shackled around the neck of modern civilization. This unrealistic theory has threatened to rob us of our intended creative purpose and the hope of a glorious future in the presence of our Maker. Only when we become free of this serious miscalculation in thinking, will we achieve our full, God-given potential. Listen to these compelling words from a prominent American engineer and mathematician, Dr. I. L. Cohen. He writes, "It is not the duty of science to defend the theory of evolution, and to stick by it to the bitter end . . . no matter which illogical and unsupported conclusions it offers. On the contrary, it is expected that scientists recognize the patently obvious impossibility of Darwin's pronouncements and predictions . . . let's cut the umbilical cord that tied us down to Darwin for such a long time. It is choking us and holding us back."[15]

There is a desperate need in our world today to expose evolution theory for what it really is, in order to protect the eager minds of young people and to point men and women toward the hope that is found in Christ alone. This need is expressed rather bluntly by Dr. Pierre Paul Grasse, who once held the coveted chair of evolution at the great Sorbonne University in Paris for some thirty years. Dr. Grasse, considered one of the greatest zoologists of modern times, explains it like this: "Today, our duty is to destroy the myth of evolution, considered as a simple, understood and explained phenomenon which keeps rapidly unfolding before us."[16]

"The heavens declare the glory of God; and the firmament shows His handiwork. Day unto day utters speech, and night unto night reveals knowledge. There is no speech nor language where their voice is not heard. Their line has gone out through all the earth and their words to the end of the world" (Psalm 19:1 4). "Since earliest times, men have seen the earth and sky and all God made, and have known of his existence and great eternal power. So they will have no excuse [when they stand before God at judgment day]" (Romans 1:20 TLB). "For thus saith the Lord that created the heavens; God himself that formed the earth and made it; he hath established it, he created it not in vain, he formed it to be inhabited: I am the Lord; and there is none else" (Isaiah 45:18 KJV). "Thus says the Lord, the King of Israel, and his Redeemer, the Lord of hosts: I am the First and I am the Last; Besides me there is no God" (Isaiah 44:6). "By faith we understand that the worlds were framed by the Word of God, so that the things which are seen were not made of things which are visible" (Hebrews 11:3). "Remember the former things of old, for I am God and there is no other; I am God, and there is none like Me. Declaring the end from the beginning, and from ancient time things that are not yet done . . . (Isaiah 46:9,10).

God Reigns: Concluding Remarks

I believe that a lack of understanding about the reality of God and the widespread absence of the fear of God, along with a stubborn refusal to obey His Word, lies at the root of every weighty problem that besets us as a human family. "All the ills from which America suffers can be traced to the teaching of evolution."[17] So said William Jennings Bryan, a leading American politician and presidential candidate in the late 1800s. "The god of this age has 'blinded the minds of unbelievers,' so that they cannot see the light of the Gospel of the glory of Christ, who is the image of God" (2 Corinthians 4:4 NIV). "You will ever be hearing but never understanding. You will be ever seeing, but never perceiving. (The hearts of these people have become calloused.) They hardly hear with their ears, and they have closed their eyes" (Matthew 13:14-15 NIV, paraphrase). And they are "always learning and never able to come to the knowledge of the truth" (2 Timothy 3:7). Now consider these powerful words from the highly revered civil rights reformer, Dr. Martin Luther King Jr., who was clearly disturbed by the way in which science has now threatened to replace faith in our culture: "Modern man has brought this whole world to an awe-inspiring threshold of the future. He has reached new and astonishing peaks of scientific success . . . yet, in spite of these spectacular strides in science and technology, something basic is missing. There is a sort of poverty of the spirit, which stands in glaring contrast to our scientific and technological abundance. The richer we have become materially, the poorer we have become morally and spiritually . . . We have allowed the means by which we live to outdistance the ends for which we live . . . Our scientific power has outrun our spiritual power. We have guided missiles and misguided men . . . If we are to survive today, our moral and spiritual 'lag' must be eliminated."[18]

Another firm rebuttal that is directed at naturalist theology was captured for us by British physicist John Houghton who aptly recorded this basic comparison: "The fact that we understand some of the mechanisms of the working of the universe or of living systems does not preclude the existence of a designer, any more than the possession of insight into the processes by which a watch has been put together, however automatic these processes may appear, implies there can be no watchmaker."[19] In 1948, while presenting his Armistice Day address at the close of World War II, the famous American general Omar Bradley concluded some of his remarks with this monumental statement: "We have too many men of science, too few men of God. We have grasped the mystery of the atom and rejected the Sermon on the Mount. Ours is a world of nuclear giants and ethical infants. We know more about war than we know about peace, more about killing than we know about living."[20] These exceptional words are ringing true more today than ever before. In conclusion, we are inclined to admit that when all of the vast evidence is thoroughly weighed, and after every last argument is systematically analyzed, it brings us to one obvious question: what is keeping any of us from getting back to the worship of the one and only true and living God, who has very faithfully revealed himself to humankind by giving us more than enough reason to believe in him? He is, therefore, the only living deity who is ultimately worthy of our sincere thanks, praise, and allegiance.

What are we teaching our precious children? Will we continue to remain silent, while allowing them to be robbed of faith in a magnificent Creator? Or will you join me in doing whatever you can to push back this terrible cloud of deception that hangs over our beloved nation. William Jennings Bryan is best known for his defense of *creationism* and his attack on evolution in the famous Scopes monkey trial at Dayton, Tennessee, in July of 1925. In this well-known court case, he recorded the following remarks: "Parents have a right to say that no teacher paid by their money shall rob their children of faith in God and send them back to their homes skeptical, or infidels, or agnostics, or atheists."[21]

Yet it is so very disturbing for me to report that this is exactly what has happened in America over the last eighty years—we have witnessed a tragic and steady decline of *faith in God* that is leading us, our children, and our grandchildren into what could become the post-Christian era of our beloved nation's history.

"And He has made from one blood every nation of men to dwell on all the face of the earth and has determined their preappointed times and the boundaries of their dwellings, so that they should seek the Lord, in the hope that they might grope for Him and find Him, though He is not far from each one of us; for in Him we live and move and have our being" (Acts 17:26-28).

You and I are no accident; He planned us and appointed us to dwell on the earth for a time and season as it pleased to him. Trust in the wisdom of God, not in the faulty and ever-changing opinions of man. "There is a way that seems right to a man, but its end is the way of death" (Proverbs 14:12). "Look to me, and be saved, all you ends of the earth! For I am God, and there is no other" (Isaiah 45:22).

Even the Old Testament promises that God can be found, and God can be known. "And you will seek me and find me when you search for me with all your heart!" (Jeremiah 29:13). Notice that Jeremiah did not say "with all your mind"! The search for God through intellect alone has led to great frustration and a lingering sense of dissatisfaction, characterized by a terrible lack of fulfillment. Ultimately, any move toward understanding, as related to the sovereign God of all creation, requires an act of faith that can never be adequately explained by human reasoning power. Jesus said, "I tell you the truth, anyone who will not receive the kingdom of God like a little child will never enter it" (Mark 10:15 NIV). The simple faith of a small and innocent child demonstrates complete humility and, therefore, is unencumbered by the misleading bias found in the intellectual rhetoric offered by the counsels of men. This humility is what God requires from each one of us.

Who can deny the reality of God Almighty? And upon what evidence will he stand? Consider the influential words of German-born rocket scientist Wernher von Braun, who became a major architect of the American space program at the height of the Cold War. Regarding the powerful evidence he would discover through his special branch of rocket propulsion engineering, Dr. von Braun became compelled to publicly acknowledge a confident belief in the reality of a super-intelligence governing the universe. He has included the following bold comments, found in a written archive that includes a letter to the California Board of Education: "As we learn more and more about nature, we become more deeply impressed and humbled by its orderliness and unerring perfection . . . One cannot be exposed to the law and order of the universe without concluding that there must be design and purpose behind it all . . . Speaking for myself, I can only say that the grandeur of the cosmos serves to confirm my belief in the certainty of a Creator . . . the creation of the fundamental laws of nature . . . they challenge science to prove the existence of God. But must we really light a candle to see the sun?"[22]

As I have previously pointed out, the massive weight of evidence uncovered by so many brilliant men of science is very clearly revealed to modern humanity. This body of evidence points us unmistakably toward the certain reality of a loving and benevolent God, who created us to become a part of his eternal family. However, make no mistake about it, we are accountable to the one who created us, and he has every right to invoke judgment for our sinfulness and rebellion against his written word, including its righteous commands. We have utterly broken his laws and each one of us stands guilty before a Holy God. "For the word of the Lord is living and powerful and sharper than any two edged sword, piercing even to the division of soul and spirit and of joints and marrow, and is a discerner of the thoughts and intents of the heart; and there is no creature hidden from his sight, but all things are naked and open to the eyes of Him to whom we must give account" (Hebrews 4:12, 13).

"But God shows his anger from heaven against all sinful, evil men who push away the truth from them. For the truth about God is known to them instinctively; God has put this knowledge in their hearts. Since earliest times, men have seen the earth and sky and all God made and have known of his existence and great eternal power. So they will have no excuse [when they stand before God at judgment day]. Yes, they knew about him all right, but they wouldn't admit it or worship him or even thank him for all his daily care. And after a while, they began to think up silly ideas of what God was like and what he wanted them to do. The result was that their foolish minds became dark and confused. Claiming themselves to be wise without God, they became utter fools instead" (Romans 1:18-22 TLB).

I will end this chapter, with one final quotation. This one comes from the famous Greek philosopher Plato: "We can easily forgive a child who is afraid of the dark; the real tragedy of life is when men are afraid of the light."[23]

There is a magnificent God in heaven, who is the only Creator of the vast physical reality that you and I have come to know. This Creator God loves us beyond measure, and we are certainly accountable to him! The evidence for the existence of the Almighty goes far beyond reasonable doubt and actually constitutes a much more intellectually sound position than that of atheism. If people do not believe in God, it is not because of a lack of evidence pointing unmistakably toward a benevolent Creator. Many People don't believe because *they don't want to believe.* In re-quoting the American Neurobiological scientist Dr. George Wald, we can see clearly why many people don't believe in God. Even though he knew scientifically that spontaneous generation was a fallacy, Wald commented, "that leaves us with the only possible conclusion__ that life arose as a supernatural creative act of God. I will not accept that philosophically, because I do not want to believe in God. Therefore, I choose to believe in that which I know is scientifically impossible: spontaneous generation arising to evolution."[24] Now that we know God is real, we must make every effort to find out who he is. Then we will need to understand exactly what God expects from us. And finally, and most importantly, we should be compelled and thoroughly motivated to do what he says! That, my friend, is what we call "fearing God," and our entire pursuit of true happiness, grounded in meaning, purpose, and fulfillment depends on it.

Chapter 9

THE MERGING OF SCIENCE AND FAITH

The Final Act—No Curtain Call

There are two critical issues facing humanity today that must be reconciled within the human heart if man is to experience true peace. The first of these realities requires every human soul to face up to his or her impending *mortality*. We must all become reconciled to the fact of our approaching death, and to fully embrace the ramifications of this uncontested reality. We are all going to decease, and no one is disputing this fact. From the moment of birth, we have been set upon a path toward our eventual demise. It has become easy for us to push this thought to the back of our minds, or to chalk it up as a matter for future consideration. People who do this have generally set out to live as though their tomorrows will never end. Inevitably, by ignoring or postponing the thought of his own mortality, man has often been able to successfully ignore the second critical issue facing humanity: *immortality*! Will the life of each individual continue to exist in some state forever as the Bible clearly teaches? This menacing question has been circling around in the back of every human consciousness. Is it possible that man will face an endless eternity when this mortal life comes to its inevitable conclusion? Like a dramatic theatrical play, the curtain of mortality will come down upon the final act__ perhaps at a time least expected. It is very unwise to ignore this ever-persistent reality, because we are all aging and the sands of time are running out, forcing each of us to face up to the certainty of our inescapable departure. We need real answers to these life-and-death questions, and the sooner we get them, the better. And we dare not settle for the wrong answers, because there is so much at stake when men and women are facing eternity every day. Therefore, if we will only consider the evidence, this will undoubtedly lead to the understanding we so desperately need in order to satisfy our deep longing for truth, meaning, and hope beyond this world.

Atheism, as a growing ideology within modern culture, is a very dangerous position to embrace. It places many individuals in the situation of having to face certain death without knowing what lies beyond. This view of life forces men and women to trust that__ if there really is an eternal existence beyond our mortality, the merits of good personal behavior in this life should be enough to warrant God's favor in the next. This, however, is a philosophical point of view that the Word of God flatly denies, and millions of people who have persisted in believing this false view would be much bettered served if they were to thoroughly understand the biblical concept of *redemption*.

There has been too much hate, war, and brutality on this planet since the beginning of man's self-indulgent occupation. Many ideas and ideals have been fought over again and again throughout the passing centuries and, even today, mankind cannot agree on how to live in peace and friendship with one another. We fail to respect our many differences__ differences that will allow our neighbors the right to life, liberty, and the pursuit of happiness, as they perceive it. The greatest single issue that divides humanity is that we cannot agree on the reality of the sovereign God who created us and who will hold us accountable for our rebellion against his Word and his authority. However, only the truth will prevail in the end, so we must ask ourselves the question, *how then shall we live?*

Science: A Powerful Witness

Albert Einstein once mused, "Science without religion is lame; religion without science is blind."[1]

Examine closely the following list of names and I am sure you will recognize some of them right away, especially if you have an interest in science as I do. Other names may seem unfamiliar to you. What you see here is a short, random listing, in no particular order, of some of the most impressive scientists of past generations, as well as many contemporary names whose scientific research has carried the bright torch of man's curiosity well into the twenty-first century.

Albert Einstein	1921	Robert Boyle
Max Planck	1918	William Kelvin
Joseph J. Thomson	1906	Sir Isaac Newton
Arthur Compton	1927	James Maxwell
Max Born	1954	Michael Faraday
Nevill Mott	1977	Johannes Kepler
Werner Heisenberg	1932	Nicolaus Copernicus
Antony Hewish	1974	James Joule
Arno Penzias	1978	Louis Pasteur
Ernst Chain	1945	Galileo Galilei
Arthur Schawlow	1981	Ernst Mayr
Christian Anfinsen	1972	Fred Hoyle
Richard Smalley	1996	Werner von Braun
Robert Millikan	1923	Michael Denton
Charles Townes	1964	Michael Behe
William D. Phillips	1997	Paul Davies
William H. Bragg	1915	Tony Rothman
Guglielmo Marconi	1909	Freeman Dyson
Isidor Rabi	1944	Frank Tippler
Erwin Schrodinger	1933	Robert Jastrow

Alexis Carrel	1912	Allan Sandage
John Eccles	1963	James Tour
Joseph Murray	1990	Henry Schaefer
Derek Barton	1969	Gregor Mendel
Walter Kohn	1998	Blaise Pascal
Ronald Ross	1902	Frances Bacon
Alexander Fleming	1945	Frances Collins
Albert Schweitzer	1952	Wolfgang Smith
Charles Sherrington	1932	Rene Descartes

What do all of the men listed above have in common? This list is only a partial group that includes a growing number of men whose dedicated study and research has shaped the world of historical as well as contemporary science. The men listed in column #1 have all been awarded the coveted Nobel Prize (date received following each name) for their major contributions to the advancement of science and a better understanding of our world. The names listed in column #2 are inclusive of many of the great scientists of the past as well as the present whose contributions have led to major advancement in our current knowledge of the basic laws of nature, along with a better understanding of organic life and the physical universe. The many contributions of these highly gifted individuals have affected our world in significant ways. All of these early and modern-day scientific pioneers listed here have one other thing in common. Each one of them believes in a creator God, and would affirm that they have gained this controversial recognition, not by the influence of any church or religious community necessarily, but through a steady search for understanding in their dedicated pursuit of science. Their great love for the knowledge of the unknown has led them to a remarkable, undeniable accumulation of reliable evidence pointing unmistakably toward this bold conclusion. These devoted men have been compelled to accept this widely controversial worldview in spite of the time-honored traditions of science that have been grudgingly cast aside in acquiring this knowledge. In fact, it has been reported that 60 percent of the Nobel Prize winners over the last century have confessed belief in a supreme power or authority who is responsible for the vast physical cosmos that had led them toward such irresistible curiosity. Why does the ongoing pursuit of empirical scientific achievement ultimately lead us back to God? In creating the universe and conscious carbon-based life on this earth, God calculated everything with such unique precision and incomprehensible complexity that man's curious discernment of even the slightest bit of understanding would inevitably point back to him.

The hope of future generations lies in the fact that science, the most powerful force in contemporary thought, is beginning to get it right. As you can see from the impressive list of names cited here, an ever-growing number of top research scientists are becoming more determined than ever before to discover the truth and reveal the facts, even if it means having to admit that over one hundred years of biased speculation has clearly led humanity down the wrong path. These brave and increasingly open-minded researchers are no longer willing to hide newly discovered scientific data for the purpose of propping up an outdated theory that has been refuted by an avalanche of new information acquired over the last seventy years or more. This new generation of determined research investigators is becoming more willing than ever before to pursue the evidence wherever it leads them, as leading scientists are putting aside their initial bias and seeking only verifiable facts in what has now become a life and death struggle hanging over the civilized world.

In this ever-increasing trend, many rational-thinking scientists are beginning to question the merits of such an obsolete theory as Darwinism. Consider these words from James Gorman, a science reporter for the *New York Times*: "Evolution is not only under attack by fundamentalist Christians, but is also being questioned by reputable scientists. Among paleontologists, scientists who study the fossil record, there is growing dissent from the prevailing view of Darwinism."[2]

Wernher von Braun was a Prussian-born scientist, who fled Nazi Germany at the end of World War II with a compelling desire to use his talent and experience to insure a more peaceful world, a world that would be freed from the terrible horrors left by the warfare he had personally witnessed in his homeland. In America, he became a world-class rocket propulsion engineer who would eventually lead the way to the development of the American space program at the height of the Cold War. Due to his outstanding leadership in structuring the American space program, he is now considered by NASA to be the "father of rocket science." This great American icon, who loved science with such great passion, was also a devoted Christian believer who viewed science and faith as comrades, not enemies. Let's consider the implication of his bold remarks that declare faith as an important virtue to any serious scientist who is willing to admit that the grandeur of the cosmos clearly points to a superior intelligence.

"Whereas all other living beings seem to find their places in the natural order and fulfill their role in life with a kind of calm acceptance, man clearly exhibits confusion. Why the anxiety? Why the storm and stress? Man really seems to be the only living thing uncertain of his role in the universe; and in his uncertainty, he has been calling since time immemorial upon the stars and the heavens for salvation and for answers to his eternal questions: Who am I? Why am I here?" Dr. von Braun continues, "The main spring of science is curiosity. But there would not be a single great accomplishment in the history of mankind without faith. Any man who strives to accomplish something needs a degree of faith . . . But many people find the churches, those old ramparts of faith, badly battered by the onslaught of three hundred years of scientific skepticism. This has led many to believe that science and religion are not compatible, that 'knowing' and 'believing' cannot live side-by-side. Nothing could be further from the truth! . . . The two most powerful forces shaping our civilization today are science and religion . . . While science tries to learn more about the creation, religion tries to better understand the Creator . . . One cannot be exposed to the law and order of the universe without concluding that there must be a divine intent behind it all . . . as we learn more and more about 'nature,' we become more deeply impressed and humbled by its orderliness and unerring perfection . . . Speaking for myself, I can only say that the grandeur of the cosmos serves to confirm my belief in the certainty of a Creator."

Dr. von Braun revealed his passion for both the spiritual and the scientific pursuits of life when he further explained the close and essential connection between the two. "The knowledge that man chose between good and evil should draw him closer to his Creator. Next, the realization should dawn that his survival here and hereafter depends on his adherence to the spiritual rather than the scientific . . . the ethical guidelines of religion are bonds that can hold our civilization together . . . Without them, man can never attain the cherished goal of 'lasting peace' with himself, his God, and his fellow man. We should not be dismayed by the relative insignificance of our planet in the vast universe as modern science now sees it . . . In fact, God deliberately reduced Himself to the stature of humanity in order to visit the earth in person, because the 'cumulative effect' over the centuries of millions of individuals choosing to please themselves rather than God had infected the whole planet. When God became a man himself, the experience proved to be nothing short of pure agony. The stage was set for a situation without parallel in the history of the earth. God would visit creatures, and they would nail him to a cross! I am certain that, were He among us today, Christ would encourage scientific research as modern man's most noble striving to comprehend and admire His Father's handiwork."[3]

While science attempts to answer for us the *how* questions, religion primarily admonishes each of us to consider the *why* questions. If we can only understand a fraction of the how and the why questions of life, we will surely experience a small measure of the fulfillment we were all meant to enjoy. Where did we come from? How did we all get here? Why are we here? Where are we going when we die? And, of course, the ultimate question that everyone on the planet should be asking themselves: what is the meaning of life, and how do I find fulfilling purpose for living out my days on this earth?

Follow the Evidence

Many men and women today, who are determined to *follow the evidence* wherever it is leading, are now finding themselves up against enormous resistance, antagonism, and provocation. It certainly takes a strong person to buck the tide and risk being discredited, denounced, and even humiliated by his or her peers; but this is what happened to men like Kepler and Galileo long ago whose brave determination and persistent pursuit of empirical scientific knowledge ultimately shaped a new scientific paradigm in their generation. This important principle first originated with Plato, and ultimately became adopted by Dr. Antony Flew who had decided that an open-minded approach to the question of origins must be engaged in by those who are sincerely searching for the truth. In Plato's *Republic*, Socrates is scripted to insist that "we must follow the argument wherever it leads."

By contrast, a firm position held by the new atheists, which is clearly represented in the written works of Richard Dawkins and others, maintains a firmly fixed and narrow-minded view of the concept of God and the origin of organic life. This rather rigid position, with respect to the modern conflict of ideas, has firmly maintained that "either you are with us all the way, or one with the enemy . . . even eminent thinkers who express some sympathy for the other side [of the argument] are denounced as traitors."[4] To call your philosophical opponent an enemy or even a trader is highly uncalled for by the proponents of atheism. Of course the argument rages onward, but these Darwinian zealots have consistently failed to address the most critical issue at stake in this highly contested cultural debate__ *the origin of life* __ with any rational argument as to how conscious life may have emerged from the interaction of lifeless chemical elements. Dawkins offers what can only be considered a weak stab at the origin of life and consciousness with a simple remark that it was based on events triggered by "an initial stroke of luck."[5]

Unfortunately, in recent decades there has been a significant public perception that modern science has buried God, and that as the undertaker, each new scientific advancement in the modern era has provided the equivalent of another nail in his coffin. This rather bizarre concept received some public support in the 1960s and 1970s but is now outdated and has become obsolete by virtue of the fact that the more man discovers, the more scientific acheivement is pointing unmistakably toward intelligence.

The contemporary Christian worldview continues to boldly assert that biblical faith and evidence are absolutely inseparable. As it turns out, faith is the natural human response to an accumulation of reliable evidence. In his world-famous biography of the life of Jesus, the first-century apostle St. John wrote the following words: "These (things) are written that you may believe" (John 20:31). John fully understood that his extraordinary eyewitness account of the life of Christ would become very powerful evidence upon which many would discover a life of saving faith. It has never been a part of the biblical worldview that certain spiritual ideals should become earnestly believed and embraced with great confidence in the absence of sufficient evidence. Just as we observe in science—faith, coupled with logic, reason, and evidence are constant intellectual companions that cannot be separated. In rejecting and condemning all faith as merely blind faith, the demeanor of militant new atheists in the modern evolutionary synthesis may have now seriously undermined any credibility they once had.

The neo-Darwinian thinkers, like Richard Dawkins and many others, have held on firmly to the erroneous and misguided notion that faith in God is blind, having no reliable supporting evidence to back it up. This is far from true! They are completely wrong in making this assertion. Faith is inseparable from any attempt at a scientific search to understand the physical reality around us. World-renowned physicist Paul Davies says it this way, "Just because the sun has risen every day of your life, there is no guarantee it will rise tomorrow. The belief that it will—that there are indeed dependable regularities of nature—is an act of faith, but one which is indispensable to the progress of science."[6] The ill-fated attempts of the new atheists to somehow cleanse the human consciousness of genuine religious faith constitute wishful thinking and, as such, they are destined to fail. These secular humanists have brought great pressure to bear upon society by insisting that faith in

God must now be restricted to the private domain, while progressive theoretical science should have completely unrestricted and uncensored access to the public consciousness in every area of human endeavor and experience.

The famous British philosopher Bertrand Russell, a winner of the Nobel Prize for literature in 1950, was an inspirational figure in the life of Richard Dawkins and greatly influenced his bold effort to carry the torch of atheism well into the twenty-first century. In a revealing book about her famous father, Bertrand Russell, British essayist Katherine Tait shares that her devoutly atheist dad was "never open to any serious discussion about the existence of God." She has written, "I could not even talk to him about religion."[7] Nevertheless, Ms. Tait, who eventually would marry a Christian minister, believed that her famous father's "whole life was a search for God . . . somewhere at the back of her father's mind, at the bottom of his heart, in the depths of his soul there was an empty space that had once been filled by God, and he never found anything else to put in it."[8] She says he had the "ghost-like feeling of not belonging, of having no home in this world."[9] However, the persistent inquiry and the continually soul-searching questions of his only daughter must have had some effect on Russell, for in a rather poignant passage he once wrote, "Nothing can penetrate the loneliness of the human heart, except the highest intensity of the sort of love the religious teachers have preached."[10]

You will not find anything remotely resembling this remark in the writings of Richard Dawkins. He has seemed very determined to champion an unrelenting and, might I say, desperate theme so common among today's atheists__ some of whom are making the contemptible claim that no scientist worth his or her salt believes in God! This provocative and outrageous view has long since been swept aside by the current tide of world-view paradigm shifting among today's top-notch scientists. Dawkins is wrong! He has made the classic mistake that nearly all evolutionists are making. They have always believed that an extremely ancient age for planet Earth makes anything seem possible, even if it's not. Those who have placed an uncompromising faith in neo-Darwinian theory, leading to the conclusion of no creator and therefore no sovereign power in the universe, have made a profound, life-altering decision based on a poor theory and flimsy evidence. With an ever-increasing amount of solid contemporary knowledge strongly supporting the time-tested creation worldview, many naturalists are becoming more and more anxious about the current widespread use of terminology and data implying *intelligent design*.

Evolutionary thinkers seem to view any claim of *intelligence* as a dangerous revival of a creationist movement characterized by an unscientific approach that is chiefly focused on a renewed attack against evolutionary thought. As an often rejected notion, the concept of a super-intelligent causation behind a remarkably complex universe is certainly not a recent phenomenon. This popular idea is as ancient as the universally prevalent sensitivities of philosophy and religion themselves. The rather commonplace belief in a theistically designed universe has stood the test of time over many millennia. Only in the last couple of centuries, due to its rather widespread dissemination in Western culture, has blind, unguided naturalism become a fairly popular worldview. Consider this offensive remark: "It is absolutely safe to say that if you meet somebody who claims not to believe in evolution, that person is ignorant, stupid, or insane (or wicked, but I'd rather not consider that)."[11] Humanists like Dawkins who adopt this kind of unwarranted, fallacious rhetoric seem to have gone off the deep end in their absurd disdain for "theism." However, I am absolutely convinced that they will gather very few followers in their misguided war against God and religious faith.

It is obvious that, at least to some degree, the driving motivation behind the current effort to widely disseminate neo-Darwinian dogma worldwide is a concerted attempt to banish the idea of God from human consciousness and from the public discourse. These misguided nonbelievers must be able to furnish arguments in support of their strictly anti-God worldview but, clearly, they have failed to do so. Instead, all they can do is train their sights on many well-known abuses in the historical past involving the world's major religions, by arguing that theology, including Christianity, has actually failed to deliver on the theme of peace and prosperity for all. Everyone would agree that many atrocities have occurred in our world under the guise of religion; very few would question this assessment. However, the accuracy of this statement does not have to be a stumbling block to those who would earnestly seek after knowledge and understanding in an attempt to find true meaning and purpose for their lives.

It is equally true that many benevolent and crucial, world-altering changes have come forth through the dedicated efforts of those who have faithfully lived out their religious conviction. For example, after many years of unwavering perseverance and personal sacrifice, William Wilberforce was finally able to prevail upon the English Parliament to end the ruthless practice of a human slave trading. This bold act of Christian love and courage literally transformed the English-speaking world. Abraham Lincoln waged a long and bitter fight to end the uncivilized practice of slavery in America, because he was completely dedicated to the biblical ideal that all men were created equal, and they were endowed by their Creator with certain inalienable rights, including the right to life, liberty, and the pursuit of happiness. Because of his unwavering commitment to this Christian virtue, Lincoln would go on to pay the ultimate price. The Reverend Martin Luther King Jr. was able to successfully lead a civil-rights movement that helped to revolutionize the American way of life forever, and this has placed us on a course toward respecting human rights and human dignity throughout the modern world. The decision by America to enter World War II was inspired by our Christian duty to champion the cause of freedom in a world in which evil men were imposing their twisted ambitions upon helpless, innocent lives. This action would lead to the liberation of the death camps of Nazi Germany, and it ended the Japanese reign of terror in the Pacific. There are many other profound examples of how faith in God and obedience to his commands has led to positive, world-altering transformation. For example, the Christian influence during the Renaissance in Western Europe resulted in the powerful emergence of music, art and architecture, creating a worldwide impact. After the founding of America, it was the Christian community that established the first hospitals, schools, colleges and universities in promoting the Christian values and moral principles upon which this new nation was founded. The virtue of Christian charity has become wide-spread throughout the entire world as American history will attest. Countless charitable organizations have emerged by way of the Christian command to *love thy neighbor as thyself.* These efforts have provided food, clean water, clothing, shelter, medicine and medical services to the underprivileged worldwide. Examples of such charitable organizations would include Feed the Hungry, the Salvation Army, Samaritan's Purse, St. Jude hospital, Habitat for Humanity, and Never Thirst, not to mention Catholic hospitals, homeless shelters, crisis pregnancy centers, and countless of other humanitarian organizations addressing human need and suffering in America and many other nations the world over.

Those of us who would sincerely seek a thorough understanding of life must be willing to look far beyond the many character flaws that reside in the hearts of men, who often hide behind the cloak of religion in order to conceal or justify their evil intentions. With free volition, man is at liberty to choose either good or evil. You would surely not condemn a monkey tree whose branches were used to fashion spears and arrows so that one native tribe might thoroughly torment, torture, and enslave another. In a few very well-chosen words from accomplished writer Mr. Roy Varghese, "The excesses and atrocities of organized religion have no bearing whatsoever on the existence of God, just as the threat of nuclear proliferation has no bearing on the question of whether $E=mc^2$."[12] Evil is and always has been born in the heart of man who alone has the power, dominion, and capacity to impose his selfish will on the less fortunate without remorse.

To a great extent, the suffering of humanity has been primarily fueled by what humans have done to one another. Don't forget that it was man and not God who invented the implements of war, torture, and slavery. The mindless, selfish actions of those who consistently disobey and disregard God's moral laws always seem to spillover onto innocent lives___ like the child out for a ride on his new birthday bicycle only to be struck down by a drunken driver, or the schoolgirl walking home after classes, who is cut down by a stray bullet in a gang-infested and crime-ridden neighborhood. The Lord God would have had to restrain or even revoke our free will, and thereby impose a robotic state upon mankind in order to prevent tragedies like these from happening to innocent victims. And, of course, this freedom of choice includes the option to carelessly disregard God's moral laws and the strong sense of decency that was wisely instilled within us by a benevolent creator.

World famous British philosopher Antony Flew was a former Oxford atheist and professor, the late son of a Methodist minister, who eventually became a decorated, internationally known scholar. Early on in his storied career, Dr. Flew professed to be an energetic left-wing socialist and even a professing communist, who led the charge of atheism for nearly fifty years. However, the most respectable thing about Antony Flew is that he became open-minded, and determined that he would live by the Socratic principle, which suggests that "we should follow the argument wherever it leads." This ultimately led him to making the wisest decision of his life. Dr. Antony Flew's primary and initial reason for denying God's existence was his inability to reconcile the problem of evil and suffering in a world with an all-loving, all-powerful God. He reasoned that if God does love us, then the existence of pain and suffering would be inconsistent with his divine nature. This argument, which has become all too common among atheists, has already been addressed in significant detail in chapter 7. Even so, people who consistently deny God have erected a new philosophical view that says, "Only statements that can be verified using the direct methods of science are considered to be meaningful." Therefore, by their very own admission, evolution is meaningless, because it has not and cannot be verified by the empirical scientific method.

Yet secular humanists have brought great pressure to bear upon society, insisting that religion and faith in God are in direct conflict with modern science and, therefore, must be restricted to the private domain, while science, including unproven evolutionary science, continues to enjoy unrestricted access at every level of modern society.

As a philosopher, Antony Flew was always privately investigating which way the evidence was leading, while he maintained a firm public view of atheism. However, as the trend toward unbiased scientific research in the late twentieth century began to reveal so much evidence that was inconsistent with evolutionary thought, Flew had remained determined to follow the evidence wherever it would naturally lead him. As it turns out, the tipping point for Dr. Flew was DNA research. The amazing data produced by these unbiased scientific investigations was the final straw that broke the camel's back in regard to Mr. Antony Flew's philosophical worldview. Dr. Flew recently wrote, "What I think that DNA material has done is that it has shown, by the almost unbelievable complexity of the arrangements which are needed to produce (life), that intelligence must have been involved in getting these extraordinarily diverse elements to work together . . . It's the enormous complexity of the number of elements and the enormous subtlety of the way they work together. The meeting of these two parts at the right time, by chance, is simply minute. It is all a matter of the enormous complexity by which the results were achieved, which looked to me like the work of intelligence."[13]

This bold statement marked a major shift from his life-long philosophical point of view, but he has clearly maintained this declaration to be consistent with the early commitment he made to follow the argument no matter where it leads. After having this new radical worldview transformation, Antony Flew remarked that "science spotlights three dimensions of nature that point to God. The first is the fact that nature obeys laws. The second is the dimension of life, of intelligently organized and purpose driven beings, which arose from matter. The third is the very existence of nature . . . the origin of life cannot be explained if you start with matter alone."[14] In the mid-to-late twentieth century, no single individual had embodied the argument for atheism more so than Antony Flew. However, after explaining his much unexpected conversion to theism in the later years of his professional career, Antony Flew has offered these parting remarks: "I have followed the argument where it led me, and it has led me to accept the existence of a self-existent, immutable, immaterial, omnipotent and omniscient being."[15] "We have all the evidence we need in our immediate experience . . . only a deliberate refusal to look (at the evidence) is responsible for atheism of any variety."[16] And now, this single man's storied career has become highly representative of thousands of scientists, philosophers and educators who have shaken off their early bias, and have now embraced the honest, knowledge-seeking principle that compels them to follow the argument, and let the evidence speak for itself.

A good man, particularly if he is a devoted scientist or philosopher, should be concerned with the facts, and should also be wise enough to follow the pathway these facts point to, even if they lead in a direction that opposes his preferred worldview. Because of this important principle, coupled with the current advances in modern-day technological research (advances that have revealed Darwin-denying complexity as never before), we have seen that worldview transformations like that of Antony Flew and others are now becoming commonplace. The discovery of the laws of physics, the fine-tuning of a vast and remarkable universe, and the absolutely transcendent complexity found in material organic design has led many unbiased, knowledge-seeking scientists, educators, and philosophers, along with other open-minded seekers of truth, to embrace the certainty of an infinitely superior mind. If we will only examine the evidence, the real truth will ultimately become clearly revealed to our hearts.

The Evidence Stands Tall

I have followed a clear trail of evidence were it would naturally lead me through many years of study and research. I have examined this unmistakable path through the many disciplines of science, over the clear and well-preserved footprints of history, and represented by a wide variety of well documented testimony gathered from scientific literature for over thirty years. What you have read throughout these pages is the focused accumulation of many thousands of hours of study, research, writing, and editing. I have been determined to make it my personal mission and lifelong aspiration to know and to understand, to some degree, the observed and revealed truth that is represented by this vast accumulation of current knowledge and information about life's most pressing questions. I can tell you with firm conviction that this diligent search has clearly directed me toward acknowledging a powerful creator God, who alone is responsible for the vast physical reality we are privileged to enjoy. We observe a material world that is filled with mystery, life, and possibility for those who were created in God's image. This all-powerful creator God has made himself known to his creation in a variety of unmistakable ways. We would be wise to open our hearts and our minds to the one who said, "Let there be light!—and there was light."

For over one hundred years now, there has been a major effort on the part of so-called enlightened individuals to circumvent the truth of the Word of God by contrasting the Holy Bible with secular public revelation in regard to scientific knowledge__ to the end that secular-minded attitudes and opinions have dominated the cultural divide between church and state. I am now convinced, more than ever, that no single issue has caused greater harm to man's perception of biblical truth than the ongoing creation-versus-evolution controversy. Three hundred years of scientific skepticism has left the message of the God's Word in doubt, to some greater or lesser degree, in the minds of millions worldwide. However, before we abandon biblical truth on the basis of biased and misguided public opinion, we must first consider the fact that the Bible has accurately revealed scientific knowledge about the physical universe, and the nature of living things, long before mankind documented so many of these fascinating details.

In my mind, this is a critical piece of the puzzle. We must thoroughly consider the false claim of many that the Bible is in conflict with science and, therefore, cannot be trusted. Evolutionary thought is a man-made philosophy, contrived by people who wanted to make their own rules. This bankrupt theory has fostered disdain for authority, has indirectly generated widespread immorality, and instills the false hope of people avoiding any and all accountability to a higher power. Can you and I really afford to risk our future on the exceedingly remote and mathematically impossible prospect that somehow impersonal, lifeless matter, directed only by random, blind chance events, is responsible for a remarkable universe? Or, should we freely admit to ourselves and others that God is real, and was the only intelligence there to witness what actually happened when life began? The God of creation has carefully recorded, for our benefit, his own account of what occurred at the dawn of history in the venerated book of Genesis, and we would be foolish to ignore it. Why do you suppose the creator God of the spirit world, who dwells beyond time and space, cares so much about feeble mankind? I believe it was because God's love for humanity (his crowning creation) was so boundless, after creating man in his own likeness, that he could not bear the thought of spending eternity without us.

Isn't it about time to put unproven, unfounded skepticism far behind us and to seriously consider what really happened when life began?

The following is only a partial list of a vast amount of scientific truth that was recorded in the biblical text thousands of years before mankind had any firsthand understanding of these facts and principles. Also included are the general dates when mankind's persistent curiosity resulted in discoveries that have confirmed these ancient written biblical details. This is nothing less than powerful scientific proof that the Bible was inspired by God.

Known scientific fact or principle	Biblical reference	Date of man's discovery
The Law of Entropy	Psalm 102:25-27	After the fall
A place in the north void of stars	Job 26:7	17th century
Earth held up by invisible forces	Job 26:7	1650
The earth is circular in shape	Isaiah 40:22	15th century
Certain animals carry diseases	Leviticus 11	16th century
Quarantine for disease control	Leviticus 13	17th century
Animal blood carries disease	Leviticus 17	17th century
Blood is essential for life	Leviticus 17:11	19th century
Oceans have natural paths within	Psalm 8:8	1854

Earth in nebular form initially	Genesis 1:2	1911
Most seaworthy ship design ratio	Genesis 6	1860
Light (photon) is a particle with mass	Job 38:19	1932
Radio astronomy (stars emit signals)	Job 38:7	1945
Oceans contain fresh water springs	Job 38:16	1920
Snow has material value	Job 38:22	1905, 1966
Number of stars cannot be counted	Genesis 15:5	1940
Dust is important to survival	Isaiah 40:12	1935
Gas particles have weight	Job 28:25	16th century
Light can be split up into colors	Job 38:24	1650
Matter is made of invisible particles	Romans 1:20	18th century
Plants use sunlight to make food	Job 8:16	1920
Stars are moving through space	Job 38:32	19th century
Description of the water cycle	Eccles.1:6,7; Job 36	17th century
Lighting and thunder are related	Job 38:25	19th century
The universe had a beginning	Genesis 1:1	20th century
Universe governed by natural laws	Job 38:33, Jer.33:25	16th-19th centuries

Having worked in the healthcare industry for nearly fifty years, my favorite Bible-science revelation is the fact that God commanded through Moses that all newborn male children from the tribes of Israel were to be circumcised on the eighth day (Genesis 17:12, Leviticus 12:3, Luke 1:59). What was so special about the eighth day? Why was it so important to wait that long before performing the act of male circumcision in Israel? As it turns out, the intestines of a newborn are sterile. It requires a number of days of breathing and feeding before an infant is able to lay down a healthy flora of natural bacteria often referred to today as "probiotic organisms." As these useful organisms accumulate in the gut of a newborn, they begin to produce vitamin K, which of course is essential for blood clotting; also, the level of an important blood-clotting protein prothrombin peaks in the newborn at this time as well. For these very important reasons, the eighth day was the safest time to circumcise a child before the current advent of modern medicine. This most critical knowledge would have prevented newborn male children from bleeding to death at the time this minor surgical procedure was performed in ancient Israel.

How could Moses possibly know it was important to wait until the eighth day to perform the rite of circumcision? That knowledge came from God (the Creator) who alone knew the unique details he had designed into the human body. In this same way, God revealed many other critical details about health, nature, and science to humanity long before man's curiosity led to confirmation of these essential facts and principles. The Bible even anticipated the eventual rise of pseudo-science, such as the evolutionary hypothesis, which contradicts the observable evidence readily available in our world today. As we read in 1 Timothy 6:20, we can clearly see that the Bible warned us in advance of this powerful deception that is so widely prevalent in our world today. "Guard what was committed to your trust, avoiding the profane and idle babble and contradictions (traditions of men that conflict with God's Word) of what is falsely called knowledge (science); by professing it some have strayed concerning the faith." And continuing in 11 Timothy we read, "In the last days perilous times will come (like many unprovoked acts of terrorism motivated by pure hatred).

For men will be lovers of themselves, lovers of money, boasters, proud, blasphemers, disobedient to parents, unthankful, unholy, despisers of good, lovers of pleasure rather than lovers of God . . . always learning and never able to come to the knowledge of the truth. But evil men and imposters (teachers of false worldviews) will grow worse and worse, deceiving and being deceived. For the time will come when they will not endure sound doctrine (biblical truth), but according to their desires, because they have itching ears, they will heap up for themselves teachers (men who reject God's eternal truth and retain beliefs that condone lustful desires__ seeking teachers and authorities who speak to them what they want to hear) . . . and they will turn their ears away from the truth, and be turned aside to fables" (like a philosophy of life that does not ultimately require moral accountability). (11 Timothy 3:1-4,7,13; chap 4:3,4).

I could cite dozens of other examples of scientific knowledge that was foretold in the biblical text long before mankind discovered these naturally ordained laws and principles, but I think the message is becoming clear that the Bible is not in conflict with science and never has been.

Many people have attempted to convince the world that science clashes with the Bible, but nothing could be further from the truth! I do not know of a single accurate fact of science that is in conflict with the biblical record. True science and Scripture are in perfect harmony, and therefore, they should be considered companions not foes.

What is information but the passage of knowledge from one intelligent being to another? Information, conveyed by letters, words, and language, can only be generated by an intelligent mind. It has nothing to do with the accidental interaction of mass and energy in a mindless universe. Information cannot exist without intelligence! Suppose you were walking along the seashore, and you came upon some very large letters scratched in the sand that spelled out "David loves Linda." Can you imagine anyone coming to the conclusion that these words appeared magically on the seashore because of some mindless, unguided process in which the natural elements came together randomly to produce an intelligent message by pure chance? It is absurd to imagine that any educated person could draw such a conclusion.

Human DNA contains around seven billion bits of information contained within about 3.5 billion chemical letters of genetic detail. This chemical code spells out many millions of details comprising a complete instruction manual for each and every person on the planet. Life is built on information and information comes from intelligence. To disallow a sovereign God as the intelligent planner and creative designer of complex organic life on this planet, one would also have to deny many truths that have been thoroughly documented throughout decades of scientific research and discovery. Which came first, the DNA or protein? Since each one requires the other, the most logical answer can only be that they both originated at the same time. This clearly infers a supreme intelligence and a creation worldview.

I find it rather strange that many scientists are constantly searching for meaningful signs of electronic communication far beyond our planet from outer space that would indicate the presence of intelligent life well beyond our world. Yet these same scientists would most likely refuse to acknowledge that the extremely complex language and information (biological communication) appearing in organic DNA points toward design by a "living intelligence." According to world-renowned physicist, professor, and writer Dr. Paul Davies, "Making a protein simply by injecting energy is rather like exploding a stick of dynamite under a pile of bricks and expecting it to form a house . . .You may liberate enough energy to raise the bricks, but without coupling energy to the bricks in a controlled and ordered way, there is little hope of producing anything other than a chaotic mess."[17]

The Demise of Darwinism

Today, after the accumulation of several hundred years of scientific investigation and much historical research, it has become more obvious than ever that evolution theory is grossly inadequate in explaining how organic life could have emerged from nonliving matter to form the complexity of living organisms that amaze us and supersede our comprehension. How then should we respond to this powerful wave of scientific and historical evidence that has cast an extremely dim view on Darwinism and has made many of the most revered scientists of the twentieth century look foolish for their outlandish claims? It is extremely presumptuous of man, with such limited knowledge, intelligence, and experience, to think that he could possibly explain events that occurred in the ancient past when Earth's history began. Evolution theory is simply a widely accepted hypothesis that attempts to explain the origin of life, not because it can be proven through a logical examination of the evidence, but because the only alternative, special creation, requires the intervention of an all-powerful supreme intelligence.

By my way of thinking, the unproven evolution model is much more difficult to believe than creation, and actually requires a great deal more faith because of its serious lack of evidence, which continues to vanish in light of today's advancing scientific knowledge. This rapidly declining explanation of origins is so unbelievable that the probability of carbon-based organic life originating by random chance alone in a mindless universe has often been compared to the unthinkable possibility of randomly producing a complete set of the *Encyclopedia Britannica* from an accidental explosion in a printing shop.

Listen again to these bold words offering a more complete quotation by I. L. Cohen, a member of the New York Academy of Sciences. He wrote, "Any suppression, which undermines and destroys that very foundation on which scientific methodology and research was erected, evolutionist or otherwise, cannot and must not be allowed to flourish . . . it is a confrontation between scientific objectivity and ingrained prejudice—between logic and emotion—between fact and fiction . . . in the final analysis, objective scientific logic has to prevail— no matter what the final result is—no matter how many time-honored idols have to be discarded in the process . . . after all, it is not the duty of science to defend the theory of evolution and stick by it to the bitter end—no matter what the illogical and unsupported conclusions it offers . . . If in the process of impartial scientific logic, they find that creation by outside intelligence is the solution to our quandary, then let's cut the umbilical cord that tied us down to Darwin for such a long time. It's choking us and holding us back . . . Every single concept advanced by the theory of evolution (and amended thereafter) is imaginary, as it is not supported by the scientifically established probability concepts. Darwin was wrong . . . the theory of evolution may be the worst mistake made in science."[18]

Was there, perhaps, a self-gratifying motivation behind a theory that leaves man in control. Listen to the confessions of two prominent atheists, each of whom have had a noteworthy influence on this debate in years past. One of them was the grandson of Thomas Huxley, who was often referred to as Darwin's right-hand man and strongest supporter ("Darwin's bulldog"). A writer and philosopher, Aldous Huxley, once wrote this: "I had motives for not wanting the world to have meaning; consequently assumed that it had none . . . and was able, without any difficulty, to find satisfying reasons for this assumption . . . For myself, as no doubt, for most of my contemporaries, the philosophy of meaninglessness was essentially an instrument of liberation. The liberation we desired was simultaneous liberation from a certain political and economic system, and liberation from a certain system of morality. We objected to the morality because it interfered with our sexual freedom."[19]

Thomas Nagel is a former professor of philosophy and law at New York University. While honestly considering his view of life as an atheist, he recorded these remarks: "I speak from experience, being strongly subject to this fear myself: I want atheism to be true and am 'made uneasy' by the fact that some of the most intelligent and well-informed people I know are religious believers. It isn't just that I don't believe in God and, naturally, hope that I'm right in my belief. It's that I hope there is no God! I don't want there to be a God; I don't want the universe to be like that . . . My guess is that this cosmic authority problem is not a rare condition, and that it is responsible for much of this scientism and reductionism of our time. One of the tendencies it supports is the 'ludicrous overuse' of evolutionary biology to explain everything about human life, including everything about the human mind . . . this is a somewhat ridiculous situation . . . it is just as irrational to be influenced in one's beliefs by the hope that God does not exist as by the hope that God does exist."[20]

Debunking evolution is not that difficult if we are willing to focus our attention on a convincing trail of evidence that is currently available. It is only those who flatly refuse to consider the evidence that are missing the truth about such a vital question as the origin of life. The teaching of evolution theory leads to a sense of purposelessness, which can have disastrous consequences. In a notable speech delivered at America's prestigious Harvard University some years ago, it was the world-famous Russian dissident Alexander Solzhenitsyn who was harshly booed by many of those in attendance when he uttered the following powerful statement, which aptly describes the general direction of nearly every culture in the Western world today: "The greatest burdens will come upon any society when they forget God!"[21]

Chinese-born scientist Dr. Kenneth Hsu speaks out boldly concerning his view on Darwinism: "We have all heard of *The Origin of Species*, although few of us have had time to read it . . . a casual perusal of the classic made me understand the rage of Paul Feyerabend . . . I agree with him that Darwinism contains 'wicked lies'; it is not a 'natural law' formulated on the basis of factual evidence, but a 'dogma,' reflecting the dominating social philosophy of the last century."[22]

According to Dr. Henry Morris, the typical mantra adamantly maintained by modern evolutionists remains the same as it always has been in the past. After absorbing the many heavy blows and powerful contradictions that objective science has dealt "the theory," through computer-age scientific advances, the basic refrain of naturalism simply will not go away. Its standard litany has always been and currently goes something like this: "We know evolution is true, even though we don't know how it works, and have never seen it happen."[23]

To the ardent evolutionist, because intelligent design is not and never can be an option, and because the fossil record has left traditional evolution without its much needed support, the only conclusion they can possibly accept is that the mechanism that is driving evolution forward must be revised to fit the currently revealed facts. This has been the typical strategy of evolutionary humanists all along—start with the various conclusions that you are confident in and have already determined to be true, and then methodically fill in the blanks by whatever means you find necessary to support your conclusions. And you must steadfastly follow this uncompromising approach even if it means that you will have to ignore, deny or perhaps minimize a growing body of evidence that increasingly lends its support to intelligent causation and a creation worldview.

The Power of Worldview Thinking

I want to strongly emphasize the critical importance of man embracing the correct worldview. Our personal view of life will hold a very powerful influence over the way we live each day. It will dominate our beliefs, attitudes, and actions in every area of our human experience. It will control our todays and determine the outcome of our tomorrows, but most of all it will serve to shape our eternal destiny. The origin of conscious, organic life is vital to our overall understanding. How we view this crucial question will prove to have profound implications on how we are likely to view the most important issues of life. The dangerous doctrine of evolution is based upon the self-serving and prideful wisdom of man, and its shaky foundation rests upon the shifting sands of time. This man-made ideology, however, is beginning to collapse right before our eyes, and the vacuum left behind must be filled by the truth, giving lasting purpose and meaning to our lives well beyond the few short years of our mortality.

Hundreds of philosophies and scores of religions have been created by the wisdom and will of man in his unrelenting effort to circumvent the Word of God. The greatest danger of evolutionary doctrine is that it ultimately leads to a universal breakdown of personal and governmental morality, resulting in a rejection of the authority of the Bible, and a failure to appropriate its many promises leading to salvation and eternal life. If human morality is grounded in evolutionary humanism, it soon becomes subjective, in which case everyone can choose their own set of values, and can impose their will upon whomever they wish. Adolph

Hitler believed he was advancing human evolution by ridding the world of inferior races and defective people, whom he believed to be unfit contributors to a superior race of men. As it turns out, he was a deranged psychopath whose choice of moral superiority became a crime against humanity rivaled only by a few other men throughout world history. Many people now believe that holding to the nonexistence of God can be seen as an escape mechanism to avoid taking moral responsibility for one's behavior in a self-centered world where many people simply do not like being told how they should live. Because of this demeanor, the people who desire to explain the origin of life without any reference to a supernatural being have eagerly embraced the theory of evolution. In becoming sort of self-proclaimed gods, who are able to personally define the boundaries of morality, humanists have always sought to repel any sense of accountability to an intelligent authority greater than themselves.

Evolution is surely the most devastating social philosophy the modern world has ever known, and it continues to be a major factor in the moral decline of contemporary cultures across the globe, including the United States of America. Evolution has provided the pseudoscientific rationale for all kinds of evil influences throughout the world, including everything from abortion to communism. Most people regard evolution as merely an abstract biological theory, with little or no consequence to their lives. However, it is really somewhat like a giant, insidious octopus with tentacles that have reached into every area of modern culture, every field of study, every level of education, and every practicing discipline, with very destructive consequences. The twentieth century was by far the deadliest century in human history in terms of the degree of carnage man has inflicted upon his fellow man (with an estimated one hundred million lives lost through human conflict alone); and much of that carnage resulted from the insidious evil of men who held to an evolutionary worldview. I do not think it coincidental that the twentieth century was also the period in history when the greatest degree of evolutionary indoctrination was thrust upon the civilized world. Evolution is not merely a crude, ambiguous biological theory but a dangerous and destructive philosophical worldview that is in direct opposition to the Judeo-Christian principles and values that gave rise to today's Western civilization. Every single life that it touches is, at least to some degree, pulled away from a sovereign and benevolent God who lovingly fashioned mankind for a noble purpose and a magnificent destiny.

Scientists Are Speaking Out

If your personal quest for truth and meaning excludes any mention of God, perhaps it is time to consider where the evidence is now leading so many of today's top-notch scientists, who have had enough with presumption and speculation that does not measure up to the facts. More than ever before, many scientists are speaking their protest toward the unfounded assumptions of evolution theory, which most of Western civilization has been dragging around like a ball and chain the last couple of centuries. Please consider carefully what is suggested by the various conclusions of these courageous and boldly outspoken men, in light of what we now know to be true.

A noteworthy French zoologist Pierre-Paul Grasse was the author of over three hundred scientific publications. He has drawn the following conclusion: "Through use and abuse of hidden postulates, of bold, often ill-founded extrapolations, a pseudo-science has been created. It is taking root in the very heart of biology, and is leading astray many biochemists and biologists who sincerely believe that the accuracy of fundamental concepts has been demonstrated, which is not the case."[24]

Loren Eiseley was an American anthropologist, educator, and philosopher, who also became well known as a natural science writer, and subsequently received no less than thirty-six honorary degrees during his outstanding career. His written works include an evaluation of the failed effort on the part of twentieth-century science to fully establish credibility for the evolution model. In regard to this clear failure to painstakingly legitimize evolution theory, he has made this assessment: "With the failure of these many efforts, science was left in a somewhat embarrassing position of having to postulate theories of living organisms which it could not demonstrate. After having chided the theologian for his reliance on myth and miracle, science found itself in the inevitable position of having to create a 'mythology' of its own: namely, the assumption that what, after long effort it could not prove to take place today had, in truth, taken place in the primeval past."[25]

Luther Sunderland served as an American aerospace engineer who worked with General Electric for many years. As a devoted creationist, he became an avid writer who thoroughly researched the question of origins and frequently published his findings. Listen to these bold remarks from his book entitled *Darwin's Enigma*: "Now, after 120 years of the most extensive and painstaking geological exploration of every continent and ocean bottom, the picture is infinitely more vivid and complete than it was in 1859. Formations have been discovered containing hundreds of billions of fossils and our museums are filled with over 100 million fossils of 250,000 different species . . . The availability of this 'profusion of hard scientific data' should permit objective investigators to determine if Darwin was on the right track. What is the picture which the fossils have given us? . . . The gaps between major groups of organisms have been growing even wider and more undeniable. They can no longer be ignored or rationalized away with appeals to imperfection in the fossil record."[26]

Louis Agassiz was a Swiss-born, European-educated biologist and geologist who was recognized as an innovative scholar in the essential study of earth's natural history. He eventually came to America, becoming a professor at Harvard University, where he taught zoology and geology for many years. After a very extensive career in the natural sciences, he made this declaration that has driven a stake into the very heart of the evolution model: "The theory [of evolution] is a scientific mistake."[27] Then he backed that statement with another prudent observation, which he wrote after many years of study, research, and investigation. "The origin of all diversity among living beings remains a mystery as totally unexplained as if the 'book of Mr. Darwin' had never been written, for no theory unsupported by facts, however plausible it may appear, can be admitted in science."[28]

Nils Heribert-Nilsson was honored among scientists as a Swedish botanist and research geneticist for his work in extensive breeding experiments as a professor of botany at Lund University. He was elected a member of the Royal Swedish Academy of Sciences in 1943. After a lifetime of work in attempting to demonstrate the process of evolutionary change in organic species he became compelled to publish the following revealing statement: "My attempts to demonstrate evolution by an experiment carried on for more than 40 years has completely failed. At least I should hardly be accused of having started from any preconceived anti-evolutionary standpoint."[29]

Chinese-born scientist Dr. Kenneth Hsu has studied geology, paleoclimatology, and oceanography, among other disciplines. After his immigration to the United States in 1948, he completed his formal studies at Ohio State University, and then received a PhD from UCLA in 1953. Dr. Hsu taught applied sciences throughout the United States for many years, while working for private industry (The Shell Oil Company) as a petroleum geologist and an environmental engineer. He became a member of the U.S. National Academy of Science in 1986. Dr. Kenneth Hsu has always been a straight shooter, and has never been afraid to report what he knew to be true. Here is another example of the bold comments he has made, which drive home the idea that Darwinism was a colossal scientific mistake: "George Bernard Shaw wisecracked once that Darwin had the luck to please everyone who had an ax to grind. Well, I also have an ax to grind, but I am not pleased. We have suffered through two wars and are threatened by an Armageddon. We have had enough of Darwinian fallacy."[30]

James Perloff is an avid writer who, among other things, has had a background and a special interest in investigative science for many years. The subject matter found in his written material includes topics such as Darwinism, U.S. politics, and world history. In his popular 1999 book, *Tornado in a Junkyard*, he made a bold assertion about evolution theory: "The evolutionary establishment fears creation science, because evolution itself crumbles when challenged by evidence. In the 1970s and 1980s hundreds of public debates were arranged between evolutionary scientists and creation scientists. The latter scored resounding victories, with the result that, today, few evolutionists will debate. Isaac Asimov, Stephen Jay Gould, and the late Carl Sagan, while highly critical of creationism, all declined to debate."[31]

Dr. David Raup was a Harvard-educated, University of Chicago paleontologist who studied the fossil record extensively for many years during a long and very fruitful academic career. He observed first-hand how weak the argument for evolution had become after the onslaught of recent evidence that has strengthened the creationist position. He has commented, "I doubt if there is a single individual within the scientific community, who could cope with the full range of [creationist's] arguments without the help of an army of consultants in special fields."[32]

At this point in the book's narrative it may be appropriate to clarify just how the role for God has been presented in the long-standing debate on origins. Support for God in the great debate has generally appeared in two different but related formats: *Creationism* and *Intelligent Design*. The term Creationism constitutes a belief that the universe and life in it have originated from specific acts of divine creation by a sovereign God as described in the biblical genesis account. The conclusion of many proponents is that evolution theory is terribly inadequate and, therefore, cannot possibly account for the history, diversity and complexity of life on Earth. This belief has been scientifically supported and aggressively promoted by a number of well-funded organizations based in the United States including the Institute for Creation Research, Answers in Genesis, and the Creation Research Society, among others. Intelligent Design, a closely related concept, constitutes the broad argument for the existence of God and is promoted as an evidence-based scientific theory about life's origin. The claim is that certain features of the universe and of living things are best explained by intelligent causation rather than by a mindless, undirected process such as natural selection. The Intelligent Design movement is commonly associated with the Discovery Institute, a politically conservative think tank based in the United States.

Dr. Phillip E. Johnson is a retired UC Berkeley law professor, whose interest in the modern creation worldview has earned him the unofficial title, Father of the Intelligent Design Movement. He became a co-founder of the Discovery Institute's Center for Science and Culture, an organization which seeks to promote the Intelligent Design hypothesis in scientific circles internationally. As a true champion of the "intelligent cause" argument he has sought to convince the scientific community to allow a role for God in scientific theory. In these remarks, he explains how the false premise of evolution has sustained itself for so long in the light of new evidence that flatly denies Darwinian claims: "It [evolution] is sustained largely by a propaganda campaign that relies on all the usual tricks of rhetorical persuasion: . . . hidden assumptions, question-begging statements of what is at issue, terms that are vaguely defined and change their meaning in mid-argument, attacks of straw men, selective citation of evidence, and so on. The theory is also protected by its cultural importance. It is the officially sanctioned 'creation story' of modern society, and publicly funded educational authorities spare no effort to persuade people to believe it."[33]

Dr. Randy L. Wysong is an American physician who served as an instructor of human anatomy and physiology for many years. He may be best known for a book he had published in 1976, entitled *The Creation-Evolution Controversy*. In the book, he had this to say about modern evolutionary ideology: "Evolution can be thought of as sort of a magical religion. Magic is simply an effect without a cause, or at least a competent cause. 'Chance,' 'time,' and 'nature,' are the small gods enshrined at evolutionary temples. Yet these gods cannot explain the origin of life. These gods are impotent. Thus, evolution is left without competent cause and is, therefore, only a magical explanation for the existence of life."[34]

Dr. Harold Urey was known for his work as an American physical chemist. He had pioneered a major work on isotopes leading to the discovery of deuterium, which earned him the Nobel Prize for chemistry in 1934. Dr. Urey went on to play a significant role in the eventual development of the atomic bomb, but he may actually be remembered most for his contribution to various theories relating to the development of organic life from nonliving matter. Although a man of his stature should be confident about a theory of origins, the following statement from Dr. Urey reveals considerable doubt. "All of us who study the origin of life find that the more we looked into it, the more we feel that it is too complex to have evolved anywhere . . . We believe as an article of faith that life evolved from dead matter on this planet. It is just that its complexity is so great, it is hard for us to imagine that it did."[35]

Michael Denton is a British-Australian author and biochemist who received his PhD in biochemistry from King's College in London, England. His examination of the evidence through a lifetime of work in biochemistry led him to write a book in 1985 entitled *Evolution: A Theory in Crisis*. This timely book has proven to be a valuable resource in the creationist dialogue. It offers a systematic critique of neo-Darwinian theory that covers a whole gamut of topics from paleontology to molecular biology. In this documentation, Denton concludes his argument with an explanation of just how a false and misleading hypothesis could have actually become such a fashionable influence on Western society. In a more complete citation of a previous quotation he wrote, "The influence of evolutionary theory on fields far removed from biology is one of the most spectacular examples in history of how a highly speculative idea for which there is no really hard scientific evidence can come to fashion the thinking of a whole society and dominate the outlook of an age . . . Ultimately, the Darwinian theory of evolution is no more nor less than the great cosmogenic myth of the 20th century."[36]

Raising the Bar on Living

In this book, I have attempted to document many reasons for and the evidence favoring the embrace of a biblical worldview. These many reasons (derived primarily from secular sources) have taken the reader beyond what he or she *should* believe by providing compelling evidence suggesting exactly *why* they should believe it. Remember, nothing in life is worth our believing unless one can demonstrate a rational and reasonable argument to support it. Naturalism or theism? There is so very much at stake in getting this answer correct. We certainly cannot afford to wait until we die to find out which worldview is true! In these few chapters, I have laid out as best I can the background and the true character of this ongoing debate. Now it is up to readers to decide for themselves what to believe concerning the mystery of life, and to choose whether or not God deserves a place in their hearts and minds, as they find their way through the difficult and sometimes overwhelming struggle of living mortal lives in a fallen world.

But let us make no mistake about it, with this ongoing creation-versus-evolution argument, we find ourselves in a life-and-death struggle for the soul of America and the civilized world. And the outcome of this struggle will, no doubt, bear eternal consequences for those who have willingly engaged in the debate, and also for those who remain oblivious to its exceptionally powerful influence over their lives. Without knowing it, millions have become indoctrinated. Consequently, many today have come to a fateful decision regarding which hypothesis will shape their lives, capture their allegiance, and control their destiny. It has been the goal of this book to refute the theory of evolution using sound reason, logic, objective science, and historical truth, all of which have been confirmed by the expert opinions of many well-qualified authorities with a wide variety of philosophical and scientific backgrounds.

No matter what we believe, or how we have come to believe it, the truth is the same for all of us. Only the truth will provide us with the lasting sense of contentment, satisfaction, and peace that we all desire. It's time for us to raise the bar, and to set a much higher standard for our families and ourselves when it comes to shaping a personal worldview that will manifest itself in every area of our lives. True faith is not a leap in the dark. It is a commitment based on evidence! You would be utterly foolish to believe in something for which there exists no valid supporting evidence based on rational logic and sound reason. This would be like an adult who has come to believe in a living Santa Claus or the tooth fairy. The very powerful, faith-filled conviction of several billion Christian believers worldwide cannot be taken lightly; this life-changing experience, based on abundant evidence, is a commanding proof of the existence and influence of the Almighty One.

You will never experience a greater sense of deep satisfaction than when you can sincerely say, "All is well with my soul"! The mystery of life will never be decided, explained, or understood through our best efforts using only human intellectual rationalization, no matter how many colleges and universities are founded in pursuit of this ideal. Although human progress and modern technological achievement continues to advance rapidly in our day, we human beings are certainly not evolving toward some ultra-advanced animal species, as evolution theory clearly teaches. You and I were created in the image of a powerful and loving creator God, and we are responsible moral beings who are accountable to our Maker. We all have the physiological capacity and intellectual potential that humanity was designed with from the very beginning of time; only the world around us with the many opportunities and stress-induced conflicts it presents has changed, and continues to do so at a rapid pace.

Like most people, I am sure you have come into contact with someone, or perhaps many people, who have eagerly explained to you what they think you should believe. What we come to believe is usually dictated by the influence of the very people who have affected our lives the most. This could be parents, siblings, friends, family, teachers, coaches, supervisors, mentors, pastors, or even professors. We may admire certain influential people who have impacted our lives in some meaningful way, but if they have failed to comprehend the truth about the mystery of life, then perhaps their best efforts have brought us only temporary resolution to our greatest worries, fears, and disappointments. After spending the better part of thirty years examining the most challenging questions about life, questions that each one of us must face at some time or other, it has been my utmost desire to assist those who may remain puzzled by the unrelenting question of what they should believe. I would certainly have very little to offer anyone on this topic if I was unable to present valid evidence and to lay a solid foundation upon which faith in the sovereign God of creation could be generated. We definitely must ask ourselves once again—what was God doing hanging on a Roman cross and how should that impact my life today? The only way I know to gain victory over the worry in living, and the fear of dying, is to make peace with God. This can be done through Christ alone!

Chapter 10

How Then Shall We Live?

Creator, Redeemer, and Judge

Most people only think of Jesus (God's eternal Son) as the Savior of humanity; but did you know the Bible also credits him as the sovereign creator God of the universe, and the righteous judge to whom all humankind will eventually answer? Our devotion to and worship of him is greatly magnified once we have fully considered what the entire Bible has to say about the magnificent God who visited humanity as a lowly carpenter's son some two thousand years ago. The Bible has declared, "For by Him [Jesus Christ] all things were created; things in heaven and on earth, visible and invisible, whether thrones or powers or rulers or authorities—all things were created by Him and for Him. He [Jesus Christ] is before all things, and in Him all things hold [are held] together" (Colossians 1:16, 17 NIV). "In the beginning was the Word, and the Word was with God, and the Word was God . . . He [Jesus Christ, the Son] was in the beginning with God. All things were made through Him, and without Him nothing was made . . . He was in the world, and the world was made through Him, and the world did not know Him, . . . and the Word [Jesus] became flesh and dwelt among us" (John 1:1-3, 10, 14). "God, who at various times and in various ways spoke in time past to the fathers by the prophets, has in these last days spoken to us by His Son, whom he has appointed heir of all things, through whom also he made the worlds" (Hebrews 1:1, 2).

That the Creator of the universe could love us enough to die for our sins (providing an atonement), which carries the potential for you and I to be restored to a right-standing relationship with God, is the best news we could possibly ever hope for. How could any person reject such a powerful demonstration of unconditional love? And yet this is exactly what millions of people are doing, while they continue to live their lives as complete strangers to the very God who created them. It was for the sake of love and relationship that Jesus became a man and identified himself with sinful humanity—experiencing our pain, sorrow and suffering. No one can accuse the living Christ of not understanding the trials they face in this mortal life. He faced more trial, sorrow, and suffering than any of us could ever imagine, when he willingly took our sin upon himself (dying in our place) so that we could know redemption, and obtain the hope of spending an eternity in his presence. *How then shall we live*? Many will live for the next big Hollywood blockbuster, the latest and greatest video game, or perhaps the next victory for your favorite team. Do these seemingly mundane and frivolous pursuits really matter in light of eternity? We would do well to focus some attention on the things that matter most!

Nearly everyone, in their heart of hearts, understands the significance of the world-changing event we will observe every year on December 25. On this day, we celebrate the miraculous appearance upon the earth of the creator God of the universe, who had reduced himself to the physical dimension in order to prove, once and for all, his undeniable love for humanity. It's offensive to hear many people complain that God does not care about their plight in life, and then, instead of running to him and seeking after him, they continue to live as though he does not even exist. They are sadly misguided! God has done everything he possibly can to prove how much he cares, even to the point that he has provided us with a sure way out of our miserable and disturbing circumstances (the many trials of living in a cursed world).

God has made the gospel truth so simple that even a small child can understand it. It goes something like this: God created us; God loves us;

and God wants to save us from the penalty, power, and presence of sin that is so clearly characteristic of our fallen world. However, he cannot do that if we continue to deny that he exists, and go about the business of inventing our own man-made truth, while completely disregarding his revealed written Word, and his sovereign authority.

Jesus himself offers a stern warning to the ungodly philosophers of our time who have assuredly caused the greatest measure of offense—an offense that has been cunningly perpetrated against the innocent young lives of children in America and around the world. The word "offend" simply means to lay a snare for, to set a trap for, to cause to stumble and fall. This is what evolutionary humanists have done in our world as a result of their massive effort to control public opinion and to shape public policy. Make no mistake about it; children believe what they are told not only by parents but also by other important figures of authority in their lives.

Jesus saw this deception coming. Evolutionary teaching, and secular humanism, has now led multiple millions toward disbelief in God and a blatant disregard for his Word. This dark cloud of deception has been very instrumental in leading us into the most sinful and corrupt time of our nation's history! When considering the many children growing up in the midst of each generation, this is what Jesus had to say, "Whoever receives one little child like this in my name receives Me. But whoever causes one of these little ones who believe in Me to sin, it would be better for him if a millstone were hung around his neck, and he were drowned in the depth of the sea. Woe to the world because of offenses! For offences must come, but woe to that man [men and women] by whom the offense comes!" (Matthew 18:5-7).

Finally, the Bible teaches that Christ has been given the authority to execute divine judgment upon those for whom he paid the ultimate prize. "I charge you therefore before God and the Lord Jesus Christ, *who will judge the living and the dead* at His appearing and His kingdom" (2 Timothy 4:1).

Dr. Henry Morris was an extraordinary student of life science and earth history. As a devoted scholar of biblical truth, as well, he worked tirelessly to connect science and the Bible as the natural outcome of rational understanding. In regard to the spiritual matters, he once wrote, "Of all the world's religions and philosophies, only orthodox biblical Christianity teaches both the supernatural creation of all things by the transcendent, yet personal Creator God, and also the substitutionary death and bodily resurrection of the Creator, the Lord Jesus Christ."[1]

A. E. Wilder-Smith was a notable British-born organic chemist who earned three doctoral degrees (organic chemistry, pharmacology, and physical chemistry). As a devoted Fellow of the Royal Society of Chemistry and a former Oxford atheist, he became challenged by several of his peers, along with the influence of C.S. Lewis, to examine the weight of physical evidence with an open mind. Wilder-Smith had concluded in like manner with Antony Flew that if a loving God really existed, he would surely not have tolerated all of the terrible injustice, suffering and heartache that is evident in the world we know. Never-the-less Dr. Wilder-Smith sought to discover the truth as revealed to him through his dedicated love for the scientific endeavor. His search for a clearer understanding brought him to the realization that a powerful personal God was the only way to explain a world as remarkable and complex as ours. Subsequent to his search for knowledge and truth, he became a devoted creationist and wrote several important books expounding on the knowledge uncovered by his devoted love of science. Through his avid research and writing this man went on to become a leading advocate and a strong proponent of creation science worldwide. Although he never used the term himself, his influence had an instrumental effect by inspiring others who eventually initiated the *Intelligent Design* movement that has become so popular today. The life-transforming power originated by his devoted love for scientific understanding has been revealed in the following personal declaration of Dr. A. E. Wilder Smith. "I believe myself in the living God who did it. I believe that this God, who supplied the information revealed himself in the form of a man so that man could understand him. We are made to understand. I want to understand God. But I can only do this if he comes down to my wavelength, the wavelength of man. I believe that God revealed himself in the form of Christ, and that we can serve him and know him in our hearts as the source of the 'logos'—all the information that is necessary to make the universe and make life itself. Look at the beauty of nature around us! When you consider that it all grew out of matter injected with information of a type I have been describing, you can only be filled with wonder at the wisdom of the Creator, who, first of all had the sense of beauty to do it, and then the technical ability. I am filled with wonder as I look at nature, to see how God technically did it . . . The Scripture teaches perfectly plainly, and it fits in with my science perfectly well, that the one who did called Himself the Logos. That Logos was Jesus. Jesus called Himself the Creator who made everything—'for Him and by Him.' Now, if that is the case, then I am very happy and filled with joy that He made the Creation so beautiful, and that He also valued me enough to die for me, to become my Redeemer as well."[2]

Why Did He Visit Earth?

I believe that people really want to know and understand the truth. It is just that so many of them do not know where to find it. Jesus said, "I am the way, the *truth*, and the life. No one comes to the Father except through me" (John 14:6). If what He said is true, then none of us will ever know real contentment if we ignore his words and deny his power to save us. Jesus came into our world to cancel the debt of sin, and to balance for all time the scales of divine justice. The King of glory—the sovereign Lord of all creation—chose to take my punishment and yours upon himself. How can anyone ever comprehend such great love as this?

As we continue to deliberate on the evidence, there is one other important question that we should all ask ourselves. Why is Jesus so popular throughout the world today, and what does this acknowledgment imply? He never wrote a book. He never went to college. He never led an army or held public office. He barely traveled as far as two hundred miles from the place of his birth, yet his astonishingly powerful words, humble life, and undeniable influence have impacted the entire world for over two thousand years. More books have been written of him by far than any other person who ever lived. More songs have been sung to honor his great name. And this one solitary life has inspired more movies, and works of art, than any other person in the history of humanity. Two millennia of time have passed from the days Jesus walked upon the earth as a wandering itinerant, and yet his popularity and monumental influence continues to flourish worldwide. All of the world's greatest leaders, military commanders, scientists, and educators combined in the history of the earth have not commanded the sheer magnetism of this single solitary life. There is only one possible way to explain this unique and commanding level of undeniable worldwide influence and popularity. This phenomenon can only be understood by the fact that Jesus truly was God in human flesh. What he said and did in three short years of public ministry has literally affected every life on planet Earth in some way or another for over two millennia. And he did it all as a lonely, isolated figure, who grew up and lived in a rather primitive culture, coming from a fairly obscure village, on the barren hillside of a tiny country. This humble servant left an undeniable trail of colossal magnetic influence, and achieved his incredible worldwide renown and prominence without the advantage of any superior technology, while basically traveling everywhere he went on foot.

The Christian faith is based upon strong historical evidence that can and has been verified as accurate and trustworthy. If a person were to believe in something for which there was no legitimate or reliable evidence to justify a rational argument, this would make him or her a fool! Christianity is not foolish speculation. If a person or group of people wanted to discredit Christianity, there is only one thing they would have to do. They would only have to disprove one single event in history. They would have to debunk the resurrection of Jesus Christ. By doing so, the entire Christian faith would crumble and fall. Many have attempted to do just that, but all have failed. The resurrection is the bedrock upon which the Christian faith rests worldwide, and it has been verified by many eyewitness accounts, and historical facts, making this event the most readily proven miracle of antiquity.

After the resurrection, Jesus appeared multiple times to human witnesses over a period of forty days. No less than six key appearances are recorded in Scripture, and corroborated by eyewitnesses, including an amazing appearance to some five hundred witnesses all at one time in the region of Galilee. Most atheists are afraid to seriously challenge the resurrection, because the evidence supporting it is rock solid. Consequently, because atheists cannot discredit the most captivating and miraculous event ever recorded (the historical event upon which Christian faith rests), the skeptics are inclined to attack the only Christian doctrine that historical facts alone cannot ultimately prove— the existence of God, and the accuracy of the early events recorded in the venerated book of Genesis. The doctrine of creation has come under much greater attack and scrutiny than any other Christian pillar of faith. By waging this war, atheists have often been able to appeal to the emotional inclination of those who want to believe there is no God. It makes things so much easier on the conscience to believe there is no accountability waiting for a self-centered life that chooses to be unencumbered by burdensome moral constraints.

This protracted warfare against God, fueled for many years by evolutionary teaching worldwide, has generated a false sense of security that would appear to many people to justify their personal position on moral issues. However, this confidence will only last for a short time. Suddenly, at the moment of death, the reality of God's existence will become very clear to all, as many deceived and unbelieving souls face an eternity of separation from their Creator, whom they have personally rejected and denied during a lifetime of self-directed living. The Bible defines death (the second death) as the separation of the human soul from the Creator forever (see Revelation 21:8).

The humanist worldview teaches that man is basically good. God's view is that mankind is sinful and separated from him. The sin of our forefather (Adam) led to a fallen world that has affected the entire human race. The Word of God has explained it like this: "Therefore, just as through one man [Adam] sin entered the world and death through sin, and thus death spread to all men, because all have sinned" (Romans 5:12). "Through one man's offense [Adam's sin, original sin] judgment came to all men, resulting in condemnation, even so, through one man's righteous act [the sacrificial death of Christ], the free gift [salvation by faith alone] came to all men, resulting in justification [as if I had never sinned] . . . For by one man's disobedience [Adam's fall] many were made sinners, so also by one man's obedience [Christ's sacrifice] many will be made righteous" (Romans 5: 18-19). The Bible states that "for all have sinned and fall short of the glory of God" (Romans 3:23). It further explains that "the wages of sin is death, but the gift of God is eternal life in Jesus Christ our Lord" (Romans 6:23).

Redemption is the central theme of the Bible. This divine act is the culmination of God's great love for humanity and it demonstrates how far he was willing to go to prove that love. Everything the Bible teaches points us toward our desperate need for reconciliation with God. When man fell into sin, his relationship with God was broken, and he now carries a debt (of sin) that separates him from his Maker. Living with guilt, and being unable to atone for it by himself, man became completely dependent upon God's grace and mercy. Only God could redeem the costly debt that all of mankind was burdened with. To reconcile that broken relationship, God determined to make the payment himself, a payment that could potentially free all men of their guilt, thus restoring that original relationship. Because man was created in the image of God, and carries free volition, it was now up to him to accept, by choice, God's offer of atonement. God was offering us a free gift of eternal value that would cost us nothing (Romans 6:23). By definition, a gift cannot be earned. The sacrifice is completely with the giver. The recipient can only choose to accept or reject the gift by an act of his or her own personal will. Only one person can save you and me from the wrath of God. Jesus, *who was without sin*, was the perfect sacrifice and God's only means of atonement for man's sinful transgressions (Hebrews 4:15, 2 Corinthians 5:21). Each one of us must decide for ourselves to accept God's gracious offer of salvation through Jesus Christ. Making no decision concerning this offer is a clear choice to reject God's plan of redemption.

To understand the gift of God, it is necessary to consider what is meant by the term "redemption." Because this concept is so central to the biblical narrative, we should thoroughly define the term so that this principle doctrine will be fresh in our minds. The word "redeem" means to buy back, to pay off, to set free upon full payment of ransom, to atone for guilt, to reclaim after recompense of a debt, to fully recover by payment and reclaim a person or thing to its original state or condition. If, for example, my wife and I had a desperate need for some immediate cash and we decided to take her valuable wedding ring to a pawn shop in order to obtain the necessary funds, the store's shopkeeper would gladly loan me a certain amount of money against the ring based on the value of the diamond. I would then have so many months to pay back the money, plus interest, in order to redeem my property and return it to my wife—in which case, it would be fully restored to its original state or condition. If, however, I failed to pay back the required amount by the due date according to our contractual agreement, in order to fully redeem the diamond, the ring would then become the property of the shopkeeper and I would have a very unhappy wife. Now, because of sin, you and I became subject to Satan (see 1 John 3:8). However, once we have accepted God's offer, and have thus become fully redeemed through faith in the blood of Jesus Christ that was shed on our behalf, the devil loses his power over us because we have been bought back, and restored to our original state or condition (to a right standing relationship with God). This is the very same condition that existed between God and man before the fall.

If you and I were never to become redeemed through a simple act of free volition, by accepting the payment offered for our sin, then we would remain under the control of Satan, and subject to an eternity with him instead of a state of bliss that could be enjoyed in the presence of God. Our original pristine state and condition (at the time of creation, when God declared his works to be "very good") was, quite sadly, disrupted, altered, and forfeited because of man's transgression. Mankind became alienated from God, and was, thereby, separated in their relationship with him. The central purpose of the Bible is to explain how God remained passionately determined to redeem mankind from this tragic curse of death and separation, thus restoring him to the original state or condition that existed before the fall. God has already done everything he is going to do about the problem of sin. The next move is entirely up to us. Will we accept his plan and the unbelievable sacrifice Christ paid to restore that broken relationship, or will we foolishly reject God's perfect plan, and attempt to concoct a salvation plan of our own?

I reject outright the idea that God (our Creator) has sent people to hell. God has done everything he possibly can to make a way for people to avoid that awful place, which was never intended for mankind. Of their own free volition, people have chosen to remain separated from the Lord by rejecting his love, grace, and forgiveness; thus, they have openly condemned their own eternal souls to a godless eternity. God does not send people to hell—they send themselves by rejecting the only remedy that has ever been offered to prevent it. Hell was not prepared for man; it was prepared for the devil and his angels (see Matthew 25:41). Men and women go there only because they reject God's love and refuse to submit to his authority. The prideful arrogance of so many will say, "I don't need God—I don't need his plan of salvation. I will save myself. I will deserve an eternal reward because of my own righteous acts and my first-class behavior." Many people seem to believe that if the good in their lives outweighs the bad, they will be fine in the end, when God examines their lives. This attitude, which remains so prevalent in the heart of mankind today, is outright rebellion against God's plan to save us. "For by grace [undeserved favor] you have been saved through faith [believing in what Christ has done for you], and that not of yourselves [not by human effort]; it is the gift of God [a gift cannot be earned], not of works [personal acts of righteousness], lest anyone should boast [making the claim that they are in right standing before God because of their own personal effort at good behavior]" (Ephesians 2:8, 9). The Bible teaches that our goodness is like filthy rags when compared to the righteousness of God (see Isaiah 64:6).

The standard that God has set for mankind is perfection. "You shall be perfect, just as your Father in heaven is perfect" (Matthew 5:48). Now, that standard may seem too high and excessively demanding. It is certainly a standard that none of us could ever hope to achieve on our own. Let's say, for example, the Grand Canyon in northern Arizona represents the wide gulf that exists between sinful man and a Holy God. Mankind needs a way to get across that expansive chasm. In 1968, the year I graduated from high school, Mexico City was the site of the most remarkable leap in the history of the Olympic long jump competition. A young American competitor by the name of Bob Beamon found himself down to his last jump in order to qualify for the finals among the world's greater jumpers. On his final preliminary jump he managed to qualify rather easily after some timely advice from his coach. Young Mr. Bob Beamon, with a boost of confidence, was determined to make his greatest leap ever and to secure the gold medal. Putting forth his best effort on his first attempt he ran as fast as possible, hit the take-off board and sailed toward the sand pit. It felt like a good jump, but to his dismay and the shock of a worldwide television audience he had not only made his best jump ever, but had eclipsed the current world record by almost two feet. Disbelieving officials were stunned as they brought out the tape to measure and re-measure a distance that was thought to be impossible. They would call it the "miracle jump" of Mexico City. Now, just suppose the fastest man alive was attempting to leap across the chasm of the Grand Canyon through human effort alone. Unfortunately, his greatest possible leap would still leave him about ten miles short of that goal. That's how futile it is for people to think that human effort alone (apart from Christ) could somehow earn them a right-standing relationship with God. The only possible way we can be found righteous before a Holy God is by crossing over on a bridge from our side to his. That bridge is Christ! (see 1Timothy 2:5). We must also keep in mind that this perfection the scripture is referring to is in the "eyes of God," not in the eyes of men. Though this perfection seems to be completely and unattainably out of reach to the human mind, the great news is that when we confess our sin to God and repent of our selfish transgressions before him, he will forgive us completely and impute to us (credit to our account) the righteousness of Christ (see 2 Corinthians 5:21). When that happens, you and I are judged as perfect in God's sight and we will never have to stand before a Holy God in judgment for our sins. This is the only way perfection will ever be found in any of us (see Philippians 3:9). Within the Old Testament the high priest would offer the same animal sacrifice again and again, year after year, but this religious duty would only provide a covering for sin for one year; it could never remove it permanently. God's final judgment for sin was completed once, permanently and for all time in the New Testament where we read these amazing words: "But when this priest (Christ) had offered for all time one sacrifice for sins, (his own death on the cross) he sat down at the right hand of God__ because by one sacrifice he has made *perfect forever* those who are being made holy" (Hebrews 10:12,14 NIV).

Many people are uncertain about the future. They are fearful, anxious, and often worry about what may lie ahead. Countless people are terrified of the thought of dying and live in distress about what may lie beyond the grave. How can man possibly conquer this tormenting fear and terrible worry that holds so many hearts and minds captive? Unfortunately, many people will never come to understand what life is really all about. And consequently, they will never be freed from these disturbing thoughts that will stalk them all the way to their grave. The Bible says, "It is a fearful thing to fall into the hands of the living God" [without knowing His forgiveness] (Hebrew 10:31). The primary doctrine of creation is the very foundation stone of Christian faith and theology (see Hebrews 11:3). It is the one Christian doctrine that the enemy of the human soul has attacked with greater vengeance than all of the others combined. Anyone who rejects special creation, denies God and goes on to demean the Bible as a man-made work in conflict with science, and full of myths, legends and contradictions that can hardly be trusted, is likely to embrace a false worldview that will lead to devastating eternal consequences.

Offering a Hope and a Future

The most amazing thing about the Bible is that it explains in easily understood terms how a person, created in God's image, can exchange their guilt and shame for His righteousness by a simple act of faith. Everyone loves a good trade! I can think of no other bargain that competes with the offer God has made to man, and I cannot understand how anyone could reject such an offer. God is offering us an exchange of our guilt, imposed by a life burdened with sin, for the very righteousness of Jesus Christ, who knew no sin. What an amazing, gracious, and merciful offer that is!

Don't be deceived! Evolution is a colossal lie! Do not let it keep you from accepting the greatest offer that was ever presented to mankind. "Professing to be wise, they became fools, and changed the glory of the incorruptible God into an image made like corruptible man—and birds and four footed animals and creeping things. Therefore God also gave them up to uncleanness, in the lusts of their hearts, to dishonor their bodies among themselves, who exchanged the truth of God for the lie [evolutionary humanism] and worshiped and served the creature rather than the Creator, who is blessed forever" (Romans 1:22-25).

The Bible goes on to explain what happens to men and women who stubbornly reject God's mercy and choose instead to adopt a false worldview. This inevitably leads to a form of personal morality that allows man to embrace a very worldly and self-centered approach to living. This trend has been captured in various catch phrases such as "looking out for number one" or "if it feels good do it." The average individual in today's high-tech, modern world, neither knows much about, nor cares about the faulty premise of evolutionary thought, and yet his or her life is continually influenced by it in a multitude of ways. This theory has led to a type of modern-day morality that regards God's Word as outdated, old-fashioned, out of touch, and with limited value in governing contemporary lifestyle choices. Many so-called enlightened members of modern society have long since cast off the moral constraints they no longer considered to be tolerable. Thus, evolution has provided mankind with a way to hide from God. Consider these thoughts from evolutionist Julian Huxley: "Darwinism removed the whole idea of God as the creator of organisms from the sphere of rational discussion. Darwin pointed out that no supernatural designer was needed; since natural selection could account for any new form of life, there is no room for a supernatural agency in its evolution."[3] Soon after Huxley made this dogmatic statement in 1960 an avalanche of new scientific data, followed by the personal testimony of hundreds of highly respected research scientists, has exposed the mistakes of the modern world's twentieth-century naturalists, who had championed the massive propaganda campaign that has sustained evolutionary thought for so long.

Evolution is a methodically crafted scheme by which the enemy of the human soul has attempted to discredit Christianity and to debunk religion and the Bible. It leaves man without the wisdom of God and with the appearance of controlling his own destiny in the absence of the accountability that was intended to safely govern his affairs. Darwinian evolution is like a corrosive acid that eats through traditional Judeo-Christian principles and values in all areas of life, and ultimately leaves people with what amounts to a revolutionary ideology. This radical worldview has led to the stubborn refusal to acknowledge divine authority and submit to moral restraint as defined for us by the Word of God.

The anti-God religion of evolutionary humanism holds sway with many people today who believe it gives them the justification they desire to pursue a life of self-gratification at the expense of the God's commands. The fruits of humanism reflect a blatant neglect of the moral foundation that has governed our Judeo-Christian nation for over two hundred years. Sinful and rebellious acts against God are the natural outcome in the lives of people who have chosen to become a law unto themselves. Pornography, fornication, adultery, homosexuality, and various other acts of sexual deviancy, along with the evil practice of abortion and euthanasia are the natural byproducts of a humanistic philosophy that says man must decide for himself what is or isn't morally acceptable within a modern culture. And now we are facing an all-out assault against traditional marriage and religious freedom sanctioned by recent actions in our government that were upheld by the courts. This sad travesty is unlike anything Americans have ever seen before. When our own government and liberal-minded courts begin to legislate morality, this is a sure sign that as a nation, we are systematically abandoning our Judeo-Christian heritage.

It would appear that the only possible hope for our beloved nation to escape the inevitable moral collapse, weakening us from within, is a fresh revival and return to the values and principles that our forefathers believed in and held dear. These were the principles that, no doubt, motivated God to bless America with great success and prosperity unlike no other nation. The great enemy of the human soul continues his work of deception to keep men in darkness, so that they may not perceive and understand the marvelous light of the gospel, nor experience the priceless gift of redemption that was purchased on their behalf by the sacrificial offering of God's own Son on Calvary. Evolutionary theory is a dark cloud of deceitfulness hanging heavily over the human mind, and placing a death grip upon the human soul. Don't be fooled by it!

No man or woman can consider themselves well educated without some practical knowledge of the Bible. Without this, man struggles to interpret life's meaning in very strange and unrealistic ways that are designed to ease the human conscience within, and to circumvent and cast off the need we all have for personal accountability. It is the growing lack of understanding of biblical truth in America that is leading us toward a cultural transformation characterized by a loss of appreciation for the values and principles that have led to our unprecedented prosperity. Diehard evolutionists have long ago predicted that the next logical step after humanism is socialism. And sadly, after having embraced Darwinism for such a long time, we are now beginning to see the public consciousness of our beloved nation trending in this direction more so than ever before.

Many people have failed to comprehend that the teaching of evolution does not leave the youth of America or any other nation in a neutral position with regard to religious persuasion, but instead, this ideology promotes the blatantly anti-biblical religion of secular humanism leading toward atheism. This deceiving secular ideology can gradually tug at the heart of man, and in many cases has pulled him away from his Creator. The unfortunate manifestation of atheism always leads feeble mankind directly toward greater government control by way of unbridled secular authority, accompanied by a very sharp decline in man's traditional reliance on and submission to the governing authority of the Word of God.

All biblical truth hinges on Genesis 1:1. "In the beginning God created the heavens and the earth." When man rejects this basic truth, it opens the door to all kinds of deception, evil, and depravity.

I have studied the Bible for my entire adult lifetime, and I have never discovered any convincing evidence that would lead me to believe it is not a God-inspired revelation of divine origin. I have come to believe and will tenaciously defend the Word of God as the foundational basis for all truth with respect to the issues that comprise the great mystery of living in a complex world. Who can confidently say, "I flatly deny the existence of God and reject the Bible as a divinely inspired record of His eternal truth"?

Christianity is an *evidence-based faith*! This genuine evidence gives us adequate reason to believe in the validity of Christian faith. It should really be accepted, not simply on the basis of what many people say to believe, but because of a vast body of evidence that points us so unmistakably toward why we should believe! What I have offered to the reader in these few chapters is only a small portion of the current and abundant evidences that thoroughly support Christian-based theology. In light of these many infallible proofs, the question we must ask ourselves is, *how then shall we live*? For those who reject the Bible as the divinely inspired, authoritative Word of God, the quest to understand "the mystery of life" will, unfortunately, never have a satisfactory outcome. Why is this? It is because by definition a mystery is that which cannot be discovered by the natural, rational searching of the human mind, but must be revealed. God—the author of life—has revealed many powerful truths to us through his Word and his creative works. Now, it's up to us to believe!

If the worldwide flood recorded in Genesis chapter 6 was actually of the magnitude and intensity as indicated in the text, then the entire elaborate scheme for an evolutionary worldview collapses in a giant heap of rubble. Why? Because evolution theory is entirely dependent upon a fossil record that must be interpreted within the framework of vast geological ages of earth history. There are some who say they believe in God, and yet support the strange view that God has used evolution to create living things. This very unfortunate and misguided compromise has required a very loose interpretation of Scripture, and, in fact, denies its literal meaning. This view relegates biblical truth to symbolic allegory, allowing men to pick and choose what is the literal truth and what is not. This is an attempt to divest God's Word of its miraculous nature in order to somehow satisfy the modern intellectual demand for a naturalistic view of life. This type of dangerous concession undermines the integrity of the God's Word, and, consequently, leaves mankind in control, allowing him to interpret the Bible in whatever manner he wishes, so that it will conform to his preferential view of life. God's inspired Word is always meant to be taken literally, unless obvious symbolism is employed.

The very height of human arrogance is telling the creator God of the universe that we are smarter than he is. We must never allow the misguided theories of men to color our minds when we are interpreting the Word of God. It seems to me that this is what people are doing when they accept certain portions of Scripture as literal, inspired, and accurate while rejecting other portions as "allegorical" or perhaps even "mythological," when the text is clearly written in a manner that is intended to be read and understood in the literal sense. Whenever man makes an attempt to interpret the biblical text, the basic rules of literary interpretation must always be applied; otherwise, the eventual understanding of the Bible passage we are examining will certainly take on a misleading or unintended significance. If you do not believe the Bible to be true in regard to the meaning of life and its purpose, then you must be absolutely certain that you are correct in this critical evaluation, because your eternal future depends on it. Life is a mystery— but this mystery has been unveiled to us by the Word of God. When we receive its divinely inspired truth, only then can we be free from our greatest fears, doubts, and unbelief. If there really is an awesome and Almighty God in the spiritual dimension, who created the entire physical dimension, then you and I are certainly accountable to him, and rightly so; for we will stand before Him in judgment on some future day when our choices, actions, and the very motives of our hearts are to be thoroughly examined. "For the Word of God is living and powerful, and sharper than any two edged sword, piercing even to the division of soul and spirit, and of joints and marrow, and is a discerner of the thoughts and intents of the heart. And there is no creature hidden from

His sight, but all things are naked and open to the eyes of Him to whom we must give account" (Hebrews 4:12, 13).

Conclusions We Should Draw

In this book, I have attempted to do everything I can to establish that the evolution model presents a false worldview that, over the years, has had devastating consequences in our world. I have endeavored to provide powerful evidence to confirm the existence of a sovereign creator God to whom we are all ultimately accountable. I have offered evidence to confirm that the Bible is indeed God's divine message to humanity—a message that will, no doubt, serve as the basis for divine judgment when each of us finally stands before the living God to give an accounting of our lives. "He who rejects Me, and does not receive My words, has that which judges him—the word that I have spoken will judge him in the last day" (John 12:48). (For a more detailed review of why we can trust the Bible as a reliable and accurate source of divine inspiration, please refer to the epilogue section at the end of the book.)

The following statements represent a list of the conclusions that I and many others have drawn based upon a remarkable amount of evidence that is pointing man, unmistakably, toward the Word of God as the primary source of information and the final authority in discovering the truth about the issues of life.

1. The one true God is very real, and he has revealed himself in many unmistakable ways to all those who remain open to the prospect of his existence (see Psalm 19:1; Isaiah 43:10, 44:6, 45:22).
2. God created everything, and is the intelligent agent who is responsible for both the spiritual and physical realm (see Genesis 1:1-30, Isaiah 45:12, Psalm 33:6).
3. Mankind was created in the image of his Maker, and became God's crowning creation—the centerpiece and focal point of his attention and affection (Genesis 1:27).

4. God's original creation was perfect in every respect, and thus reflected the awesome nature of his divine character and extraordinary imagination (see Genesis 1:31).

5. In his relentless desire for personal relationship, God was compelled to create man with free volition (the unique ability to choose his own path) (Genesis 1:27, 2:17, 3:17).

6. Mankind chose to use this freedom to rebel against the authority of his Creator (Genesis 3:1-19).

7. The tragic fall of mankind corrupted not only his personal relationship with God, costing him full dominion and authority over the planet, but the whole of creation was drastically altered by man's sin (Genesis 3:17-19, Romans 8:19-23).

8. The terrible consequence of sin resulted in the curse of death and decay that has come upon the entire physical dimension (see Genesis 2:17, Romans 8:19-23).

9. God's everlasting love for humanity has prompted Him to reach out to mankind by preparing and executing a brilliant plan of redemption (Genesis 3:15, John 3:16).

10. The overall purpose of God's unmistakable love for his image-bearing sons and daughters was to *redeem them* to become a part of his eternal family and also restore, to as many as received him, that which was lost when mankind originally chose to rebel against his Maker by disregarding divine authority (Revelation 21:1-4, 22:1-5).

11. As a result of this divine plan, the redeemed of God (those who have entered into a God-fearing relationship with the Creator by faith in Christ) have now become the rightful heirs to everything that God has created, and will enjoy his manifest presence throughout eternity (see Romans 8:16-18).

"Happily ever after" is not just in fairy tales. God's plan is to make this magnificent dream a reality in the life of every human soul he has created, loved, and died for.

You and I can choose to believe these conclusions about life and reality or not. Each and every person must decide for themselves and embrace his or her own personal worldview, and each one of us must live with the consequences of our decision. However, I can guarantee you, based on thirty years of study and research that this is the direction the evidence is pointing toward and we would be foolish to ignore it. We all know that death is inevitable for each one of us. If the Word of God is true (and I know that it is) then heaven and hell are very real places, and each one of us will be judged by the higher power that so many have been determined to ignore. The meaning of life is one question none of us can afford to get wrong. Let's get the real truth settled in our hearts and minds now, while we still have hope, because after we die, we will all know for certain how very real God is—only then it will be too late to change and convert, if we have ignored and rejected God's love all of our mortal lives. Those who choose to reject him and his Word in this life are destined to carry that devastating choice into eternity, and it will cost them everything when they ultimately become separated from their Creator's blessings forever.

Mankind has struggled through the centuries to discover true meaning in material living. And those who are completely honest with themselves will have to admit that the competitive pursuit for power, prestige, possession, and pleasure leaves the human soul very much empty of the essential elements that would define a gratifying and purpose-filled life. If there really is a living God to whom we must all give account, as the evidence strongly suggests, then you and I cannot afford to be ignorant of who he is, of what he has done, and of what he expects from us. What possible justification can there be for anyone to reject him, deny him, and refuse to acknowledge his divine power and unmistakable authority?

If I were to ask the question, what do you long for the most in this life? I believe an overwhelming majority of people would express a desire to be loved and accepted. We need to feel that their life has significance to other people. We were created with the need to love and to be loved. This reflects the fact that we were created in the image of a personal, loving God because this is undoubtedly the top priority of our Creator as well__ to love and to be loved. He has designed you and me to become a part of his eternal family, and he desires for each of us to have a personal and ongoing relationship with him. We were created by a purpose-driven God who longs for that kind of relationship with every one of his image-bearing sons and daughters. Ultimately, however, the decision to return God's love is ours alone.

God has already completed everything he plans to do about the problem of sin. God's commitment to us was fulfilled when his one and only Son was hung to die on a cruel Roman cross. Now, the decision to respond is up to us. What will you and I do about the man called *Jesus*? In the final analysis, the Son of God becomes the focal point of the knowledge and information I have shared with you throughout these many pages! He is the ultimate answer and the central resolution to *the mystery of life*!

There is no logical reason why we should deny him. There is no scientific reason to deny him. And there is no historical reason to deny him. Only the prideful human heart and that brash unwillingness to submit to his authority will keep people living in unbelief. You may be thinking, *Why should I invest my devotion and allegiance to a worldview I cannot possibly explain?* My short answer to that question is, because this mortal life on planet earth is totally and completely unexplainable apart from God! Many people simply give lip service to God, but have never (in their hearts) given him the glory that he alone deserves. In referring to Isaiah, Jesus said, "as it is written: this people honors Me with their lips, but their heart is far from Me. And in vain they worship Me, teaching as doctrines the commandments of men. For laying aside the commandment of God you hold to the tradition of men" (Mark 7:6-8).

Perhaps you should also consider this question as well: can I explain how evolution theory actually works and point to an abundance of validating evidence that would suggest exactly why this concept should capture my allegiance and dominate my worldview? Before you answer this question, consider the penetrating words of Dr. Collin Patterson, who held a very distinguished position for many years as a senior paleontologist with the British Museum of Natural History. In an honest moment of confession, he has provided us with some candid remarks concerning the current state of evolution. "For over 20 years, I thought I was working on evolution . . . but there was not one thing

I knew about it . . . So for the last few weeks I've tried putting a simple question to various people, the question is: 'Can you tell me any one thing that is true' [about evolution]? I tried that question on the geology staff at the Field Museum of Natural History and the only answer I got was silence . . . I tried it on the members of the Evolutionary Morphology Seminar in the University of Chicago, a very prestigious body of evolutionists, and all I got there was silence for a long time, and eventually one person said, 'Yes, I do know one thing, it ought not to be taught in high school'. . . Over the past few years you have experienced a shift from evolution as knowledge to evolution as faith . . . Evolution not only conveys no knowledge, but it seems somehow to convey anti-knowledge."[4]

Is a time-tested historical theory that is confusing, frustrating, and unexplainable to so many of the world's greatest evolutionary experts really where we should invest our personal faith?

When I was a young college student studying for my undergraduate degree at the university, I once attended a church service next door to my college campus in Seattle, Washington. When listening to the message that day, I was rather stunned to hear the preacher admonishing the congregation that if you were born and raised in America, you are a Christian. He may have gotten this strange notion from the fact that America, up until recently, has most often been viewed as a Christian nation. However, to say that you qualify as a Christian if you were born in America is like saying you qualify as a cow if you were born in a barn. It was a ridiculous, false, and utterly misleading statement, which I have never quite forgotten. Everything that has happened to me since that day has confirmed to my heart and mind that each and every one of us must choose to become a Christian—it's not a birthright!

God alone is the real answer to everything you need and desire for yourself and your family, now and throughout eternity. Every breath of air you take is because of Him. Every bite of food, every drink of water, every bird that sings and tree that grows, every ray of sunlight, every drop of rain, it is all because of him and him alone. On the other hand, every deadly disease, every tear of sorrow, and every dying breath is because of us! We are the cause of a cursed world that does not reflect the original intent of its Maker. We alone have rejected his truth and despised his authority, and now we are all living with the terrible consequences of those tragic choices. I personally do not understand how anyone could cut out of his or her life the only source of hope we have to be set free from a world that is reeling under the curse of death and decay.

Revelation 3:17 speaks of a man who thought he was totally self-sufficient, could depend completely on his own resourcefulness and ingenuity, and was in need of nothing from anyone, including God. He was blinded by the devil's deception. He was full of pride in his own success, and was prepared to live out his days in leisure and luxury. This was God's response to an arrogant and reckless way of living. "You do not realize that you are wretched, pitiful, poor, blind, and naked." How many people have slipped into eternity leaving everything they have worked for to others, only then to discover that their lives have been void of any eternal treasure beyond this world?

God is saying the same thing today to all of those who have decided that they can handle life just fine on our own, having no need of a power greater than ourselves. How many people are like this today? I fear the number is staggering! They must be reminded of the God to whom they will give account, and the fact that their days on this earth are numbered. There is no logical reason for any of us to remain in a self-centered state of isolation and separation from the Creator of the universe. Three verses later, in Revelation 3:20, God says to all of us, "Behold, I stand at the door and knock. If anyone hears my voice and opens the door, I will come in to him and dine with him and he with me." In other words, God is offering us the opportunity to experience a restored relationship with him. This is the only way we will ever find peace and security in a troubled world ravaged by sin and death. When we say yes to God, he gives us the power to live the Christian life we were meant to have. Only his power will enable us to truly love him in return, and to love our neighbor as ourselves.

Jesus said, "You will know my disciples by their love for one another" (see John 13:34, 35). There is no question that we were born to know and to love God as we also know and love one another. But what about the multitudes that do not believe they are in need of God's love? How do we deliver a message of hope to them? After the crucifixion, the few disciples of Christ were huddled together, cowering behind closed doors. They were confused, fearful, and disillusioned, being still unaware that the crucified Christ had actually risen from the dead. Soon after this, the resurrected Jesus presented himself to his disciples on a day when the apostle Thomas was not among them. When all the disciples who were present told Thomas that Jesus was alive, and had been resurrected from the dead, his immediate response was, "I will not believe until I see the marks in his hands and put my hand in his side [where he was pierced]" (John 20:25, paraphrase). This incident became the source of the familiar term "doubting Thomas." Thomas was waiting for the physical evidence. He surely wanted to believe, but he needed proof to dispel the powerful doubt in his mind. When Jesus finally appeared among them again, while Thomas was in attendance, an interesting thing happened. Jesus could have rebuked Thomas for his unbelief but instead he gladly showed him the nail marks in his hands and the scar in his side (John 20:27). Why did he do this for the unbelieving disciple? He did it because the evidence is what Thomas needed to bolster his faith? The following bold expression revealed Thomas's response to the evidence: "My Lord and my God!" (John 20:28). Doubting Thomas was thoroughly convinced by the evidence even though he could only marvel at what he saw without knowing how to explain what had happened. This disciple, along with all of his companions, was transformed with boldness and courage and went on to share his faith far and wide, and ultimately gave his life for the cause of Christ when he died the death of a martyr.

Christianity is an evidence-based faith. When I think of all the multitudes that just need to "see the evidence" to bolster their faith, I am reminded once again of what has compelled me to write this book. In response to the evidence presented in these pages, are we prepared to declare as Thomas did so long ago, "My Lord and my God!" I definitely believe that if we will show people valid evidence for the reality of God and his unmistakable love for fallen humanity, genuine faith will naturally follow. This wide living world and the vast seemingly unknown universe reveals far too much evidence for a Creator to possibly believe otherwise. Are you now ready to say yes to God's offer to exchange your sin for his righteousness? It's very hard to imagine why anyone would ever refuse such an amazing offer as this.

Not Too Good to Be True

Now that evolution theory has been thoroughly exposed for the monstrous deception that it is, proof for the existence of God has been thoroughly examined, and the true nature of the Bible as a document of divine origin has been adequately discussed, "how then shall we live"? Many will continue to live their lives as though God does not exist and ultimately will face his wrath in the coming judgment by trusting in their own goodness to save them. Others will place their faith, hope, and trust in the eternal Word of God, after acknowledging that all have sinned against the God of creation, have broken his laws, and have disobeyed his commands. This kind of thinking is the first step toward true repentance__ to acknowledge God, to fear his judgments, and to feel a sense of remorse for one's own sinful acts and attitudes that have grieved our Maker. Why would anyone take a chance and gamble their eternal soul on the faulty, constantly changing "wisdom" of man. All we have to do is to ask God to reveal himself to us in a personal way. If he is powerful enough to create the world around us, he can surely reveal himself to us, if only we would care enough to ask him.

God is certainly not expecting each of us to be perfect in and of ourselves because he knows that this is humanly impossible. He is, however, expecting us to acknowledge who he is, confess that we have rebelled against him by transgressing his laws, and choose to repent before him and forsake our sin. We are all God's children through creation, but we must also become his children by means of redemption, or we will never partake of his priceless promises and eternal rewards. If we only decide to consider the evidence for God without ever offering an adequate response, then it is perfectly understandable why we would have no excuse when we stand one day before our Maker in judgment (see Romans 1:20).

With eternity at stake, you and I cannot afford to be indifferent and to ignore such a life-and-death matter as this. We must respond to the truth once we understand it, because no decision is a choice to reject God and his undeniable love for each of us. There really can be no neutral ground in this debate; either we are with him (submitting to his astonishing love and atoning death), or we are opposed to him. Don't miss out on the single greatest blessing afforded to us in this lifetime— the priceless opportunity to know for certain, before death comes, that our sins will never be counted against us. Be assured that you possess, by faith alone, a certain hope, and a magnificent future that is guaranteed and secured far beyond the mundane physical reality that you and I have experienced during our mortal lifetimes. The voluntary, sacrificial death of God's only Son on a Roman cross was generously offered to all of us out of our Creator's overwhelming love for humanity, and the compelling desire of a relationship-seeking God to spare humankind of eternal judgment.

If you think your belief system is the right one, and you are currently not living the Christian life, there is one sure way to test what you believe to determine if it really is worthy of your allegiance. Ask yourself this question: believing as I presently do, am I prepared to die at this moment with the belief system I currently embrace, or do I have some nagging doubt about whether I am ready to face what lies beyond the grave? If you can honestly say that you have some serious doubt, then you are certainly not ready to face death while holding fast to your present view of life. The reality is that much of the world does not want God to be the answer to their need. They do not want Jesus Christ in their life! They have remained unwilling to admit that their sin has grieved the Holy Spirit, nor are they willing to accept the accountability God requires of them. Why would anyone not want to receive God's priceless gift of redemption, which requires only a willful act of believing faith on the part of each new recipient?

As I see it, each of us has two choices. We can examine the evidence now and discover the truth while it is still able to impact our lives in a positive way, or we can wait until we die, and then the truth will become very clear to each one of us. However, if we push God aside and wait 'til the end, it will be too late to repent, and all hope for a meaningful future will be forever gone. If you should die tomorrow and face the prospect of eternity—tell me why God should welcome you into heaven to remain in his presence forever? There can be only one answer, and it's not because you have been a good person! Our goodness is like filthy rags as compared to the righteousness of a Holy God. The only possible answer could be that God would welcome you because you have not relied upon your own merit, which you and I know to be completely inadequate with respect to God's high standard, but you have relied only upon the sacrificial death of Jesus Christ on your behalf. He paid our penalty and has offered us a full pardon by laying down his sinless life to satisfy God's divine justice in regard to our sin.

I have repented of my sin and have trusted completely in the atonement God has provided, knowing that it was never possible for me to earn my own way to heaven. My reconciliation (restoration to right standing) with God is because of Christ alone, and not because of anything I have done, or ever could do, to deserve it. There is absolutely nothing you and I could ever do on our own to merit salvation! All we can do is trust in His promises and say yes to God—the rest is up to Him.

In the Old Testament, a sacrifice offered by the high priest would secure a covering for sin for one year. In the New Testament, the blood of Christ was offered for the sin of all mankind, but this was not a temporary covering. The death of Jesus Christ was the final sacrifice that did away with the debt of sin in the lives of all who believe. I am reminded of the word "expunge." It means to erase, to delete or to blot out and remember no more. The Bible says that when we repent our sins are removed from us as far as the east is from the west (see Psalm 103:12 and Jeremiah 31:34).

Any person who thinks they have no need for God's love—that they have life all figured out, and that Christianity is just some crutch for weak-minded people to lean on—should seriously consider the following questions. In light of the evidence presented in this and other books, can I really afford to take a chance knowing I may be wrong about God and the Bible? What if there really is a supreme God who created all living things, and will hold me accountable one day when I face his righteous judgment?

Nobody wants to face the wrath of a Holy God, which the Bible says will be poured out upon all who do not know God and refuse to obey the gospel of Jesus Christ (see 2 Thessalonians 1:6-9 and 1 Peter 4:17). Do I really believe that heaven and hell are not real places and that there is no life after death, when the Bible clearly teaches otherwise? What if the Bible is the truth and, when I die, I will become separated from God and everything he provides, forever, because I stubbornly chose to reject his words and deny his love? Perhaps God really does love me enough to send his only Son into the world to die for my transgressions, making it possible for me to be reconciled to a right relationship with my Maker. Can I afford to ignore the clear message of scripture and take a chance that trying to be a good person will be enough to save me from the wrath of God, when the Bible clearly denies any such claim (see Titus 3:5)? The Bible says, "It is appointed for men to die once, but after this the judgment" (Hebrews 9:27). This means that there will be no second chance for reconciliation with God after death. Therefore, the most important question I can ask myself is, am I ready to face the righteous judgment of a Holy God in the current condition of my eternal soul?

Do not stake your future and all of eternity on personal opinion or a comfortable, popular philosophy of what life is all about, when you do not have the evidence to back it up. In the end, it is only God's opinion that will count, and it is his opinion that we have all sinned and have fallen short of his glory (see Romans 3:23).

Some people would suggest that the Christian faith is foolishness, and the great miracles of Scripture are far too outlandish to believe, if taken literally. God anticipated their reaction when his inspired Word declared, "But God has chosen the foolish things of the world to put to shame the wise, and God has chosen the weak things of the world to put to shame the things which are mighty" (1 Corinthians 1:27). "For the message of the cross is foolishness to those who are perishing, but to us who are being saved—it is the power of God" (1 Corinthians 1:18).

"For what will it profit a man if he gains the whole world, and loses his own soul?" (Mark 8:36; see also Matthew 16:26).

The Bible says, "If you confess with your mouth the Lord Jesus, and believe in your heart that God has raised Him from the dead, you will be saved. For with the heart one believes unto righteousness, and with the mouth confession is made unto salvation" (Romans 10:9, 10).

The tremendous popularity of Facebook, Twitter, and other social media outlets have demonstrated, without question, that people all over the world are seeking desperately after the approval, acceptance, and the admiration of family, friends, coworkers, neighbors and perhaps even complete strangers. The only problem I see is that, in many cases, some individuals could be substituting this kind of human acceptance for the unconditional acceptance that only a personal loving God could provide for them. God's amazing, unrestricted, and impartial forgiveness can only be found through an act of personal repentance, by our demonstrating genuine faith in Jesus Christ as the mediator between God and man (see 1 Timothy 2:5). The result will become (through spiritual growth) an unselfish life set on a new path of submission and obedience to God's precepts and his commands. Instead of accepting the living God on his own terms, however, many people in today's me-first generation will often expect God to accept them on *their* terms, by overlooking their sin, and tolerating personal choices that are made with little or no regard to his divine judgments. I can't think of any possible reason why we should not give God a chance in our lives. What do we have to lose?

Just because someone offers you a gift, does not make it yours—you must actually reach out and receive a gift to take ownership of it. Just because Christ died on the cross to pay the penalty for man's sin does not mean your sins are automatically forgiven—you must actually accept this gift of God's grace in order to take ownership of it. Reconciliation with God is a decision that must come from the heart, not just an acknowledgment of the mind. It's like a young lady, standing before a man who is proposing marriage to her. She must, of her own free will, give a response to the offer that has been presented to her. To be silent would mean that she is either unsure of her decision, or is declining the offer. Even her possible indecision will have to be settled and a final choice made—otherwise the answer is no. Some people think that they can demonstrate unresponsiveness toward God, and remain undecided about the meaning of life and eternity. However, God surely understands the actual choice people are making by their indifference and indecision. To remain uninterested and unresponsive to God's free offer of salvation does not make a person any less accountable when they finally face his righteous judgment. Jesus told his disciples, "If you do not believe that I am He, [the Messiah sent by God] you will die in your sins" (John 8:24).

While driving in Orange County, California, on a very bright, sunny afternoon, I was pulled over by a police officer who informed me that I had run through a red light. Several excuses crossed my mind as to why I may have failed to stop at the intersection. However, none of them would have held up to the serious scorn of the authority figure that was holding me accountable. The truth is, I was clearly guilty, and no excuse was good enough to justify my action; consequently, I had to pay a stiff penalty and go to traffic school for breaking the law. The Bible says that we have all broken God's laws and that each one of us stands guilty before him. What parent would not do anything and everything to protect their young children from harm, pain, and suffering? That is how God feels about us. He was acting just like a good parent when he identified certain selfish behaviors as sinful. These are behaviors that cause harm, pain, and suffering, at some level, to the guilty party, and in most cases to someone else at the same time. God has established moral guidelines to protect us! He did this because he loves us, and he wants the very best for our lives. In the very same sense that we are held accountable to obey traffic laws, we are also held accountable to obey God's moral laws as well.

You and I are responsible to God in the same way that any young child would be answerable to his or her earthly father. With this said, God should be treated with respect, reverence, and fear as the authority figure to whom we all must answer. Evil is conceived in the mind of man, generated through the heart of man, and acted out by the will of man. The Bible teaches that all men have broken God's laws, and stand condemned to be judged for doing so. However, the good news that we can all rejoice in is that Christ has taken our place and received the penalty that was due for our self-centered transgressions, so that we could, in turn, receive God's forgiveness and be restored to a right and lasting relationship with him. No one can or ever will earn the favor of God and thereby escape his wrath through the merits of his or her own personal effort at good behavior (see Ephesians 2:8, 9). The only way we can escape the penalty for our transgressions against a Holy God is for someone else to take our punishment for us. This is exactly what Christ did when he took our sins upon himself to fully satisfy the righteous justice of God.

If we stubbornly reject or ignore this substitutionary act of grace, the wrath of God will remain upon us, and we will be accountable to pay the penalty for our own sins (see John 3:36). It would have been great for someone else to voluntarily step in and pay my traffic fine, but nobody was there offering to pay the penalty for me. The good news is that this is not the case with regard to the debt we owe before a righteous God. *We have a substitute, an intermediary to pay our sin debt.* The debt you and I owe before a Holy God cannot be excused from our account without full payment offered; neither can it be paid for by another guilty party (for all have sinned). For this reason God sent his only Son, who knew no sin, to pay the debt for us. All we have to do now is accept it! Has there ever been a better offer than this?

A New Birth Certificate

God is calling men and women everywhere to repent; for he is not willing that any should perish, but that all should come to repentance (Acts 17:30 and 2 Peter 3:9).

What should our response be to the evidence presented in this book and recorded in a thousand other books that document many valid reasons in support of Christian faith? What God has offered humanity seems almost too good to be true, but it's not! When someone (like God) longs for a relationship based on mutual love and respect, he will do whatever it takes to secure that relationship; and in our case, it required the death of his only Son on a cruel Roman cross. What we should and must do in response to this extremely undeserved measure of unconditional love are the following:

1. Acknowledge the living God as our creator, provider and ultimate judge.
2. Confess that we have broken his laws, and stand guilty before him for doing so.
3. Admit that we cannot save ourselves from the wrath to be poured out upon unrepentant humanity.
4. Believe that God sent his only Son to do for us what we could never do for ourselves.
5. Repent of our sins before a loving and merciful God who offers us more than we derserve.
6. Receive Jesus the living Messiah into our lives by faith knowing that he has provided the atonement for sin, and is the only mediator between a Holy God and fallen humanity.
7. Decide to allow the Holy Bible (God's Word) to become our instruction manual, which explains in vivid detail how we should live and how we can begin to grow in our personal relationship with Christ.

If you are deciding, for the first time, that God is real and he loves you enough to send his Son into the world to die for your sins, then I hope you agree that now is the time to offer a sincere response to an amazing, merciful offer for your life. If you have never experienced a right relationship with God, by accepting the only provision that was ever made to eliminate your sin, then I would encourage you to carefully consider the following pages and apply your signature as a way to acknowledge your decision to accept God's redeeming grace for your life. Jesus said to Nicodemus in John 3:3 that a man will never see the kingdom of God without experiencing a "new birth." This occurs when we repent of our sin, and receive the atonement God has provided, by faith. The crucifixion was the ultimate price a Holy God required to recompense the penalty for the many offenses you and I have committed against him. Jesus, of course, was speaking to Nicodemus about the spiritual birth that takes place when we acknowledge our sin and receive the provision God has made for us by sending his only Son to an agonizing death in order to redeem the debt owed by each and every human life burdened by guilt. To explain the miracle of the new birth, Jesus offered this in response to the confusion of Nicodemus: "The wind blows where it wishes, and you hear the sound of it, but cannot tell where it comes from or where it goes. So [he said] is everyone who is born of the Spirit" (John 3:8).

Dr. Henry Morris understood early in life that science and faith are to be embraced as companions, not as foes, as many misinformed scholars are teaching today. Dr. Morris clearly explains the tragic dilemma that is facing humanity and what a loving Creator God was prepared to do about it. "The Creator has imposed the law of decay and death on his whole creation, because of the rebellion of its human stewards. Therefore, only he can defeat death, and this only by paying the redemption price himself, dying for sin, and then rising victoriously from the dead . . . Thus, the great miracle of the resurrection requires the great prior miracle of supernatural creation . . . the omnipotent, omniscient Creator cannot fail in his creative purposes, even though man's sin has brought the universal reign of death into the world. Therefore he must conquer death and redeem his creation. This he can only do by his incarnation, his dying for sin, and his resurrection."[5]

The following words may be used as a personal confession of believing faith and spiritual commitment:

I believe in the only true God, the Creator of heaven and earth, who has revealed himself to the world through nature, the cosmos, and the Holy Scriptures. I now understand that according to God's Word, I must have a personal relationship with my Maker in order to gain the hope of eternal life when I die. This requires me to experience what the Bible calls "redemption." The Bible reveals that everyone has sinned and has fallen short of God's righteous standard. To have peace with God, I need the assurance that my sins have been forgiven. "God sent his Son into the world, not to condemn the world, but that the world through Him might be saved." Jesus died in my place, taking my sin and condemnation upon himself, so that I could experience right standing with God in this life and the next. By offering his only Son for my sins, God did for me what I could never do for myself through human effort and my own good works. God is offering me the free gift of eternal life, made possible only by the death of his Son upon the cross. It is my understanding that there is nothing I have done or ever could do to earn this priceless gift. I also acknowledge that a gift does not belong to me until I have personally received it. The Bible declares, "As many as received Him, to them gave He power to become the sons of God" (John 1:12 KJV). By receiving the risen Christ into my life, I recognize that his death was necessary to satisfy God's justice in regard to my sin. I believe Jesus has risen from the grave, victorious over death, giving me the assurance that he was indeed God in human flesh. Although I know little about God and the Bible, I now understand that I cannot save myself from the penalty of sin, which is death. The Bible has defined death as eternal separation from God in a horrible place that was specifically prepared for the devil and his many fallen angels. By applying my signature to this document, I am affirming my personal decision to receive Jesus Christ into my life, and I freely acknowledge that what Jesus did on the cross was necessary to save me from the wrath of God. Today, I will experience the forgiveness of sin and a new relationship with God, which the Bible promises to all who believe. I know that if I had rejected God's generous offer (the provision made for me that required the death of His Son) and instead depended on my own good works to merit heaven, the Bible clearly teaches that I would have no hope beyond this life. God's Word plainly states, "Jesus is the way, the truth, and the life and no one comes to God the father, except through Him." I have decided to accept God's offer of forgiveness by receiving Christ today and, by making this decision, I now join millions of others from around the world who have gladly accepted God's amazing grace into their lives. I will closely examine the following Scriptures for a better understanding as I begin a new life of faith at the direction of God's Word: Romans 3:23, 6:23, 10:9-10; Mark 8:36; John 1:12, 3:3, 3:16, 14:6; Acts 4:12; Ephesians 2:8-9; and Hebrews 9:27. As I pray the following prayer out loud before God, this document now becomes my *New Birth Certificate.*

I _____ choose to accept you, Jesus, into my life today. I confess that I have broken God's laws, and I deserve his judgment. But today I repent of my sins and receive your forgiveness, knowing that the precious gift of eternal life is promised to all who believe. I am now just beginning a new purpose-filled life of devotion and service to God, and I look forward to becoming your true disciple as I gradually grow in the knowledge and fear of God's Word and His ways. Today, _____, is my spiritual birthday!

If you have prayed this prayer for the first time, consider the words of 2 Corinthians 5:17: "If anyone is in Christ, he is a new creation; old things have passed away; behold, all things have become new."

Creation is the foundation stone for all biblical truth. On the other hand, evolutionary theory, and the humanist worldview has laid a foundation for all kinds of evil, sin, and corruption. Consider once again some final words from Dr. Henry Morris, PhD: "Evolutionism has been the chief opponent of the saving gospel of Christ, undermining the faith of multitudes in the Bible and its promises. It is not too much to say that evolutionary theory, in one form or another, has provided the pseudo-rationale for all that is false and harmful in the world (the real cause, of course, is the innate sinfulness of the human heart, with its rebellion against the Word of God) . . . all who opposed the true God must always resort to some kind of evolution, for this is the only possible alternative to special creation by a transcendent God."[6]

"Lift your eyes and look to the heavens: Who created all these things? He who brings out the starry host one by one, and calls them each by name. Because of his great power and mighty strength, not one of them is missing . . . Do you not know? Have you not heard? The Lord is the everlasting God, the Creator of the ends of the earth. He will not grow tired or weary, and his understanding no one can fathom. He gives strength to the weary and increases the power of the weak. Even youths grow tired and weary, and young men stumble and fall; but those who hope in the Lord will renew their strength. They will soar on wings like eagles; they will run and not grow weary, they will walk and not faint" (Isaiah 40:26, 28-31 NIV).

Can we really use evolutionary theory or any other man-made ideology to hide ourselves from the Lord God Almighty? Not so, according to Hebrews 4:13, where we consider some very penetrating words: "And there is no creature hidden from His sight, but all things are naked and open to the eyes of Him to whom we must give account."

Yes, of course, we are accountable before a transcendent God, but our Creator is a God of amazing grace, unconditional love, and unimaginable mercy. Every one of us wants to be loved and accepted. The problem is that a Holy God cannot accept our sin with impunity. God's justice requires that the debt of sin must be paid. That is why he sent his Son to the cross to pay the debt for us—so that we can be delivered from the wrath of God to be poured out on the unbelieving world. That's how much he loves us! He was willing to pay the debt on our behalf—taking our punishment upon himself, allowing us to be set free from the penalty of sin and to become partakers within his eternal family. Our acceptance of this unspeakable gift of unconditional love is certainly not a difficult decision to make. We must not let pride and unbelief stand in the way of God's plan to save us and to give each one of us the certain hope of spending an eternity of pleasure, joy, and fulfillment in his presence.

Yes, you and I were created for the purpose of relationship. We were designed to have relationship with God and relationship with each other. If, in our effort to find meaning in life, we only discover personal relationship with one another and do not seek out personal relationship with the loving God who created us, then we are sure to miss out on the very best that life has to offer, and the hope of an endless eternity in the presence of our Maker. We must acknowledge him, seek him, and know him!

This book was intended to be another contribution to the current lethal assault that is being waged against the dangerous deception of secular materialistic atheism__ a movement that was born out of the false and misleading ideology of evolutionary humanism.

Please remember that God loves you more than you can possibly comprehend and He has done everything that was necessary to rescue us from the terrible curse of death and decay upon this world.

With this said, I am reminded once again that God's image-bearing sons and daughters all carry free volition, and can certainly choose a worldview that denies the powerful truths I have presented in these many pages. But one thing is certain if they do—they can no longer depend on science, history, and logic to justify their position.

The Human Race

I looked into the world I see and
searched for answers desperately.
I found the truth and set my course
to serve the God who is my source.
And though the days grow weary
as I face a world of strife,
I have my Lord's assurance
that I possess eternal life.
Temptation came to knock upon
the door-gate of my heart.
I had the choice to live for self
or as God's servant do my part.
So by his grace I stood my ground
refusing compromise,
to live for self would rob me
of a great eternal prize.
So when I stand before my God
and look upon his face,
I will have to give account
of how I ran the human race.
If I live my life unto myself
a failure I will be.
But if I can touch a dying world
perhaps I'll help to set men free.
Few people understand this life
and that seems very odd.
My purpose is to glorify
the true and living God.

(Hebrews 12:1)
David E. Peeples

Epilogue

In researching and writing *The Mystery of Life* I have been compelled to make a strong case for the undeniable connection between science and faith. The narrative addresses the greatest culture war of our time and proposes a worldview that places the sovereign, eternal God of the Bible at the center of the discussion. This awesome, benevolent and infinite Creator God is believed to be the designing agent and sustaining power behind a material, physical world in which human life is center stage. Any knowledge and understanding we have gained in our struggle to survive is because of our complete and absolute dependence on Him and all that He provides for us.

Evolutionary thought has led humanity directly toward humanism, a man-centered religious ideology that became the breeding ground for all sorts of evil, racism, corruption, immorality, hatred and violence__ not to mention mass genocide. After all, if there is no sovereign personal God as humanistic atheism has proposed, that means there is no sin, no heaven or hell, and no human accountability to a power and authority greater than ourselves. If this is the case, then what possible difference does it make if I take whatever I want in this life at the expense of those around me? Who restrains me if I decide to covet my neighbor's wife or embezzle money in a shady business deal? After all, it's all about "survival of the fittest," right? Years ago, I can recall briefly observing a display of popular publications at a local book store. On this occasion I was rather surprised to observe that one of the best-sellers that year was a book entitled *Taking Care of Number One*, This is what humanism does to people; it gives them a license to act upon selfish impulses without restraint__ to consistently place one's own needs, wants, and desires before those around us leading to self-centered lives. This has ultimately led fallen mankind into moral corruption as morally impoverished humanity makes up his own rules, rules that are typically designed to satisfy the desires of the flesh__ desires and impulses that are at war with God.

The greatest obstacle for humanity imposed by the false and misleading view of evolution has been the generation of significant doubt and widespread skepticism toward biblical truth as trustworthy and reliable. This profound skepticism has generated much rebellion in the heart of man toward the authority of God as creator, provider, and the benevolent sustainer of the physical dimension in which we live. This false and misleading theory has gradually but steadily eroded man's confidence in the Bible as the trusted, authoritative Word of God, and has become the greatest single obstacle hindering the advance of the gospel of Jesus Christ and his saving power over human lives for multiple generations.

I will tell you why the message of the gospel seems so utterly fantastic and too unbelievable in the hearts and minds of many people in this generation. What we experience in this physical world through our five basic senses is not total reality, although many sincere people view it that way. Everything we naturally think, experience and feel in this material realm is influenced by the limitations of a fallen, three dimensional world. However, the nature and characteristics of this present age do not even come close to reflecting the quality, beauty and perfection that the earth once had when God declared that his creative handiwork was "very good"! We are born, we live out our days, and we experience much joy and satisfaction throughout our lives on earth, but in the end, we will all face disease, pain, and even loneliness followed by certain death. This is all we have ever known, like every generation that came before us. Now, even though evolution has clearly failed to deliver on its grandiose prediction of a more advanced, healthier, stronger and more disease-resistant humanity, many people have still been coerced into believing that this pain-ridden world is all there is. So the best we can hope for, in the materialistic way of thinking, is to convince ourselves that there is no greater power to which we must give account when this mortal life is over. To do this, people must be able to deny a living God by explaining away any consideration and by denying any mention of a supernatural creator. So many of the elite within today's modern culture have claimed that a divine presence is totally outside the natural world of man's intellectual, rational, and sophisticated way of thinking. By denying any possibility of the supernatural, people struggle to make sense out of lives without purpose and meaning that last for only a few short years followed, supposedly, by nothingness. The gospel of Jesus Christ is often rejected because the concept of supernatural power was dismissed from many human minds long ago, when they embraced evolutionary thought. However, the total reality, which has been largely forgotten in this generation, began with a perfectly created cosmos and will end with a perfect recreation of the same. What we know and experience today is only a very brief intermission in the reality that began with a personal loving God and will continue with the same benevolent creator when his plan and purpose for this present world is complete.

Only by believing in the supernatural and submitting our lives to the Word of God (the Bible) are we able to comprehend the deep mysteries of life that have baffled the world's greatest minds for thousands of years. As we examine the Scriptures, we can begin to understand why there is life and death, why there is love and hate, war and peace, marriage and divorce, truth and falsehood, and heaven and hell. God intended for his revealed Word to be our instruction manual to guide us through life__ a way to clear up the confusion and misunderstanding that has plagued mankind throughout his occupation of this earth. With this said, the vast majority of humanity either knows or perhaps suspects that the Holy Bible is a truthful and reliable source of divinely inspired revelation. Even though many people will seldom open their Bible, they suspect that it contains the wisdom and provides the understanding for the most difficult challenges we face. The many grueling and life-altering problems mankind has created for himself have always resulted from a stubborn unwillingness to submit our lives to God's truth, which represents the authority of our creator over his creation. And whenever we reject this truth we find ourselves in open rebellion against that authority.

The trustworthiness and genuine authenticity of the biblical text is clearly not the central theme of *The Mystery of Life* narrative, and the topic would certainly require many bound volumes of its own in order to adequately address this crucial subject matter. However, because the biblical narrative text is paramount to the primary theme of this publication, I feel obligated to address this issue at least in some brief dialogue in order to give the reader confidence that the Bible can be trusted. Therefore, allow me to summarize in this epilogue section the many reasons why we can trust the Bible and confidently believe that it is a reliable revelation of God's wisdom and will as intended for the beneficence of humanity.

In nature, we have clearly seen the brilliant handiwork of a master design engineer. Our instinct and personal conscience reveal to us that we were created as moral beings that are accountable to a power and authority much greater than ourselves. However, these avenues of understanding can only give us a general revelation of who God is and what He is like. Even though the evidence of a benevolent creator is very impressive in and of itself, it does not provide us with any detailed knowledge about the loving personal nature of God and why He has placed such a high value upon human life. It tells us nothing about his love, grace, mercy, and compassion, for example. For this reason, man was in great need of a more specific and detailed revelation from above. If God is truly real, and he desires a relationship with man, then it is entirely up to him to communicate his word and his will to us. Therefore, the question is, has God taken the initiative to communicate divine truth to mankind? Is the Bible a revelation of divine origin? Can we trust the Scriptures as the complete, authoritative Word of God? What evidence, if any, would lend support to its authenticity and reliability as a supernatural communication from the sovereign creator of heaven and earth? Even though close and constant observation of the magnificent beauty and design that surrounds us has revealed the splendid handiwork of a creative supernatural force at work, the sovereign God is a personal being who desires an intimate relationship with all those whom he has lovingly created in his own image. Therefore, we need much more knowledge and clear understanding of this sovereign Lord of creation in order to relate to him personally as he has intended us to. As the centerpiece of God's creation, we humans were primarily designed for relationship that would include both God and our fellow man. God has given us the biblical narrative so that we could understand who we are, and how we can learn to live in peace and harmony with each other. But most of all, we need to understand the true character of the one who created us, and to learn what it takes to relate back to Him on a personal level. Without the Bible, we would never be able to understand what it takes to know God in the way he desires to be known. Because you and I were created to experience personal relationship, it has always been God's desire to have an unbroken friendship with man that would allow us to become a permanent part of his eternal family.

The manufacturer of any complicated machinery or inventive device will always provide a precise instruction manual in order to explain how their product works properly and how to troubleshoot if problems arise. The Holy Bible is our *instruction manual* for living. It reveals in great detail the God of creation, why we are here, how we can find purpose for living, and what will happen when we die. All of the most challenging and difficult questions man has struggled with over the centuries are addressed in God's revelation. And yet people so often ignore its truth and many choose to go on living troubled lives without real meaning and without purpose. Why not just read the instruction manual so that we can live out our lives the way they were meant to be lived?

In considering the mystery of life, we should start where the Bible starts, with creation. The high value, dignity, and great worth that God places on human life is deeply rooted in the fact that we were created in his image. God has chosen us humans to represent his character on earth. This high-calling and privileged purpose makes sin all the more tragic as our separation from God, due to sin, prevents man from fulfilling his intended creative purpose. Earlier in *The Mystery of Life* narrative, I mentioned that evolutionary thought threatens to undermine the message of the cross. Let me explain more clearly hear what I meant by that. When Satan uses the evolution theory to convince humankind that random, naturally-occurring events are the only realistic way to explain why you and I exist, this is an all-out assault on the fundamental Christian doctrine of creation. The rational goes something like this: If there is no creation by intelligent design, then there can be no creator. If there is no creator, then there is no sin-induced separation from that creator. If there is no separation from a benevolent power greater than ourselves, then there is no need for a savior to rescue mankind from his fallen condition. And if there is no need for a redeeming savior, then the message of the cross of Jesus Christ amounts to pure nonsense in the minds of those who have embraced a humanistic worldview.

In her popular book *Total Truth*, Nancy Pearcey explains it like this: "It is because humans are the masterpiece of God's creation that the destructiveness of sin produces such horror and sorrow."[1] Only when man comprehends that sin has separated him from his Creator, will he begin to recognize the need for a savior. Because we have become the sons and daughters of God by creation first and foremost, you and I were designed to reflect the character of God in the physical dimension, and to give back to Him the glory that He alone deserves. To so many Americans living in a secularized, hedonistic culture, the concept of sin makes no sense whatsoever. This is why the strange notion of evolution theory must be thoroughly exposed for the satanic lie that it has become within modern cultures throughout the civilized world. The pathway to redemption that was opened up wide to mankind by the death and resurrection of Jesus Christ restores men and women to their original high-calling as sons and daughters of the Most High. Only then can we rediscover our true identity and appreciate the immense value that God places upon our lives. As the true image of a benevolent God is fully renewed in us, we can once again reflect God's character on the earth as powerful witnesses to a sick and dying world. Now, because we have all sinned against a Holy God, we need an instruction manual so we can understand what God has done for us and how to be restored to Him. This is why we have the Bible. It is the instruction we need to relate back to God across the great divide between the physical and spiritual worlds.

Because evolutionary thought is so widespread in our culture and has thoroughly infiltrated every institution within modern society, many people see no need for the Bible. They simply do not believe in a personal God that every human is required to answer to. The modern philosophy that humankind has intellectually outgrown any alleged need for God and, therefore, is able to manage his own personal affairs without divine interference has now become the underlying cause of many of the major problems the world is facing today. The devil will typically do his dirty work through pure deception. By twisting and distorting the truth, he has been able to control the masses in an all-out effort to thwart the plan of God to save mankind. Therefore, I encourage you to *examine the evidence* and to decide for yourself if the Bible we hold in our hands can be trusted to give each of us a certain hope and a promising future when we respond with conviction to its central message. What clear evidence, if any, has God left for us to solve this great mystery? If he is truly all-powerful and all-knowing then perhaps he would leave a clearly divine signature upon his written revelation to humanity. With eternal lives at stake, a personal loving God would surely leave little room for doubt that divine intelligence was at work in recording the sacred Scriptures. The truth about biblical inspiration, therefore, is the final battleground of engagement between the church and the world. The Christian faith stands or falls upon this highly controversial question regarding the divine inspiration and authority of the Bible.

How did the Bible get from the mind of God to the heart of man?

How did we get the biblical narrative, and can we really trust it to reveal the divine truth to us about a personal loving God and our relationship to him? You and I should be highly motivated to determine for ourselves if the Bible is the authentic Word of God. We certainly cannot afford to rely upon our feelings and emotions or even upon societal preferences when it comes to the serious question of the veracity of the Scriptures, because if the Bible we hold in our hands is God's eternal Word, then we will surely be judged according to what it has to say. The conclusion to the long-standing debate of whether or not the Bible is the inerrant Word of God giving clear instruction on this earth to every man, woman, and child is surely of eternal importance.

First of all, God has chosen to use man to reveal his thoughts, will, actions and intentions to everyone with a willingness to hear them and an open heart to receive them. The truth of scripture was delivered from the mind of God by way of the Holy Spirit to the heart of certain men whom God had chosen. We call this "Revelation"! In Ezra chapter 1:1, we read this example of how God directed man: "In the first year of Cyrus king of Persia, in order to fulfill the word of the Lord spoken by Jeremiah, *the Lord moved the heart* of Cyrus king of Persia to make a proclamation throughout his realm and put it in writing."

And in Jeremiah 1:9 we read: "Then the Lord put forth His hand and touched my mouth, and the Lord said to me: behold *I have put my words in your mouth*." Another example of how God communicated His words to man is found in 2 Peter 1:20,21 which explains that "above all, you must understand that no prophecy of Scripture came about by the prophet's own interpretation. For prophecy never had its origin in the will of man, but men spoke from God as they were *carried along by the Holy Spirit*."

Second, God called these specific individuals by divine appointment to document in writing the revelation he had given them for the beneficence of all humankind. We call this "Inspiration"!

And, finally, the record of God's revelation in written form was preserved and safe-guarded by a specially chosen nation of people, while the divine message was made available to the multitudes__ the subjects of God's endless love and devotion. As searching mankind would hear, learn, and understand the heart of God through his written revelation, the Holy Spirit allows the message to penetrate the heart of man and transform him from within. We call this "Illumination"!

There are a number of supernatural elements that have been recognized in the Bible providing all the proof we need that it can be trusted as the inspired revelation of God's eternal truth. Let's take a look at these supernatural elements that set the Bible apart from all other books.

Supernatural Element 1: God's instrument of revelation

God chose one unique nation of peculiar people to whom he would choose to directly reveal his divine thoughts, words, and actions. This imperfect nation of often rebellious souls was entrusted with the responsibility of not only recording God's eternal Word, but also were commissioned with the awesome task of protecting, preserving and passing on accurately this sacred narrative to each new generation until the whole world could be reached with God's divine truth. In chapter 8, we have already considered the miraculous beginning and survival of the Jewish nation of Israel whom God had set apart unto himself to be the instrument by which he would reveal his true character in great detail to the whole earth. Through one miracle after another God established this unique nationality, commissioning them to receive his divine oracles and, ultimately, they would introduce the promised Messiah into the world. Without God's miracles, there would be no nation of Israel, and without Israel we would have no Bible and no Messiah.

Supernatural Element 2: Unique origin-amazing continuity

The Bible is a thematically unified message system with *redemption* as its central theme. As you will see, God left no possibility for collusion between the writers of Scripture. The Bible was written in three languages__ Hebrew, Aramaic, and Greek. It was recorded on whatever writing material was available at the time, such as clay tablets, stone, papyrus, parchment, leather, and even certain metals. The forty-four separate writers of Scripture came from diverse and widely different backgrounds__ they were kings, fisherman, shepherds, a statesman, a cupbearer, a tax collector, a physician, and multiple prophets of Israel for example. The Holy Scriptures were recorded on three separate continents with these men having little or no knowledge of one another. They wrote in the dessert, on the hillsides, on craggy cliffs, in dungeons and jails, in the temple, on a deserted island, in the city of Babylon, in

Rome, in Egypt, and throughout the region of Asia Minor, spanning 1,600 years and some forty generations of human history during times of great conflict and times of peace. How is it even possible that forty-four different and isolated writers, who had never written before, could maintain the same general theme over a period of 1,600 years? This could only be done by divine inspiration with writers revealing God's truth as it was illuminated to their hearts and minds and by divine oversight in that the combined volume of sixty-six books would form a unified message system woven together to make one continuous and progressive revelation of God's eternal truth. No other religious revelation even comes remotely close to the diverse circumstances God used to record his eternal Word. The Koran was written by one man__ Mohamed. The Analects of Confucius are the work of one man. The religious works of Buddha were fashioned by one man. The Book of Mormon was compiled and published by one man__ Joseph Smith. We would undoubtedly expect religious books that have had a primary responsible agent to be consistent in the thematic content they present, but God chose many men and extremely diverse circumstances to deliver a unified message to mankind in a manner that defies collusion and requires an explanation beyond human intellect, so that we would recognize very clearly that divine origin would be the only way to explain its existence.

With diverse background characteristics, God has insured that the unique continuity and thematic consistency found from Genesis to Revelation could only point to one thing__ divine origin. The Bible speaks with amazing unity, conformity and exceptional harmony on the most controversial topics from cover to cover. The first writer is thought to be Moses, who recorded his contribution around 1500 BC, and the last writer of the Old Testament, Malachi, recorded his revelation about 400 BC. This left a widespread gap between the last writer of the Old Testament and the first writer of the New Testament of somewhere between four and five hundred years. This gap was also a part of God's divine plan. By leaving this wide gap in revelation between the Old and New Testaments, God insured that there could be no collusion between the prophets of the Old Testament revelation and the appearance of Messiah, who was the primary subject of their prophecies. The entire revelation of God's Word was recorded beginning around 1492 BC and was completed with the last book of New Testament around AD 80 or slightly before. These ancient Hebrew Scriptures have clearly helped mankind to fully understand that ultimate reality in the physical dimension we occupy is not isolated only to the activities of man and the organic life-forms that surround him. These eternal words reveal to us the activities of God and Satan both interacting with mankind, with an emphasis on three general locations__ heaven, hell, and earth. Due to the very unusual and extremely unique circumstances surrounding the origin of the Bible, one would certainly expect that the total combined volume of sixty-six books would demonstrate much confusion, contradiction, and a general lack of unifying subject continuity. However, perhaps the most amazing thing about the Bible is that the subject narrative of every book and every author throughout the combined volumes blends together quite cohesively, forming one continuous revelation of God's divine truth. It is certainly not a heterogeneous jumble of myths, legends, and superstitions as many atheists would have us believe, but a harmonious collection of knowledge and details that obviously originated from a single divine source. There is no other way to explain its unique origin than to acknowledge that the Holy Spirit has orchestrated all of it. Considering that the Bible addresses the most sensitive and controversial topics from Genesis to Revelation with harmony and agreement throughout, provides us with our initial evidence that the text was the work of God and not that of man. Imagine, if you will, the jumbled mess of conflicting points of view that would appear in a blended book narrative written under similar circumstances today by a select group of widely diverse writers working independently of one another. Let's say, for example, they were assigned to create a collection of family resource material addressing all of the most challenging moral issues of our time. Does that objective not seem like an overwhelming task? And yet our unique biblical collection of sixty-six books compiled by forty-four writers over 1,600 years focuses on virtually every moral issue of our time with astonishing harmony from cover to cover as the work of each individual writer reinforces the message of the others and the theme of the Old Testament is dramatically fulfilled in the New. It is apparent then that man could never have compiled a volume of books with the unifying qualities of the Bible by human effort alone.

Supernatural Element 3: Divine perspective of the Bible

The Bible is a progressive revelation that begins with the creation of heaven and earth, and ends with the creation of a new heaven and a new earth (Revelation 21:1). The Bible gives us God's description of the origin of the universe and relates to us how life began. It provides a detailed account of the nature of God, the fall of man, the way of redemption and God's eternal plan and purpose for the ages. The New Testament was never meant to take the replace of the Old. It was, however, meant to offer a fulfillment of the underlying promise of the ancient Hebrew text. In many cases, the New Testament was actually needed to fully understand the Old. For example, we cannot thoroughly understand Leviticus without Hebrews, or Daniel without Revelation. Also, Isaiah 53 would be difficult to comprehend without the gospels of Matthew, Mark, Luke, and John. But if the Bible is truly from the mind of God, and not the mind of man, then we could certainly expect the Scriptures to be recorded in such a way as to reflect God's point of view in the narrative. Is the Bible written from the standpoint of God speaking to man? If the scriptures were merely the result of human achievement, as the skeptics believe, it is quite unlikely that the Bible would reflect God's perspective. Phrases like "Thus saith the Lord" and "The Word of the Lord came unto me saying" appear over two thousand times in the Old Testament (see Jeremiah 1:9). Also, keep in mind that the Old Testament refers to itself as being the Word of God some 3,800 times, and the New Testament writers, including Jesus, made reference to Old Testament events at least 160 times by quoting directly from more than 240 Old Testament passages. This is certainly the type of narrative we would expect to find in a sacred message that originated from the mind of God. 2 Timothy 3:16 tells us that *"all scripture is God-breathed* and is useful for teaching, for rebuking, for correcting and for training in righteousness." God has chosen and has divinely directed certain gifted individuals to receive and to record divine laws, historical facts, doctrines, poetry, and the prophetic warnings that he intended for mankind to know of. And he accomplished this goal without endangering the accuracy of the message, because the sovereignty and divine providence of an all-powerful God insured that His communication with man, although written by human hands, would accurately reflect divine truth, and could, therefore, be trusted as reliable and authentic. The writers of Scripture used their own personal faculties, and wrote in their own individual style; yet God preserved them all from error while allowing them to express his words in their own unique way without distorting the divine message.

We must keep in mind that the words recorded by mankind from his own human intellect are always limited to the author's personal knowledge, understanding, and unique experience. However, from what we read in the Bible text, it has become apparent that the writers of Scripture did not always understand the significance of what they were writing. This in itself is strong evidence that the Bible is not the result of human thought and planning. "This salvation was something the prophets did not fully understand. Though they wrote about it, they had many questions as to what it could all mean. They wondered what the spirit of Christ within them was talking about, for he told them to *write down* the events which, since then, have happened to Christ: His suffering and His great glory afterwards. And they wondered when and to whom all this would happen" (1 Peter 1:10, 11 TLB). The fact that God has previously revealed his word to men and instructed them to record it is clearly seen by the words of the prophet Jeremiah: "In the fourth year of Jehoiakim, son of Josiah, king of Judah, this word came to Jeremiah from the Lord: Take a scroll and write on it all the words I have spoken to you concerning Israel, Judah and all the other nations from the time I began speaking to you in the reign of Josiah till now" (Jeremiah 36:1, 2). God was so serious about maintaining the accurate nature of his revelation to man that he left a stern warning to us all that no one was to add or take from his divine message. Scripture records this warning at least three separate times. "You shall not add to the word which I command you, or take from it, that you may keep the commandments of the Lord your God which I command you" (Deuteronomy 4:2). "Every word of God is pure; He is a shield to those who put their trust in Him. Do not add to His words, lest He rebuke you, and you be found a liar" (Proverbs 30:5, 6). "For I testify to everyone who hears the words of the prophecy of this book; If anyone adds to these things, God will add to him the plagues that are written in this book . . ." (Revelation 22:18).

As we have already discussed, man is incomplete and basically unfulfilled without a personal living relationship with the God who created him. If the Bible is indeed the authoritative Word of God, it is essential that we feed upon its divine truth if we should ever hope to truly understand what human life on planet earth is all about. "But He answered and said, it is written, 'Man shall not live by bread alone, but by every word the proceeds from the mouth of God'" (Matthew 4:4).

Supernatural Element 4: Impartial content of the Bible

People often wonder why God favors Israel over other nations. Is this true? Definitely not! God chose Israel and he used them in a remarkable way to accomplish his divine purpose. But he loves all people the same. A closer look at the Bible text reveals that God was completely impartial when he instructed the recording of details concerning the history of both nations and the individuals who became his main messengers to a dying world. For example, the detailed history of the Jewish nation that was recorded in Scripture is one of stubborn rebellion, idolatry, and deceitful wickedness. Now, since all of the writers of the Old Testament were Jewish ethnicity, it does not make sense that if they were writing the history of their own beloved nation, they would choose to record it as a despicable record of ingratitude, idolatry, and unbelief. This naked detail could only have been inspired by the sovereign mind of a very impartial God who favors no living soul over another. The Bible speaks with complete honesty and with a total absence of favoritism when it comes to the heart of God for humanity. The biblical narrative provides a detailed and unmerciful account of the personal sins of those who wrote it. For example, the sins and personal failures of some of the greatest men in world history are clearly exposed for the entire world to know of. The worst sins of Adam, Abraham, Isaac, Jacob, Moses, David, Solomon, Hezekiah, Elijah, Peter, and Paul, for example, are clearly detailed for our common knowledge; yet through repentance and the merciful forgiveness of the Almighty, these men accomplished more for God in their lifetimes than probably anyone else in world history. It does not make sense then that the writers of the Scriptures would emphasize their own personal sins and failures, as well as their national sin, if they were writing from their own individual thoughts and perspective.

Supernatural Element 5: All-inclusive nature of the Bible

The Bible starts at the beginning with the creation heaven and earth, and continues through seven human dispensations of history in which God is dealing with humanity, followed by the final act of God's plan and purpose for the ages when He recreates the heavens and earth in preparation for the perfect age in which the redeemed of God enjoy the presence of their Maker uninterrupted forever.

These human dispensations include the following from the perspective of God's dealing with man.

1. "The Edenic Dispensation" the *Age of Innocence* that ends with the fall of man.
2. "The Antediluvian Dispensation" the *Age of Conscience* prior to the great flood.
3. "The Postdiluvian Dispensation" the *Age of Human Government* after the flood.
4. "The Patriarchal Dispensation" the *Age of God's Promise* spoken thru the patriarchs.

5. "The Legal Dispensation" the *Age of Divine Law* through God's servant Moses.

6. "The Ecclesiastical Dispensation" the *Age of God's Grace* also called the Church Age.

7. "The Messianic Dispensation" the *Kingdom Age,* also the Millennial Reign of Christ.

8. "The Dispensation of the Fullness of Times" the future *Perfect Age* that will never end.

It is appropriate for us to consider that numbers are very meaningful in the Bible. The number seven is God's number of fulfillment or completion. Thus, we see that God's plan and purpose in dealing with humanity is completed or fulfilled in seven dispensations of time. The number eight in the Bible is the number of "new beginning." Thus we see that after God's faithful dealing with humanity, He recreates heaven and earth and a perfect age (new beginning) ensues with the fullness of time that has no ending.

Supernatural Element 6: The remarkable transmission

Let us consider for a moment whether or not the Bible, as we know it today, reflects the same thought and intent of the original manuscripts. Considering the turbulent history of the Jewish nation, to whom the oracles of God were entrusted, it seems that the Bible would have had little chance to survive with its original language intact. Many original manuscripts of the most ancient Hebrew text have not survived to the present day for a couple of reasons that we will discuss in a moment. However, this is not the case with the New Testament documents. We still retain within church archives 24,633 original handwritten manuscripts representing the preservation of either all or part of the early New Testament, which have actually survived from antiquity. By comparison, the next closest surviving literature from the ancient days__ Homer's Iliad __ can claim only 643 handwritten copies. With these extremely valuable copies on hand, scholars are able to compare and contrast the textual purity of contemporary printed narratives of the same text that are currently available in wide circulation. The sacred documents forming the New Testament had to be copied and recopied for centuries until the advent of the printing press. And after centuries of copying, one might expect the Bible to contain many errors and omissions, resulting in a serious loss of its original meaning and vitality. However, with so many original surviving manuscripts with which to compare current copies, the accuracy and textual purity of the New Testament today has been firmly established and this recognized inerrancy and purity of the sacred Scriptures from ancient time until the present day cannot be denied. Thus, our abundance of manuscript evidence attesting to the accuracy of current New Testament documents makes our modern translations very reliable renderings of the original language.

The case of the Old Testament transmission of the Holy Scriptures presents a quite different story altogether. The reason we do not have many ancient copies of the Old Testament today is primarily two-fold. First of all, these documents were copied onto perishable material such as parchments, papyri and animal skins, which were terribly inferior to the reliable writing material we possess today. This would certainly account, in part, for a lack of preservation through the centuries. However, a more resounding reason for a significant lack of original copies of the Hebrew text is because of the way these documents were handed down from ancient time. In fact, in the case of the Old Testament, the reason there are so few surviving documents from ancient work with which to compare and contrast currently circulating material is actually a real testament to the reliability and accuracy with which these manuscripts were duplicated and then transmitted to future generations. The explanation for this is found in the extreme diligence and meticulous care with which the Old Testament documents were copied and transmitted. Since all ancient documents could only be preserved by handwritten copy, the accuracy in textual transmission was solely dependent upon the special care with which these ancient manuscripts were handled. Because the early writing materials were continuously subject to decay, a special class of people was employed to constantly replace the worn and dilapidated copies with newer ones. Within ancient Jewish culture the extreme care used to preserve the sacred writings of the Old Testament patriarchs and prophets was such an important part of their national pride and cultural identity that an entire class of men were trained whose sole duty it was to accurately preserve and to transmit the Holy Scriptures with the most precise exactitude humanly possible. This class of professionals are identified as the Talmudic and Masoretic scribes. In the copying process, these men were pledged to fulfill twenty separate criteria in completing their work to insure the precise accuracy of textual transmission. For example, the number of lines, words per line and letters per line were counted to match the original. This is only a fraction of the many detailed tests that each newly copied manuscript was subjected to. At the completion of each copy, if more than three misplaced strokes of the pen were found, the copy was immediately destroyed. The primary reason that we have so few handwritten copies of the ancient Hebrew Scriptures handed down to us today is because these scribes did not keep the worn out older copies from which the new documents were produced. The reason is that the older documents were destroyed or burned after copying was completed because, in the scribe's commitment to textual purity, they could not allow any worn out copies to remain that might possibly be misread at some point by others resulting from a loss of visual integrity due to blurred and indistinct lettering. This could lead to miss-copied documents at a later time. These scribes were determined that not one jot or tittle, or the least stroke of the pen would be lost from the original documents.

God chose the Jewish people, not only to record his sacred Word, but he also entrusted and divinely charged them with the responsibility of protecting, safe-guarding, and preserving the accuracy of his divine message. The question is, how well did these scribes do at fulfilling their grand commission to pass along divinely accurate manuscripts to future generations without compromising the original language? The accuracy of the copied Hebrew documents was considered to be in serious doubt by many scholars until the accidental discovery of many ancient scrolls in some caves near the Dead Sea by a Bedouin shepherd boy in 1947.

While searching for a lost goat, this young shepherd tossed a rock into a cave on the west side of the Dead Sea only to hear the sound of breaking pottery. Then upon closer inspection, he discovered some large ancient-looking jars containing leather scrolls that were carefully wrapped in linen cloth. The jars had been sealed in such a way as to protect these ancient scrolls from decay for an indefinite period of time. As these Old manuscripts were diligently studied and carefully photographed it became apparent to Hebrew Bible scholars that this find had been the most significant archeological discovery in the Holy Land in modern times. The Dead Sea scrolls have provided scholars with an extremely rare opportunity of comparing recently discovered documents with the oldest Hebrew manuscripts available to them at that time. This most fascinating discovery would surely help scholars determine the accuracy of textual transmission from ancient times to the present. The scrolls contained fragments from every book of the Old Testament text, with the exception of Esther. Also included were some extra-biblical works of great worth and a few valuable biblical commentaries as well. Through the providence of God, these rare documents had survived totally undisturbed for nearly 2,000 years. Up until this amazing discovery the oldest Old Testament manuscript in existence was dated at around AD 900. The Dead Sea scrolls have afforded textual scholars the unique opportunity to compare these AD 900 documents with their newly discovered ancient counterparts that have been dated back as far as 125 BC. With this momentous opportunity scholars were able to test the accuracy of textual transmission of the Hebrew Old Testament since before the time of Christ. The transmission accuracy of the ancient Hebrew Scriptures could now be examined as never before in human history. One of the ancient leather scrolls, dated at 125 BC, included a complete manuscript of the Hebrew book of Isaiah, certainly one of the most beloved books of the Old Testament cannon. When this document was compared to the Isaiah manuscript dated at AD 916, scholars were absolutely amazed at the results. Even though over 1,000 years of time had separated the two documents, they were virtually identical when compared word for word. For example, of the 166 words comprising the fifty-third chapter, only one single word was in question__ a word that did not affect the meaning of the original language. The Dead Sea scrolls have now erased any lingering doubt as to whether or not the Old Testament of today is to be considered accurate when compared to documents dating before the time of Christ. Outside of some insignificant variation in spelling and grammar, we can be certain that today's modern copies of the biblical text do not differ substantially from the content of the original narrative. By divine providence, a sovereign eternal God has clearly protected and preserved his revelation to humanity for the beneficence of all generations. Of those who deny the trustworthiness of the Bible and are skeptical about its reliability today, perhaps they simply do not want it to be a truthful revelation of God's heart for mankind.

Supernatural Element 7: Miraculous survival of the Bible

Even though the works of many non-biblical writers lend full support to the trustworthiness of the Scriptures, many bold attempts have been made to discredit the authority of the Bible. Through the avenue of textual criticism, many liberal-minded theologians and biblical critics have attempted to undermine the veracity of the Scriptures by questioning the authorship and the dates of the biblical writings, as well as questioning historical details in an effort to discredit the written content. This has been an effort to generate doubt as to the reality of the people, places, and events they were describing. Historically, however, the New Testament is primarily a collection of first-hand accounts written by men who witnessed the events they wrote about or had received first-hand the powerful words of the Lord through intimate personal contact. Nevertheless, this relentless assault by the higher critics to condemn the biblical text continues to be exposed as nothing but a malicious attack upon the divine authority of Scripture, in light of a profound advance in archeological research over the last century. Needless to say, the Bible has survived the attacks of the higher critics, becoming more thoroughly vindicated today than ever before in history. The Bible has faced far more persecution than any other known work of literature in history by far. It has been defamed, burned, banned, and outlawed from the early days of the Roman Empire up until the recent attacks of humanistic liberalism, of communism, and of an insidious element within modern-day Islam. For example, in AD 303 a wicked Roman emperor named Diocletian had proclaimed in an edict that all Christians and their sacred book were to be destroyed. He sent Roman soldiers throughout the empire burning churches to the ground and destroyed all the Scriptures they could find. However, this edict didn't last long for it was only twenty five years later that Constantine succeeded this evil emperor and commissioned some fifty copies of the Holy Scriptures at government expense, while declaring Christianity to be the official religion of the Roman Empire. During the dark ages of religious persecution Christian monks were forced to sew copies of the Scriptures into the lining of their clothing to avoid prosecution as they moved from place to place sharing the hope of God's love for humanity. In the 1700s, an infidel Frenchman by the name of Voltaire became a bitter enemy of Christianity and the Bible. As he began to persecute the church and the Scriptures, Voltaire ultimately vowed that Christianity and the Bible would be eradicated from the earth by the end of the nineteenth century. However, as divine providence would have it, some fifty years after he died in 1778, the house of Voltaire became occupied by the Geneva Bible Society and was transformed into a Bible printing and distribution center. Ironically, they used the infidel's own printing press to produce copy after copy of the sacred Scriptures for wide distribution. Men like Thomas Paine, Adolf Hitler, Joseph Stalin and many others have tried to rid the world of the church and the Bible, but the persecution has only made the Scriptures more valued and treasured. Throughout the centuries of time many evil men have sought to destroy the Scriptures and to persecute those who profess Christianity, but every attempt has been unsuccessful while the Bible has endured to become influential worldwide despite the efforts of a few infidels. The enemies of truth pound away until their hammers break, but God's anvil still stands firm. Satan would certainly not go to such great lengths to destroy the Holy Bible unless it posed a serious threat to his control over the hearts of men. If the Bible is not God's Word, it would have been forgotten and forsaken long ago.

The Bible is surely the most despised book ever written. Hatred for the Word of God runs deep in modern cultures where men and women prefer not to be confined by burdensome moral constraints. It is still illegal in some countries to own, read, publish, sell or translate the Bible. None of this should be a surprise because the devil does not want people to read and understand inspired Scriptures, which lead men to salvation and eternal life. The Bible has inspired great music, art, architecture and culture. If you were to take away the biblical influence over Western culture, you would destroy the inspiration for the greatest advancement, success, and achievement in the history of the world. The Bible we hold in our hands today is the only physical thing that we can point to on this earth that is eternal in nature. The Bible has survived the ravages of war, famine, disease, pestilence, and persecution. And it will remain long after the earth as we know it passes into history. "The grass withers, the flower fades, but the word of our God stands forever" (Isaiah 40:8). "Heaven and earth shall pass away, but my words will by no means pass away" (Jesus__ Matthew 24:35). Yes, the pages of the Bible represent the most intimate possible connection and communication between heaven and earth.

Supernatural Element 8: Universal circulation & influence

Has the Bible received the degree of public circulation and the universal influence we would expect from a book of divine origin? We do not have to look far to discover that no other book in the history of mankind can even begin to compare with the Bible in terms of its universal influence and circulation throughout the world. The Bible is by far the most dearly beloved book of all time. As the world's all-time best seller, it is the most widely read and the most extensively translated literature in all of human history, having a worldwide circulation that is now approaching one copy for every person on the planet. The Bible has clearly received more attention and has been quoted from more often than any other work of literature by far. The Bible was the first book to come off the printing press, and the first book to be translated from one language into another. As of 1979, the Bible had been translated into more than 1,500 known languages and dialects. At that time, the translation rate included 95 percent of all human languages. Today there are very few languages, dialects, and remote tribes that do not have at least some of the Bible available to them in a format they can understand. It is important to note that the Bible can be translated into any language without losing its vitality and spiritual power. The message of the Bible has so inspired the thinking of man that the number of books and commentaries that have been written in response to it has been equally impressive. And the profound influence the Bible has had upon the civil affairs of mankind has been nothing short of astonishing. This is, of course, what we would expect if it truly was a divinely inspired message of hope and promise that originated from the mind of God.

Supernatural Element 9: Textual harmony with science

The Bible has proven to be scientifically accurate in its entire content. This quality of the Scriptures is powerful evidence that God's hand has directed the writers he chose. They recorded great knowledge and information that was beyond the understanding of mankind at the time, and only an omniscient God would have known. Although the under-appreciated harmony of the biblical text with true science has already been adequately dealt with in the main body of this narrative within chapter 9, we will touch on it just briefly again here. For many years, claims were made that the written text was in direct conflict with what we understood about science. However, as it turns out, the problem was not with the Bible but man's lack of knowledge about the physical world, because mankind's discoveries had not yet caught up to the Bible. For example, for a very long time, men believed and taught that the earth was flat, when all along, the Bible said it was circular (see Isaiah 40:22). For many years, under the influence of Aristotle, it was believed that the sun rotated around the earth. This was the prevailing view of the day until about the sixteenth century, when Kepler and Galileo put an end to that outdated paradigm. Johannes Kepler was a strong believer in God and the Bible. He once declared that "science is simply thinking God's thoughts after him."[2] Mankind didn't even know that blood circulates through the body until around 1650 when William Harvey discovered the circulatory system. During the middle ages, the Bubonic plague ravaged Europe killing one-fourth of the entire population before it ended. This death occurred because mankind did not adequately understand germs, contagious disease, and quarantine. People had failed to appreciate the importance of cleanliness and the appropriate use of running water. Victims of the plague were not isolated from healthy individuals, so others quickly became infected. But the book of Leviticus chapter 13, written several thousand years before these tragic circumstances unfolded was packed with knowledge that could only have come from a loving personal God, and would have saved millions of lives then, as it does today.

The wise-men of ancient Egypt had believed that the earth was held up by five pillars. This was the prevailing view in that culture, during the Egyptian dynasty. However, they didn't read Job 26:7. For centuries it was believed that there were only a few more than one thousand stars in the universe. Now we know there are an infinite number of stars that cannot even be counted. They didn't read Jeremiah 33:22. For hundreds of years, it was thought that bleeding a sick person would improve health whenever people became gravely ill. It was called bloodletting. This procedure is what led to the death of George Washington. Leviticus 17:11, however, tells us that the life of every creature is in its blood. How could Moses possibly have known that if it had not been revealed to him by the Creator? Now, we give people blood transfusions to save lives. The Bible records only the truth. It is pure nonsense to say the Bible is scientifically inaccurate. People who say this know little about science, and even less about the Bible. Today, we now know that every known fact of science mankind has discovered to date is in complete harmony with the Bible. God Almighty established the laws of nature so they would stand firm over his creation (Psalm 148). Wisdom suggests that we should acknowledge this truth. What we should take away from the revealed harmony between science and the Bible is that only God would have known these scientific facts before mankind confirmed the truthfulness of this revelation.

Supernatural Element 10: Historical accuracy of the Bible

Among other things, the Bible is a work of historical literature. Because of this, we can now compare the biblical record with many known facts of history obtained through scientific and historical research and investigation. If the Bible is truly the Word of God, we would expect it to present absolute accuracy in every recorded detail of history. It would surely take numerous publications to provide a thorough summation of the vast degree of historical and archeological evidence that lends its prevailing support to the accuracy of the Bible as an historical document. This evidence is such a profound witness favoring the trustworthiness of Scripture that it must be addressed at least briefly in this epilogue. The following material provides a small sampling of the many names, places, and historical details mentioned in the biblical narrative that have been clearly identified through diligent historical research. This research includes non-biblical sources such as ancient inscriptions, historical manuscripts, and engraved tablets, pots, and monuments. For more than a century and a half, scholars from various institutions, including both public and private universities the world over have successfully led research teams on thousands of major archeological expeditions throughout the biblical Middle East. The fascinating discoveries these devoted scholars have uncovered has proven far beyond doubt that the Bible is reliable and accurate in its historical narrative whenever it has been put to the test. Through the progressive knowledge science has obtained by uncovering the past, we have accumulated a great deal of valuable information that strongly influences our collective confidence in the biblical record.

Many attempts have been made to discredit the veracity of the Bible's historical record, but one by one, these erroneous claims have met with disappointment in the light of modern archeology. Are the historical figures, events, and places recorded in the Bible to be accepted as real history in the literal sense? When Jesus was entering the city of Jerusalem on the back of a donkey, as recorded in Luke 19: 36-40, the people began to shout out praise. The pious Pharisees were indignant, and told him to silence the crowd by rebuking his disciples. Jesus gave a very direct response: "if these people should hold their tongues, the stones will immediately cry out." Well, the stones have cried out, but not immediately, yet their voice has declared a resounding shout throughout the world now for nearly two centuries. Again, we are touching on a major topic, which has become the subject material for hundreds of books over the last century or more, as the facts uncovered by the scientific discipline of archeology in the last couple of centuries are nothing short of astonishing. You and I do not have to look far to see that archeological research, undertaken in the Holy Land, has provided unwavering support for the accuracy of the ancient biblical text. Many prominent authorities agree that historical research has added convincing support to the biblical account of history. Let us consider here just a few biblical references receiving archeological and historical confirmation.

Various Bible critics have attempted to discount the life and journeys of the Old Testament patriarch *Abraham*. However, the extensive excavation at Ur of the Chaldees has uncovered positive proof of his life and activity. Apparently, Abraham was well-known throughout the region as a record of his activity was discovered in the excavation of Babylonia as well. Other discoveries have helped man to confirm the migration of Abraham from Ur of the Chaldees to Canaan as recorded in the book of Genesis. Still many other excavation projects have positively confirmed the biblical historical record of many kings and rulers associated with the biblical narrative. Particularly impressive is the confirmation of the reign of *King Solomon*. The Old Testament record of his extensive building endeavors has been validated by an abundance archeological evidence. For example, according to 1 Kings 10:26, we understand that King Solomon commanded a staggering number of horses and chariots. The modern excavation of the ancient fortified city of Megiddo has resulted in the positive identification of Solomon's stables that were extensive enough to accommodate an armory of horses and chariots. The excavation of another location under Solomon's rule has revealed an ancient blast furnace, which undoubtedly has a positive connection with the record in 2 Kings that mentions Solomon's casting of metals. Also regarding King Solomon, Mideastern archeology expert Dr. Nelson Glueck has explained that "the whereabouts of Solomon's lost city of Ezion-Geber was for centuries an unfathomable mystery, because no one paid attention to the biblical statement that it was located 'beside Eloth, on the shore of the Red Sea, in the land of Edom'"[3] (1 Kings 9:26). This ancient city was found exactly where the Bible recorded it to be.

On December 18, 1995, the featured article of *Time* magazine was a narrative entitled "Is the Bible Fact or Fiction?" This article, from a popular publisher that typically leans heavily toward the liberal view of humanistic evolution, presents the Bible as containing "some truth." Although it acknowledged some archeological discoveries that validate the historical accuracy of Scripture, it left the reader with the feeling of skepticism by suggesting that unless a biblical event can be proven through historical research, it cannot be considered trusted and reliable information. Hebrews 11:6 tells us that without faith, it is impossible to please God. I would reject the idea that we should only believe what we can conclusively prove. None of us live that way. We all exercise a degree of faith in what we do and why we do it. You and I will only cross a bridge in our car if we have good reason to believe that the bridge will hold us up; and we would certainly never jump out of an airplane unless we had the faith to believe that whoever packed our parachute knew exactly what they were doing. Therefore, when we look at a topic like the veracity of Scripture, we are looking for a consensus of evidence that will point us toward belief that is "beyond reasonable doubt." If the true and living God is the magnificent sovereign that he claims to be in the Bible, then you and I cannot discount the possibility that his transcendence enables him to preserve the veracity of Scripture for the benefit of those to whom he was communicating. With this said, let's take a closer look at more historical Bible facts, and determine if the evidence is indeed mounting in favor of the divine origin of the Scriptures.

The amount of archeological evidence that supports the historicity of the Bible is so vast in terms of volume of documentation that we can go all the way back to the Garden of Eden to begin our overview of material that has been uncovered by historical research. The following information can be found in Haley's Bible handbook between pages 68 and 90.

The Temptation Seal__ Found in Babylonia, this engraved relief depicts the temptation of Eve by the serpent in the Garden of Eden.

The Adam and Eve Seal__ From Assyrian archives, this ancient artifact depicts the sorrow and dejection of Adam and Eve (walking with heads down) after falling to temptation and subsequently being forced out of the Garden of Eden.

The Weld Prism__ As the oldest known outline of world history from around 2170 BC it lists eight rulers before the great flood and reveals knowledge of long life spans during that time.

The Gilgamesh Seal__ Archeological evidence abounds for a cataclysmic worldwide flood and can be found in the historical traditions of every major culture in early human history. This is especially true upon examination of the ancient Babylonian civilization as seen in the *Epic of Gilgamesh* revealed by the inscription text found on the Gilgamesh Seal.

Pre-flood cities uncovered__ The excavation of pre-flood cities in Mesopotamia (Ur, Fara, Susa, and Kish among other sites) has revealed some very interesting circumstances. At many ancient sites in the Middle East, archeologists commonly find that one city is built on top of the ruins of a previous one. In 1929, a joint expedition commenced between the University of Pennsylvania and the British Museum under the direction of Dr. C. L. Woolley. This research team had set out to complete a thorough search through the ruins of Ur, the original home of the biblical patriarch Abraham. They uncovered numerous layers of human occupation beginning near ground level, followed by an eight foot thick layer of water laid sediment containing no human artifacts at all. As they continued to dig down through the sediment layer, they eventually uncovered another distinct layer of human occupation. What they found below the sediment layer was a pre-flood civilization that had been buried by a great cataclysmic event. According to Dr. Woolley, "that eight feet of sediment implied a very great depth and long period of water; it could not have been put there by any ordinary overflow of the rivers, but only by some such vast inundation as the Biblical Flood."[4] Further excavation of the general area also revealed that this eight feet of sediment was universal throughout the entire region, as confirmed in the uncovering of other pre-flood locations. Halley's Bible handbook reports the following information based upon the excavation of multiple pre-flood sites in the vast region of ancient Mesopotamia: "The fact of a vast flood covering the whole area of early civilization is established by the eight foot layer of silt which cuts through the 'culture levels' of all the Euphrates Valley sites."[5] This fascinating revelation has provided some very impressive evidence favoring the authenticity of the ancient biblical flood of Noah as recorded in Genesis 6-8. At the original pre-flood site of Ur Dr. Woolley has reported that some magnificent discoveries were made among the human artifacts uncovered there, indicating that early man possessed a very high level of intelligence, artistic skill, and inventive ingenuity.

Tower of Babel Ruins__ More than two dozen very early Ziggurat-type tower structures from ancient Mesopotamia have been excavated, including that of the Genesis 'Tower of Babel', where, according to the Bible, God confused the speech of man, forcing him to scatter abroad across the face of the earth.

Ur of the Chaldees__ As stated above, world-renowned archeologist C. L. Woolley excavated the Mesopotamian birthplace of the Bible patriarch Abraham beginning in 1922. He, and those who were under his direction, uncovered one of the best known ancient sites of all time__ a city that was at the height of its splendor when Abraham left there to follow God's command leading him toward Canaan and a new land of promise.

The Code of Hammurabi__ Discovered at ancient Susa by a Frenchman in 1902, this very early code of inscribed laws identifies Hammurabi, the most famous of the early Babylonian kings, and it dates all the way back to the time of Abraham. This discovery represents the oldest known legal system in the world and demonstrates that early human culture was already far advanced as a civilization.

Other biblical archeological research has identified evidence confirming the following major events:

Abraham's sojourn into Egypt (Gen. 12), Abraham's battle with the Kings (Gen. 14), the commonly known destruction of Sodom and Gomorrah (Gen. 18-19), The events involving Joseph and Potiphar's wife in Egypt (Gen. 39), The seven years of famine in Egypt while Joseph ruled over the house of Pharaoh (Gen. 41), Israel's sojourn into Egypt to escape famine in Canaan (Exodus 1), the birth of Moses (Exodus 2), the death of Pharaoh's first-born (Exodus 12), Israel's Exodus from Egypt under Moses (Exodus 12), the defeat of Jericho (Joshua 6), the reign of King Saul (1 Sam. 1), the prosperous reign of King David and his many conquests (2 Sam. 1), and as mentioned the reign of King Solomon, including his gold, stables, furnace, and naval fleet (1 Kings 7-14).

Other identified sites include the building of Samaria, the rebuilding of Jericho, Shishak's invasion, Ahab's House of Ivory, Jezebel's cosmetic box, Assyrian captivity of the Northern ten tribes of Israel, Hezekiah's tunnel, Manasseh's reign, Queen Ester's palace, Babylonian captivity of Judah, the reign of Belshazzar, the fall of Babylon, the Edict of king Cyrus, and the repentance of Nineveh.

Again and again the independent sources have corroborated the historical facts of the Old Testament biblical text. Archeology, ancient literature, and many historical records have confirmed the accuracy of the Scriptures concerning the identity of many kings, places, and events that are recorded.

According to Dr. Nelson Glueck, who is considered the most eminent Jewish archeologist of the last century, over twenty-five thousand names and locations documented in the Old Testament have been clearly identified. He made this statement in 1955. This number has certainly grown substantially over the years as new Bible details are being identified throughout Israel and other middle-eastern locations on a regular basis in this century also. Research scholars have never identified a single piece of ancient artifact, which can be pointed to with confidence that disproves any statement recorded in the Scriptures. Dr. Nelson Glueck explains it this way: "It may be stated categorically that no archeological discovery has ever controverted a Biblical reference. Scores of archeological finding have been made which confirm in clear outline or in exact detail historical statements in the Bible. And by the same token, proper evaluation of Biblical descriptions has often led to amazing discoveries."[6] Nelson Glueck had remained close to the forefront of biblical historical research throughout his entire lifetime, and, after an outstanding career of accumulating and categorizing first-hand knowledge from archeological research throughout the entire region of the Middle East, the world-famous archeologist documented his work in a book entitled *Rivers in the Desert*.

Another respected scholar, Dr. J. O. Kinnaman, said this about Middle Eastern archeology: "Of the hundreds of thousands of artifacts found by the archeologists, not one has ever been discovered that contradicts or denies one word, phrase, clause, or sentence of the Bible, but always confirms and verifies the facts of the biblical record."[7] As a brilliant language scholar and former professor of linguistics at Princeton Theological Seminary, Dr. Robert Dick Wilson mastered forty-five different languages and dialects during his long career. Dr. Wilson was considered, by far, the most qualified Old Testament linguist of the twentieth century. He made the following statement after a full career of studying the biblical text from a linguistic point of view: "After forty-five years of scholarly research in biblical textual studies and in language study, I have come now to the conviction that no man knows enough to assail the truthfulness of the Old Testament. When there is sufficient documentary evidence to make an investigation, the statement of the Bible, in the original text, has stood the test."[8]

As already mentioned, the Dead Sea caves have yielded a treasure trove of well-preserved ancient Bible manuscripts. And of the many caves discovered, cave #4 alone housed fifteen thousand fragments from 574 manuscripts, predating any previous copies of Old Testament documents by as much as one thousand years. These very valuable manuscripts were believed to be hidden by a community of Jewish scribes called the Essenes, an isolated religious sect living and working at Qumran near the shores of the Dead Sea from 200 BC until well after the life of Jesus Christ played out in dramatic fashion on the ancient Jewish landscape. The Old Testament copy and dedicated preservation tradition of the Essene community is described in the writings of the ancient historians Josephus and Philo.

The March 5, 1990, issue of *Time* magazine published an article entitled "Score One for the Bible" in which documentation was reported concerning the research excavation of ancient Jericho in 1930 and 1936. Joshua 6:20 records that at the direction of God, the people gave a loud shout and the walls of the city fell down flat__ meaning they fell outward and down the hillside instead of collapsing inward upon themselves as was typically the case whenever fortified city walls were breached by battering rams in ancient times. By falling down flat, this allowed the Jewish invasion force to proceed rapidly up over the rubble and into the city with minimal resistance to secure an easy victory. These two excavations proved historically that the walls of ancient Jericho fell down flat, outward and away from the city, exactly how the Bible so accurately described it.

In 1846, historical explorer Austen Henry Layard discovered a black obelisk among the ruins of ancient Nimrud, located in what is now present day Iraq. This exciting discovery has recorded the military exploits of the biblical King Shalmaneser III, who historically chronicled his army's defeat of King Jehu of Israel.

In another incident Hezekiah, King of Israel, had ordered emergency fortification of the walls of Jerusalem in order to repel an invasion from Sennacherib the King of Assyria in 701 BC. This event is recorded in 2 Chronicles 32:1, 2, and 5. After the considerable damage and destruction from the famous six day war of 1967, a team of researchers from Israel's Hebrew University were successful in locating the ancient ruins of this wall construction that King Hezekiah had ordered in urgent preparation for the expected Assyrian invasion.

Another nineteenth century archeological discovery found in Iraq yielded a clay cylinder bearing the decree of King Cyrus allowing the Jews to return to their homeland, ending the seventy-year captivity imposed by God for Jewish rebellion. The event was recorded in Ezra

1:1-3. This cylinder find provided a clear confirmation of one of the most astonishing events recorded in the Scriptures. It is fascinating to note, as well, concerning the Persian King Cyrus, of how God used this pagan ruler to fulfill his divine purpose. I think we can all agree that only God knows the future before it happens. In the case of King Cyrus, God predicted, through the prophet Isaiah, the birth of this man, including an accurate foretelling of his very name and what was predetermined for him to accomplish nearly 150 years before he was born. King Cyrus was a very important person in Scripture, whom God used in a powerful way. His name is recorded some twenty-two times in the Bible. This is certainly fascinating proof that God spoke very clearly to the men he chose to record his divine revelation to humanity. King Cyrus is the man who founded the Persian Empire. In Isaiah 44: 24, 26-28, God declares himself the Creator and Redeemer and predicts very clearly that he will use a (yet to be born) man named Cyrus to restore the ruined city of Jerusalem. However, when this prophecy was spoken, Jerusalem was still a prospering and thriving city that would not even be destroyed until more than one-hundred years later by a Babylonian king named Nebuchadnezzar. This direct and precise fulfillment of Bible prophecy that was historically confirmed is proof that the sovereign God of Scripture does exist, and that He certainly has the providential power and authority to control and shape the present and future destiny of humanity.

The Roman historian Tacitus, who was known to be hostile toward Christianity, recorded in the Annals of Tacitus xv. 44. a clear record of the life of Jesus, Pontius Pilate, and Tiberius that dates between AD 115-117.

The Jewish Rabbinical writings of the Sanhedrin 43a, written between AD 70-200, records the event of Jesus' death on Passover eve as described in the New Testament.

King David's rule has been confirmed by the discovery of some engravings on a basalt monument unearthed at Tel Dan in 1993. The fact that ancient Israelites were in bondage to Egypt, as the Bible records, was confirmed by a discovery in Thebes in 1895. The *Merneptah Stele* uncovered in Pharaoh Merneptah's tomb dates back to the Jewish slavery in Egypt, and records the presence of the Israelites during his reign. Pharaoh Merneptah is believed by some to be the Pharaoh of the Exodus. In fact, an autopsy of his remains confirmed the cause of death was drowning. Could it also be that the multiple broken bones identified along with the drowning death resulted from a deadly pursuit of the Israelites into the Red Sea, where Pharaoh's entire army perished according to Scripture?

Dr. Robert Dick Wilson's book *A Scientific Investigation of the Old Testament* documents the historical identification of twenty-nine kings. Included among them were some rulers over Egypt, Assyria, and Babylon. In the discovery of ancient monuments honoring their reign, every name transliterates as it appears in the Old Testament.

The *Moabite Stone*, also called the *Mesha Inscription*, which was discovered in 1868, dates back to 830 BC. In 2 Kings 3, we read of Mesha, a vassal king of the Moabites who paid tribute to Israel. This monument records some of his extensive military campaigns. Still other inscriptions uncovered in the Middle East confirm the reign of various biblical kings, along with other nations and places as recorded in Scripture. The following is a list of some of those biblical confirmations (just to name a few).

Sargon II __ Sennacherib __ Nebuchadnezzar __ Belshazzar __ Ahab __ Jehu__ Ahaz __ Omri __

Hezekiah __ Hoshea __ Jeroboam __ Manasseh __ Pekah__ Joash __ Menehem __ Ahaziah __ Uzziah

Jehoiakim __ Shalmaneser III__ Nahor __ Haran __ Nineveh __ Elam

Yes, the science of archeology has gradually confirmed the ancient historical record set forth in the Bible. The accuracy of the Old Testament has become well-established by the continuous excavation of ancient ruins, leading to the discovery of recorded history on various tablets, pots, and monuments.

The basis for the faith and hope of millions of Christians worldwide is solely dependent upon the truthful reliability of modern New Testament documents. For this reason, the monumental effort of Bible scholars, researchers, and even scientists to help validate the accuracy of the New Testament is unparalleled in the history of ancient literature. Let us look briefly at some of the pain-staking work that has been completed. Keep in mind that thousands of people, who were eye witnesses of the events surrounding the life, death and resurrection of Jesus Christ, were still living when the gospels were written. If the truth had not been recorded accurately, they would have refuted those documents as fraudulent. Thousands of early Christians were tortured and martyred for their faith, yet no record exists that any of them had ever denied the accuracy of the Scriptures; and once the Scriptures were translated and copied for widespread distribution and usage, it would have been impossible to corrupt the text or to introduce any fraudulent misinformation.

Thanks to modern archeology, nearly all of the ancient cities recorded in the book of Acts have now been located and positively identified as well. Other New Testament sites that have been identified include the court where Jesus was tried by Pilate, the Pool of Bethesda, the ancient temple area, and the Pool of Siloam. These are some of the exact locations where many profound New Testament events transpired nearly two thousand ago. However, even though modern archeology has greatly helped to substantiate the New Testament record, its most impressive support has come from written documents of a non-biblical variety that have survived to this day. Researchers have identified numerous non-biblical historical texts that have survived from ancient times referring to the person of Jesus Christ, including the many events surrounding his activity and ministry as an itinerate preacher, his trial and crucifixion, his resurrection from the dead, and the early Christian movement that ensured. A number of these nonbiblical ancient scholars and early historians are listed here for you consideration: Ignatius, Polycarp, Irenaeus, Clement of Alexandria, Tertullian, Justin Martyr, Eusebias, Tacitus, Lucian, Josephus, Seutonius, Origen, Aristides, Philo, Thallus, Phlegon, and Plinius. As stated earlier, according to Dr. Gary Habermas, author of *The Historical Jesus*, when the writings of these and a few other ancient texts are combined, we have a very accurate accounting of the life of Jesus without even referencing the New Testament record at all. The historical existence of Jesus Christ, and the movement he began with his sacrificial death and resurrection, is not in question. There has been no other person in history whose existence has been so thoroughly documented. Only infidels bent on destroying the Christian faith have had the nerve to question the historical evidence verifying the life of Jesus of Nazareth.

According to the outstanding biblical scholar and researcher Sir Frederick Kenyon, "The interval then between the dates of original composition and the earliest extant evidence becomes so small as to be in fact negligible, and the last foundation for any doubt that the Scriptures have come down to us substantially as they were written has now been removed. Both the authenticity and the general integrity of the books of the New Testament may be regarded as finally established."[9] Because of historical and archeological research, we are rapidly reaching the point where the question is no longer__ what of the recorded details of the Bible have been historically identified? The question is now rapidly becoming__ what biblical names, events, and places have not been identified? The convincing evidence of modern archeology certainly does not prove conclusively the divine origin of the Bible. However, what it does prove is that the Bible is absolutely trustworthy and historically reliable from the standpoint of recorded history. If we can indeed trust the biblical record in regard to the historical figures, events, and places detailed, this would certainly be a good indication that it should be equally reliable and exceptionally trustworthy in other areas of divinely inspired revelation. Considering the amazing harmony between the Bible and the current treasure trove of uncovered historical details from the past, we must conclude that the Bible easily passes the test of historical accuracy.

Supernatural Element 11: Prophetic purity of the Bible

If God wanted to communicate a solemn message to mankind, how would he do that in such a way that man would know for certain the information had a divine origin? Well, for one thing, he could record history in advance, hundreds, or perhaps a thousand years or more before the events recorded came to pass. It is certain that only an all-knowing and all-powerful God knows the future before it happens. This is exactly what God did with the Bible. His prophetic fingerprints are all over its pages, from Genesis to Revelation. This very impressive supernatural quality of Scripture is perhaps the most obvious reason why we know that the Bible came from the omniscient mind of God. It certainly would have been risky to be a prophet in ancient Israel__ why__ because according to Jewish law you would have to be accurate 100 percent of the time or you were branded a false prophet and put to death.

We can trust the Bible because it is prophetically accurate. Of the many predictions recorded in the Old Testament, over three hundred refer directly or indirectly to the promise of a coming Messiah dating as far back as 1,500 years before his incarnation. We will examine carefully some of the more familiar Messianic passages of Scripture later in this section of material. The Bible not only presents to us a unique revelation of the past and present, but it is also the only revelation ever written that goes well beyond the current world situation and predicts for us the major events that will culminate in the future as God fulfills his plan and purpose for the ages. Perhaps the strongest evidence ever presented to verify the supernatural origin of the Bible comes from the study of Bible prophecy. Let us now briefly examine the matter of fulfilled prophecy to determine what additional strength this may add to the mounting evidence that the Bible is the work of God, and not that of man. If God is the source of all biblical revelation, and God is all-knowing (omniscient), then we could expect the prophetic passages of Scripture to receive a very precise and literal fulfillment. According to Dictionary.com, the word *prophecy* means "a foretelling or prediction of what is to come__ a divinely inspired utterance or revelation." As we briefly consider this topic in some detail, we should keep in mind that the God of the Bible, who declares himself the creator of heaven and earth, is the only one with all knowledge. This omniscience means that only God has total unlimited knowledge of the past, present, and future. When his revealed word to man makes many predictions of what is to come, and those predictions receive a precise fulfillment in the course of history, there is absolutely no doubt that God has spoken, and his signature of prophetic truth is all over the Bible. "As for the prophet who prophesies of peace, when the word of the prophet comes to pass, the prophet will be known as one whom the Lord has truly sent" (Jeremiah 28:9). The fascination of our world with the practices of the occult stems from the age-old desire of man to contact the spiritual world and to know the future before it happens. The best way to contact the spiritual world is to read the Bible. It is packed full of prophetic declarations__ predictions of the future that were each forecast hundreds of years before the events they describe were fulfilled. Few people realize that the content of the Bible, according to scholars, is upward of 33-35 percent prophetic in nature. With a solid one-third of the biblical text seen as consisting of prophetic revelation, most of which having already been fulfilled over time, we can easily examine the outcome of many of these ancient predictions and see how they compare with accurate historical records. The Bible text contains approximately 2,700 detailed predictions throughout its narrative. Of these many revelations, over 2,200 have already received complete fulfillment. This understanding certainly gives us confidence that the remaining 500 or so predictions, concerning the second coming of Christ, will also be fulfilled to the letter, and, perhaps within our lifetime. "For I am the Lord. I speak, and the word which I speak will come to pass . . . I will say the word and perform it, says the Lord God" (Ezekiel 12:25). "For assuredly, I say to you, till heaven and earth pass away, one jot or one tittle will by no means pass from the law till all is fulfilled" (Jesus__ Matthew 5:18).

Many of the predictions that were revealed by God through the ancient Hebrew prophets of the Old Testament were directed toward ancient biblical cities of the Middle East. Here we shall examine one of these ancient passages of scripture in detail to see how well the Bible corresponds with recorded history. Approximately six centuries before Christ, God revealed through the prophet Ezekiel, a judgment that he was declaring upon the ancient city of Tyre__ a city that was located in what we know as modern-day Lebanon. In the ancient world, Tyre was one of the great trade and commercial centers of its time. The citizens of Tyre had excelled as merchants, mariners, and explorers. As a strongly fortified city along the western shore of the Mediterranean Sea, this ancient metropolis was prospering and thriving during the time that Joshua led the children of Israel into the conquest of Canaan. Centuries later, during the time of the prophet Ezekiel, God declared divine judgment on Tyre because her people had rejoiced at the fall of Jerusalem. This ancient prophecy by Ezekiel was one of the most detailed predictions recorded in the Old Testament. For centuries, it seemed as though it would never see a clear fulfillment. In the twenty-sixth chapter of the book of God's ancient prophet, a pronouncement against Tyre is recorded for our examination. The prophet revealed that several nations would rise against Tyre's fortifications, and they would ultimately destroy her massive walls and break down her gates and towers.

God's word, penned by Ezekiel, predicted that a foreign adversary would remove her timbers and foundation stones and actually scrape away the debris and rubble to make the city like a bare rock. It predicts that the rubble and debris from the fallen city, and even the dirt, would be cast into the sea. The prophecy specifically stated that Nebuchadnezzar, king of Babylon, would lay siege on Tyre from the north, and would eventually conquer the city. The prophet declared that other nations would participate in the destruction of Tyre, and that a great spoil would be taken from the wealth of this city, causing many other nations to fear greatly at her downfall. The prophecy also recorded that ancient Tyre would become a place for the spreading of nets in the midst of the sea, and foretold that the original site of the city would never be rebuilt. This prophetic passage included some very strange details that seemed rather unlikely to ever be accurately fulfilled.

Ancient Tyre was a prominent and powerful city along the northern coast of what would eventually become known, in later years, as Palestine. When Ezekiel recorded God's judgment on this wealthy commercial trading center, it was at that time inhabited by the sea-faring Phoenicians. In the year 586 BC, Nebuchadnezzar, the King of Babylon, laid siege to the fortified Phoenician capitol. His arduous campaign for conquest lasted for thirteen years until finally, in 573 BC, the city yielded to his control. However, no treasure of consequence fell into enemy hands because the citizens of Tyre had secretly transported their merchandise and wealth onto a small island fortress about a half mile out into the Mediterranean Sea. Although the city was destroyed and left in ruins, Nebuchadnezzar profited little and was unable to pursue the Phoenician treasure to its new strategic location. Nevertheless, a portion of the ancient prophecy had been fulfilled. With the wealth of the mainland city now deposited safely on a nearby island, the Phoenicians went about the task of building their island citadel into one of the great trade centers of the ancient world. For some 241 years, the mainland city of Tyre remained in a heap of rubble just as the Babylonian army had left it. Later, however, when Alexander the Great began his extensive military campaign, Greek legions swept across the land conquering and subduing everyone they faced. Although fearing the strong Phoenician naval fleet, Alexander moved south to conquer the wealthy island fortress of Tyre. In 322 BC, his Grecian forces approached the fortified island citadel. Alexander called upon the wealthy rulers of Tyre to open their gates to him at once. Upon their refusal, Alexander became enraged and determined to overtake the city by any means possible. Not having a naval fleet, however, left him at a disadvantage. Alexander struggled to devise a plan that would allow him conquest of the island treasures he so greatly desired. Finally, however, he formulated a plan by which he believed the conquest of the wealthy island fortress was within his grasp. Alexander decided that he would build a land bridge from the shore of the mainland out to the nearby island that would allow his troops to invade the wealthy Phoenician capital. Even though the Phoenicians had a superior naval fleet with which to harass and to keep the enemy at bay, Alexander commanded his legions to remove all of the rubble and debris from the overthrown mainland city to be used for constructing a causeway that would connect the mainland to the island fortress. The broken down debris of stones, timbers, pillars, and even the very dust of the original mainland city was cast into the sea leaving the once-thriving metropolis as a bare rock.

After many months of difficult labor, marred by costly setbacks imposed by the Phoenician naval forces, the causeway was finally completed, and Alexander marched his army across dry ground to ultimately conquer the wealthy metropolis. The island citadel of Tyre was reduced to rubble, and the financial wealth of the once great city fell into the hands of the Greeks. The fall of Tyre caused such fear in neighboring cities that they opened their gates to Alexander, and, without opposition, submitted to his conquest. The island city eventually recovered from the Greek invasion, but, years later it was once again destroyed by another foreign invader by the name of Antigonus. In time a new commercial harbor was opened up along the Red Sea and the trade routes shifted so that the great wealth that had formerly flowed into the port of Tyre now found its way to Alexandria instead. Thus, Tyre had received its final blow__ the permanent loss and the demise of a once flourishing ancient metropolis. The city of ancient Tyre has never regained the prominence of her past glory. Today the ancient trade center has become a popular haven for fishing boats, and, upon the very ground where the Phoenician merchants once traded their fine goods to gain wealth, fishermen are now spreading their nets to dry in the afternoon sun. The prominent city of Tyre, the trade and commercial center of the ancient world for centuries, was subdued by the hand of Almighty God, and the freshwater springs that had once supplied the needs of the original mainland metropolis still flow today. And although it remains an excellent location with enough fresh water to supply a large modern city, the site has never been restored in more than 2,600 years as Ezekiel accurately predicted. Even though this ancient prophecy seemed very unusual, history confirms that it was accurately fulfilled down to the minutest detail. Thus, we have convincing proof of the accuracy of God's Word spoken through His ancient prophet Ezekiel.

If the prophet had recorded this series of predictions using only human foresight, without a divine impartation of future events, what would the remote probability be that every detail of this prophecy would have randomly come to pass in the course of time? Based on probability estimates, it has been calculated that the chance fulfillment of these unusual prophetic details is placed at one chance in seventy-five million.[10] It is, therefore, certain that only an omniscient God could foretell, years in advance, events such as this with such precision.

Many more detailed Bible prophecies were directed at other cities of the ancient world, such as Babylon, Edom, Sidon, Ammon, Samaria, Nineveh, Jericho, as well as Jerusalem for example. These other prophecies have also been fulfilled with amazing accuracy. The fulfillment of these unusual prophetic details concerning Tyre, along with many other ancient cities of the Old Testament stands as indisputable evidence of the divine origin of the Old Testament record. Since we now know for certain that the prophetic accuracy of the Bible has been well established, we can only conclude that the Bible is truly the result of God's own planning and design.

An Address in History

If you were trying to identify me, for example, how would you do it? Well, you could start with my name, check out my birth certificate, and discover my address, narrowing it down to street number, street name, city, county, state, and country. You could search for my social security number, a photo perhaps, employer, phone number and email address. This would pretty much complete the search. The Bible is about the Messiah, who would come to bridge the wide gulf between a Holy God and fallen humanity. Therefore, it is rather important that God identifies for us who the Messiah will be. What is his address in history? To start with, the Bible says that he will be the offspring of a woman (an allusion to the virgin birth). We know this because, throughout the Bible, genealogies always use the father to document lineage. This statement in Genesis 3:15 is a very unusual exception to that standard practice. He would be of the lineage of Shem, of the seed of Abraham, the son of Isaac, of the line of Jacob, and the tribe of Judah, from the family of Jesse, and of the house of David. The gospel of St. Luke chapter 3 traces the lineage of Jesus all the way back to Adam, the first man. This gives us a pretty good start in identifying the Messiah, sent by God, who was to bare the sins of the world. But this was not enough identification for God. He chose to pinpoint the Messiah for us so precisely that there could be no doubt whatsoever who he was. That is why the God of Heaven revealed over three hundred prophecies in the Old Testament that would unmistakably identify the true Messiah when he came into the world. The following is only a short list of these many prophecies that God used to pinpoint the Messiah. They were all precisely fulfilled in the life of one man. Each prediction lists the Old Testament prophecy followed by its fulfillment documented in the New Testament.

Messianic Prophecy	Old Testament Reference	New Testament Fulfillment
Born in Bethlehem of Judea	Micah 5:2	Matthew 2:1
To be born of a virgin	Isaiah 7:14	Luke 1:26-31
He would be called Immanuel	Isaiah 7:14	Matthew 1:23
Slaughter of the innocence	Jeremiah 31:15	Matthew 2:16-18
He would come out of Egypt	Hosea 11:1	Matthew 2:14, 15
He shall be called a Nazarene	Isaiah 11:1	Matthew 2:23
Be a light to the gentiles	Isaiah 9:1, 2	Matthew 4: 13-16
Receive praise of children	Psalm 8:2	Matthew 21:15, 16
Preceded by a forerunner	Isaiah 40:3, Malachi 3:1	Matthew 3:1, 2
He would be a prophet	Deuteronomy 18:15	Acts 3:20-22

He would speak in parables	Psalm 78:2	Matthew 13:34, 35
He would enter Jerusalem on a colt	Zechariah 9:9	Luke 19:35-37
He would be betrayed by a friend	Psalm 41:9	Matthew 10:4
Sold for thirty pieces of silver	Zechariah 11:12	Matthew 26:14, 15
Money thrown in House of God	Zechariah 11:13	Matthew 27:3-5
Money used to buy potter's field	Zechariah 11:13	Matthew 27:5-7
His betrayer to be replaced	Psalm 109:7, 8	Acts 1:16-20
Forsaken by his disciples	Zechariah 13:7	Mark 14:50
Accused by false witnesses	Psalm 35:11	Matthew 26:59, 60
Would be silent before accusers	Isaiah 53:7	Matthew 27:12-14
Would be beaten and bruised	Isaiah 53:5	Matthew 27: 26
Would be smitten and spat upon	Isaiah 50:6, Micah 5:1	Matthew 26:67, 27:30
Would be mocked by the crowd	Psalm 22:7, 8	Matthew 27:29
His hands and feet pierced	Psalm 22:16	Luke 23:33
His side would be pierced	Zechariah 12:10	John 19:34
Would die by crucifixion	Psalm 22:14, 15	Luke 23:33
Be crucified among thieves	Isaiah 53:12	Matthew 27:38
Intercedes for his persecutors	Isaiah 53:12	Luke 23:34
Rejected by His own people	Isaiah 53:3	John 7: 5 John 1:11
He was hated without a cause	Psalm 69:4	John 15:24, 25
Garments parted and lots cast	Psalm 22:18	John 19:23, 24
Gall and vinegar offered to drink	Psalm 69:21	Matthew 17:34
Would be forsaken by God	Psalm 22:1	Matthew 27:26

Would commit himself to God	Psalm 31:5	Luke 23:46
No bones would be broken	Psalm 34:20	John 19:32, 33
His heart would be ruptured	Psalm 22:14	John 19:34
His death would be voluntary	Isaiah 53:12	John 10:11
He would die for others	Daniel 9:26	Matthew 20:28
His death, a sacrifice for sin	Isaiah 53:5-12	Romans 5:6-8

According to Peter Stoner, a mathematical professor and the author of *Science Speaks*, the chance fulfillment of just eight of these major Messianic prophecies (if written by the wisdom of man without divine input) is estimated (based on the principle of compound probability) to have a combined chance occurrence of 1×10^{28}, and the chance that all eight prophecies would be fulfilled in only one man he places at 1×10^{17}. He goes on to estimate the chance fulfillment of sixteen of these prophecies in the life of one man at 1×10^{45}, where the chance occurrence of 1×10^{50} is now considered to be scientifically impossible. He doesn't stop there, however, but also gives us the estimated chance fulfillment of forty eight major prophecies coming to pass in the life of one man at 1×10^{157}. To give some perspective to these probability figures, Professor Stoner relates that if you covered the entire state of Texas two feet deep in silver dollars that included only one checked coin in the entire massive collection, the chance that a blindfolded man could randomly select the checked coin on the first try is estimated at 1 chance in 10^{17}. This is the same chance that only eight of these prophecies would be fulfilled randomly in the life of one man. If we then consider the probability of forty-eight major prophecies being randomly fulfilled in one man with a chance of 1×10^{157}, we are talking about mathematical nonsense here with a chance fulfillment far exceeding the probability that a blindfolded man could find a single checked electron in an entire universe full of the same. And yet God has revealed over three hundred prophetic details to identify exactly who the Messiah would be. He left absolutely no room for doubt.

The outline above includes only forty-four of several hundred prophecies written about a coming Messiah by the prophets of the Old Testament five hundred to a thousand or more years before the actual birth of Christ, and yet every one of these detailed predictions was amazingly fulfilled in the life of only one man__ Jesus. Could anyone actually believe that this was coincidental? This is why God used prophecy throughout the Bible to predict future events with precise accuracy. I've listed only a few of the prophecies informing mankind about the promised coming Messiah that was predicted throughout the Old Testament. We could also list hundreds of more prophecies that were directed at various people, places, cities, nations, and rulers that were also fulfilled with precise accuracy. The only logical way to explain history written five hundred to fifteen hundred years in advance of the events they had described is to admit to ourselves that this information required a divine impartation of knowledge from the Holy Spirit of God to the faithful writers of the Scriptures.

It's certainly very interesting to note here that King David, writing in Psalm chapter 22 more than a thousand years before Christ, gives us an excellent description of the agony and suffering of one who is put to death by hanging on a cross. There is certainly no actual way that King David could have known of this event by himself, however, because at the time he recorded these details, a sentence of death by crucifixion as a means of capital punishment was unknown to the Jewish nation. During David's time, death was routinely carried out by stoning. Crucifixion, as a form of lawful execution for a capital crime, was introduced by the Romans who gained preeminence over the Jewish nation nearly a thousand years later, well before the time of Jesus. It is quite obvious then that these prophetic details required a divine impartation of knowledge that would not have been available to the writer by any other means. The Christian faith was never established based on wishful thinking, blind acceptance of church tradition, or the feelings and emotions of the writing contributors. It was firmly founded on a vast body of objective evidence that can be explained only by a divine revelation. The study of Bible prophecy demonstrates that there is an abundant of evidence to support the authenticity and truthfulness of God's Word. This evidence is widely available to all those who are willing to consider it. However, no degree of evidence will ever be sufficient enough to persuade those who are unwilling to believe.

As a young man, William Ramsay, an English research scholar, traveled to the Middle East in an attempt to disprove, based on historical research, the accuracy of Luke's gospel and the book of Acts as recorded in the New Testament. As a young skeptic, who was out to disprove the Bible, he spent many years digging up evidence and detailing research throughout the vast region of Asia Minor. After many decades of exploration, however, Dr. Ramsay was finally forced to conclude that the many accounts and statements recorded by Saint Luke in the New Testament were found to be astonishingly accurate down to the smallest possible detail. Based upon his own discoveries and the research of others confirming the recorded facts from the New Testament, Dr. William Ramsay became a Christian and ultimately a great Bible scholar. His scholarly books have become classics on the historicity of the New Testament and he was eventually knighted in his home country of Great Britain, becoming Sir William Ramsay.

Dr. William F. Albright, whose expertise ranks him as one of the world's most renowned biblical archeologists, has claimed that there is no basis at all for dating any book of the New Testament after AD 80. Further evidence suggests that they were most likely all completed by AD 75. This means that the New Testament documents were recorded by the pen of those who had first-hand knowledge of the events they were documenting.

Confirmation of the life of Joseph in ancient Egypt, as recorded in the historical record of Genesis, has come down to us in a most interesting fashion. A previously overlooked cache of ancient Egyptian coins, stashed in the vaults of a museum, have now confirmed the biblical record of Joseph, and the role he played in government service to the pharaoh of Egypt long ago. Although originally discovered a century earlier, in 2009 this cache of ancient coins was rediscovered by authorities at the Egyptian National Museum. Shortly afterward, a local Cairo newspaper had printed that the coins in question reportedly bear the name and image of the biblical Joseph. The conclusion of the team of antiquities researchers is that the coins had originated at the time when Joseph served as Pharaoh's treasurer during the seven years of plenty, followed by the seven years of famine, as predicted by Joseph when he was called upon to interpret Pharaoh's dream recorded in Genesis chapter 41. There was one particular coin that bore Joseph's effigy as the minister of treasury in Pharaoh's court. Inscribed on another old coin bearing Joseph's image, his name appears twice; written in hieroglyphs, his Hebrew name is inscribed and also the Egyptian name that was given to him by Pharaoh when he was appointed to be the treasurer of Egypt. Still another coin displayed an inscription on it and bore the image of a cow, which would have, most likely, symbolized Pharaoh's famous dream of the seven fat and seven lean cows. What an amazing confirmation this has been of the biblical events documenting the life of Joseph, dating back to around 2000 BC. Further confirmation of the life of Joseph, and the seven years of plenty followed by the seven year of famine in Egypt was discovered on a marble tablet inscription. This marble tablet was uncovered in the nineteenth century within the ruins of an ancient fortress in what is now present-day Yemen. This was dated around eighteen centuries before the birth of Christ. An abundance of valid evidence also confirms the life of Moses as a leader of the Jewish throng in ancient Egypt. And Flavius Josephus even records that two Egyptian priest-scholars, named Manetho and Cheremon, left a record identifying the Jewish presence in Egypt and their sudden exodus under the leadership of Moses.

There is clearly no shortage of astonishing biblical confirmation available today. Everyone who is willing should consider the vast evidence suggesting that the Holy Scriptures are and were divinely inspired, and that the real architect of the Bible was none other than the Holy Spirit. He has selectively illuminated the willing hearts and minds of specifically chosen men in ancient times, who faithfully recorded God's divine revelation. Archeologists have discovered that ancient governing authorizes, historians, kings and rulers will often leave behind accurate cultural records in the form of ancient seals and stone inscriptions. These and other written documents often record the military exploits, decrees, proclamations, and additional historical narratives that bear witness to human exploits throughout the Middle East region. According to the biblical scholar and historical expert Mr. Grant Jeffrey, "Anyone who carefully examines the ancient, extra-biblical historical records with an open mind cannot honestly hold on to the belief that the Bible is nothing more than a collection of legends, fables, and myths."[11]

Witness of the Disciples and Apostles

As we have already discussed in a previous chapter, the resurrection of Jesus was the pivotal event in the formation of the Christian church that began in the first century and continues to expand the world over with unyielding passion. The documents and evidence surrounding the resurrection of Jesus involve facts that have never been refuted. Therefore, we will not spend additional time on this matter now as the topic could certainly fill an entire book. What I would, however, like to call to your attention is concerning the lives of the disciples of Jesus and their dramatic reaction to the events surrounding his resurrection. The disciples of Jesus surely knew him better than anyone else who ever lived. After the crucifixion, the Scriptures paint a bleak picture of the Lord's disciples cowering behind locked doors, in fear for their lives. However, after the resurrection of Jesus from the dead, we can observe a remarkable transformation of these men into bold ambassadors for the cause of Christ, whose witness could not be silenced by any law, power or authority. As they went forth with supernatural courage to share the truth about what they saw and heard, no force on earth could deter their bold proclamation. The result was the beginning of a rapidly spreading fire of passionate faith that ignited throughout the ancient world and will never be quenched by any forces of evil on the earth. According to the writer Eusebius, an early church historian of the fourth century, the contemporary disciples and apostles of Jesus became scattered across the entire ancient world, spreading the gospel of Jesus Christ everywhere they went. With the exception of the apostle John, these brave souls would all face a terrible martyr's death for the righteous cause of the resurrected Christ. The only way to explain the passionate zeal that led to their premature death is to understand that their motivation for missionary service was based on the facts they witnessed concerning the resurrection of Jesus. The historical records confirm that these men all faced their fate without ever denying faith in Jesus Christ and what he accomplished on behalf of fallen humanity.

Only a fool would die for a lie if they knew it was a lie, but a good man might dare to die for the truth, if they knew it was the truth. James (the son of Zebedee) was beheaded at Jerusalem for his faith. Andrew was crucified in Greece after being beaten with a whip. Bartholomew (Nathanael) had preached the good news throughout Asia Minor and was flayed to death with a whip in Armenia. Thomas was speared to death in India after a very successful missionary journey. Peter was crucified upside down, believing he was unworthy to die in the same manner as his Lord. Phillip was hung to death. Thaddeus was killed by arrows in Armenia. Jude was put to death by arrows in Persia. James (brother of Jesus) was thrown off the pinnacle of the temple in Jerusalem. After discovering that he had survived the fall, his enemies beat him to death with a club. Matthew was killed with a sword in Ethiopia. Matthias, the disciple chosen to replace Judas Iscariot, was stoned and then beheaded. Mark was dragged through the streets of Alexandria with a rope until he died. Luke was hanged to death in Greece. Barnabas was stoned by the Jews in Cyprus. The apostle Paul was imprisoned and tortured by the Roman Emperor Nero. After enduring a lengthy imprisonment, during which time he wrote important parts of the New Testament, he was beheaded in AD 67. John, whom Jesus loved, was the only living survivor of the severe persecution faced by the early church leaders. He was thrown alive into a pot of boiling oil and expected to die. After surviving the ordeal, which left him severely disfigured for life, he was banished to the isle of Patmos, to live like an animal. It was there that this great apostle wrote the prophetic book of Revelation. He was the only disciple to die of old age. The disciples of Jesus, and the followers to whom they witnessed, would ultimately turn the ancient world upside down by introducing a new faith. Christianity was birthed in the cause of truth, love and freedom as expressed through the life, death, and resurrection of Jesus Christ. This hope and promise was for all who would dare to believe that God had, in the person of his only begotten Son, provided the redemption for mankind as promised so long before.

Supernatural Element 12: Miraculous events of the Bible

One cannot truly believe the Bible is God's divine Word, and in the same breath, deny the miracles and supernatural events it records. To deny miraculous events is simply to deny God. If God is who he claims to be, then the recording of supernatural events is what we would expect to find. It would be inconceivable to believe in God and, at the same time, to deny any possibility of supernatural events. The God of the Bible is a God of the miraculous. Skeptics routinely scoff at and ridicule anyone who actually believes in the great recorded miracles of Scripture. Many people consistently claim that the Bible is full of myths, legends, and fables. They hide behind a pseudoscience and the bold claim of naturalists that anyone who believes in miracles should have their head examined. But I do not believe this debate should ever start with the question, are miracles possible? Because when it comes to the understanding of miraculous events, the only question we need to ask ourselves is, have any miracles occurred? If no inexplicable supernatural events have ever been recorded, then the atheist might have a leg to stand on. Unfortunately for humanism, this is not the case. The Bible records many supernatural events that have occurred in God's interaction with mankind over the course of history. If physical and historical evidence confirms that the miraculous events recorded in the Bible have occurred in history, then the question "Are miracles possible?" becomes an insignificant query. Throughout this book, the goal has been to present valid evidence worthy of consideration. In our brief deliberation into the topic of the veracity of Scripture, again, we must follow the physical and historical evidence and we will, ultimately, be led to the truth. With the powerful evidence we have examined throughout this epilogue section, many would contend that the Bible itself is a miracle, along with the creation of the universe around us. A strong consensus of evidence, supported by the supernatural elements I have documented, suggest that the physical realm and the Bible have both originated from the mind of God. And when we seriously consider the topic of miracles, there is no single event in the annals of mankind that has been more thoroughly scrutinized than the "resurrection." There are a number of helpful books in print that have presented all the arguments concerning the resurrection. The evidence presented strongly confirms that this event was a fact in history. Everything I have encountered in my research over the last thirty years, confirms to me that the truthfulness and rationality of the resurrection of Jesus Christ has been thoroughly established. Every attempt to deny this event has been met with agonizing defeat, because the monumental evidence that was left behind to validate this historic event is indisputable.

Here is a very brief overview of some evidence for us to consider. For example, the death of Jesus was thoroughly confirmed at the cross. He was placed in hewn-out tomb and the entrance was sealed. A guard of trained soldiers was posted at the scene to insure that nobody had access to the grave site. There was an earthquake and a bright flash of light that astonished the soldiers. Afterward, the tomb was found to be empty. Nobody, neither friend nor foe, could ever produce the body. The chief priests bribed the soldiers to lie about what they saw. Jesus appeared multiple times to his disciples after he arose from the grave, and on one occasion he was seen by some five hundred people at one time. His followers were so thoroughly transformed by what they saw that they went out with supernatural boldness and changed the world forever. These men were so sure of the truth about the resurrection that they were willing to face a martyr's death before denying what they heard and saw. The resurrection is a well-documented fact of history, and this event was historically documented by non-biblical sources as well. Therefore, it is a sure thing that miracles have occurred and they are possible, but only by the power of the living God.

Another miracle in history that has been scoffed at relentlessly for centuries is the biblical worldwide flood in the days of Noah, as recorded in Genesis chapter 6-8. With the evidence supporting evolution theory rapidly disappearing with new up-to-date research, in terms of empirical science and documented historical findings, many scientists are beginning to take another look at the biblical claim of a universal flood. They are discovering that the monumental devastation described in the biblical text is perfectly compatible with what historical, geological, and anthropological science has encountered over the last century. Archeological evidence alone reveals more than two hundred accounts of a one-time massive worldwide flood that wiped out nearly all of humanity and the animals. For a thorough understanding of how God could have preserved animal species aboard Noah's Ark during the universal flood, do a little research of your own and visit the Ark Encounter in Williamstown, Kentucky where you will discover a life-size replica of Noah's ark and learn how it preserved life through that devastating ancient cataclysm.

The nation of Israel is a miracle, as we have already discovered in a previous chapter. Still other supernatural events recorded in the Scriptures have also received confirmation based on the findings of historical and archeological research. These events would include, for example, the diversity of human language associated with the Tower of Babel incident. A clay tablet discovered in Babylon references a temple that was once destroyed with the people scattered and their "speech made strange." The famous Oriental language scholar Max Mueller claims that all human languages can be traced to an original one. This professional testimony suggests that the confusion of language by God at the Tower of Babel is a feasible explanation for why there are so many languages in the world today. Other verified miracles of antiquity would include a three hour period of darkness at the death of Christ, the unusual manner in which the walls of Jericho fell, and the supernatural destruction of Sodom and Gomorrah. In addition to these events, there is also extra-biblical evidence supporting the biblical account of the "ten plagues of Egypt," as recorded in the book of Exodus. The Ipuwer Papyrus, which is housed in the Dutch National Museum of Antiquities, is something of a poetic lamentation. This ancient document describes great disasters that took place in ancient Egypt. The record is dated at around 1400 BC, placing it close to the time of the Exodus (circa 1446 BC). This ancient papyrus makes a fascinating reference to the plague of blood throughout the land, the death of the livestock, the plague of hail and fire, the extended days of darkness, and the death of the first born of Egypt.

Supernatural Element 13: Its life-changing power

Does the Bible have modern-day relevance to our lives? If it is the Word of God, we can expect it to address the needs of people in every generation with life-changing power and influence. In the midst of the increasing confusion and uncertainty all around us, we can still turn to an open Bible, and find the words of help and encouragement we so desperately need. The Bible clearly addresses normal human needs, actions, and attitudes, while expressing above all God's love and impartial devotion for every human soul. It disturbs the complacent, comforts the sorrowful, rebukes the proud, reforms the sinful, strengthens the weak, and brings hope to broken lives. The Bible is uniquely different than all other books. It is very much alive and fully empowered by the Spirit of God for the life-changing benefit of every man, woman and child. Its powerful God-breathed narrative seems to have a remarkable way of penetrating the very soul of man to reveal our spiritual need in the sight of a loving personal God, who is attentive to his creation. "For the word of God is living and powerful, and sharper than any two-edged sword, piercing even to the division of soul and spirit, and of joints and marrow, and is a discerner of the thoughts and intents of the heart" (Hebrews 4:12). The Bible is somewhat like a powerful mirror into which we look and observe ourselves the way we really are, the way God sees us. Unfortunately though, throughout history men have tried to judge the Bible rather than allowing it to judge them. The Bible contains all the information necessary to fill the deepest longing within every human soul__ that longing for a relationship with our Creator that gives lasting peace to the inner man and a certain hope beyond this life. What could be more important than that? As we have previously discussed, the central theme of God's book is the *redemption of mankind*. It offers a personal petition to the heart of every individual, and requires a response on the part of each one of us. Everyone must choose to accept or reject God's plan of redemption. Nobody can abstain; we either choose life or we choose death depending on how we have responded to the free gift of God's grace that is offered to every man, woman, and child through the blood of Jesus Christ and his personal sacrifice on our behalf. God's eternal love for every member of the human family required the voluntary death of his only son on Calvary. The biblical narrative has never become outdated. Its message is as fresh, meaningful, and life-changing today as it was during the days of the early church.

The earth-shaking and world-altering power of the Holy Scriptures is clearly evident as we look at the significant impact it has had on great personalities and world leaders. No evil tyrant or murderous dictator has ever been a friend to or an advocate of the Bible. On the other hand, history reveals that no successful, highly revered world leader has ever been an enemy of the Scriptures. Therefore, to deny the authority and authenticity of the Bible is to set oneself firmly against the values and principles held by many great leaders of Western Civilization. The following is a very brief list of what some notable world leaders have had to say about the Bible's influence.[12]

George Washington: "It is impossible to rightly govern the world without the Bible."

Benjamin Franklin: "Young men, my advice to you is that you cultivate an acquaintance with, and a firm belief in, the Holy Scriptures."

Patrick Henry: "This is a Book worth more than all the others that were ever printed."

Andrew Jackson: "That book, sir, is the rock on which our Republic rests."

Abraham Lincoln: "But for this Book we could not know right from wrong. I believe the Bible is the best gift God has ever given to man."

Theodore Roosevelt: "No educated man can afford to be ignorant of the Bible."

Woodrow Wilson: "The Bible is the one supreme source of revelation of the meaning of Life."

Sir Isaac Newton: "We account the Scriptures of God to be the most sublime philosophy. I find more sure marks of authenticity in the Bible than in any profane history whatsoever."

Michael Faraday: "Why will people go astray when they have this blessed Book to guide them?"

Chiang Kai-Shek: "The Bible is the voice of the Holy Spirit."

Winston Churchill: "We rest with assurance upon the impregnable rock of Holy Scriptures."

H. G. Wells: "The Bible has been the Book that held together the fabric of Western civilization . . . The civilization we possess could not have come into existence and could not have been sustained without it."

"The law of the Lord is perfect, converting the soul; the testimony of the Lord is sure, making wise the simple." (Psalm 19:7)

No Lack of Communication

The Bible has revealed to us invaluable information that we would not otherwise know. It gives us knowledge about the origin of life and the physical world; it reveals to us the nature of man whom God created in his own image, and it relates the existence and character qualities of God and the relationship between God and man. It also reveals to us God's perfect plan and purpose for the ages, as he interacts with humankind, who is the centerpiece of his vast creative works. Because of sin, mankind became separated from his creator in terms of relationship. This left mankind totally at the mercy of God to bridge the wide gulf that now separated the spiritual and the physical worlds. The purpose, therefore, of the divine communication in the Bible is to reveal to us how well God has accomplished bridging this gap, and what it means to mankind in terms of our response to the redemptive work God has performed on our behalf. Of all God's vast creation, only mankind is equipped to relate to him on a personal level. God has always desired to have a loving, intimate relationship with man without violating the free will with which man was created. We all know for certain that a personal loving relationship between mutual friends cannot exist without freedom of choice.

In communicating his plan and will for mankind, it became necessary for God to authenticate his revealed Word in a way that would distinguish it from all other written works that might lay claim to divine origin. Our Christian faith is built upon and around the Holy Bible; without it we would be lost, wandering souls without hope and without purpose. In examining how God has thoroughly authenticated his communication to mankind, we soon discover that the Bible is a fully integrated message system that was carefully designed and engineered by a personal loving Creator. The evidence of design throughout the Bible is a clear demonstration of this divine authorship. Not only can we trust the Bible thoroughly, but because of the immense effort with which God has undertaken in communicating it to us, you and I will also be held accountable for what it has to say (see John 12:48).

When we think about it from a logical point of view, we should each ask ourselves the following important question: if Jesus was not the son of God and the promised Messiah of Israel, how could he possibly still command such wide influence and powerful magnetism over human lives two thousand years after he lived? How could a poor wandering Jew, from an obscure village of the ancient world, in the first century, gain such a profoundly strong influence over the world's population so far removed from his lifetime? The man called Jesus had no political power. He had no formal education. He never wrote a book, led an army or held public office. And yet after only three short years of public ministry two thousand years ago, he has commanded a Christian movement that continues to multiply with every generation. Today, he is reported to have several billion followers worldwide. There is absolutely no logical explanation for this fact, unless he is exactly who he claimed to be__ the eternal Son of God.

The vast body of evidence that supports the Bible as a trustworthy and authentic message of divine origin is rock solid. There should be no valid reason for anyone to deny that the Bible is an inspired communication that came to us by divine impartation. The Bible text embodies all the knowledge and information man needs in order to fill the deep longing of his eternal soul__ to know the truth about the Creator and find answers to the most challenging questions he will face in this world. It is the blueprint owner's manual of the Master Architect, and only by following its instruction, can we have the full and satisfying life we were created for. The orthodox view of the Christian faith holds that the biblical text alone is the inspired, illuminated revelation of truth from God to mankind, and is the sole basis of divine authority for all true believers. The Bible introduces us to the Christian faith, which is not just one of many worldview philosophies we may choose from. When people reject the Holy Bible and Christianity, they are not rejecting a philosophy__ they are rejecting a person named Jesus Christ. And this person is God's only provision for the problem of sin that has ravaged our world with death, disease, sorrow, and unimaginable pain and suffering. This is our only way out of the terrible mess we are all in! Religion is all about *man's effort* to gain favor with God. Christianity, on the other hand, is about *God's effort* to provide fallen humanity with the means by which to be restored to a right-standing relationship with his Maker. All we have to do is to accept God's generous offer of *redemption*. The rest is up to Him! We cannot afford to be ignorant of the Word of God, and we will pay a terrible price for neglecting it.

Supernatural Element 14: Evidence for our generation

In his 1997 best-selling book *The Bible Code*,[13] the American journalist and author Michael Drosnin introduced the world to a fascinating new feature within the text of the Old Testament Torah. This new revelation could only have been discovered in this modern generation because it required sophisticated computers, utilizing math-related statistical analysis, which has allowed textual scholars and researchers to scrutinize the Hebrew text of the venerated Torah with remarkable efficiency as never before. This captivating research has revealed secret hidden messages in the Old Testament cannon that are highly relevant to human history, and prove beyond doubt, that the human mind was entirely incapable of the mathematical genius required to design such a breathtaking feature as *the Bible codes*. These secret messages encoded within the text of the Old Testament Torah are called ELS codes (equidistant letter sequence) and have generated a great deal of interest from Bible scholars and researchers all over the world. These messages reveal remarkable details about historical events that have transpired thousands of years after the venerated text of the Hebrew Bible was written. This textual evidence revealed to our generation proves once again that the Scriptures are supernatural in origin. Perhaps God placed these fascinating codes within the text of Scripture to be discovered by a very skeptical generation such as ours at a time when the whole civilized world is leaning heavily toward casting off the Word of God as the overriding inspiration for governing our national and individual lives. In examining this unique feature of the Bible, it became immediately obvious that these encoded messages could never have appeared by random chance alone. Contained hidden within the venerated Torah are unique messages that chronicle major events of world history, such as Hitler's death camps, the Gulf War, and the French Revolution, for example. The Hebrew text written as much as 1,500 years before Christ has revealed the ELS encoded name of *Yitzhak Rabin* adjacent to the word *assassination*. This was discovered while Mr. Rabin was still serving as the Israeli Prime Minister and a warning was sent to him, which he quickly disavowed. He was assassinated in 1995.

Other ELS codes included the adjacent words: *Napoleon, France,* and *Waterloo,* as well as *Shakespeare, presented onstage, Hamlet, and Macbeth.* Researchers had also discovered the common name of certain modern inventions of technological achievement, such as the *light bulb* and the *airplane.* Adjacent to these words were found the name of each inventor. In another section of Scripture researchers discovered the following encoded words associated with the Third Reich of Nazi Germany: *Hitler, Nazi, slaughter, Eichmann, the ovens, extermination, Zyklon B.* Adolf Eichmann was the Nazi SS official tasked with facilitating and managing all the logistics required to carry out the mass deportation of the Jews to ghettos and extermination camps in German-occupied Eastern Europe during World War II. Eichmann was captured by the Israeli secret service in Argentina in 1960. After a lengthy trial in Israel was completed, he was convicted of war crimes against humanity and hanged to death in 1962. Zyklon B was the gas that Nazi Germany used to exterminate the Jews.

Jewish scholars at the famous Hebrew University in Jerusalem have explored the Hebrew text of the Old Testament using computer algorithms in a way that previous generations never dreamed of. These complex ELS codes are earthshaking in terms of their significance, because they reveal a staggering level of mathematical genius that could never have been produced by the unaided human mind. After examining and researching these complex ELS codes found in the Hebrew text of the Bible, a leading mathematician at Yale University, Dr. Ilya Piatetski-Shapiro, had this to say: "There is no way within the known laws of mathematics to explain seeing the future . . . What we're talking about here is some intelligence that stands outside . . . I think the only answer is that God exists."[14] Michael Drosnin has called this phenomenon the first scientific evidence that some intelligence outside our own does exist. __ In short, this recent discovery has provided us compelling mathematical evidence that the Hebrew Scriptures were inspired by a supernatural intelligence far beyond the capacity of the unaided human mind. By analyzing the text with modern computerized sophistication, researchers have discovered electronically the sequencing of letters that spell out messages of particular significance from human history. For example, imagine, hypothetically, that a passage of scripture subjected to computer analysis reveals a meaningful phrase within the broader context of the passage with consecutive letters appearing equidistant from each other in a repeating sequential order. Suppose that computer program targets each significant letter of a word or phrase that appears evenly spaced every ten or every twenty characters within the sample text. Then, when all the letters are combined into meaningful words, by computer-generated analysis, they reveal a distinct message, such as, for example, "Hitler__ Death Camps." It is particularly significant to note that these researchers have been unable to detect any significant ELS codes in any other Hebrew text outside of the Bible.

These fascinating Bible codes give God glory, and leave researchers scratching their heads in great awe and disbelief at the mathematical genius of the God of the Bible. For nearly seventeen centuries now, beginning with the conversion of the Roman Emperor Constantine in AD 312 until the twentieth century, the Bible has been revered by the vast majority of those within Western culture as the inspired, authoritative, and inerrant Word of God. Sadly, however, over the last century or more, corresponding very closely with the rapid rise of evolutionary thought in today's modern culture, we have witnessed an unrelenting assault upon the authority of Scripture by the intellectual elite of an increasingly secularized society. The academic community, the secular media, evolution-minded scientists, and even some liberal theologians have constantly mocked and allegorized the Bible, stripping it, in the minds of many, of its convicting power over human lives. No other generations have been as skeptical as ours and stands in greater need of additional scientific evidence for God. Perhaps when presented with the discovery of these amazing secret codes built into the Hebrew text of the Bible, other hearts will be turned back to Him. According to renowned author and Bible scholar Mr. Grant Jeffrey, who has had a significant apologetic influence on this generation, of particular interest is the biblically encoded appearance of the name *Yeshua* (The Hebrew equivalent for Jesus) that appears over and over again throughout the Old Testament text. Grant Jeffrey has pointed out that scholars have now discovered this phenomenon in virtually every one of the major prophetic passages foretelling of a coming Messiah in the Torah text.

They virtually all contain the ELS encoded name *Yeshua.* Yes, history really is *His-story.* The Bible Code phenomenon has left a very significant message to consider for those who are open-minded in this generation___ that the Bible is truly supernatural in its textual revelation, and it was inspired and directed by an ingenious providential intelligence___ an eternal sovereign God who has gone to great lengths to demonstrate that His Word can be trusted.

The Hidden Gospel Message

Did you know that the message of the Christian gospel is hidden within the pages of the very first book of the Bible? Once again, we see the providence of God at work as the Holy Spirit has orchestrated another surprise appearance of the fingerprints of God upon his divine Word. The true gospel message is found in the genealogy of Noah. This was no accident! It's hard to believe that any Jewish rabbi would dare conspire to hide the Christian Gospel within the pages of the venerated Torah! But there it is in Genesis chapter 5. There are ten names listed here that complete the genealogy of Noah, beginning at creation, and ending with preparation for the great flood. Most people skip right over the genealogies of the Bible, but they are important and we need to take a closer look at this one in Genesis 5. In the Bible names are significant and their meaning is often very relevant. Abraham, for example, means "Father of Many," and he became the father of many nations. Jesus means "Savior," Christ means "Anointed," and He was the Messiah___ the anointed savior of the world and God's appointed atonement for sin. Now, what do the ten names in Genesis chapter 5 actually mean, and what is their significance in the grand scheme of God's design? The very first name we encounter is <u>Adam</u>, which means "*man*". Adam's son carried the name <u>Seth,</u> which means "*appointed.*" Seth had a son and named him <u>Enosh</u>, which means "*mortal.*" Enosh bore a son whom he named <u>Kenan</u>. The name Kenan or Cainan denotes "*sorrow*." Kenan bore a son whom he named <u>Mahalalel</u>, which translates "*the Blessed God*." Mahalalel's son was named <u>Jared</u>, which means "*shall come down*." Jared bore a son and named him "<u>Enoch</u>," which means "*teaching*." Enoch's son was named <u>Methuselah</u>. This unusual name translates "*His death shall bring*." Methuselah lived and begot a son whom he named "<u>Lamech.</u>" His name means "*the Despairing*." Then Lamech bore a son and called him "<u>Noah.</u>" The word translates "*comfort*" or "*rest*." Now, when we put the meanings of these ten names altogether we find the hidden message: "<u>Man</u> (is) <u>appointed</u> <u>mortal</u> <u>sorrow</u>; (but) <u>the Blessed God</u> <u>shall come down</u> <u>teaching</u> (that) <u>His death shall bring the despairing rest</u>." Isn't that fascinating! So man was appointed mortal sorrow (because of sin); but the Blessed God (Jesus) came down from heaven, teaching us that his death would bring those living in despair the rest they were longing for__ giving peace and comfort to their troubled souls.

Testing for Divine Revelation

Suppose that a friend wanted to introduce me to a book that he believes contains divinely inspired revelation from the mind of God. I would say, okay, I'll take a look, but first let me tell you the rigorous tests that book will have to be subjected to in order to qualify as divine revelation.

1. It must be written by multiple individuals over a long period of hundreds of years or more, with each contributing writer working independently of the others, so as to prevent any possibility whatsoever of collusion between them.
2. It must address, with consistent unity throughout the combined narrative, the most challenging and controversial topics that have ever come before the councils of men.
3. The collective works of these many diverse writers must be in complete harmony and agreement with one another on each and every topic addressed.

4. It must address with impartial honesty the sins and failures of those who have penned the words, including their national sin and record of disobedience to God's commands.

5. It must reach out to the intended audience in a style of writing that would be indicative of God speaking personally to his human creation.

6. It must speak forth the truth concerning every issue of consequence to man and be in complete agreement with the Bible on every matter addressed.

7. It must have survived to this day with its divine message intact and basically unaltered as compared with the original recorded documents. No editing changes shall be found when compared to the original written manuscripts.

8. It must have suffered an incredible history of hatred and persecution at the hands of the enemies of God without ever succumbing to the ignorance of men. It must, ultimately, rival the Bible as the most prolific, beloved and popular literature in the history of mankind.

9. Its message must be so profound that it becomes translated into every known human language for the benefit of all humankind over the course of time.

10. It must become the very foundation upon which societies of free men are established and the affairs of men are based. This profound influence must, ultimately, be reflected in government, education, culture, and civil law.

11. It will not contain a single detail of informative revelation that can be proven to be false by the progressive advance of human knowledge through science and education.

12. It must be saturated with prophetic words written months, years, and even hundreds of years in advance of the precise fulfillment of each and every prediction. This will make it obvious to all that the message could only have come from an omniscient God.

13. It must record profound supernatural events, which can only be explained by the work of an omnipotent Creator, and a significant number of these profound events must be verifiable by means of eye-witness accounts, physical evidence and historical documentation.

14. The narrative must clearly state that its origin is of a divine nature and this fact will be demonstrated by textual evidence upon close scrutiny and examination.

15. This book must profoundly and forever transform the lives of those who have accepted and embraced it as a message of divine truth.

16. This book must clearly point mankind to the redemptive plan and purpose of a loving, personal God and its theme must be absolutely consistent with the theme recorded in the biblical narrative.

These are the criteria God has used to deliver his eternal truth to the human lives that where created in his image and likeness. The Bible, and no other published work, fulfills this detailed criteria outlined here. The profound magnitude of the biblical narrative and the life-changing qualities that have made it the most beloved and controversial document in the entire history of humanity have been presented for your careful thought and sincere examination. Nothing else even comes close to matching the obvious fingerprints of the Holy Spirit that are all over this divinely inspired classic.

A Verdict is Reached!

People often disbelieve things that are true because they don't want them to be true. The real question we should be asking ourselves is, in my current circumstance, do I believe in something that represents the final authority in my life, and upon what foundation can I stand to give me the hope of a promising future when my days on earth are completed? If what you believe is in direct conflict with the Bible when it is taken a face value, then don't trust it. Do not trust your feelings and emotions. They can mislead you. The powerful evidence that favors the Bible alone as the inerrant Word of God is what makes it so worth believing. We are admonished in scriptures to "test all things; holding fast to what is good" (I Thess. 5:21). Will you trust in the Word or the world? I believe the Bible is the only anchor you can always count on in the storms of life! The self-centered human heart often says, "I want to be the boss. I want to do things my way and not be restricted by any burdensome moral constraints." In our rebellious nature, we want to exclude anyone else from being the lord over our lives. We want to be in control and do things our own way. This is why God has given us the Bible. He knew we would need an instruction manual, or we would never figure out how to live the way we were intended to, allowing us to experience that elusive peace, joy, satisfaction, and fulfillment we all desire. Don't let your free will get in the way of knowing the God of the universe and living out your intended creative purpose on this earth. Who is the final authority in your life? Is it God or you? If you are not currently experiencing the fulfillment you desire, then take a stand on the promises of God. The Bible cannot help you if you refuse to believe it and remain skeptical, and the death of Christ cannot save you if you refuse to accept that it was God's only means of atonement for your sin. If the Bible is not the truth, then you and I would have no hope in a fallen world that is full of death, disease, pain, and suffering, with no way out from under the curse that is upon this planet. The Bible gives us clear instruction on the sure way out of the mess we humans are in. Accept it as the inspired Word of a loving God, and make it the final authority in your life. As you love it, learn it, and live it, the Bible will radically transform who you are from the inside out (see Romans 12:2). We could actually pass a law that says you must love your neighbor, but as creatures exercising free will, we will only love our neighbor if it is in our hearts to do so. Only God can give us that unconditional love for others, and only the Bible can tell us how get it! (John 8: 31, 32).

In this brief summary, we have barely touched on the broad topic of biblical veracity. However, the evidence we have examined here overwhelmingly supports the firm belief of many that the Bible alone is

God's divine revelation to mankind. It is a widely used publication that, when taken seriously, will transform us from the inside out, making us into the people God created us to be. Perhaps the most profound evidence that the Bible is God's Word is that when we read it with an open mind and open heart, these powerful words somehow jump off the page to penetrate our very souls, thus transforming our thinking, conduct, and worldview; and ultimately it will shape the lifestyle we choose to live as the Holy Spirit of God illuminates its message to our hearts. God's divine purpose in giving us the Bible was to reveal to mankind those things that would have otherwise remained unknown to us. God took the initiative to communicate clearly with mankind (his crowning creation), and in doing so, he provided us with a divine standard to live by__ an instruction manual that will lead us into a fulfilling relationship with himself. The Holy Bible was never intended merely for literary enjoyment. Even though it has always been valued and treasured as a great work of literature, the true value of the Bible text is found in its message, not its style. Those of us who have accepted the authority of biblical truth have found it to satisfy our deep desire to answer each and every troubling question about life; and more importantly we have discovered the fulfillment of a personal relationship with our Creator God. Yes, the Bible is truly the authentic, inspired Word of God. It has provided us with a progressive, harmonious collection of divine thought and knowledge, which constitutes a complete, unified revelation of God's eternal plan and purpose for humanity. The Bible is reliable, and we can stake our lives on it. We should embrace it with great appreciation and reverently fear the God who gave it to us, because this will be the standard by which our lives will be judged when each of us faces our Creator one day. If we believe and hold fast to the promises of God, we will never have to wonder or struggle with the thought of whether we are good enough to make it. Our salvation is not and never will be based on what we have done, but our hope is based solely on what He has done for us.

The numerous documentation of reliable evidence that we have thoroughly examined in this epilogue section overwhelmingly supports the unwavering conviction of many that the Holy Bible is God's divine revelation to mankind.

The Bible says that God cannot lie, and the word of the Lord is true (Hebrews 6:18, Psalm 33:4, Proverbs 30:5, and, Psalm 12:6). I think we would be wise to believe it!

"Beware lest anyone cheat you through philosophy and empty deceit, according to the traditions of men, according to the basic principles of the world, and not according to Christ. For in Him dwells all the fullness of the Godhead bodily; and you are complete in Him, who is the head of all principality and power" (Colossians 2:8-10).

"You are worthy, O Lord, to receive glory and honor and power. For You created all things, and by Your will they exist and were created" (Revelation 4:11)

Recommended for further reading:

How We Got Our Bible	by Ralph Earle	1971
The Resurrection Factor	by Josh McDowell	1981
The Flood	by Alfred Rehwinkel	1951
Science Speaks	by Peter Stoner	1969
Examine the Evidence	by Ralph Muncaster	2004
The Signature of God	by Grant Jeffrey	2010
That Manuscript from Outer Space	by H. L.Willington	1974
Many Infallible Proofs	by Henry Morris	1974
Science and the Bible	by Henry Morris	1986
Evidence That Demands a Verdict	by Josh McDowell	1992
New Evidence That Demands a Verdict	by Josh McDowell	1999
Rivers in the Desert	by Nelson Glueck	1959
Seven Reasons Why You Can Trust the Bible	by Erwin Lutzer	2015
A Skeptic's Search for God	by Ralph Muncaster	2000
Jesus: The Great Debate	by Grant Jeffrey	1999
The Life and Times of Jesus the Messiah	by Alfred Edersheim	1993
Manual of Biblical Archaeology, Vol. 2	by Carl F. Keil	2010
A Scientific Investigation of the Old Testament	by R. D. Wilson	1926

Topical Index

167, 173–74, 267, 287, 291, 293, 313

G

geological timescale, 54–55, 120
geologic column, 46–47
gradualism, 47–48, 55, 59
Grand Canyon, the, 52, 307–8
Great Diaspora, the, 224

H

Halley's Comet, 22
Hell Creek formation, 152
hemophilia, 97
Hominid fossils, 75
Homo sapiens, 68, 71, 74, 76
Hubble Telescope, iv, 8, 101
humanist worldview, 304, 332

I

incarnation, 225, 233, 330, 373
inferior races, 133, 289
Institute for Creation Research, 27, 73, 75, 158, 293
intelligent design, 2, 7, 9, 19, 22, 27–28, 41, 80, 95, 105, 108, 111, 116, 131, 134, 154, 200, 242, 273, 287, 293–94, 301
internal combustion, 143, 254
irreducible complexity, 19, 22, 25, 96

J

Java man, 67
Judeo-Christian heritage, 4, 140, 215, 311

M

macroevolution, 4–5, 59, 103, 127, 173
metamorphosis, 26
microevolution, 4, 103
missing links, 12, 57–60, 62, 67, 75
Mount Rushmore, 111, 199
Mount St. Helens, 51
Museum of Natural History, 27, 52, 61, 63, 172, 318–19
mutations, 35–41, 43–44, 97, 104, 158

N

naturalism, 2, 6, 18, 32, 36, 51, 75, 80–81, 103–4, 106, 113–14, 129, 132, 138, 144, 150, 154, 161, 168, 173, 176, 184, 192, 195, 204
naturalistic evolution, 6, 59, 242
natural selection, 4, 6, 11, 15, 17, 20, 22, 26, 35, 42, 44, 58, 63, 103–5, 132, 135, 146, 158, 167, 174, 210, 213, 254, 293, 310
Neanderthal man, 73–74
Nebraska man, 69–70
neo-Darwinian theory, 4, 103–4, 272, 295
new atheists, 209, 254, 270–71
nucleotides, 91, 93, 97–99

O

ocular perception, 22
Orce man, 71
ozone layer, 24, 189

P

paleontology, 48, 56–57, 59, 65, 129, 152, 172, 174, 295
Peking man, 69
peptide bonds, 85–86
photosynthesis, 24–25
physics, laws of, 22–23, 28, 142–43, 161, 172, 187, 202, 252, 255, 278
Piltdown Man, 67–69, 74
Planned Parenthood, 133
polypeptides, 84–86, 99, 107
population dynamics, 124–25
primordial soup, 106, 109, 111, 118
probability analysis, 14, 83, 87–88
probiotic organisms, 282

R

Ramapithecus, 70
recapitulation theory, 76
redemption, 229, 231, 264, 299, 305, 312, 316, 322–23, 330, 342, 345, 348, 387, 391, 394
ribonucleic acid (RNA), 89, 93, 96, 99, 107, 201

S

scientific materialism, 134
scientific pioneers, 8, 30, 113, 266

secular humanism, 130, 132, 135, 147, 159, 167, 300, 312
secular worldview, 16
sedimentary deposition, 48, 121
sickle cell anemia, 41
special creation, 7, 17, 56, 62, 126, 140, 172, 204, 242, 285, 309, 332
spontaneous generation, 4–5, 89–90, 99, 101, 103, 108, 111, 116, 188, 262
survival of the fittest, 11, 17, 36, 212

T

theism, 18, 32, 176, 273, 277, 295
theistic design, 204
thermodynamics, laws of, 32–33, 203
transitional links, 50, 61–63, 75
Transit of Venus, 23
transmutation of species, 15
Tyrannosaurus rex, 53

V

variation of species, 12
vestigial organs, 78–79

W

Western civilization, xxi, 3–4, 7–8, 113, 209, 215, 290, 391–92

Reference Notes Index

Chapter one

1. Dr. Lee M. Spetner, (American Physicist- MIT graduate) "Not By Chance" (Judaica Press, Inc: Brooklyn, New York 1997) preface viii.
2. Charles Darwin, (1809-1882) (British Student of Theology who left Cambridge to become a self-taught naturalist and became instrumental in popularizing the theory of evolution through reliance on *natural selection*) "The Origin of Species" (John Murray Publishing: London, England 1859) p. 84. see "The Battle for Truth" David A. Noebel (Harvest House Publishers: Eugene, Oregon 2001) p.120,121.
3. Charles Darwin, "The Origin of Species" (P.F. Collier and Son Corp: New York, NY 1909) p.20.
4. Ibid. p.169. also see "Examine the Evidence" Ralph Muncaster (Harvest House Publishers: Eugene, Oregon 2004) p. 48.
5. Ibid. p.170. also see "Examine the Evidence" (op cit) p.48.
6. Ibid. p.169.
7. Charles Darwin, "The Origin of Species" (John Murray Publishing: London, England 1859) p.292. "The Origin of Species" (London, England 6th edition, 1902) p.341-342. see "The Battle for Truth" (op cit) p.342. and "Dawkins God" (Blackwell: Oxford, England 2005) p.81.
8. Desmond Morris (British Zoologist) "The Naked Ape: A Zoologist's Study of the Human Animal" (1st American ed. McGraw-Hill: New York 1967) see the book review condensed in *Reader's Digest* magazine, July 1968.
9. *Time Magazine*: Cover story "How Man Became Man" (November 7, 1977).
10. *Time Magazine*: "Puzzling Out Man's Ascent" (November 7, 1977) p.77.
11. Julian Huxley (1887-1975) (British evolutionary biologist and a strong proponent of the *natural selection* hypothesis) "At Random" a television preview, which aired on November 21, 1959. see Sol Tax, *"Evolution of Life"* (University of Chicago Press: Chicago, Illinois 1960) p.1. see "The Battle for Truth" David Noebel, (op cit) p.118.

12. Julian Huxley, "Evolution: The Modern Synthesis" (Harper and Brothers Publishers: New York 1942) p.457. "The Long War Against God" Henry Morris, (Master Books: Green Forrest, AR. 2008) p.322.

13. Carl Sagan (1934-1996) (American evolutionary astronomer and cosmologist), "Cosmos" (Random House Publishers: New York 1980) p. 27. see "The Battle for Truth" (op cit) p.118.

14. Carl Sagan, "The Dragons of Eden: Speculations on the Evolution of Human Intelligence" (Random House Publishers: New York 1977) p.6. see "The Battle for Truth" (op cit) p.120.

15. Isaac Asimov (1920-1992) (a former professor of biochemistry at the Boston University school of medicine) "Science and Creationism" ed. Ashley Montague, (Oxford University Press: Oxford, England 1984) p.183. see "The Battle for Truth" (op cit) p.118.

16. Corliss Lamont (1902-1995) (a left-wing socialist philosopher from Columbia University), "The Philosophy of Humanism", rev. ed. (Frederick Ungar: New York 1949, 1982) p.120. see "The Battle for Truth" (op cit) p.121.

17. George Gaylord Simpson (1902-1984) (American born paleontologist from Columbia University and a major participant in the *modern evolutionary synthesis*) "The Meaning of Evolution" original 1949. (Yale University Press: New Haven, Ct. 1971) p.345. see "The Battle for Truth" (op cit) p.117.

18. Rene Dubos (1901-1982) (French born American microbiologist and a strong advocate for humanist evolutionary philosophy) "Humanistic Biology" (the *American Scientist*, vol. 53, March, 1965) p.6. see "Scientific Creationism" Dr. Henry Morris, (Creation-Life Publishers: San Diego, California 1978) p.10.

19. Julian Huxley, *Education and Humanism*, "Essays of a Humanist" 1964 p.125.

20. Humanist Manifesto I (Prometheus Books: Buffalo, New York. 1933, 1980) p.8. see "The Battle for Truth" (op cit) p.117.

21. Humanist Manifesto II (Prometheus Books: Buffalo, New York 1973, 1980) p.17. see "The Battle for Truth" (op cit) p.117.

22. Carl Sagan, "Cosmos" (Random House: New York 1980) p.4. see "God's Undertaker" John Lennox, (Lion Hudson Pub: Oxford, England 2009) p.30.

23. Michael Denton, (British-Australian biochemist & author) "Evolution: A Theory in Crisis" (Adler & Adler Pub: Bethesda, Maryland 1985,1986)

p.342. (British printing, Burnett Books Ltd,: London, England 1985) see "The Long War Against God" Henry Morris, (Master Books: Green Forest 2008) p.277.

24. Richard Dawkins, (British biologist and prominent evolutionary philosopher. Oxford, England) "The Blind Watchmaker" (W. W. Norton & Co: New York 1986) p.43. see "Is There Really a God"? Ken Ham booklet (*Answers in Genesis*: Florence, Ky. 1998) p.7.

25. Michael Behe, (American biochemist and biomolecular researcher from Lehigh University, known for introducing the design principle of '*Irriducible Complexity*': a single system which is composed of several to many well-matched interacting parts that contribute to the basic function, where upon the removal of any one of the parts causes the system to effectively cease functioning. *"Darwin's Black Box: The Biochemical Challenge to Evolution"* (The Free Press: New York 1996) p.252-253. "Darwin's Black Box" 2006 edition, p.39. J. Buell & G. Hearn, eds. "Darwinism: Science or Philosophy"? (Dallas, Texas: Foundation for Thought and Ethics, 1994) p.68-69. see "The Case for Faith" Lee Strobel (Zondervan Publishing: Grand Rapids, Michigan 2000) p.101.

26. Charles Darwin, "On The Origin of Species" (John Murray Pub: London, England 1859) p.219. facsimile of the 1st ed. (Harvard University Press: Cambridge, Mass. and London, England 1964) p.189. also see "The Origin of Species" 6th ed. (New York University Press: New York 1988) p.154. cited in "Total Truth" Nancy Pearcey, (Crossway Books: Wheaton, IL. 2005) p.187.

27. Charles Darwin, "On the Origin of Species" (J.M. Dent & Sons Ltd: London, England 1971) p.167. see the discussion on adaptations in "Creation Facts of Life" Gary Parker, (Master Books: Green Forrest, AR. 1994) p.80-81. this material from "The Origin of Species" is found in Darwin's chapter entitled 'Difficulties With the Theory'.

28. Michael Behe, "The Edge of Evolution: the search for the limits of Darwinism" (Free Press: New York 2007) p.166. cited in "God's Undertaker" John Lennox, (Lion Hudson Publishing: Oxford, England 2009) p.120.

29. Bertrand Russell, (1872-1970) (British writer & philosopher - Nobel prize for Literature in 1950) see the "History of Western Philosophy" (Routledge: London, England 2000) p.570. see "God's Undertaker" (op cit) p.84.

30. Colin Patterson, (1933-1998) (a former paleontologist at the British Museum of Natural History-London) spoken in an address at the *American Museum of Natural history*, (New York, Nov 5, 1981) see "Creation Facts of Life" Gary Parker, (Master books, Green Forrest, Ar. 1994) p.107.

31. Duane T. Gish, (1921-2013) (former biochemist - UC Berkley, an officer of the *Institute for Creation Research* and a strong prominent of creationism during the 20th century. Known for confronting many evolutionary biologists in formal debate) "Evolution: The Fossils Say No"! (ICR Publishing Co: San Diego, California 1973) p.3.

32. Henry Morris, (1918-2006) (a highly regarded earth scientist, and a former college professor with multiple PhDs who became a young earth creationist and directed the *Institute for Creation Research* for many years while authoring more than twenty books as a highly regarded scientific Christian apologist) "Many Infallible Proofs" (Master Books: El Cajon, California 1974) p.249.

33. Ibid. p. 249.

34. Galileo Galilei, (1564-1642) (early scientific pioneer - physicist & astronomer) In a letter to Grand Duchess Christina, 1615. cited in "The Language of God" Francis Collins (Free Press: New York 2006) p.158.

35. James Tour, (American scientist highly regarded as a synthetic organic chemist, specializing in nanotechnology-Rice University) see Candace Adams article, "Leading Nanoscientist Builds Big Faith" (The Baptist Standard, March 15, 2000) cited in "The Case for Faith", Lee Strobel, (Zondervan Publishing: Grand Rapids, Michigan 2000) p.111.

Chapter Two

1. Ernst Mayr, (1904-2005)(a leading evolutionary biologist of the twentieth century) "Populations, Species and Evolution" (Harvard U. Press: Cambridge, Mass. 1970) p.102. cited in "Scientific Creationism" Henry Morris, (Creation-Life Publishers: San Diego, Ca. 1978) p.54.

2. Corliss Lamont, see chapter one, reference 16, (2nd citation) for emphasis.

3. Werner Gitt (German engineering professor and a young earth creationist) "In the Beginning was Information" (Master Books: Green Forrest, AR. 2005) p.93.

4. George Gaylord Simpson, "The Non-prevalence of Humanoids" (*Science* vol. 143, 1964) p.772. (pathlights.com/creation - evolution encyclopedia) 2014.

5. Lee Spetner, "Not By Chance: Shattering the Modern Theory of Evolution" (The Judaica Press: Brooklyn, New York 1997) p.131.

6. Ibid. p.138.

7. Pierre-Paul Grasse, (1895-1985) (French zoologist of the 20th century and author of over three hundred publications) "Evolution of Living Organisms: Evidence for a New Theory of Transformation" (Academic Press: New York 1977) p.87. see "Creation Facts of Life" Gary Parker, (Master Books, Green Forrest, AR. 1994) p.109.

8. Ibid, p.87. (op cit) Gary Parker, p.109.

9. Pierre-Paul Grasse, "Evolution of Living Organisms" (Academic Press: New York 1977) p.103. (soulwinners.com.au/8.html) 2014

10. Pierre-Paul Grasse, "Evolution of Living Organisms" (Academic Press, New York 1977) p.38. (pathlights.com /creation - cvolution cncyclopedia) also see (2christ.org/quotes) 2014

11. Jonathan Sarfati (PhD in chemistry and a young earth creationist/author working with Creation Ministries International (CMI) a non-profit Christian apologetics ministry) " Refuting Evolution", (Master Books, Green Forrest, AR. 1999) p.40,41. (antibiotic resistance) see also C. Wieland on, 'Superbugs: Not Super After All', *Creation Ex Nihilo*, 20(1): p.10-13 (June-August 1992).

12. Albert Szent-Gyorgyi, (1893-1986) (the Cambridge educated Nobel Prize winner –biochemist/physiologist who discovered vitamin C) see "Creation Facts of Life" Gary Parker, (Master Books: Green Forrest, AR. 1994) p.109.

13. Gary Parker, (PhD in biology with a specialty in geology and paleontology. biology professor, author and former atheist) "Creation Facts of Life", (Master books: Green Forrest, AR. 1994) p.122.

14. Thomas Nagel, (American Philosopher) 'Philosophy and Public Affairs' *Wiley Inter Science*, vol. 36, (2), 20, 2008 p.199. see "God's Undertaker" John Lennox (op cit) p.120.

15. Notice the genetics discussion – Richard Goldschmidt/Norman Macbeth's "Darwin Retired" (Dell publishers: New York, 1971) p.33,154. see "Total Truth" Nancy Pearcey, (Crossway Books: Wheaton, Illinois 2005) p.160.

16. Richard Goldschmidt, (Zoologist/Geneticist-UC Berkley) in Norman Macbeth's "Darwin Retired" (Dell publishers: New York, 1971) p.33,154. also see ('Material Basis of Evolution' Yale University Press) (2christ.org/quotes) 2014.

17. Jeremy Rifkin, (social theorist- specializing in technological and environmental change) 'Algeny' (Viking Press: New York 1983) p. 134. see "The Long War Against God" Henry M. Morris, (Master Books: Green Forrest, Ar. 2000) p.160.

18. Gordon Taylor, (American microbiologist) "The Great Evolution Mystery" (Harper & Row Publishers: New York 1983) p.34,38. (2christ.org/quotes) 2014.

19. Michael Behe, (professional observations cited by John Lennox "God's Undertaker" 2007) p.110.

20. Stephen J. Gould, (1941-2002) (former professor of Evolutionary Biology & Paleontology, Harvard University – a leading evolutionary spokesman of the 20th century) "The Return of Hopeful Monsters" *Natural History*, vol. LXXXVI(6), June-July 1977, p.28. (creation.org/articles/quotes) 2014.

21. Nils Heribert-Nilsson, (1883-1955) (Swedish Botanist/Geneticist) 'Synthetische Artbildung' (Verlag CWK Gleerup Press: Lund, Sweden 1953) p.174. (2christ.org/quotes) 2014.

22. Stephen J. Gould, 'The Return of Hopeful Monsters' article published in: '*Natural History*' June/July, 1977 also see "The Panda's Thumb: more reflections in natural history", (Penguin Press: London, England 1980) (with reprint 1990) p.158. (pathlights.com/creation-evolution encyclopedia) 2014.

23. F.H.T. Rhodes, H.S. Zim & P.R. Shaffer, "Fossils" (Golden Press: New York 1962) p.10. see "Scientific Creationism" Henry Morris, (op cit) p.97.

24. John Woodmorappe, (American geologist/biologist and young earth creationist) see discussion- CRS Quarterly vol. 18, No. 1, p.46-71. (2christ.org/quotes) 2014.

25. David Raup, (1933-2015) (Former University of Chicago paleontologist and curator at the Field Museum of Natural History, Chicago) quoted from 'Conflicts Between Darwin and Paleontology' (Field Museum of Natural History Bulletin, vol. 50 (1), 1979) see "Creation Facts of Life", G. Parker, (op cit) p.143.

26. Duane T. Gish, "Evolution—The Fossils Say No"! (ICR Publishing Co: San Diego, Ca. 1973) p.17.

27. Ibid. p.41.

28. Henry M. Morris, "The Remarkable Birth of Planet Earth" (ICR Publishing Co: San Diego, Ca. 1972) p.22.

29. David B. Kitts, (1923-2010) (professor of geology-University of Oklahoma, Head Curator with the dept. of geology, Stoval Museum and a well known evolutionary paleontologist) "Paleontology and Evolutionary Theory" *Evolution*', vol. 28, Sept. 1974. p. 467. see Genesis Park used by permission ("Examine the Evidence" Ralph O. Muncaster, (Harvest House: Eugene, Oregon, 2004) p. 53. cited at (2christ.org/quotes) 2014.

30. Stephen J. Gould, "The Panda's Thumb" (W.W. Norton: New York 1980) p.238-239.

31. Stephen J. Gould, *The Episodic Nature of Evolutionary Change* "The Panda's Thumb" (W.W. Norton: New York 1985) see "God's Undertaker" John Lennox, (op cit) p.114.

32. Gary Parker, "Creation Facts of Life" (Master Books: Green Forrest, AR. 1994) p.208.

33. Niles Eldredge, (biologist/paleontologist - a curator at the American Museum of Natural History - dept. of invertebrates) 'Progress in Evolution'? *New Scientist*, vol. 110, 1986, p.55. (quote mine project/ eldredge) 2014.

34. Peter L. Forey, (1945-2016) (paleontologist with the British Museum of Natural History) 'Neontological Analysis versus Paleontological Stories' (Academic Press: London, England 1982) p.120-121.

35. Brian Sykes, (professor emeritus of Human Genetics, Oxford) *Nature*', vol. 352, August 1, 1991, p.381.

36. Carl Sagan, "The Dragons of Eden" (Random House Publishers: New York 1977) p.6. see "The Battle for Truth" D. Noebel, (op cit) p.122.

37. Steven M. Stanley, (American paleontologist and evolutionary biologist – U. of Hawaii) "Macroevolution: Pattern and Process" (W. M. Freeman pub: San Francisco, California 1979) p.39. see "The Long War Against God" Henry Morris, (Master Books: Green Forrest, AR. 2008) p.27.

38. David Woodruff, (1943-2015) (biology professor - UC San Diego) *Science*' vol. 208, 1980, p.716.

39. Mark Ridley, (British zoologist, Oxford University /doctoral advisor: Richard Dawkins) 'Who Doubts Evolution'? *New Scientist*, vol. 90. June 25, 1981) p.831.

40. Gary Parker, see (ideacenter.org), (2christ.org/quotes) and (goodreads. com/author/quotes/garyparker) 2014.

Chapter Three

1. John Lennox, (Oxford Professor of mathematics, philosopher of Science - a prominent Christian apologist who has lectured and debated throughout the world on 'the origin of the physical dimension' and 'the existence of God') see his book "God's Undertaker, has Science Buried God"? Lion Hudson Pub: Oxford, England 2009.

2. Jerry Adler & John Carey: 'Is Man a Subtle Accident'? *Newsweek*, vol. 96, No. 18 Nov. 3, 1980 p.95. (2christ.org/quotes) 2014

3. *Newsweek*, Jerry Adler & John Carey, 'Is Man a Subtle Accident'? November 3, 1980 p.95-96. Reporting on the: 'Macroevolution' conference -- Chicago Field Museum of Natural History.

4. Chester A. Arnold, (1901-1977) (professor of botany and curator of fossil plants- University of Michigan) in "An Introduction to Paleobotany" (McGraw-Hill Publishing Co: New York, 1947) p.7. (2christ.org/quotes) see at "Scientific Creationism" Henry Morris, (Creation-life Pub: San Diego, Ca. 1974) p.86, 87.

5. Eldred Corner, (1906-1996) (professor of botany- Cambridge) A.M. MacLeod & L.S. Cobley, eds. "Evolution in Contemporary Botanical Thought" (Quadrangle Books: Chicago, IL. 1961) p. 95, 97. from Bird, L. p. 234. see "Creation Facts of Life" Gary Parker, (op cit) p.148.

6. Steven M. Stanley, "The New Evolutionary Timetable: Fossils, Genes, and the Origin of Species" (Basic Books: New York 1981) p.95.

7. Douglas Futuyma, (American evolutionary biologist) "Science on Trial: The Case for Evolution" (Pantheon Books: New York 1983) p.82.

8. Colin Patterson, (in a letter to Luther D. Sunderland, April 10, 1979) as appearing in "Darwin's Enigma: Fossils and Other Problems" by Luther Sunderland (Master Book Publishers: Green Forrest, AR) (4th edition printing El Cajon, Ca. 1988) p.89. see "Refuting Evolution" Jonathan Sarfati, (Master Books: Green Forest, AR. 1999) p.48.

9. Albert Fleischmann, (1862-1942) (former German professor of zoologist and comparative anatomy) 'The Doctrine of Organic Evolution in the Light of Modern Research' Journal of the Transactions of the Victoria Institute 65, 1933. p.194-95, 205-6, 208-9. (nwcreation.net/ evolutionquotes) 2014.

10. Stephen J. Gould, 'Is a New and General Theory of Evolution Emerging'? an article appearing in *Paleobiology*, vol. 6(1) Jan. 1980, p.127; p. 40 as

cited in Genesis Park. see "Examine the Evidence" Ralph O. Muncaster, (Harvest House Publishers; Eugene, Oregon 2004) p.54.

11. Java-man fraud/Eugene Dubois retraction, "Evolution- The Fossils Say No!" Duane T. Gish (ICR Publishing: San Diego, California 1973) p.85-88.

12. Duane T. Gish, (expert on the fossil record exposes the fraud of Piltdown Man) "Evolution-The Fossils Say No!" (ICR Publishing: San Diego, California 1973) p.92.

13. Solly Zuckerman, (1904-1993) "The Amazing Story of Creation" Gish (ICR Pub: El Cajon, Ca.1990) p.84.

14. Solly Zuckerman, "Beyond the Ivory Tower" (Taplinger Publishing Co: New York 1971) see "The Amazing Story of Creation" Duane T. Gish (op cit), p.84.

15. Richard Leakey, (paleoanthropologist son of Louis Leakey and director of the National Museums of Kenya) *The Weekend Australian* magazine May 7&8 1983, p.3. (creation.org/articles/quotes) 2014.

16. Charles Oxnard, Reference 13 above, p.84. also see quotation in "Creation Facts of Life" Gary Parker, (Master Books: Green Forest, AR. 1994) p.162-3.

17. Duane T. Gish, Reference 12 above, p.103.

18. Timothy White, (paleoanthropologist- University of California, Berkeley) see Ian Anderson article 'Hominid Collarbone Exposed as Dolphin's Rib' *'New Scientist'* April 28, 1983. p.199. (creation.org/articles/quotes) 2015.

19. Greg Kirby, (Senior lecturer in population biology at Flinders University) quoted from an address to the biology teachers Association, South Australia. 1976. see (chick.com/evolution) by Chick Publications, Jan/Feb, 1987.

20. Stephen J. Gould, "The Panda's Thumb" (W.W. Norton publishers: New York 1980) p.126.

21. Henry M. Morris, "Science and the Bible" (Moody Press: Chicago, Illinois 1986) p.61.

22. Robert Wiedersheim, (1848-1923) (German Anatomist) writing in 'The Structure of Man: An Index to His Past History' 1893. 2nd edition. (translated by H. and M. Bernard) (Macmillan and Co: London, England 1895) see (wikipedia.org/wiki/robert_wiedersheim) 2014.

23. Horatio Newman, (1875-1957) (a zoologist from the University of Chicago who offered a written statement read into evidence at the famous *Scopes Trial* of 1925) Darrow, Clarence & William J. Bryan (1997)

'The World's most Famous Court Trial: The Tennessee Evolution Case Published' The Lawbook Exchange, Ltd. p.268. found at (wikipedia.org/wiki/robert_wiedersheim) 2014.

24. Henry Morris, "The Long War Against God" (Master Books: Green Forrest, AR. 2000) (4th printing) 2008 p.113.

25. Wolfgang Smith, (mathematician, physicist, philosopher- MIT, UCLA, OSU) 'Teilhardism and the New Religion: A Thorough Analysis of the Teachings of Pierre Teilhard de Chardin' (Tan Books, Rockford, IL. 1988) p.5-6. see "The Long War Against God" H. Morris (op cit) p.161.

26. David A. Noebel, (American religious leader, Christian philosopher and avid writer) "The Battle for Truth" (Harvest House Publishers: Eugene, Oregon 2001) p.146.

27. Lee Strobel, (American journalist, Christian author and apologist) "The Case for Faith" (Zondervan Publishing House: Grand Rapids, Michigan, 2000) p.91.

Chapter Four

1. John Lennox, (Oxford mathematician and philosopher of science) "God's Undertaker: Has Science Buried God" (Lion Hudson Pub: Oxford, England 2nd edition 2009) p.127.

2. Ibid. p.129.

3. Michael Behe, J. Buell & G Hearn, eds. *Darwinism: Science or Philosophy* ? Dallas, Texas: Foundation for Thought and Ethics, 1994. quoted in: Stephen C. Meyer, 'The Explanatory Power of Design', p.126. see "The Case for Faith" Lee Strobel, (Zondervan Publishing: Grand Rapids, Michigan 2000) p.101.

4. I.L. Cohen, (engineer & mathematician/ New York Academy of Science) "Darwin Was Wrong: A Study in Probabilities" (New Research publications: 1984) p.205. (Greenvale, NY. ed. 1985) p.6-8, 209-210, 214-215. see the creation - evolution encyclopedia at (pathlights.com) 2014.

5. Fred Hoyle, (1915-2001) (British astronomer and professor, Cambridge University) 'Hoyle on Evolution'. *Nature*, vol. 294, Nov 12, 1981, p.105. see "The Case for Faith" Lee Strobel (op cit) p.101.

6. Fred Hoyle, ' The Universe, Past and Present Reflections' *Annual Review of Astronomy and Astrophysics*: vol 20, 1982. p.16. *Engineering and Science* 1981 p.12, quoted in Holder, 'Is the Universe Designed'? *'Nature'* Nov 12,

1981 vol 294: p.105. partial quote, see (godandscience.org/apologetics/ quotes) 2014.

7. Christian de Duve, (1917-2013) (Nobel Laureate, Belgian Cytologist/ Biochemist) 'A Guided Tour of the Living Cell' *Scientific American Library Series* Nov. 1984. see science quotes at (simpletoremember.com) 2014

8. Kenneth Ham, (conference speaker, educator, author and Christian Apologist) 'Is There Really a God?' booklet (*Answers in Genesis,* Florence, KY. 1998) p.23.

9. Edgar Mitchell, (1930-2016) (American Pilot- NASA: decorated Apollo 14 Astronaut and the sixth person to walk on the moon) see (simpletoremember.com/science-quotes) 2014.

10. Francis Collins, "The Language of God" (Free Press: New York 2006) p.1-2.

11. Richard Dawkins, "Genetics: Why Prince Charles Is So Wrong" (checkbiotech.org Jan. 28 2003) see: "Total Truth" Nancy Pearcey (Crossway Books: Wheaton, IL. 2005) p.191.

12. Nancy Pearcey, (evangelical author, Frances Schaeffer scholar, Christian philosopher and apologist serving at the Discovery Institute Center for Science and Culture) "Total Truth" (Crossway Books Wheaton, IL. 2005) p.197.

13. Ibid. p.198.

14. Francis Collins, (director of the Human Genome Project) "The Language of God", (Free Press: New York 2006) p.1. (paraphrase) cited by Marilyn Adamson "Does God Exist- Six Reasons to Believe" p.5. (everystudent. com) 2013.

15. Francis Collins, "The Language of God" (Free Press: New York 2006) p.3. Nancy Pearcey, 'Copying the Human Script: Genome Project Raises Hopes, Fears' *World* July 8, 2000. see "God's Undertaker" J. Lennox (op cit) p.176..

16. Michael Denton, (Btitish/Australian microbiologist and author) "Evolution: A Theory in Crisis" (Burnett Books Ltd: London, England, 1985) p.334. see quotes by men of science (simpletoremember.com/ science-quotes) 2013.

17. Werner Gitt, (director: German Institute of Physics and Technology) "In the Beginning was Information" CLV, (Bielefeld, Germany 1997) p.79. see "Is There Really a God"? Ken Ham booklet (*Answers in Genesis* 1998) p.26.

18. Ibid. p.107. see "God's Undertaker" John Lennox (op cit) p.145.

19. Bill Gates, (Chairman- Microsoft Corporation) "The Road Ahead" 1995, (Penguin: London, revised) (Blue Penguin: Boulder 1996) p.228. see "God's Undertaker" J. Lennox (op cit) p.145.

20. Walter T. Brown, (American engineer and young earth creationist-MIT) "In the Beginning: Compelling Evidence for Creation" 7th edition (Phoenix: Center for Scientific Creation 1986) p.6. see "The Battle for Truth" David Noebel (Harvest House 2001) p.141.

21. Molecular Configuration: 'Chirality' requirements in organic physiology. see "Examine the Evidence" Ralph O. Muncaster (Harvest House: Eugene, Oregon 2004) p.110-115.

22. Francis Collins, "The Language of God" (Free Press: New York 2006) p.90-91.

23. Michael Denton, "Evolution: A Theory in Crisis" (Adler & Adler, Bethesda, MD. 1986) p.250. see "The Battle for Truth" D. Noebel (op cit) p.140. and "God's Undertaker" J. Lennox (op cit) p.122.

24. Walter L. Bradley, (advocate of Intelligent Design- former professor of engineering: Baylor University) interview with Mr. Lee Strobel "The Case for Faith" (Zondervan Publishing: Grand Rapids, Michigan 2000) p.109.

25. Richard Dawkins, 'The Necessity of Darwinism' New Scientist, 1982 vol. 94 (April 15) p.130. see Ken Ham "Is There Really a God"? booklet by (Answers in Genesis 1998) p.9-10.

26. Stephen C. Meyer, (history/philosophy of science graduate at Cambridge, director of the Center for Science and Culture: The Discovery Institute "The Message of the Microcosm: DNA and the Death of Materialism" Cosmic Pursuit Fall 1997 p.41-42. see Ralph O. Muncaster "Examine the Evidence" (op cit) p.117,123.

27. Michael Behe, "Darwin's Black Box" (The Free Press: New York 1996) p.193,243,251. see "The Case For Faith" Lee Strobel (op cit) p.90-91.

28. Michael Denton, "Evolution: A Theory in Crisis" (Adler & Adler: Chevy Chase, Maryland 1985, 86) p.77. see "The Case For Faith" Lee Strobel (op cit) p. 87.

29. Michael Denton, "Evolution: A Theory in Crisis" (op cit) p.62,358. (nwcreation.net/evolutionquotes) 2014.

30. Ibid. p.249-50. also see "God's Undertaker" J. Lennox (op cit) p.122.

31. Ibid. p.250. and "God's Undertaker" J. Lennox (op cit) p.122,123.

32. Jacques Monod, (1910-1976) (French Biologist: Nobel Prize winner 1965) 'Chance and Necessity: An Essay on the Natural Philosophy of Modern

Biology' (Collins Press: London 1972) p.134 see "God's Undertaker" J .Lennox (op cit) p.123.

33. Michael Behe, "Darwin's Black Box" (Simon & Schuster: New York 1996) p.39. see "God's Undertaker" J. Lennox (op cit) p.123,124.

34. Ibid. p.193. see "God's Undertaker" J. Lennox (op cit) p.125.

35. Frederick Hoyle, "The Intelligent Universe" (Michael Joseph pub: London, England) (Holt, Rinehart, Winston: reprint New York 1983) p.20,21,23.

36. Wolfgang Smith, "Teilhardism and the New Religion: A Thorough Analysis of the Teachings of de Chardin" (Tan publishing: Rockford, IL. 1988) p.1-2. "The Long War Against God" Henry Morris (partial quote op cit) p.279.

37. Charles Darwin, 'The Life and Letters of Charles Darwin' 1887, vol. 2. p.229. see famous quotes from famous evolutionists at (anounted-one. net/quotes) 2014.

38. Ilya Prigogine, (1917-2003) (Russian born, Belgian physical chemist and decorated Nobel recipient- 1977) 'Physics Today 25' by Prigogine, Gregair, & Babbyabtz, discussion p.23-28. (simpletoremember.com) 2014.

39. Paul Davies, (award winning British Physicist- professor at Arizona State University) "Superforce: The Search for a Grand Unified Theory of Nature" (Simon & Schuster: New York 1984) p.223. see "The Battle For Truth" David Noebel (op cit) p.140.

40. Ibid. p.243 (godandscience.org/apologetics/quotes) 2014.

41. Richard Dawkins, "The Blind Watchmaker" (W. W. Norton & Co: New York 1986) p.287. see "Total Truth" Nancy Pearcey (op cit) p.168.

42. S C Todd, 'A View from Kansas on the Evolution Debate', *Nature* 401 Sept. 30, 1999 p.423. see "Total Truth" Nancy Pearcey (Crossway Books: Wheaton, Ill. 2005) p.168.

43. Richard Dawkins, "The Blind Watchmaker" (W.W. Norton & Co: New York 1986) p.1. (emphasis added) see "Total Truth" N. Pearcey (op cit) p.183.

44. George Wald, (1906-1997) (American evolutionary scientist, professor emeritus of Biology/Harvard- Nobel recipient specializing in Neurobiology) 'Innovation and Biology' *Scientific American*, vol. 199, Sept. 1958, p.100. (famous quotes from famous evolutionists, groups. google.com/forum) (the quote mine project) 2018.

45. Theodosius Dobyhansky, (1900-1975) (Ukrainian-American geneticist and evolutionary biologist) Review of Evolution, 'Creation and Science' by F.L. Marsh 1945. *The American Naturalist* p.75,79.

46. Nancy Pearcey, "Total Truth: Liberating Christianity from its Cultural Captivity" (Crossway Books: Wheaton, IL. 2005) (study guide edition) p.168-169.

Chapter Five

1. For detailed information on the use of radiometric dating methodology refer to: "Scientific Creationism" by Dr. Henry Morris (Creation Life Publishers: San Diego, Ca. 1974) beginning with p.137.

2. Robert H. Rastall, (economic Geology- Cambridge) Encyclopedia Britannica, vol. 10 (William Benton Publishing: Chicago, IL. 1956) p.168. (2christ.org/quotes) 2014.

3. Ronald R. West, (assistant professor of paleobiology, Kansas St. University) 'Paleoecology and Uniformitarianism' Compass, vol. 45, May 1968, p.216. see (creationism.org/articles/quotes) 2014.

4. Niles Eldredge, "Time Frames: The Rethinking of Darwinian Evolution and the Theory of Punctuated Equilibia" (Simon & Schuster: New York 1985) p.51,52 see the Quote Mine Project: Gould, Eldredge, etc. quotes 2014.

5. A. E. Wilder-Smith, (British organic chemist, and former atheist) "Man's Origin, Man's Destiny" (Harold Shaw Publishers: Jan. 1968) (9) p.127-128. (paperback by Bethany House publishing, 1975) (2christ.org/quotes) 2014.

6. Henry M. Morris, "Scientific Creationism" (Creation Life Publishers: San Diego, Ca. 1974) p.155. see also: Stuart E. Nevins article: 'Evolution: The Oceans Say No'! ICR *Acts and Facts*, Impact Series #8, October, 1973.

7. Ibid, p.158.

8. Ibid, p.157-158. see also: Dr. Thomas G. Barnes article: 'Origin and Destiny of the Earth's Magnetic Field' (ICR publishing: San Diego, Ca. 1973) p.64.

9. Ibid, p.151-153. see also: Hans Pettersson, (Swedish oceanographer) 'Cosmic Spherules and Meteoric Dust', *Scientific American*, vol. 202 February 1960) p.132.

10. Ibid, p.153. (ocean salt content)

11. Ibid, p.167-169. (see the mathematical calculation of population dynamics based on the old earth scenario)

12. Ibid, p.169 for a further study of evidence supporting a young earth as compared to the billions of years demanded by evolution theory, I refer the reader to: Dr. Henry M. Morris, "The Biblical Basis for Modern Science" (Baker Publishing, 1985) p.477-480.

13. Colin Patterson, (1933-1998) "Evolution" (Cornell University Press: Ithaca, New York 1978) p.150. (pathlights.com creation/evolution encyclopedia) 2014

14. L. H. Mathews, (evolutionary biologist) 'forward' to Charles Darwin, 'Origin of Species" 1971 edition, (J. M. Dent & Sons, Ltd: London, England) p. x,xi. see "Scientific Creationism" Henry M. Morris (Creation Life Publishers: San Diego, Ca. 1974) p.6.

15. Pierre-Paul Grasse, "Evolution of Living Organisms" (Academic Press: Nerw York 1977) p.107. he adds: (Natural selection is a conservation mechanism rather that a creative process. It serves to hinder the spread of harmful mutations through a population, keeping the status quo) as cited in "The Long War Against God" Dr. Henry Morris (Master Books: Green Forest, Ar. 2000) p.161.

16. Theodore Roszak, (1933-2011) (professor emeritus of History) California St. University 'Unfinished Animal: the Aquarian Frontier and the Evolution of Consciousness' 1975, p.101-102. (nwcreation.net/evolutionquotes) 2014.

17. Dean Kenyon, (Biochemist: San Francisco St. University) see Walter T. Brown, "In the Beginning" (Phoenix: Center for Scientific Creation, 1986) p.6. cited in "The Battle For Truth" D. Noebel (op cit) p.142.

18. Wolfgang Smith, 'The Universe is Ultimately to be explained in Terms of a Metacosmic Reality' Margenau and Varghese (eds): *Cosmos, Bios, & Theos* p.113 quotes from famous evolutionists (anointed-one.net/quotes) 2014

19. Louis T. More, (Professor of Paleontology- Princeton) "The Dogma of Evolution" (Princeton University Press: Princeton, New Jersey 1925) 2nd printing p.160. also see "Darwin's Enigma: Fossils and Other Problems" Luther D. Sunderland (Master Books: Santee, Ca. 1988) p.27. and "Mind Siege" Tim Lahaye (Word Publishing, 2000) p.140.

20. Julian Huxley, Humanist Assoc. membership brochure (San Jose, California) 'What is Humanism'? Humanist Community of San Jose. features Julian Huxley. see also "Scientific Creationism" (op cit) p.197.

21. Henry Morris "Scientific Creationism" (op cit) p.197. (see Justice Abe Fortas comment in connection with US Supreme Court ruling striking down Arkansas anti-evolution law).

22. David A. Noebel, "The Battle for Truth" (Harvest House Publishers: Eugene, Oregon. 2001) p.147.

23. Michael Ruse, (science philosopher- Florida State University and a leading anti-creationist advocate) (1) 'Saving Darwinism from the Darwinians - How evolution became a religion: creationists correct'? *The National Post* May 13, 2000, p.B1,B3,B7. (2) 'Mystery of Mysteries: Is Evolution a Social Construction'? (Harvard University Press, Cambridge, Mass. 1999) cited by Nancy Pearcey "Total Truth" (Crossway Books, Wheaton, Illinois. 2005) p.172. These statements by Dr. Ruse are in stark contrast to his testimony at the Arkansas 'Balanced Treatment Bill Trial of 1981/82' where he and other anti-creationists denied the claim that evolution should be accurately viewed as an anti-God religious dogma.

24. Ibid. (1) (op. cit) (2) p.172.

25. Dr. R. Kirk, as cited in 'The Rediscovery of Creation' (*National Review*, May 27, 1983) p.641. (google: quotes reveal the credulity of evolutionists) also see S. Jaki, 'Cosmos and Creator' 1982. (nwcreation.net/evolution) 2015.

26. Marjorie Grene, (American philosopher of science with a particular emphasis on biology) 'The Faith of Darwinism' *Encounter*, November 1959, p.49. reprinted in Grene, Marjorie "The knower and the known" (University of California Press: Berkley, Ca. 1974) p.187. retrieved – google books Sept. 17, 2014.

27. David Coppedge, 'Speaking of Science, Creation Matters', May/June 2003. (debunking evolution) (newgeology.us/presentation32.html) 2015.

28. Colin Patterson, (quoted from a letter to Luther D. Sunderland, April 10, 1979) (talkorigins.org) 2014. see "Darwin's Enigma: Fossils and other Problems" Luther D. Sunderland, (Master Books: San Diego, Ca. 1984) p.89.

29. Richard Bliss, (Professor of Biology-Christian Heritage College) 'It Takes a Miracle for Evolution' *Christian Heritage Courier* 1 (March 1979) p.4. cited by Tim Lahaye in "Mind Siege" Word Publishing (op cit) p.142.

30. Klaus Dose, (director of the Institute for Biochemistry, Gutenberg University, West Germany) 'The Origin of Life: More Questions than Answers', *Inter-disciplinary Science Review*, 13, 1988. p.348. see "God's

Undertaker" J. Lennox (op cit) p. 133 & "The Case For Faith" Lee Strobel (op cit) p.107.

31. Walter L. Bradley & Charles B. Thaxton, "Information and The Origin of Life" *The Creation Hypothesis* (Intervarsity Press: Douners Grove, Illinois 1994) p.194. see also 'Life from the Heavens? Not This Way' Fazale Rana & Hugh Ross, *Facts and Faith*, Quarter 1, 2000. cited by Lee Strobel in "The Case For Faith" (op cit) p.107.

32. Julian Huxley, (evolutionist and former president of UNESCO) (statement taken from a television interview questioning J. Huxley about the rapid rise in Darwinian thought in the 20th century. (late 1950's) cited by Dr. Henry M. Morris in "The Troubled Water of Evolution" 1974, p.58.

33. Nancy Pearcey, "Total Truth" (Crossway Books, Wheaton, IL. 2005) p.176.

34. Richard Lewontin, (research professor – Museum of Comparative Zoology, Harvard University) "Billions and Billions of Demons" (New York Review of Books, Jan. 9, 1997) p.28,31. cited at (ucsb.edu/fscf/FAQ/ evolution) review of Carl Sagan's book "The Demon Haunted World: Science as a Candle in the Dark", (New York Review of books, Jan 9, 1997) also see "God's Undertaker" J. Lennox, (op cit) p.35,36.

35. Julian Huxley, "Evolution: The Modern Synthesis", (Harper & Bros. Publishers: New York 1942) p. 457. see "The Battle for Truth" D. Noebel (op cit) p.118.

36. Gary Parker, "Creation Facts of Life", (Master Books: Green Forrest, AR. 1994) p.122.

37. Norman MacBeth, (Harvard trained attorney and out-spoken critic of the neo-Darwinism) "Darwin Retired", (Gambit Books: Boston, Mass. 1971) (forward) also see "Creation Facts of Life" Gary Parker (op cit) p.122.

38. Phillip Johnson, (former law professor: University of California-Berkley) "Darwin on Trial", (Regnery Gateway: Washington DC 1991)

39. Norman MacBeth, "Darwin Retired: An Appeal to Reason" (Gambit Books: Boston, Mass. 1971) (forward)

40. Johannes Kepler, (1571-1630) cited in Morris Kline "Mathematics: The Loss of Certainty" (Oxford University Press: New York 1980) p.31, as cited by J. Lennox, "God's Undertaker: Has Science Buried God"? (Lion Hudson Publishing: Oxford, England 2009) p.21.

41. Galileo, (1564-1642) 'GG ll Saggiatore', (1623) as translated in 'The Philosophy of the 16th & 17th Centuries' 1966 by Richard Henry Popkin,

p.65. see Morris Kline's book "Mathematics: The Loss of Certainty" (1980) cited by John Lennox, "God's Undertaker" 2009 p.24.

42. Keith Ward, (British philosopher, theologian and scholar) "God, Chance, and Necessity" (One World Publications: Oxford, England 1996) see "God's Undertaker" J. Lennox (op cit) p.63.

43. Henry F. Schaefer, (highly decorated professor-University of Georgia - computational and theoretical chemist, a five time nominee for the Nobel Prize) J.L. Sheler & J.M. Schrof, 'The Creation', *U.S. News & World Report* (December 23, 1991) p.56-64. (godandscience.org/apologetics/ quotes) 2014.

44. Kurt Godel, (world renown Austrian mathematician, logician, & philosopher) Palle Yourgrau, 'A World Without Time: The Forgotten Legacy of Godel and Einstein' (Basic Books: New York 2005) p.104-105. as cited by Antony Flew in "There is a God" (Harper Collins Pub: New York 2007) p.167.

45. John Lennox, "God's Undertaker" (Lion Books: Oxford, England 2009) p.63.

46. John Lennox, Ibid. p.65.

47. John Lennox, 'U-tube debates' an illustration often used by J. Lennox in many of his debates concerning the question: 'has science eliminated the need for God'?

48. Stephen Hawking, 'ABC Television's 20/20' 1989 as cited by J. Lennox "God's Undertaker" (op cit) p.63.

49. Arno Penzias, (America physicist and radio astronomer who won a Nobel Prize in 1978) In Denis Brian, *Genius Talk*, (Plenum: New York, 1995) see "God's Undertaker" J. Lennox, (op cit) p.75.

50. Charles Townes, (highly decorated American Nobel Prize winning physicist 1964) 'Making Waves' *American Physical Society*, 1995. see "God's Undertaker" J. Lennox (op cit) p.69.

51. Julian Huxley, 'At Random' a television preview aired on Nov. 21, 1959. cited in "The Battle For Truth" David A. Noebel, (op cit) p.124.

52. Junior High biology textbook, "Matter- Its forms and changes" 2nd edition (Brandwein, Stollberg, Greenstone, Yasso, Brovey) Junior High School textbook, Los Angeles City Schools (Harcourt Brace Jovanovich, Inc: (New York, Chicago, San Francisco, Atlanta, & Dallas) 1972.

53. High school textbook, "BSCS Biology: A Molecular Approach" 8th edition, Jon Greenberg (revision editor) (Everyday Learning Corp: 2001) p.446. as cited in "Total Truth" N. Pearcey, (op cit) p.169.

54. High school textbook, (Neil A. Campbell, Jane B. Reece, & Lawrence G. Mitchell) "Biology" 5th edition. (Addison Wesley: Reading, Mass. 1999) p.426. see "Total Truth" N. Pearcey, (op cit) p.169.

55. College level textbook, Douglas Futuyma, "Evolutionary Biology" 3rd edition textbook, (Sinauer Co: Sunderland, Mass. 1998) p.15. see "Total Truth" N. Pearcey, (op cit) p.169.

56. University textbook, "Evolution" 2nd edition (Sudbury, Jones & Bartlett, 1996) p.62. see "God's Undertaker" J. Lennox, (op cit) p. 87.

57. Douglas Futuyma, (Evolutionary Biologist) "Science on Trial: The Case for Evolution" 1983, p.82. also see: "Evolutionary Biology" 2nd edition (Sinauer Co: Sunderland, Mass. 1986) p.3. as cited in 'God's Undertaker' John Lennox, (op cit) p.87, & "Total Truth" Nancy Pearcey, (op cit) p.200.

58. Richard Lewontin, cited by D. Futuyma "Science On Trial" (Sinauer Co: Sunderland, Mass. 1995) p. 161. see "God's Undertaker" J. Lennox, (op cit) p.99.

59. The Humanist magazine, 'A Religion for a New Age' J. Dunphy *The Humanist* Jan-Feb 1983, p.23,26. (emphasis added) cited by Wendell R. Bird, Origin of the Species – Revisited, vol. 2 p. 257. see "Refuting Evolution" J. Sarfati, p.20-21, and "Mind Seige" Lahaye p.170.

Chapter Six

1. The documentary film "Expelled: No Intelligence Allowed" was directed by Nathan Frankowski and hosted by Ben Stein. 2008.

2. A Professional '*textbook critique*' by Mills, Lancaster & Bradley: 'Origin of Life- Evolution in Biology Textbooks- A Critique' *The American Biology Teacher*, vol 55, No. 2, February, 1993, p.83.

3. Tim Lahaye, (Christian minister and apologist, distinguished author, expert educator in Biblical escatology) "Mind Siege-The Battle for Truth in the New Millennium" (Word Publishing: Nashville, TN. 2000) p.153,154.

4. M.H. Armitage and K.L. Anderson, *Acta Histochemica* 115, 603-608: (intellihub.com/Scientist-terminated) 2013.

5. Nancy Pearcey, 'Scopes in Reverse' *Washington Times*, July 24, 2000. cited in "Total Truth" Nancy Pearcey (Crossway Books: Wheaton, IL. 2005) p.173.

6. *Reader's Digest* magazine- a response from the editors to an ICR article publication request. (Institute for Creation Research News Letter Jan 1982. El Cajon, Ca.)

7. Luther D. Sunderland, "Darwin's Enigma: Fossils and Other Problems", 4th edition. (Master Books: Santee, Ca. 1988) p.7,8. (2christ.org/quotes) 2014.

8. Henry Morris, (author of more than twenty books on science and faith) "Many Infallible Proofs" (Master Books: El Cajon, California 1974) p.246.

9. Albert Einstein, Max Jammer, "Einstein and Religion" (Princeton University Press: Princeton, NJ, 1999) p.48. see "There Is a God" Antony Flew, (Harper & Collins Publications: New York 2007) p.99.

10. Antony Flew, (Professor of Philosophy/Oxford) 'Atheist Becomes Theist: Exclusive Interview with Former Atheist Antony Flew' at Biola University. see interview at (godandscience.org/apologetics/quotes) 2015.

11. Wernher Von Braun, (rocket scientist and space pioneer) as quoted by James Perloff, "Tornado in a Junkyard" (Refuge Books: Arlington, Mass. 1999) p.253. see (nwcreation.net/evolution quotes) 2015. also see T. McIver, 'Ancient Tales and Space-Age Myths of Creationist Evangelism' 1986. *The Skeptical Inquirer* vol. 10: p.258-276. 'Gone Bananas' *World* Sept. 7, 2002. (godandscience.org/apologetics/quotes) 2015.

12. Wernher Von Braun, *This Week Magazine* Jan 24, 1960. p.2.

13. Kenneth Ham, 'Is There Really a God'? 1998. booklet by Answers in Genesis, Florence, KY. p.33.

14. Albert Fleischmann, "Witnesses Against Evolution" by Mr. John F. Meldau (Christian Victory Publishing: Denver, Co. 1968) p.13. see citation at (nwcreation.net/evolutionquotes) 2014.

15. Henry M. Morris, "The Long War Against God", (Master Books: Green Forrest, AR. 2008) p.256 (4th printing)

16. Ibid, p.32.

17. Frank Tipler, (mathematical physicist and cosmologist – Tulane University) "The Physics of Christianity" (Doubleday publishing: New York 2007)

18. William Paley (1743-1805) (Christian apologist and philosopher) This is a variation of an original quote from his book "A View of the Evidences of Christianity" 1794. (this quotation is often confused and has sometimes been mistakenly credited to a Mr. Herbert Spencer.)

19. Niles Eldredge, "Time Frames: The Rethinking of Darwinian Evolution and the Theory of Punctuated Equilibria" (Simon & Schuster: New York 1985) p.44. "Time Frames: The Evolution of Punctuated Equilibria" (Princeton University Press: Princeton, New Jersey 1985) p.144-45. cited in "God's Undertaker" J. Lennox (op cit) p.114. (famous quotes from famous evolutionists) 2014.

20. Arthur Keith, (anti-Christian physical anthropologist) writing in the 'forward' to the 100th anniversary edition of Charles Darwin's 'Origin of Species, 1959. see Google Groups- famous quotes from famous evolutionists. cited at (soulwinners.com.au/8.html) 2014.

21. Frances Crick, (British molecular biologist & Nobel Laureate for his epic DNA discoveries/ research) "Life Itself, Its Origin and Nature" (Futura pub: London, England 1981,82) p.88 (Simon & Schuster: New York 1981) p.88. cited in "God's Undertaker" J. Lennox, (op cit) p.133.

22. Roger Haines Jr. (research attorney- Ca. Third District Court of Appeals) 'Macroevolution Questioned' *Creation Research Society Quarterly*, Dec 1976, p.169.

23. Edmund J. Ambrose, (professor of cellular biology, University of London) "The Nature and Origin of the Biological World", (John Wiley & Sons, 1982) p. 164. (anointed-one.net/quotes) 2014.

24. Mark Czarnecki, (evolutionary paleontologist) 'The Revival of the Creationist Crusade' *MacLeans's* Jan. 19, 1981, p.56. (The TalkOrigins Archive- Quote Mine Project) also see (anointed-one.net/quotes) 2014

25. Robert Jastrow, (American astronomer, physicist, cosmologist and a leading NASA scientist) "The Enchanted Loom: Mind In the Universe" (Simon & Schuster: New York, 1981) p.19. (anointed-one.net/quotes) 2013.

26. Stephen J. Gould, 'Evolution's Erratic Pace' *Natural History* vol. 86. (May 1977) p.14. (The Talk Origins Archive -Quote Mine Project) (talkorigins. org) 2014.

27. Allan Sandage, (widely regarded as the world's greatest living cosmologist: winner of the Crawford prize in astronomy) J.N. Willford: March 12, 1991. 'Sizing up the Cosmos: An Astronomers Quest' *New York Times*, p.B9. also see "God's Undertaker" J. Lennox (op cit) p.66. (godandscience. org/apologetics/quotes) 2014.

28. H. J. Lipson, (Professor of Physics, University of Manchester, UK) 'A Physicist Looks at Evolution' *Physics Bulletin*, vol. 31. 1980 p.138. (emphasis his) Is evolution religion? (nwcreation.net/evolution) 2014.

29. Wolfgang Smith, "Teilhardism and the New Religion: A Thorough Analysis of the Teachings of de Chardin" (Tan Books & Publishers: Rockford, IL. 1988) p.1-2. (2christ.org/quotes)(wordpress.com) 2014.

30. Frederick B. Burnham, (theologian and professor-history of science) quoted from an appearance on ABC's Nightline with Ted Koppel, April 24, 1992. quotes for creation (english.sdaglobal.org/research/qotcratn.htm)2014.

31. Sir William Dawson, "The Story of Earth and Man" (Harper & Brothers: New York, 1887) p.317,322,330,339. (nwcreation.net/evolutionquotes) 2014.

32. Henry M. Morris, "The Long War Against God" (Master Books: Green Forest, AR. 2008) p.199.

33. Ernst Chain, (1945 Nobel Prize winner- Isolated and Purified Penicillin) (Jerry Bergman, Ph.D. April 2008. 'Ernst Chain: Antibiotic Pioneer' Acts&Facts, vol. 37, No. 4, p.10-12.) quotes 1 & 4 (A) Clark, R.W. 1985. 'The Life of Ernst Chain: Penicillin and Beyond' New York: St. Martin's Press, p.147. quotes 2&3 (B) Chain, E. 1970. 'Social Responsibility and the Scientist in Modern Western Society' (Robert Waley Cohen memorial lecture) London: 'The Council of Christians and Jews' p.25. Dr. Ernst Chain, along with Alexander Fleming and Howard Florey, all received the Nobel Prize for their discovery and development of penicillin__ a medical breakthrough that would prove to be an invaluable asset to the world community at large.

34. Robert Jastrow, "God and the Astronomers" (W.W. Norton & Co: New York, 1978) p.115-116. in Moreland J.P. ed., 'The Creation Hypothesis', 1994, p.292-293 (godandscience.org/apologetics/quotes) 2014.

35. Arno Penzias,"Science and Christianity" Henry F. Schaefer p.49. also see A. Penzias quoted by Malcolm Browne, 'Clues to the Universe's Origin Expected' New York Times, March 12, 1978, p. 1. see "The Language of God" Francis Collins (Free Press: New York 2006) paperback edition p.76.

36. Soren Lovtrup, (Swedish Biologist/Embryologist) "Darwinism: The Refutation of a Myth" (Croom Helm pub: London/New York 1987) p.422. (2christ.org/quotes) and (nwcreation.net/evolutionquotes) 2014.

37. Louis Bounoure, (Professor and Director of Research at the French National Center of Scientific Research) 'The Advocate' March 8, 1984. p.17. (2christ.org/quotes) and (nwcreation.net/evolutionquotes) 2014.

38. T. N. Tahmisian, (former Atomic Energy Commission physiologist) '*The Fresno Bee*', August 20, 1959. as quoted by N. J. Mitchell 'Evolution and the Emperor's New Clothes' (Roydon Publications: United Kingdom 1983) title page. (2christ.org/quotes) and (nwcreation.net/evolutionquotes) 2014.

39. John Lennox, "God's Undertaker" (Lion Books: Oxford, England 2009) p.210.

Chapter Seven

1. Julian Huxley, "Evolution after Darwin' Sol Tax. edition, (University of Chicago Press: Chicago, Illinois 1960) cited in "God's Undertaker" J. Lennox, paperback edition (op cit) p.87.

2. Nancy Pearcey, (fellow - Discovery Institute) "Total Truth" (Crossway Books: Wheaton, Illinois. 2005) p.189.

3. Stephen Hawking, (award-winning British astrophysicist) 'A Brief History of Time' (Bantam Press: New York 1998) p.210. (1988 ed. p.175) cited by Francis Collins, "The Language of God" (Free Press- paperback 2007) p.62.

4. Paul Davies, 'A Brief History of the Multiverse' *The New York Times*, published on April 12, 2003. cited in "Total Truth" Nancy Pearcey, (op cit) p.189.

5. Paul Davies, "God and the New Physics" (Simon & Schuster: New York 1983) p.145. cited in "Mind Siege" Tim Lahaye, (Word publishing: Nashville,TN 2000) p.143.

6. Paul Davies, 'The Just So Universe' Walter L. Bradley, *Touchstone*, July/August 1999, p.72.

7. John O'Keefe, (planetary scientist and NASA Astronomer) F. Heeren, "Show Me God" (Searchlight Publications: Wheeling, IL. 1995) p.200. see (godandscience.org/apologetics) 2014.

8. John Polkinghorne, (theologian & professor of mathematical physics-Cambridge, a leading voice explaining the relationship between science and religion) 'Science Finds God' Sharon Begley, *Newsweek* Magazine July 20, 1998 p.48. see "Mind Siege" (op cit) p.138.

9. Sir Frederick Hoyle, "The Intelligent Universe" (Michael Joseph pub: London, England 1983) p.220. see (english.sdglobal.org/research/qotcratn) 2014.

10. Steven Weinberg, (American physicist and Nobel Laureate in High Energy Physics 1979) writing in the journal 'Scientific American' see quotation at (simpletoremember.com/science-quotes) 2015

11. Edward Harrison, (British astronomer and cosmologist) "Masks of the Universe" (Collier Books: Macmillan, 1985) p. 252,263 science quotes (godandscience.org/apologetics/quotes) 2014.

12. George Greenstein, (American Astronomer) "The Symbiotic, Universe: Life and Mind in the Cosmos" (Williams & Morrow: New York, 1988) p.27. see "Total Truth" (op cit) p.189,190.

13. Alexander Polyakov, (Soviet mathematician) S. Gannes, *Fortune Magazine* October 13, 1986. p. 57. see (godandscience.org/apologetics/quotes) science quotes 2014.

14. John Lennox, U-tube video doc. 'Design of The Universe?' 9/28/2007 John Lennox 'the birth of science' lecture, see also "God's Undertaker" (op cit) p.70. (accuracy comparison by Dr. Paul Davies)

15. John Lennox, "God's Undertaker" (Lion Books: Oxford, England 2nd edition (paperback) 2009) p.70.

16. Arno Penzias, "Cosmos, Bios, and Theos" H. Margenau, R. Varghese, ed. (Open Court pub: La Salle, IL. 1992) p.83. also see 'Our Universe: Accident or Design' (Wits 2050, S. Africa: Starwatch, 1992) p.42. quoted by Walter Bradley in the 'Just So' Universe- the fine-tuning constants and conditions in the cosmos. "God's Undertaker" John Lennox, (op cit) p.58,73.

17. Henry F. Schaefer, (five time Nobel nominee) quoted in his essay: 'Stephen Hawking, The Big Bang, and God' (godevidence.com/2010/08/quotes) 2014.

18. Alan Sandage, (highly decorated American astronomer) "Sizing up the Cosmos: An Astronomers Quest" J.N. Willford, *New York Times*, March 12, 1991, p.B9.

19. Charles Darwin, (the most predominant founding father of evolution theory, British naturalist and author) "The Autobiography of Charles Darwin" Nora Barlow edition (Collins Co: London 1958) p.92,93. as quoted in Antony Flew's book "There is a God" 2007 p.106. also see Kenneth R. Miller, "Finding Darwin's God" (HarperCollins: New York 1999) p.287. and "The Language of God" Francis Collins, 2007, p.99. (emphasis added)

20. William Paley, (18th century clergyman, naturalist and Christian apologist who first championed the teleological argument for the existence of God

long before the recent advent of evolution theory) "Natural Theology: or Evidences of the Existence and Attributes of Deity, Collected from the Appearances of Nature" publish date 1802. (material reprinted in 1972 by (St. Thomas Press: Houston, TX) p.3.

21. Isaac Asimov, 'In the Game of Energy and Thermodynamics You Can't Even Break Even' *Smithsonian Institute Journal*, June 1970. p.10. (creation. org/articles/quotes) 2014.

22. Antony Flew, (former long-time atheist and advocate of materialism) "There is a God, How the world's most notorious atheist changed his mind" (Harper Collins pub: New York 2007) p.126.

23. Richard Feynman, (American theoretical physicist- Nobel Prize recipient 1965 for his work in quantum electrodynamics) "The Meaning of it All: Thoughts of a Citizen-Scientist" (Basic Books: New York. 1998) p.43.

24. Julian Huxley, see (gospeloutreach.net) 2014. "Does God Exist" Rolaant L. McKenzie August 2007, p.3.

25. *Time Magazine*, April 1980. 'Modernizing the Case for God' April 7, 1980. as quoted in "There is a God" Antony Flew, 2007, preface p. xv.

26. Jim Holt 'Science Resurrects God' fascinating article from The Wall Street Journal, (December 24, 1997) Dow Jones & Co., Inc. (quotes from scientists - design of the universe) (godandscience.org/apologetics/quotes) 2014.

27. Sir Isaac Newton, (1643-1727) (widely recognized as one of the most influential scientists of all time and a key figure in the scientific revolution) 'Symmetry in Plants' 1998 Roger Jean & Denis Barabe (part 1) p. xxxvii (a translation of a Latin phrase Newton wrote in his student's notebook) see (wikiquote.org/isaacnewton) 2014. Newton (part 2) …"Human Nature: An Interdisciplinary Biosocial Perspective' vol 1, Issues 7-12, 1978, p. 47.

28. Paul Davies, (a highly regarded British astrophysicist, professor and author, winner of the Templeton Prize 1995, Faraday Prize 2002) "The Cosmic Blueprint: New Discoveries in Nature's Creative Ability to Order the Universe". (Simon & Schuster: New York, 1988) p.203. (godandscience .org/apologetics/quotes) 2014. see partial quote in: "God's Undertaker" (op cit) p.71.

29. Max Planck, (Nobel Prize winning Physicist and founder of Quantum Theory) 'Religion and Natural Science' (lecture - 1937) Scientific Autobiography and Other Papers. translated by F. Gaynor. New York, 1949. p.184.

30. Antony Hewish, (British physicist and radio astronomer- Nobel Prize recipient-1974, for his work on pulsar research and high energy physics) Dr. Hewish has consistently argued that religion and science are complementary as noted in the forword to John Polkinghorne's book "Questions of Truth" (Nicholas Beale, Jan 16, 2009) (John Knox Press: Westminster) p.12. (retrieved 7/27/12) (see fifty one responses to questions about God, science, and belief).

31. Tony Rothman, (American physicist, cosmologist and scientific writer) J.L. Casti, "Paradigms Lost" (Avon Books: New York, 1989) p.482-483. (godandscience.org/apologetics/quotes) 2014.

32. Paul Davies, "The Mind of God" (Simon & Schuster: London, England 1992) p.232. see "God's Undertaker" J. Lennox, 2009, p.59.

33. Bertrand Russell, "Religion and Science" (Oxford University Press: Oxford, England 1970) p.243. cited in "God's Undertaker" (op cit) see introduction to chap 2. p.31. & p.40,41.

34. Fyodor Dostoyevsky (Russian writer and intellectual) quoted by John Lennox (Veritas Forum – Duke University) March 1, 2012. Addressing the subject: 'Is God Rendered Irrelevant'? (www.veritas.org) 2012.

35. John Lennox, U-tube lecture 'Common Objections Atheists Make' June 2011.

36. Richard Dawkins, as quoted by John Lennox in a U-tube debate with Dawkins on the topic 'Is There a God'?

37. Alexander Solzhenitsyn, (world famous Russian dissident) as quoted by John Lennox: U-tube debate 'Is There a God'? 2008 apologetics.com.

38. Jurgen Habermas, as quoted in a U-tube lecture by John Lennox 2/15/2011 on the topic 'Is Faith Delusional'?

39. Rolaant L. McKenzie, (business and learning specialist) 'Does God Exist'? August 2007 as cited at (gospeloutreach.net) p.4. 2013.

40. C. S. Lewis, (British novelist, literary critic, and Christian apologist who wrote the highly acclaimed fictional novel series: The Chronicles of Narnia) quotation from (thoughtfulchristianity.net) 2014.

41. William Lane Craig, (Analytical Philosopher and Christian Apologist - never outmatched in over 100 debates addressing the C/E cultural war in America) as stated in a 1998 debate vs Antony Flew: Madison, Wisconsin.

Chapter Eight

1. Grahame Clark, (British Archaeologist and Ancient Literature specialist) as quoted by John Lennox in a U-tube debate with Victor Singer. 'Is there a God'?

2. Rev. Billy Graham, (highly esteemed as the world's greatest preaching evangelist of the 20th century) "Salvation: The Reason for My Hope" (Thomas Nelson Publishing: Nashville, TN. 2013) p.77. (W Publishing Group)

3. Henry Morris, "The Long War Against God" (Master Books: Green Forrest, AR. 2000) p.277.

4. Peter Hitchens, (British Journalist and influential writer) 'Darwin's bizarre cult' *The International Express* (UK) Jan 5th 2000. (creation.com/ darwin-bizarre-cult) 2015.

5. Rick Warren, 'Meditations on the Purpose-Driven Life' Inspirio, a division of Zondervan publishing. 2002.

6. Frank Tipler, (esteemed professor of mathematical Physics) F.J. Tipler "The Physics Of Immortality" (Doubleday Books: New York, 1994) preface p. ix cited at: (godandscience.org) & (allaboutscience.org) 2014.

7. Frank Tipler, (former atheist) *"The Physics Of Christianity"* (Doubleday Books, New York 2007) (Introduction) (godandscience.org/apologetics/ quotes) 2014.

8. Arthur L. Schawlow, (Nobel Prize winner in 1981 for his work on laser spectroscopy/Stanford University) H. Margenau & R. Varghese, eds. "Cosmos, Bios, and Theos: Scientists Reflect on Science, God, and the Origins of the Universe, Life, and Homo Sapiens" (Open Court Pub: La Salle, IL.1992) p.107 (godandscience.org/apologetics/quotes)

9. Ibid. p.107. also see "God's Undertaker" John Lennox, (Lion-Hudson pub: Oxford, England 2009) p.210.

10. Ravi Zacharias, (Indian-born Christian apologist and an international champion for evangelical truth) as quoted in *Servant* magazine, spring issue, 1999, p.8. "The Case For Faith" Lee Strobel (Zondervan: Grand Rapids, Mi. 2000) p. 247. (thepoachedegg.net/ravi-zacharias) 2014.

11. Ravi Zacharias, "A Shattered Visage: The Real Face of Atheism" (1994, 2004) as quoted in 'Scorned for God-Part 1' (Let My People Think Podcast).

12. Albert Einstein, Max Jammer, 'Einstein and Religion' (Princeton University Press, Princeton, NJ 1999) p.93. see 'There is a God' Antony Flew, 2007, p.102.

13. Albert Einstein, "The Quotable Einstein", ed. Alice Calaprice, (University Press: Princeton, NJ. 2005) p.195-6. "There is a God" Antony Flew, (HarperCollins pub: New York 2007) p.102,103.

14. Albert Einstein, as quoted in *'The Saturday Evening Post'* Oct. 26, 1929.

15. I. L. Cohen, (American engineer and mathematician) "Darwin Was Wrong: A Study in Probabilities" 1984/1985 (Greenvale, New York: New Research Publications, Inc.) p.6-8, 209,10. 214,15.

16. Pierre Paul Grasse, "Evolution of Living Organisms" (Academic Press: New York 1977) p.8. see "The Long War Against God" (op cit) p.278.

17. William Jennings Bryan, (1860-1925) (American Politician and Attorney) 'Quotations on Free Thought and Religion' (about.com) 2015.

18. Martin Luther King Jr., (1929-1968) (famous American Baptist Minister & Civil-Rights Leader/ Nobel Peace Prize Winner 1964) as stated in his Nobel Prize acceptance speech, Olso, Norway 1964. at age 35.

19. John Houghton, "The Search for God – Can Science Help"? (Lion Publishing: Oxford, England 1995) p.54. see "God's Undertaker" (op cit) p.91.

20. Omar Bradley, (famous American military General) quoted from his 1948 Armistice Day Address at the end of World War ll. (christianity.co.nz/science) 2015.

21. William Jennings Bryan, (statement offered into recorded testimony in the famous Scopes monkey trial at Dayton, Tennessee) July 16, 1925.

22. Dr. Wernher von Braun, (former director, Marshall Space Flight Center-NASA) comments included in 'My Faith' *American Weekly* Feb. 10, 1963, 'a letter to the California St. Bd. of Education' September 14, 1972. and a personal untitled essay on Science and Christian Faith. 1976. (Creationsafaris.com/wgcs_4vonbraun) 2014.

23. Plato, (well-known classical Greek philosopher and mathematician, student of Socrates and teacher of Aristotle) 427 BC - 347 BC see quotation citing at (thoughtfulchristianity.net) 2013.

24. George Wald, partial quotation repeated for emphasis from chapter four, reference 44.

Chapter Nine

1. Albert Einstein, see famous quotation at (goodreads.com/author/quotes/einstein) 2014.

2. James Gorman, (science reporter - the New York Times) 'The Tortoise or the Hare?' *Discover*, October 1980, p.88 (evolutionfacts.com/evolution-handbook) 2014.

3. Wernher von Braun, (1912-1977) from an untitled essay written as a forward to a paperback book by Harold Hill, "From the Goo to You by Way of the Zoo" (Logos International: Plainfield, New Jersey 1976) (creationsafaris.com/wgcs_4vonbraun)(emphasis added) 2014.

4. Roy Varghese, (in reflecting on the 'new atheist' position of all or nothing adherence led by R. Dawkins) "There Is a God" Antony Flew, (HarperCollins Pub: New York, 2007) preface p. xvi

5. Ibid. preface p. xvii see R. Dawkins "The God Delusion" (Bantam books: London 2006) p.140.

6. Paul Davies, "The Mind of God" (Simon & Schuster: London 1992) p.81. see 'God's Undertaker' John Lennox (op cit) p.62.

7. Katherine Tait, (British author/essayist, only daughter of Bertrand Russell) "My Father, Bertrand Russell" (Harcourt Brace Jovanovich: New York 1975) p.189. see "There Is a God" Antony Flew (op cit) (preface by Roy Varghese) preface p. xx.

8. Katherine Tait, (op cit) p.189. (op cit) Antony Flew (Varghese) preface p. xxi.

9. (op cit) p.189. (op cit) preface xxi

10. Bertrand Russell, (British Philosopher- Nobel Laureate) "The Autobiography of Bertrand Russell" (George Allen & Unwin: London 1967) p.146. see "There is a God" Antony Flew, (preface by Roy Varghese) 2007 preface p. xxi.

11. Richard Dawkins, 'Put Your Money on Evolution' *The New York Times Review of Books* April 9, 1989. p.34,35. cited in "God's Undertaker" (op cit) p.95.

12. Roy Varghese, preface "There Is a God" Antony Flew, (HarperCollins Pub: New York, 2007) preface p. xxiv.

13. Antony Flew, (decorated and world known British philosopher and a former champion for the atheistic worldview before undergoing a profound transformation near the end of his career) "There Is a God: How the world's most notorious atheist changed his mind" (HarperCollins Pub. New York, 2007) p.75.

14. Ibid. p.88-89.

15. Ibid. p.155.

16. Ibid. p.163. (emphasis added)

17. Paul Davies, "The Fifth Miracle" Allen Lane, (Penguin Press: London 1998) p.61.

18. I.L. Cohen, (engineer, mathematician and a member of the New York Academy of Sciences who served as an officer of the Archaeological Institute of America) "Darwin Was Wrong – A Study in Probabilities" (New Research Publications: Greenvale, New York. 1984) p.6-8, 209-210, 214-215.

19. Aldous Huxley, (grandson of Thomas Huxley [Darwin's Bulldog] and a brother to Julian Huxley) "Confession of a Professed Atheist" *Report* June 1966.

20. Thomas Nagel, (a professor of philosophy and law at New York University) "The Last Word" (Oxford University Press, Oxford, England 1997) p.130-131.

21. Alexander Solzhenitsyn, (world famous Russian dissident) spoken in a commencement address to Harvard University students and faculty on June 8, 1978.

22. Kenneth Hsu, (Chinese born geologist and environmental engineer) "Sedimentary Petrology and Biologic Evolution" (Journal of Sedimentary Petrology 56 September 1986) p.730.

23. Henry M. Morris, "The Long War Against God" (Master Books: Green Forest, AR. 4ᵗʰ printing, April 2008) p.24

24. Pierre Paul Grasse, "Evolution of Living Organisms" (Academic Press, New York 1977) p.202 (pathlights.com/evolution/encyclopedia) 2014.

25. Loren Eiseley, (American anthropologist and natural science writer) "The Immense Journey" (Vintage Books, a division of Random House, New York 1957) p.199.

26. Luther D. Sunderland, (American aerospace engineer and avid science writer) "Darwin's Enigma: Fossils and Other Problems" 4ᵗʰ edition (Master Books, 1988) p.9 (allaboutthejourney.org/evolution-and-the-fossil-record) 2014.

27. Louis Agassiz (former longtime Harvard University professor of natural sciences) cited in H. Enoch, "Evolution or Creation" (Evangelical Press, 1986) p.139. (evolutionfacts.com/Evolution-handbook) 2014.

28. Louis Agassiz, on "The Origin of Species" *American Journal of Science*, 30 (1960) p.154. (pathlights.com/ evolution/encyclopedia) 2014.

29. Nils Heribert-Nilsson, "Synthetic Speciation" 1953, p.31. (evolutionfasts.com/evolution-handbook) 2014.

30. Kenneth Hsu, "Reply" *Geology*, vol. 15 (1987) p.177. (pathlights.com/ce_encyclopedia/Encyclopedia) 2014.

31. James Perloff, "Tornado in a Junkyard: The Relentless Myth of Darwinism" (Refuge Books: Arlington, Mass. 1999) p.241. (freerepublic.com/focus/f-bloggers)(quotes reveal the credulity of evolutionists) 2014.

32. David M. Raup, (University of Chicago paleontologist, expert on the fossil record) "Geology and Creation" *Bulletin* of the Field Museum of Natural History, vol.54, Mar. 1983, p.18 (freerepublic.com/focus/f-bloggers)2014.

33. Phillip Johnson, "Objections Sustained: Subversive Essays on Evolution, Law and Culture" (Intervarsity Press: 2000) p.9. see "Mind Siege" by Tim Lahaye, (Word Publishing: Nashville, TN 2000) p.143.

34. Dr. Randy L. Wysong (instructor of human anatomy and physiology) "The Creation-Evolution Controversy" (Wysong Institute, Inquiry Press, 1976) p.418.

35. Dr. Harold Urey (Noble Prize winner for chemistry: UC San Diego) quoted in the "*Christian Science Monitor*" January 4, 1962 p.4.

36. Michael Denton, "Evolution: A Theory in Crisis" (Adler & Adler Pub: Bethesda, Maryland 1986) p.358. (mountainretreatorg.net/apologetics) 2014.

Chapter Ten

1. Dr. Henry Morris, "The Long War Against God", (Master Books, Green Forest, AR. 2008) p.300.

2. Arthur E. Wilder-Smith, PhD,Dr.Sc.,Dr.es.Sc., "The Natural Sciences Know Nothing of Evolution" (Master Books/ICR, Santee, California: 1981) p.154.

3. Julian Huxley, (professed evolutionary atheist) "At Random, A Television Preview" appearing in *Evolution after Darwin* 1960, p.41. (evolutionfacts.com/Evolution-handbook) 2014.

4. Collin Patterson - in an address at the American Museum of Natural History, New York City, Nov. 1981. (freerepublic.com/focus/f-bloggers) 2014.

5. Dr. Henry Morris (op cit) 299.

6. Dr. Henry Morris (op cit) 303.

Epilogue

1. Nancy Pearcey, "Total Truth", (Crossway Books (study guide edition), Wheaton, Illinois) 2005

2. Johannes Kepler, AZ Quotes.com/author/quotes. 2014. (use in the public domain)

3. Nelson Glueck, "Rivers in the Desert: A History of the Negev" (Farrar, Straus and Cudahy: New York 1959)

4. Henry H. Halley, "Halley's Bible Handbook", Zondervan Publishing, 1961, p.77

5. Ibid p.80.

6. N. Glueck, "Rivers in the Desert: A History of the Negev" (Farrar, Straus and Cudahy: New York, 1959) p.31.

7. J.O. Kinnaman, found at (geocities.com/Heartland/7234/quotes) accessed October 2009. cited in Grant Jeffrey, "The Signature of God" (Water Brook Press: Colorado Springs, Co. 2010) p.57.

8. Ibid p.57

9. Sir Frederick Kenyon, "The Bible and Archeology" (Harper and Row: New York 1940) p.288-289. cited in Josh McDowell- a Christian evidence study guide 'Research in Christian Evidences' 1979, p.30

10. Peter Stoner, "Science Speaks" (Moody Press, Chicago, Illinois. 1968) p.79.

11. Grant Jeffrey, "The Signature of God" (Water Brook Press: Colorado Springs, Co. 2010) p.70.

12. H. L. Willmington, "Manuscript from Outer Space" (Riverside Book and Bible: Iowa Falls, Iowa. 1974) p.35-37.

13. Michael Drosnin, "The Bible Code" (Simon and Schuster, New York 1997).

14. Dr. Ilya Piatetski-Shapiro, (former Yale University mathematician) cited article: 'The Bible Code' Is it for real, and if so, does it provide new evidence of the supernatural origin of the Bible? Appearing at (Christinprophecy.org/the-Bible-code) accessed Jan. 2018.

Printed and bound by PG in the USA

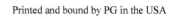

USA2019PG1L